CONFESSIONS OF A DOPE DEALER

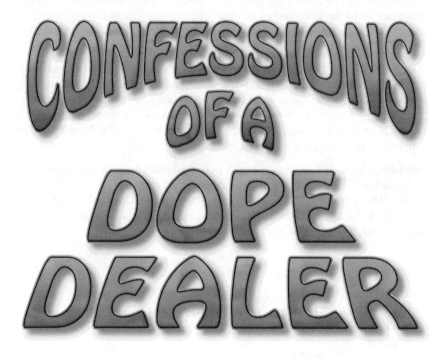

CONFESSIONS OF A DOPE DEALER

By Sheldon Norberg

Ronin Publishing, Inc.
Berkeley, California

Book design by Pete Masterson, Æonix Publishing Group, www.aeonix.com.
Cover art by Alan Forbes.

Author's note: While no subjective impression can be hailed as "truth," this story is the truth as far as I remember it, except in those places where certain points of fictionalization were deemed necessary. In the case of a personal history, many events must be condensed or extracted to create a readable work. In our repressive and litigious society, I have also found it necessary to alter the names and identities of people, change geographic locations, and mask historical fact, in order to protect the privacy of those involved.

Publisher's Note: It is our intention in publishing this book to help promote a dialogue about drugs, their effects, and their place in society, not to promote emulation of the author's abuse. Reading, or knowledge of, this book, shall indemnify the publisher against any claim by, or on the behalf of, someone dumb enough to repeat the actions of the author. (Don't try this at home, kids!)

Publisher's Cataloging-in-Publication

Norberg, Sheldon
    Confessions of a dope dealer / by Sheldon
  Norberg. — 2nd ed.
    p. cm.
    LCCN: 2005905984
    ISBN: 1-57951-032-9   Includes bibliographical references.
    ISBN-13: 978-1-57951-032-9

    1. Norberg, Sheldon. 2. Narcotic dealers—
California—Biography. 3. Drug traffic—
California. I. Title.

HV5805.N67A3 2000   363.45'092 [B]

Published by
Ronin Publishing, Inc.
Berkeley, CA
www.roninpub.com

Printed in the United States of America
Printed on recycled, acid-free paper. The soy-based ink, however, has been dosed.

Dedication

To everyone who contributed to my delinquency. Thanks for treating me like an adult.

Contents

Acknowledgments

This book would never had existed without the friendship, guidance, and love of Mary Swanson. Thanks also to: Francesca McCartney, for the tools I needed to rebuild my life; Dr. Wu, for all things Chinese; Uncle Forresty, for insight and laughter; Ken Solomon, for floating and support; Tom Reid, for listening, sharing, and the North Mountain; Hal Bennet, for invaluable instruction in what it is to write, as well as editing, oversight, and dreams; Pete Masterson, for solid design and an anchor in the sea of publishing. **Everyone** who lived through these years with me; and of course, my family: Doris, my swingin aunt, who made this all possible; Gnome, my expatriate sister—(sorry to eliminate you from the map of my consciousness) my brothers, (who left the rake out for me), and my parents, who survived me being their son.

In this second edition, I find it important to thank Sylvia Thyssen for bringing me up to date, Carla D for demanding that I get back to work, my shamanic teachers for helping me reformat my mind, and Suzanne for not reading this book and loving me anyway and giving me a new world in our son, Gryphon, who I can hopefully teach to avoid my mistakes.

The Characters

The Characters (of import, introduced chronologically):

{The Discussions}   Huang Ti - The Yellow Emperor, codifyer of
                  Chinese Medicine
                  Chi Po - Huang Ti's personal physician

{Wood}   My Parents
                  David/Dave - My eldest brother
                  Ivan/Ive - my other elder brother
                  Mr. Ching - my creative writing teacher
                  Pam - a recreation leader

High School: Mark Mackie - my chem partner
                  Don - my neighbor
                  Ed Darrow - my buzz buddy
                  David Wails - a cool guy
                  Clay - my best friend
                  Paul Beach - a partier
                  Garry Jackson - action

Barrington: Stymie - The Master
                  Art - a dope scientist

{Fire}

The Dorms: Bob Bitchin - a golden boy
                  Cindy Threadgill/Thrillwell - my neighbor
                  Paula - a gymnast
                  Rock-it Rod - a talent
                  Kip - my upstairs pal
                  Chunk - a partier
                  Chuck - Rod's friend
                  Eileen - Chuck's girlfriend
                  Craig - my partner

The frat: Jared Tate - an alcohol absorption machine
                  Droz/The Phi - the president of the house
                  Wyckoff/Wyck - a philosophy major
                  Ken - my "big brother"
                  Merle - a helping hand
                  Speck - a coke dealer - a pledge brother
                  Carson - a pledge brother
                  Chico/Bob - a pledge brother
                  Barry Benson/Thomas - a nerd - a pledge brother

Krajkowicz/Krajk/Scott - a pledge brother
Sharky - a pyrotechnician - a pledge brother
The Hawk - a tilesetter - a pledge brother
Bam-Bam -an unstoppable force - a pledge brother
Dane Watson - a tragedian
Quick Carl - a wit - Dane's "younger brother"
Terry- Rod's girlfriend
Mina - Terry's best friend
Natalie - a waitress

Berkeley: Rachel - Dave's girlfriend
Manny - Stymie's pal
Bagel - a rude boy
Willy Went - a hanger out
Ruth - Rachel's younger sister
Bill Crooks - a freaky hippie

Dead tour: The Grateful Dead/The boys - a psychedelic band
    Jerry - lead guru
    Phil - intestinal rumblings
    Bob/Bobby - rhythm and weirdness
    Brent - keyboards and youthful optimism

{Earth}
Humboldt: Ben - Stymie's land partner
Mulehorn - Stymie's other land partner
Bernard - Stymie's asshole land partner
Dan/the Cowboy - a legend
Lidya - his wife
Grunt - a wild man
Beetle - a Freak Brother
Taco Sauce/TS - a Freak Brother

Barrington: Derek - a lothario
Luigi - a pal
Oblio - a marketing major
Clark - an adventurer

Dead tour: Dennis the Menace - a rager
Spin - a taper
BT - an acid maker
Mex - an acid maker
Slag - an acid dealer
Hogarth - a dope dealer
Jan - the liquid connection

Foreweird

I had imagined I'd be famous before I wrote this, but contrary to my personal tendencies, dope dealing demands a certain level of anonymity. As legendary as you may get, your objective is to stay out of the news. Dope dealing has been around for centuries, since the first spices were brought out of the east, at a profit. Rum runners, pirates, the tea trade, The Boxer Rebellion, these are all parts of the long and colorful history of dope dealing, which, despite its nefarious air, has long been the power tool of empire building.

Before I conceived of my gloriously benign rule, however, I had a recurring dream. It started when I was about five. My dad would take me to the dentist's, where they'd lock the door so I couldn't get out, go behind the pebbled glass into the office, and confer in sinister whispers. Then they'd bring me in, strap me in the chair, put the mask on me and turn on the laughing gas. This was before I ever had a cavity or anything, so I must have seen it in a cartoon. I'd be floating in the room, watching them from above. They'd have my skull opened up so they could mess around in my brain and my Dad would be telling me, "You will be normal," as if I were hypnotized. From then on I knew that I had to pretend to be normal to keep my brain intact.

WOOD

It is written that Huang Ti, the Yellow Emperor, began a series of discussions with Chi Po, his chief physician, who described the natural order of the five elements that make up the world and the body. These discussions formed the foundational text of Chinese Medicine, The Nei Ching.

"The first element," began Chi Po, after setting down his teacup and collecting his thoughts, "is Wood. That is, if there can be said to be a first in a cyclical and interactive pattern. Wood is the beginning of everything, the chi of springtime. When you walk through the Imperial gardens in Spring, what do you see?"

"I see the shoots breaking from the limbs, and the green of new leaves," replied Huang Ti.

"Yes, you see the energy that brings forth life, pushing it from the ground in its newborn color of green. What do you feel?"

Huang Ti thought a moment, "I feel the wind, blowing from one direction and then another."

"This is true. The movement of the Wood energy not only expands, but like the wind it scurries from point to point. What do you hear?"

"I hear the shouts of children, excited to be outdoors again."

"Yes, the sound of Wood is shouting, as the energy is brought forth quickly, and without control."

"Where does Wood come from?" the emperor wondered aloud.

"Wood is the child of Water, which collects throughout the still winter to give birth again."

"But how is Wood borne in the body," Huang Ti inquired.

"Wood in the body is manifested in the Liver, which controls the outward movement of energy. When the Wood is imbalanced, pains scurry about the surface of the body, or lodge in the middle burner, causing discomfort in the stomach. The Wood element rules the tendons, and the flexibility of the body is dependent on its chi flow. The Wood element also rules the eyes, bringing vision, and tears. When the liver becomes stagnant, or weary, the vision succumbs."

"How does one affect the liver, making it weary?" Huang Ti asked.

"As with all organs, the primary cause of health or illness is emotion. The emotion of the Liver is Anger. Anger causes shouting. Anger blinds us to the truth. Anger tightens the body. When we cannot be gentle with others, we cannot be gentle with ourselves, and brittleness occurs. The Liver must be treated with care, for its function ranges widely. It houses the dream body, which roams the inner world to bring you truth. When the Liver has no rest, the dream body has no home, and its wanderings bring no peace."

1

"Bobby? Cindy? Karen? Randy? ...Sh ... Sheldon?" My kindergarten teacher, Miss Banner, looked around the room that first day. I raised my hand, excited to be acknowledged, but not before registering her struggle, the questioning tone of her voice. "Sheldon?" I had noticed people having difficulty with my name by then, which seemed odd, since it was clear to me at five that it was spelled phonetically, and I expected adults to be able to read. It certainly read easier than Michael, or even Thomas, but somehow it seemed enigmatic, as if I were from a foreign land. Growing up in San Leandro, a bay area suburb, I met no one who could recognize my name as the near lowest rung in the Jewish hierarchy of names, something slightly less nebbish than Myron, or Schlomo, but nowhere near as respectable as Abraham or Isaac, and perhaps that was a good thing. I was not exactly Jewish myself, my mother merely married someone who had been, probably putting her on the outs with her parents for the rest of time. "Sheldon" was, despite various rhyming insults like Sheldon Smelldon, indefinable to my neighborhood children. It had no cultural basis, such as Henry or Charles, which could be grasped and categorized. I enjoyed this sense of rarity, and cultivated it, from that tender age, into a proud sense of uniqueness.

I was a bright child, and my parents read to me often, when they weren't dealing with my older brothers, who also shared in the formation of my talents. The three of us were close as children, despite the gap of six years between us. Ivan and David had followed each other in the biannual spacing of planned parenthood, with plenty of time to themselves before I came along. Yes, I was a mistake, insofar as the universe makes mistakes, the unexpected fusion of sperm and egg in a time abortion pills were the idle dream of a not-so-idle mother. My parents had waited a long time to get married, and even longer to have children. They told me once that they were disturbed by their friends falling in love and rushing into marriage, and found that they were the only ones rational enough to maintain their sensibility. Eventually this led to the decision that they were compatible, and that raising rational children might be its own reward. Perhaps it was in reaction to such rationalism, solidarity amongst the oppressed class, which brought the three of us boys into alignment.

I loved my brothers more than anything in the world, despite their taunts of "Baby of the family," and continued inference that I had in fact been adopted. In my infinite trust I was subject to various wounds caused both by their mirthful trickery and my own mistaken expectation that they were looking out for me, but I always forgave them. I'd have done anything for them, to repay them for their guidance, but being so much younger, there wasn't much I could do. On some internal level though, I pledged my life to them, and to upholding their teachings. I followed them as much as our age difference would allow, but there were so many things I couldn't do until I got older. So I watched and listened as they played their pranks, saw them get into trouble, or not, and I learned.

I developed a stronger bond with Ivan, my middle brother, than with Dave, the eldest. When playing street football, my Fred Belitnikoff played slightly harder to secure the win for Ivan's Raiders than my Paul Warfield did for Dave's Dolphins. It wasn't that I didn't love Dave, it was just that Ivan was so—slick. From Ivan I learned how to feign attention, ignorance, remorse, how to lie boldly, how to fake out anyone, (mostly by being a sucker for his gags) and most importantly, how not to get caught. This was an important thing to know, considering the alternative.

My father was a rather sullen man, a powerful, brooding intellect of six feet in a 46 long single breasted, whose behavior toward us was as intimidating as his Hebraic nose was to the general populace. He had a great love for classical music, which was our dinner accompaniment every night. I can still hear the somber tones of Kodaly's cello sonatas whenever I smell spaghetti and garlic bread, and I feel the darkened wood emotional quietude the music brought with it. In '68, about the time I became cognizant, my father was disemployed from his engineering position due to an industrial accident on his shift, for which he was blackballed. It wasn't particularly his fault, and I realized later that his employers were probably looking for an excuse to fire him, due to his tendency to treat everyone like ignorant savages. Not even his elders were immune, for he couldn't stand the idea of anyone doing anything incorrectly, which was, in his view, how most people did everything. When an encyclopedia salesman came to the door one day, my father's desire to provide the world for his children took a turn for the literal, and being unable to afford the books outright, he began a career as an encyclopedia salesman. This gave my father, who had long had considered himself rather intellectual, an immersion into how ignorant people really were. He would come home completely baffled by people's low prioritization of their children's education, and decided that large segments of the populace were simply idiots. Perhaps this made him a less effective encyclopedia salesman than he could have been, but I respected his air of condescension, and eventually employed my own with glee.

Almost as much as I loved my brothers, I loved those books, which now took prominence in our house. I read the encyclopedia from cover to cover, and the dictionary as well, absorbing everything I could, like Gumby exploring the world page by page. Still, the encyclopedia provided no articles on developing social skills of boyhood, so I relied on my own gregariousness, and my brothers. My father's focus was on our cultural development; classical music, chess, museums, stuff that makes even bright kids feign illness. I guess we just had different ideas of what culture was. The bros taught me how to ride a bicycle, at an age my parents forbade it, one of their peculiar rules being that no child should have a bike before the age of 10. They taught me to spit, to climb a tree, to throw a baseball, a football, a newspaper, a Frisbee. Hell, I can put your eye out with a dirt clod. Most importantly, they taught me how to fight, a skill they knew I'd need, since they had been through the hurly-burly of elementary school already. Implicitly and explicitly, they taught me that fear was the killer, and that I should never back down.

Our father espoused a nonviolent stance, (when he wasn't beating us) but it was certain that actions defying rationality would be punished, if discovered. Discretion was never Dave's strong suit, since he believed, as we were told, that honesty would always protect him. I wasn't a liar, my sense of honesty as a characteristic of self-hood was well formed, but I learned through observation that honesty was no way to avoid my father's wrath. Perhaps I was too young for him to challenge my sense of self, but when it came to confronting my father directly I wisely chose the slippery path of avoidance and denial. This stylistic difference in dealing with our father was apparent early on, when my father caught us all in some anti-rational act, for which we were spanked. I fell upon the idea of screaming as loud as I could after a swat or three, in an effort to burst his eardrum, which proved quite effective. Prancing back to the bedroom, I was soon joined by Ivan, and together we laughed our escape. Dave, on the other hand, felt obliged as the eldest son to challenge the conceptual basis of the need for punishment, as well as our father's ability to dole it out. I remember watching out the window in bewilderment as he attempted to mutely defy the purposelessness of the beating until our father's hand fell off, which never occurred, although it was probably sore by the time Dave was retired to non-sitting. Despite the grudging pride that Dave may have maintained after suffering the loss, it was obviously a no-win situation.

Maybe it was our birthright, as brothers, to go about things so differently. Dave had always been the good child, the quiet child, the martyr. Our parents were so pleased with him that perhaps he was duped into thinking he should please them too. His middle name was Adlai, after Adlai Stevenson, great democratic statesman and presidential hopeful. Another shining light of America's political failure, it was a very liberal thing to name a boy. "Son, I want you to be a brilliant failure!" Thinking Dave was so great, and probably just to bug the McCarthyites, they named their next son Ivan. There is only one adjective that attends Ivan. Terrible! So our parents moved from one self-fulfilling prophecy to another. Ivan always cried, until he was old enough to convert his anger into antisocial behavior. It was pretty clear that I was the unplanned for child, and Ivan told me that I was named (in the Jewish tradition) after an uncle, who had (not in the Jewish tradition) committed suicide. I believed this for most of my life, "Son, if abortion were legal in 1962 you'd have spent your extremely short formative years squirming around in a dumpster." I suppose my prophesized death influenced my early yearning to become one with the universe, but maybe it was just me. (It turns out that Sheldon was my father's best friend from high school. He had become a doctor and mysteriously died of a morphine overdose. No karmic remnants there.)

2

"I'm gonna be a jet pilot when I grow up," my best friend, Jack, stated with clear intention. "What are you gonna be?" Astronaut flashed through my mind, but as exciting as Star Trek was, it was obviously a few hundred years away. Being an astronaut without meeting aliens would be too dull. The standard choices of fireman and policeman seemed far too mundane for me. Adventurous perhaps, but with a dozen years to go before I'd hear Frank Zappa's, "Help I'm a Rock," I still couldn't imagine life in a blue uniform. A highly trained government assassin, that I could see, but really, I didn't want to be anything. Being me seemed like all I could ask for. I did want to be a star of some kind, a movie star perhaps, but as much as acting appealed to me, I wanted most to live the kind of life that movies were made about.

I imagined myself becoming rich and famous, perhaps leading some secret double life as well, but it was more about doing then being. I figured I'd learn five, maybe seven languages, earn humanities and science degrees, travel the world, see everything I'd ever read about in the encyclopedia, and do whatever needed doing to make my millions. Mostly, I'd have adventure. I'd skydive and scuba dive, mountain climb and spelunk, cliff dive in Acapulco, trek Nepal, climb the pyramids and raft the Amazon. I'd see lava spewing volcanoes, meteor showers, eclipses, tornadoes, ball lightning and the Aurora Borealis, whatever there was to see. I didn't yet know that I wanted to knock off women like James Bond, or James West, but I knew I wanted to experience life, the highest highs and the deepest depths, and whatever it took to do that, I'd do.

When I was eight years old, I answered an ad in the back of a comic book, and started my first job, selling seeds door to door for the American Seed Company. Young and full of patriotic Horatio Algerism, I took to the streets to provide my neighbors with the best in flowers and vegetables. "Good afternoon Mrs. Johnson," I'd begin in my high pitched but confident tone, " I see you've been growing some Petunias here. I'm selling seeds for the American Seed Company, and I have quite a variety of flowers that could enhance your garden, perhaps Marigolds. I also have lots of vegetables, and if there are any seeds you'd like that I don't have, I can order them for you." Despite starting with the average mix of seeds, I was quickly able to parlay my small investment into the more lucrative varieties, by developing a knowledge of my clients' interests. It was here that I learned the basics of sales, the satisfaction of finding a need and filling it, and so became an agri-capitalist. I kept certain flowers and veggies for myself, and helped my mom grow them in our garden, which begat another facet of industry I would eventually call into use, but at the time sales looked good to me. Greeting cards, band candy, Mason shoes, you name it—I sold it. It shocks me to think that I must have been emulating my father, but I suppose I was young enough that his distancing behavior hadn't yet dispelled my pride in him. After all, he did teach me the salesman's adage, "Always sell a product that sells itself." Like encyclopedias?

Seed sales lasted a couple seasons, but greeting cards were even more seasonal, and fifth grade found me in a state of penury. I never had an allowance, for the simple fact that there wasn't money for it. I was out walking with a couple friends one day, down by the market, when this little kid walked up.

"You guys want five dollars?" he asks us.

"Suuuuure," we responded, as if there was anything else to say to a goofy five year old. He pulled a five-dollar bill out of his pocket, handed it to us, smiling like he'd made some new friends, and ran back home toward another neighborhood. We were incredulous! Five Dollars! We bought ten candy bars and still had a dollar thirty-five each! After gorging ourselves we split up and each took our loot home with us. The next day at school we discussed the thrilling event and what we might do with our money. A couple hours into the day, the three of us were called into the principal's office. I couldn't imagine what was up. Greg and I were pretty good students and did some extracurricular stuff, so maybe he wanted us to do something special, but Matt wasn't into that. We waited outside until he called us in, one by one.

Mr. Lee was an old Southern gentleman, I had met him many times, occasionally for fighting, but usually for some accolade, since I was a top student. I was surprised to see two police officers in his office. The old venetian blinds were turned down, bringing a closeness to the room. Mr. Lee looked sternly from behind his big oak desk, "Sheldon, these officers came in with a boy and his mother this morning. The boy looked through the class pictures, and identified you, Greg and Matt as having beaten him up and taken five dollars from him. Do you want to tell me what happened?" I was stunned, but I trusted Mr. Lee, and knew I hadn't done anything wrong. I told them exactly what happened, after which Mr. Lee replied in his measured drawl, "Now Sheldon, we know you're lying." How could he say that to me! I knew enough not to get caught doing things kids do, but I had never lied in my life. I was a straight A student! Hadn't

Greg come in and said the exact same thing? I just stood there, flushing with anger, wishing my gaze could burn a hole through Mr. Lee's head. "You obviously beat that boy up and took the money." His mother obviously beat him for giving away her cigarette money, dummy! That was what I wanted to say, but instead I was suspended and sent home to get the dollar thirty-five I had left. Needless to say, my regard for authority took a major hit.

I realized that there was no easy money after that, and followed in the bros' footsteps by getting a paper route when I was 11. It was the San Francisco Chronicle, so I was up every morning at four A.M., and I loved it. I could go anywhere and do anything. I indulged in my share of delinquent behavior, but I was well trained by Ivan, and never got caught. There was something else about the morning though, something free. You could see the stars, and the blackness, and you knew that you were all alone, except for an occasional cat, and that was good. The chill morning air, turning your breath into fog below the street lights, as the flutter fluh fluh fluh pop! of a paper flying in to the porch broke the silence. There was an incredible power there, having the world to myself, and I basked in it. I suppose in some ways I began to crave it, this power of freedom. I had always been pretty independent. Even without my brothers I would go off adventuring in the creek or the fields, building forts and playing war, catching frogs or lizards or mice, staying out too late for whatever time I was supposed to be back. When I was ten I told my mom, because her concern for me wore on her, and that bothered me, "Mom, don't worry about me. Whatever I'm doing, wherever I go, I'll be okay. Just don't worry about me." My sense of invincibility had been clearly established, I just needed somewhere to take it.

Despite not playing an instrument himself, my father had expected each of us to take one up, which led to a somewhat noisy household. At the end of the chain, and needing to make as much noise as possible, I started on trumpet. By this time, the bros were getting a little older, into jazz and rock, so I got to hear a much greater variety than they had at my age. I could feel the power and the presence in that music, and it excited me. Not that classical is without its sensitivity, but even at its most powerful it doesn't exactly wail. We were into wailing. It's a process getting through enough years of band to figure out how music works, but I was definitely committed. I was into being on stage from the first time I got there, in second grade, and music was a direct road. It was different, in that acting or speaking opens you up to guiding a whole room, while music creates an organism that you all become part of. In either case,

23

there is a point where the definitions get blurred, and you find yourself in the flow of things, taking the audience along with you. The music in movies is amazing like that. It can be some dumb movie that's boring the hell out of you, but the right music can make you feel things that you don't even want to feel. Music is power, a doorway to another world, but it's a power that doesn't come without practice.

I had a driven need to know how these transient powers worked, and I developed a deep interest in esoteric subjects. Perhaps it was from watching all those horror movies on Creature Features and Chateau Noir, but I was intrigued by magic, not just sleight of hand, but real magic. I studied ESP and parapsychology, swamis and fakirs, the Bermuda triangle, aliens, Van Daniken, vampires, lycanthropes. I was prepared to head into a career in parapsychology, providing one could be had, because these things held an unbreakable grip on my consciousness. You see, with my parents religious division, we were raised as atheists. Not that it mattered, but it gave me room to study all these questions of superstition or science without any religious controversy. My mom and I had already been meditating with the Maharishi and his whole TM deal since I was ten, and I really wanted to ascend to some mystical guru state of consciousness, but you know how when you meditate you sometimes get stuck on something? I was at this group meditation, with my mom, in a room full of beaded, bearded, TM guys, and I just kept hearing this song lyric, "I'm proud to be an Okie from Muskogee," (which, in that space was deliriously funny) and I could not stop laughing. —Now I recognize that finding such humor in one's meditative awareness is probably a sign of enlightenment, but at the time they asked my mom to take me home. Still, I was intent on discovering every way to harness the power of my mind, or expand it.

I used to spend a lot of my free time in the school library, and it was probably sixth grade when the hip librarian let me see the dope paraphernalia kit. It was a big fold out binder, with inset areas for each drug, covered in plastic so no one would steal them. I spent a lot of time with it in the library, inspecting the "roaches" and joints, the dexies, bennies and meth, the "goofballs"—yellowjackets and reds, and of course the burnt spoon and needle. I studied it all, researched it, and bought the government propaganda hook, line and sinker. By seventh grade, when it was actually shown to the general population, I was giving presentations to my class on the dangers of drugs: the chromosome damage, psychological addiction, the smell of burnt leaves, the craving for sweets, not to mention the legal ramifications. Possession, sale, trafficking; two-to-five, five-to-ten, ten years to life in prison, plus fines. I was a hard core anti-drug crusader in the making.

Overcoated figures haunted my imagination; lurking in shadowy alleys, exchanging crumpled cellophane baggies for schoolchildren's lunch money, but the actual insidious reality of drugs proved no further away than the breakfast table. As America was beginning to wake up to the dangers of coffee and caffeine, my parents decided it would be healthful and economical to quit. I'd never thought of coffee as anything other than the evil bitter black liquid that adults drank every morning, but I became aware, as my parents shuffled disconsolately between coffee substitutes, that they were now incredibly agitated. I remember my father complaining mercilessly about the horrid attributes of Kava, "This damn crap tastes like battery acid!" and grimacing his desire to spit it out. What I couldn't figure out was why they didn't just stop drinking it. If they wanted to quit drinking coffee, why didn't they just stop drinking coffee? It hit me like a ton of bricks, coffee is a drug, and they're having withdrawal symptoms. My parents are coffee addicts! I watched them very carefully after that, and I vowed, never, to drink coffee.

I came home from school one day and went through Dave's desk drawer. I don't know what I was looking for, but it sure wasn't what I found. A bag of weed! I flipped! I had to tell my folks, who knew what kind of filthy degenerate he was gonna turn into? But they weren't home yet, so I waited nervously until Ivan showed up. Ivan was the level head of the family, he'd know what to do.

"Ivan, Dave's got weed in his drawer."

"What are you talking about," he says.

"C'mere, I'll show you."

"No, you're supposed to go trim the hedge before mom gets home, hurry up."

"Okay, but check it out." So I go outside and trim the hedge, and I come back in to show him. I open Dave's drawer and there it is, a bag of… pencil shavings???

"Do you mean this?" Ivan asks, inferring that I'm an idiot.

"No way, I swear to God it was weed, why would he put pencil shavings in there?"

"To remind you to stay out of his drawer you stupid little asshole!" Man that freaked me out. I swear it was weed. And Dave was getting to be more of a hippie, too. Going to Cal, wearing that greasy leather headband and shit. Ivan and I were pretty merciless about hassling him, even though he was the oldest. One time I cut off some of my hair and got up early on Saturday morning, while Dave was still asleep. I crept across the room and worked the scissors by his head while dropping hair on his face. He popped up so fast I almost accidentally put his eye out, then he proceeded to blacken mine. That hippie peace shit only went so far.

I guess he had to retaliate somehow, he certainly took enough punishment from my dad. Since the spanking incident Ivan and I had noticed Dave's pattern of suffering through my dad's abuse. We just couldn't understand it. It would have been equally pointless to fight him, yes, but anything was better than simply enduring it. It turned out that my dad was at his worst when he'd take you for a drive and demand that you explain to him why you did whatever it was that was not rational. You never had any idea why you did these things that were driven by a situation, an emotion, an impulse, or a reaction, but Dad would be glowering at you,

"You're going to tell me why you did this!"

"I don't know."

"What do you mean you don't know? You did it, didn't you?"

"Yeah, I guess."

"What do you mean, you guess?" It was hard to be certain of anything in that situation, your head began to feel like a balloon attached to a tiny little body somewhere in the distance. Those interrogations were fucking unbearable. It seemed that my father was worried that any non-rational act on our part would reflect poorly on his stature as a rational man, and that would not be tolerated.

Stealing his most bizarre punishment from an old Star Trek episode, he once took Dave into our room and demanded, "Slap yourself." Dave didn't really respond. So he repeated it. "Slap Yourself!" The first one was pretty weak. "Harder!" he yelled, and Dave's slap made some noise. "Harder!" Dave didn't slap himself as hard as Captain Kirk did, but he wasn't being controlled by aliens, or acting. Ivan and I watched through the keyhole and it was unbearably funny for a moment, the idea, and the fact that Dave would do it, but it got to a depressing sign of what might lie ahead for all of us.

In the summer after sixth grade my buddy from across the street convinced me to cut my typing class and come to his creative writing class because the teacher was so cool. It was the first time I ever cut class, and it probably cost me my secretarial career, but this teacher, Mr. Ching, was unlike any I'd ever had. First of all, he was Chinese, and not much taller than we were, but he carried himself like no one I'd ever met. Some of the kids in class thought they were pretty tough, but he had them worried that he knew kung fu, because he was Chinese. When a kid told him he would bring his gang over to beat him up he said, "That's alright, but you know I always carry my .357." He was totally bullshitting these guys, but he could lie to them so well that you could almost see their brains spinning. The amazing thing about him was that he asked us to talk about whatever we wanted, and to write about it too. We'd go out to the park by the school to sit on the lawn and talk about what was up with us. There on the nervous edge of adolescence we had a free place to talk about school, our parents, whatever. He also expected us to think about things, to look at our reactions, and try to understand what they were based on. He definitely opened some doors for people trying to express themselves, but he also clarified to me just how to examine people's motivations, to know when they were lying, and question why. He got dismissed from his teaching position after a girl told her parents that he had allowed us to talk about sex in class. It wasn't a big problem for him, since he was the principal of an independent school, but it alerted me to the fact that something was fucked up in the general educational system. The first teacher I ever had who spoke to us honestly and intelligently was being terminated. Hmmm. That was about the time that Ivan, who was working as a teacher's aide, found out I had been cutting and told my mom. I was shocked that he'd do such a thing, but maybe he thought Mr. Ching was some kind of weirdo. I guess he thought he was looking out for me.

4

Having survived our family for 20 years, it was no surprise when Dave eagerly moved to Berkeley at the end of that summer. Ivan left soon after, to USC, and in a sense, I was alone for the first time. About a month after Ivan left, Dave asked me if I wanted to go out canoeing at Lake Chabot, cuz he had wanted to talk about a few things. Ivan had been his kid brother for all the years before I came into the picture, and without him around, I guess Dave realized our need for each other. We were having a great day, just paddling around the lake, when Dave says to me,

"You know, I've been smoking pot for a few years now, and I thought you should probably know about it." I just about jumped in the lake.

"Don't you know what that stuff does to you!"

"Man, that's all government bullshit, me and Ivan have been smoking pot for years."

"What! Ivan smokes pot?"

"Oh yeah, we'd smoke-out in the bedroom after you were asleep sometimes." There I was, a reverse Bill Clinton. I'd been inhaling it without ever trying to smoke it.

"What about that weed I found in your drawer?"

"Oh yeah, good thing Ivan caught you, he went out to the garage and sharpened all our pencils, then filled a bag with it. Fooled you, huh." I couldn't believe it. My brothers, dopers! The guys who taught me to ride a bike, play football, crap in a plastic bag and leave it on someone's porch,

"You guys are smokin dope?"

"Yeah, I've been taking LSD too. It's pretty cool, but you're a little young for that. If you ever wanna try pot though, we can get high together."

I knew at the time that some of my classmates were throwing away their lives by smoking weed, but I didn't have any preparation for my brother's admission that he was "a filthy dope smoking hippie!" All that time in the same room and I had never known. I was mortified. But I started to think about it. The kids at school who got high were the same assholes I had to fight every year cuz I was too smart. They all smoked pot to be cool. I didn't really feel like I wanted to be cool, if hanging out with them was cool. But my brothers were smart, and they were hanging out with smart guys and getting high. And weren't they the one's who had always told me the real truth about things? I was in a quandary. I had always felt like my life should be some kind of incredible adventure, and this was a scary question. Could weed unlock some part of the mind? With my background, adventures of the mind seemed like the ones to have, so one Saturday I told my mom I was gonna go visit Dave at Cal.

I took BART out to Berkeley, and got out at the bubble, that landmark of urban architecture. I remember all the vendor carts parked there, selling smoothies or coffee & donuts, back before Odwalla and Starbucks were even a dream. Dave met me there, and we walked back to the co-op where he lived, the infamous Barrington Hall! It was an amazing place, a playground for big kids. All the hallways were painted in murals. So were most of the rooms. Dave took me up to the top floor, the 3rd floor, where we went to his friend's room. He put "Mars Hotel" on the stereo, and got out some Thai weed. He had this poster on his wall of a corner in Ann Arbor, Michigan, where these two streets cross, Nixon and Bluett. They fired up a pipe, passed it to me, and I nervously took my first of a lifetime's worth of hits. I don't think it quite affected me the way I was expecting though. I still felt pretty clear. I wasn't tasting the music or seeing trails, but I had the most curious sensation going back downstairs, like I weighed 300 pounds, and it was kinda cool. Dave and I talked about LSD too, and he promised to take some with me when I turned 21, but that was a long way off. I started making weekend jaunts to Barrington every month or so, smoking pot, and hanging out with Dave and his college buddies. What more could you ask for in seventh grade? I kept it together at home though. I realized I couldn't tell anybody what I was doing. My friends were still completely straight, and the cool kids who smoked dirt weed had me pegged for a narc, which was fine by me. The one decision I made about smoking weed was that if it ever affected my health, I'd quit.

I was still pretty civic minded in those days, so I took on a volunteer position with the rec department that next summer. My weed smoking was limited to occasional excursions to Berkeley, but that was fine. I ended up working at the Watson Elementary School, which was a couple miles from my house, but right next door to the junior high where I took summer school. The rec leader was a woman, which wasn't what I was expecting, but she was cool. Her name was Pam. She had a great sense of humor and a classic old VW Beetle, classic in the sense that it had the original worn powder blue paint and cracking vinyl upholstery. Pam took care of most of the art stuff and games while I kept an eye on the playground sports. Being summer, there were hours and even days that no kids would show up. We'd sit around talking, to the point that we became fairly intimate. Pam wanted to know if I'd had any girlfriends, and took it upon herself to introduce me to the concepts of sex. I was already leaning toward perversion, having scoped out Matt's dad's porn mags and bought some filthy newspapers on the streets of Berkeley, but I hadn't ever discussed it with a girl. We started with simple question and answer sessions, where she would answer my inquiries, but one day after we left the playground, she suggested we just go sit in the field. She pulled out a copy of "My Secret Garden," a collection of women's sexual fantasies that was popular at the time. Every day after we were done on the playground we would take turns reading those fantasies to each other. It was pretty exciting. We went out for ice cream cones one day and she stopped me when I started eating mine. She suggested that I should practice licking it, as if it were a woman's tit. Fudge Ripple Nipple became a favored flavor, and as usual, I displayed great academic prowess. At the end of summer we had a day trip planned to Chabot Park. I don't think we were trying to vibe the kids out, but none of them signed up, so it became a picnic for the two of us.

It was a weekday, so the parking lot was almost empty, and without even looking we found a site devoid of human company. There was a picnic table in a small clearing where we put our stuff down. We sat on top of the table, the summer sun warming us from above despite the protective ring of forest that secluded us. We were talking about what had transpired over the summer when Pam looked at me intently, "Is there anything you want to do?" I was not so conscious of the physical sensations of lovemaking that I thought about kissing her. I was more directed toward actually seeing the tangible monuments to feminine design which were constantly obscured by garments. At that age my only glimpses of real tit were occasional exposures of my mom as she scuttled toward the bathroom. Pam was twice my age, but she was a far cry from my mother!

"Take off your shirt," I told her, nervously navigating the boundary between asking for a present and taking one that's offered. Her fiesta patterned bikini top prevented my eyes from resting on the objects of my desire, but her well-tanned skin and smile of anticipation emboldened me. I felt her smooth belly while my mind raced through the possible approaches to garment removal, but quickly realized that the nexus of freedom was a knotted string beneath her shoulder blades. I climbed around her on the table, held her arms, grabbed the string with my teeth, and pulled my head away until the knot released with a pop. I worked my way back around, nuzzling her skin until I could lift her top and reveal her breasts. They were fabulous! Although lacking sugar sweetened flavor or chocolate chips, they were a temperature sensitive taste treat, with their own textural gradient, moving from the smooth skin to the bumpy areola to the ever-hardening nipple. Far from any inanimate training device, they had responses all their own. Sucking on Pam's hardening nipples beat the hell out of any Maraschino cherry I had encountered, which despite it's ability to elicit gleeful squeals from children, has no effect like the moaning that Pam was beginning to exhibit.

I savored them for a long time, but eventually, as their largess is only a physiological reminder of other things, I got tired of them. I sat back, to inhale them visually once again, and pride myself on my work. "Is there anything else you want to do?" she asked seductively. A glance at the fringe of thread on her cutoffs, making a white contrast to her tanned thighs, was all the symbolism I needed to realize that she wanted me to fuck her. How many times I've relived that day, trying to wash away the stark terror that struck me at the time, a time at which **I hadn't yet started puberty! Fuuuuuuuck!** World is my oyster and me without a shucking knife! Damn!

As close as we had become, it was still far too embarrassing to tell Pam this, and I could feel her incredulous disappointment when I sheepishly told her "No." She put her top back on, we had our picnic, walked and talked, and my decision was never questioned. Before we left though, she asked me to do her a favor.

"Anything," I told her.

"You're going into junior high now, and I want you to promise me something."

"What's that?"

"Promise me you won't try smoking pot." Of all the things we had talked about and done together that summer, I guess we hadn't talked about pot. How could I keep such a promise? Pam obviously cared about me, and I had certainly had more intimate discourse with her than anyone ever, but that was treading on my secret life with Dave, my brother! Here, in the same park that he had told me that smoking dope was cool, the person who was trying to reveal an equally adult factor in life was telling me that it wasn't. I had to assume that she didn't really know the score, since there was so much misinformation floating around, and she seemed so earnest in her concern for me. I suppose I equated it to mothering, on some level, because it left me with only one choice. I hated to do it, but I lied to her. "No, no, don't worry about me."

5

Pam ended up working at my old elementary school that fall, but I didn't see her too much. I was pretty busy with my paper route, jazz band, concert band, honors program, my occasional weekends in Berkeley; I was just avoiding her until I could convince my dick to catch up with my mind. Otherwise I'd be gnawing on frustration. There was the whole testosterone lowering scare that had led Dave's high school friends to start calling him "raisins," in reference to his potentially shriveled scrotum. Could it be that smoking pot had ruined me already? I didn't dwell on it that much, I had the whole social ordeal of junior high to think about, which added its own level of pressure. There were more smart kids to hang out with, my friends from the mentally gifted program, who were also craving experience. The few I told about smoking weed trusted me, and wanted to check it out, since they were mostly outcast from the cool crowd too. So I made my first mistake, I got my friend Brian Bates high. We had hung out for years, doing model rockets & shit, and he had a paper route, too. I had introduced him to various forms of early morning dereliction so I figured it was okay. The very next day after we smoked some pot, he was hanging out with this asshole older kid from his street, acting cool, cuz now he smoked dope. Fuck. I really had to back off after that. The social pressure was just too much to deal with. I think it's even harder on the nerds, cuz we're so used to being outcast that any opportunity to join society has to be latched on to. It wasn't about getting high, or reaching some state, it was all about the social order.

It was cool going out to Berkeley, though, Telegraph Avenue & People's Park, the underground comix store, the head shops. I bought my first bong in the Indian Imports store. I didn't quite understand the concept, so when I took the first hit I neglected to carb it. I just kept inhaling until my lungs exploded. I wasn't quite ready for that. It had this big 'ol party bowl on it, and I never took the bong away from my mouth, so it shot this load of burning weed and bongwater right into my eyes. Yeah, I guess I was stoned! But even though I bought the best Colombian I could afford, the $15 an ounce stuff, it didn't seem to be doing that much. The allure of hanging out with college kids at Barrington was just as big a draw.

I guess I must have let my grades slip a little that year, doing algebra in my head got my math teacher pissed off, and my parents were getting a little edgy about things in San Leandro. My grandma had had a stroke earlier that year, and my mom spent a bunch of time taking care of her.

They seemed relieved to send me away to Matt's new home in Utah for the summer, just knowing I'd be out of their hair, but when I returned I found out the real reason. They had purchased my now deceased grandma's house and we were moving the next week. Fuck! I had a pretty good thing going. I was acting, in band, in the gifted program, had lots of friends, I could go off to Berkeley and get high. Fuck! I considered running away. I thought maybe I could go to Berkeley and enroll in Berkeley High or something. But at thirteen, I didn't quite have it together, so I moved to Roseville, the Bicentennial All-American City.

6

In my entire history of visiting my grandmother, which was at least once or twice a year, I had never seen another kid in Roseville. Nothing but old people and creaking trains. It had some quaint aspects, but those hardly balanced out my seething. So I started school there, right down the street from my house, and I hated it. There really weren't very many kids in my neighborhood, but those that were there at least knew everyone else, which put me at the bottom of the social ladder. This was the year that Prop 13 started to cut the schools apart, but it wasn't necessary at Roseville High, my junior high had a far more serious music program, drama program, gym equipment, cultural opportunities, academic rigors, you name it. I was cast into hell, and for all I could see everyone was straight too. I was all set for a life of lonerhood.

The first week of PE class they were picking teams for football. It went around and around, and nobody knew me, so I was left with the fat and lame guys. Admittedly, my donut and Slurpee excesses from having a paper route had made me sort of pudgy. One of the captains, Tyson, looks us over and asks me, "You smoke pot?" I replied with an affirmative grunt, and he says, "Okay, you're on my team." These guys were serious stoners in ninth grade, out in the parking lot every morning buying Js of Colombian, already headed for continuation school, exactly the folks I spent my previous life avoiding, and now I was on their team. They were all from Rocklin, the next town over, so I really didn't spend any time getting high with them, but now I knew that people were getting high out here, and pretty soon I began talking it up with my chemistry partner, Mark Mackie. We were always singing Fly Like an Eagle to get us through class. "Time keeps on slippin, slippin, slippin." We never got high though. He had to take a bus home after school, and even with a stash of Colombian in my drawer, I wasn't sure I wanted to get involved in the whole scene.

Interestingly enough, there was a kid living right next door to me, Don. I think he was introverted enough for me never to have seen him in previous years, although he hadn't moved there until he was ten or eleven either. Don was pretty cool, in a smart is cool way. He was into interesting shit. His dad was a real hardcore about mowing the lawn, it had to be picture perfect. Don took his skills into the marketplace, mowing all the old ladies lawns in the neighborhood for a couple bucks apiece. He'd take his money down to the Roseville Auction, which had this giant flea market where he would buy books. He had the best library of anyone I'd met. Of course it was all science fiction, but that was fine. He was also into chess, so we'd retire behind his father's precisely stacked cords of wood, yet another project, to play in privacy. Although it was hard to appreciate at the time, Roseville was a nice, dull place. You could still feel the trees swaying in the breeze while you wandered the gravel alleys, backed by the endless groaning of the trains making their way through town. It had its oddities too. There were real hobos, who hopped freights beneath the old railroad-bridge a block away. You could find stuff in their little camp under the bushes. Tins of beans, beer bottles. I once found a porn mag, but it was kinda skanky so I left it for the next hobo to use. You never saw them though, they arrived and departed with the night.

There were a couple of guys, maybe not homeless, but crazy guys who used to wander the streets in a fairly regular rotation. Pimp Man and Binocular Man were Roseville's finest freaks. Pimp man was an older guy, white haired but not feeble, who wore a white suit and white patent leather shoes all the time. He'd walk his circuit through town in a sort of proud way, like the eccentric son of a railroad baron who had been left in place by the airlines. He definitely had that "not all there" look. Binocular Man made slightly less regular appearances. Perhaps he lived in the hobo shacks I was yet to discover at the edge of town, but he came through for supplies once in awhile. He was a black guy, in his thirties or forties, maybe a vet. He always had his knuckles taped with white athletic tape, although it was usually sort of ragged. Of course, he never appeared without his signature pair of binoculars. He would sit on benches around town watching the world proceed through the magnification of his namesake. You could watch him for long stretches as he eyed the world this way. He never seemed to notice he was being watched as he watched others, so it always made you wonder just what it was he was watching.

At Thanksgiving both Dave and Ive came to visit, and we all went down to our relatives in Oakland. I drove with them and we stopped off at Dave's friend's house on the way. Dave had been hanging with this guy who was bringing Kona Gold over from Hawaii, back in '76, when it had just started. I think that both Dave and Ive wanted to provide a serious experience for me, so they loaded me a bowl on this gas mask bong and cranked up Pink Floyd's "Welcome to the Machine." By now I had bonging figured out, but I don't think I was ready to be transported into space. After a couple hits I thought I was flying this bong like some kind of astronaut, the music was exploding and raining colors on me, luminous, and everything I touched felt deeper, thicker, and now, now I was

HIGH! We took the Landau top off for the drive back to town. I, with my head lying between the back speakers, staring at the sky, not even thinking, just knowing I wanted to be like this for life. I scored some of that weed from Dave, it was way more expensive than Lumbo, but it was really what I had been searching for; an E ticket.

When I got back from vacation I told Mackie about this weed, and he wanted to get some, as did this other girl I knew. I decided I could recoup my expense by selling them a couple of buds. Now, in my grandma's little Roseville house I shared my bedroom with my parents' office. There was a big bookcase dividing it, so I had some privacy, and the back door led out into the laundry room, which also adjoined the kitchen. I got this weed out of my desk, wrapped a couple buds in foil, put them in my jacket pocket, and **Whoa!** My mom starts walking in outta the laundry room! I hadn't even heard her go in there. I threw the bag of weed into my drawer and slammed it closed, and then tried to be nonchalant, "Hey mom," which is a bit of a problem when your heart is beating 20 times a second. I had to go to school right then so there was nothing I could do about it, just hope that it would be okay. So I went about my day, inching my way into the wonderful world of paranoia. What if she looked in my drawer? Fuck Fuck Fuck Fuck Fuck! I sold $10 worth of this bud to Sherry, and went home. I had been thinking about this episode of the Nancy Walker Show that I had watched the month before with my parents. Nancy's son had stashed his pot in a tea jar in the kitchen, and she boiled some up and got high. A ridiculous premise, but entertaining enough for television in 1976. My parents laughed pretty hard. Maybe they'd be cool about it. After all, they were liberal democrats. Maybe my mom hadn't even noticed me being weird. Maybe…. Not!

She looked in my drawer and yes, they were freaked out. I get the impression that I thought of myself as an independent entity earlier than most, but I'm sure you had that discussion with your parents where you realized they thought of you entirely as being controlled by them. I guess it's just part of parenting to freak out about your thirteen year old smoking pot, but hey, this is America. I tried to bring up the humor of that Nancy Walker episode, but it just didn't seem funny to them at the time. My father demanded to know what I was doing taking it to school. "I sold some to my friend Sherry." They made me call her to let them talk to her parents. Fortunately her parents weren't home, so I arranged with her to buy it back the next day. Then came the real brutal part; "Where did you get this?" I told them that Dave had given it to me, which was what they already suspected, but it really seemed to freak them out. "What else has your brother been doing with you?" my father demanded. "What **else** has he been doing with you?" I really had no idea what he was shouting about, but it was freaking me out. Several years later Dave told me that he had decided he was gay at that point, and in keeping with the family tradition of mindfucking the parents, he had told them. So there I was, completely in the dark, while my parents were thinking I was some sort of cannabis catamite, which was probably no easier on their twisted minds than their suspicion was on mine.

The whole thing with Sherry got really weird. I went over her house the next day after school to get the weed back and she just freaked out on me.

"I've heard about people like you. Your parents make you sell dope to people then threaten to turn them if they don't give it back, and you keep the money."

"What are you talking about? They're freaking out on me, and now you're all paranoid. Here's your money."

"Just don't ever talk to me again." This totally sucked. She was kinda cool, or, I sort of liked her. Probably better off to see her freak out early on, knowing what I know now, but I thought that there might have been some possibilities there. At that age, when guys were trying to have sex with farm animals, any possibility of getting in with an actual girl was pretty exciting, and I was finally starting to mature. Oh well, fucked that one. Here I am trying to develop something, and my now-afraid-I'm-a-bender parents screw it up for me. Ha!

Well, they flushed all that Kona down the toilet, so I quit pot. It seemed to be a total bust, and they were watching me pretty close, so what options did I have? I got serious about school, and started getting heavy into debate and speech, the only positive aspect of my academics at Roseville. I played some tennis, but mostly I was bored. Ivan came up around Easter for a visit, slickly avoiding, as usual, any of the folks' suspicion that he was a contributor to my delinquency. He hadn't yet dropped out of USC, as Dave had from Cal, but he was headed down that road. He had really wanted to stick it to our dad on that trip, he told me later, but found their conversation to be less than thoroughly destructive.

"Well son, what's new?"

"I've started shooting heroin, dad."

"That's nice, want to play some chess?" I guess the old man was becoming numb to it all, and just considered Ivan another shard of his shattered dream of rational child rearing. At least he wasn't a fag.

He wasn't shooting dope either, but he couldn't think of anything more potentially devastating to our dad, whose rock-like reaction didn't make him feel very successful, so we went out for a walk. Ivan had joined a frat at SC, and felt like dispensing some brotherly wisdom.

"You smokin cigarettes yet?"

"Hell no, I quit smoking pot, why the fuck would I smoke cigarettes?"

"They have their own attraction. You drinking?"

"I mix martinis for mom and dad, but they taste pretty nasty." We had ambled over to the Shortstop by this point, so Ivan went in and procured a half-pint of Black Velvet and some Marlboros. He broke out a couple cigs, lit them, and handed one to me, taking up an instructive tone.

"The most important thing about smoking cigarettes is knowing how to flick your ash. People who can't flick their ash properly are a disgrace to smoking."

"I don't smoke."

"Well, you're young," he replied confidently. He cracked open the whiskey and took a slug, handing me the bottle. Now this I could appreciate. I hadn't really done any serious drinking before, but I took a big swallow, which I managed to get down before the stinging wrenched me into a coughing spasm.

"Whhheeew," I finally sighed in a now tattered voice.

"Takes practice," Ivan said, nursing down a slug. He displayed to me the proper format for holding a cigarette and flicking off the ash, and despite my lack of desire to drink much more whiskey, probably considered the evening a successful contrast to being stonewalled by our father.

That year went by pretty normally. I made a couple more friends. In the fall I had this guy Ed in my English class. He was the center for the football team. We used to argue about everything, but it was good. I started meeting some more people through him. I was playing water polo, which was killing me, but good. It was after Thanksgiving that Dave came up for a visit, which was a little strained with the folks. I wasn't even thinking about getting high, but I was swimming a mile every morning before school and I asked him to come along. It was the only chance we had to talk privately about the whole bust thing, so it was kind of a relief. Of course, he had some pot. He said this was this new kind of pot grown here, Sinsemilla. It was a peculiar variety called "Purple Creeper." I really didn't think I wanted to get back into it, but it was some attractive looking bud, so we sat in the park and fired up a bowl. Nothing happened.

"Aahh this ain't doin nothin."

"No, no, try some more." It tasted pretty good, but I felt completely straight. So we went to the pool and I dove in for some sprints. I got about fifteen yards in and wham! I spent the next hour floating on my back in the pool, totally spaced out. And then, for the first time, I went to class high. I thought it would be a bust, but it was totally cool. My mind was thoroughly occupied with nothing in particular while my teachers droned on, and I was able to respond almost as fast as ever to their questions. This was entertaining!

But Dave split, and I had no money, and nobody even had the kind of pot I wanted, so no biggee. I just kept it cool with the folks and in school. Being something of a wiseacre, I began to draw more sarcastic people to me. My friends Tim & Tom, the twins, were a lot of fun, albeit straight. They were part of a large contingent of Air Force brats who went to Roseville. They played tennis and water polo and debated, so I saw a lot of them. I managed to meet a lot more people that fall, despite being socially uninvolved. I didn't go to games or dances or any of that shit. In fact I was stunned by the whole rah rah concept. Do you people really care? Is your esteem actually based on this shit? I was still looking for something higher in life. Turning my grades around for the year had eased my folks' paranoia, and they agreed to let me spend my Christmas vacation with Dave. That way I'd be out of their hair, and could see my old friends from home.

Back in Berkeley I got a hold of my best friend from Jr. high, Walter Carlson. I had promised to turn him on while we were still in school together, but my opportunities had been limited. Meanwhile, he had availed himself of many others, and gave me a detailed description of inhaling PAM in a bag. "It made the music break up into separate notes that bounced around off the walls." Like me, he still hadn't taken acid, so Dave got us a hit of Gold Dot, some heavy shit. We spent the whole day wandering around Cal, which, even in Winter break, seemed like an incredible carnival. What can I tell you about the first time I dosed? The world felt alive, like it was actually breathing. The buildings, the ground, the sky, the trees, everything was breathing. I was beyond my body, but inside it too. I could feel all the space around me, and my sensations varied between being totally discrete points and continuously flowing over me. Everything was synchronistic, you were thirsty and a drinking fountain appeared. Maybe your brain saw it first and reminded you that you were thirsty, but it sure didn't seem like that. I think the key was that I felt totally free to explore these places. We found this sculpture, a metal pyramid all strung with wire, hanging from a tree by the creek. As it slowly rotated in the breeze the sun would strike the wires and send refractive spectrums all over this shady dell, into the creek and onto the bridge, across all the leaves and right through us, it was just magnificent. Everything was amplified, intensified, cool, unless it pushed your thinking in the wrong direction.

We walk into the Sather Tower, to go to the top and hear the Carillon. We're standing there, in the sort of smallish entry room, feeling cramped, waiting for the elevator. Finally the elevator arrives and we get on, silently. We can't speak to anyone else, but it's okay, cuz we seem to be communicating telepathically. Waiting for the old guy who had run the elevator forever to close the door and go up is taking a looong time, and he's staring at us. He points to this little fare box and says "It's ten cents." We both scrounge through our pockets and I come up with one quarter. We look at each other—and we look at the old guy—and at each other—and at the 10 cent sign on the fare box—and the hair is rising up on the backs of our necks—and this little old elevator guy has some kind of uniform on and—he's gonna bust us cause we don't have a "dime," AAAAHHHH! So we run the hell outside, not realizing that we probably could have just tipped him a nickel, and we sit outside with our backs to the Tower, trying to recover. We eventually sort of turned around to look at it, and—you know how perspective works, we look up and up and up and up and up and up and up and, Oh My God! It's falling over on us! After running away from that, things seemed pretty cool again. Amazing sunset from the roof of Barrington. The sun sank behind the Golden Gate and sat on the bay for a million colors and then poof! It just fell off the edge of the world. That's when we realized we should go, cuz Walter's mom would be waiting with dinner.

We started walking to Berkeley BART, not far, we could see the bubble down the street, but the more we walked, the farther away it got. We looked at each other, cuz we were having exactly the same trip, and we started walking faster. And it was getting smaller. We're walking faster and it's getting smaller, and we're passing people and it's getting farther away, and we're practically running and it's shrinking and we're sweating and panting and bing! Here's the underground entrance. We're just across the street. Hmmm. So we go down and get on the train. Rush hour. Packed. Maybe not like Tokyo, but totally Sardinian. And everyone's face is melting. I look at Walter, and he looks at me, and he's Walter, but he's lookin at me like, check this out! The businessman next to us has a bird head, and the lady next to him is all froggy. We start laughin and laughin and pointing at these people—Check out the lizardman! We're dying and we haven't even gone one stop yet. Somehow we survived that ride, giggling until snot was running down our faces. We got back to his house and his mom, in her transcendent momly wisdom, had made us a batch of… spaghetti. Ever eat spaghetti while you're frying? There is no end. It's infinitely good. You can't tell if it's going in or coming out. Is it alive? It's all bloody. I'm chewing on a giant skinny worm. Thank God his mom had already eaten and left us to our own devices, cuz when you have no sense of time it can be very embarrassing having people ask you why you're still chewing.

Walter was the first person I knew to have cable TV, so after a back-yard doobie to refresh our high, our evening drew to a conclusion with *A Clockwork Orange.* I have to admit, I was probably irreparably scarred by that. *"But Oh My Brothers,"* now I knew that life held some infinitely greater potential than I had ever imagined, and I swore that I would take LSD once a year for the rest of my life.

7

I think this resolution made school a little more tolerable, and studying Nadsat gave me a new bent. Knowing my interests, Tim and Tom suggested that I meet David Wails. He… was really cool. His name fit him perfectly. Wails was number one on the tennis team, but I had never talked to him my first year, because I sucked, and I wasn't playing in my sophomore year. I devised some corny premise, hanging out by his locker to borrow some tennis balls, which he always had, because I needed to teach someone how to juggle. One of those strangely socially ept people, he summed me up pretty quickly, asking if I wanted to get high after school. We drove out the highway in his green LTD and smoked some of the then ubiquitous Santa Marta Gold, and it was good. Wails, like me, was something of a mistake, but his parents were in their 60's. They also took care of his grandfather, which absorbed enough of their time that they pretty much let David run. Which he did. Not only was he high all the time, he was scoring on all the hottest babes. A good guy to be tagging along with. We used to drive out after school and get high, then he'd come back to play a match and whip these dudes. All the time wearing those green aviator shades. The tennis coach was also my debate coach, and it was interesting to see how Wails handled him. I took a lot of lessons that year, and it began to work for me socially.

Ed had this big party while his parents were away, and I was gonna go with Wails. He ended up having to go somewhere with his parents though, so he gave me a quarter oz bag of weed and told me to get everybody high. I went on a mission, sort of an emissary of highness. I borrowed a face mask pipe from another crazed friend of Ed's, Garry Jackson, on the afternoon before the party, then set out to smoke dope with everyone there that was cool. I was beginning to be a little better known, as a smart guy, a show off, kinda crazy. I'd always been ready to do anything, and always had an instantaneous demented verbal repartee, so I was having some fun. We were all getting fucked up, going out to a vacant lot through a hole in the back fence, where a couple of slats were missing, to smoke pot. At one point, I heard that Jackson, who I really wanted to smoke some pot with, was back there. I went running through the fence and totally tagged my head on the top crossbeam. You know how in the cartoons people's legs go straight up and they drop flat on their back? It was like that. Everybody cracked up. I popped up like one of those inflatable punching dummies, and was even more manic to go smoke pot. I think that's when it dawned on me, that I had a new format for entertaining people. If I could just get high with them and do the crazy shit I do, maybe they'd like me.

Well, back at school Monday it seemed that my entertainments had not gone unnoticed, and I stepped up a peg in the social world. Certainly no closer to getting any chicks, but acknowledged. It was that spring in my general speech class with Ed that I met Clay, who turned out over time to be my best friend. Clay was the sort of good looking, athletic, all American guy that I never pictured hanging out with. But the lines had sort of broken down at Roseville. Sure you had your nerds, your jocks, and your stoners, and in Roseville we had cowboys too, but I think the '70s did something to the general social reality so that more of the jock types ended up smoking pot. None of my nerd friends got high, so I was hanging out with more stoner jocks. Clay was pretty well rounded, he played tennis too, and was one of the mysteriously existent kids in my neighborhood. His parents were divorced, so we'd go to his house after school and pretty much do whatever. Mostly get high and munch out all the Wheat Thins and Triscuits. His mom must have bought a new box every day. She was pretty cool, even when she was at home we'd go out to the garage and get high. Clay had a job as a busboy at Cattleman's, so he was doing alright. He'd buy pot every week and we'd be smokin it every night. I just did whatever the hell it was that made me so entertaining.

Wails graduated and moved not long after that, but we kept in touch, writing stories about high-brained comic adventures. My parents let me go back down to the city that summer, to see a concert and stay with Mr. Ching. They appreciated my interest in music, so even though they didn't particularly like what I listened to, they let me go anyway. Mr. Ching had moved to Berkeley, where he was living with his wife and two sons. He gave me a bunch of this killer Thai weed that he grew in his back yard to take to the show. It was the hardcore rock & roll Day on the Green; AC/DC, Cheap Trick, Blue Öyster Cult, Journey, and Ted Nugent, and it was fuckin awesome. Angus, in his schoolboy knickers, running out into the audience and wailing on Problem Child, Rick Nielson peeling licks from his checkerboard guitar on Surrender, Blue Öyster Cult crushing the place with Godzilla, Journey hadn't yet wimped out entirely, and Ted was just a fucking maniac. I remember smoking a pipe load of this weed with some guy halfway through Ted, and I was just paralyzed, glued to my seat while the Richter scaled vibrations made my body twitch. I had serious doubts about whether I could get up and walk back to BART, but I managed. Mr. Ching was a great one for acknowledging life's simple pleasures though. The next day he took me out in his back yard and we picked a breakfast of fresh blackberries, which we ate with cream and sugar, before he told me he was moving up to the mountains. I had a pretty reasonable sense of geography, but when he told me he was moving to Garberville, which I had never even heard of, let alone seen on a map, I knew I'd probably never see him again. It was with some sense of loss that I got on the bus back home.

A few weeks later I was aimlessly wandering around the neighborhood when I noticed a hippie dude out on his front lawn chipping plastic golf balls into a hula hoop. He had longer hair and a bigger beard than anyone I had seen in Berkeley, owing to his adult status, and his presence amazed me. I had seen him around town before, but I had no idea he lived in my neighborhood. We looked each other over before I asked him,

"What are you doing in Roseville?"

"What does it look like, I'm working on my golf game."

"I just didn't think they allowed relatively cool people here."

"Oh, didn't they tell you?"

"No, what?"

"They keep me around to corrupt the morals of youngsters like yourself."

"It's a little late for that."

"Oh, then you play golf?"

"Naaah."

"Shoot pool?"

"Yeah."

"C'mon in." Glenn had a full sized pool table on the back deck, which he had purchased as a church related expense when you could still get away with claiming Universal Life Church ministry as a tax deduction. He had also held services from the end of a tow rope, which made his ski boat a church expense too. We hit it off immediately. He was on disability from an accident at work, which turned into a lawsuit, but he was one of those guys who had figured out the whole system of how they would try to screw you long before they tried. "I just go in there nodding my head like I'm just another hippie dippie dumbfuck, and they treat me real nice until I hand over the stuff my lawyer's drawn up. Then I sit back and watch them crack." He gave me a beer, which he had brewed himself, and we shot pool.

"You smoke weed?"

"Of course." He broke out some stuff he had, which he liked to smoke in an old long stemmed wooden pipe. I'd go over to his place every couple days, drink beers, shoot pool, and smoke weed. He'd tell me his stories about the various ways Uncle Sam and others had fucked him over while he was in the Army, naively doing his duty. He taught me to shoot pool pretty well, demanding that I shoot left handed instead of behind my back. "Quit bein left hand retarded! Did they teach you that in school?" Like Mr. Ching, he had the insider view on other people's motivations, and loved to pull their chains. He was a pretty wise old dude, and I spent my summer taking lessons.

I had met another guy at Ed's party, Paul Beach, who I ran into at the Day on the Green concert, too. Beach was a serious bonger, and by fall we were hanging out a fair amount. Beach used to drive a truck with one of those hunting scene screens on the back window, so you could see out and no one could see in, and we'd sit in the faculty parking lot, doing bong hits and checking the mirrors for the vice-principal. Beach actually sold weed, and I used to watch him cut it up and deal it out. He began training me in the capitalistic reality of the black marketplace. Beach's Law: You got it, you smoke it! was an unarguable truth. If you didn't turn your product over fast enough, you'd inhale your profit. I learned plenty from hangin around with Beach, watched the various levels of business, and got around to more parties! By fall I had a regular routine. Go to Clay's, get high, go to school, go to Clay's, get high, eat all the Wheat thins and watch cartoons, or go to Glenn's, get high, shoot pool, go home, eat dinner, go to Clay's, get high, do Algebra homework, listen to Floyd. Some nights I'd go out with Paul on his Suzuki, which he would promise my mom to drive safely before we got on, then pop a wheelie and ride us away from my parent's house at a 45 degree angle. Wait for the weekend. Go to some party at some ranch house, get all high, drink a keg, go home, take some incredible piss in the neighbor's yard so I wouldn't wake my parents at 4 A.M. Fit whatever entertainments and wildness I could into the rest of my college prep schedule, and come to think of it, that was a college prep schedule.

Now, forgive me if my brain is too tattered, but wasn't the whole focus of society at that time getting fucked up. This was before the word party had been verbed. You went to parties, but you didn't party, you got fucked up! Movie stars were getting fucked up, rock stars were getting fucked up, everyone you modeled yourself after and the media itself was fucked up. Cheech & Chong were fucked up, Belushi & Ackroyd were fucked up, Billy Carter was fucked up. Hell, Betty Ford was fucked up! Roseville was not completely outside the general American cultural trends, so like everyone else, I started going out and getting fucked up. But I could see there was a difference between these different states, getting high, stoned, and fucked up. I think it's good to differentiate between them. Being high has a more cerebral tone, you're checking out the mental effects, you're engaged with your surroundings—or with your internal dialogue on the surroundings. Being stoned is sort of dulling, more like a mental bondage, where everything slows down and you let it roll by. It was about this time that I first began to differentiate the effects of various weeds into the high and stoned categories. It was obvious that the green weeds, the sinse bud, the Kona, the Santa Marta, these got you high! It was the brown weeds, the lumbo & Thai & Mexican, that got you stoned. You could also see the social difference in who was using what, not just economic stratification, but mentally. The burnouts were smoking brown while the highbrains were smoking green. But in the end, we'd all get together to get fucked up! Drinking is primary to getting fucked up. No matter what other drugs you've taken, you're never completely fucked up until you've consumed some staggerfying amount of beers, JD, Peppermint Schnapps, tequila, or for the young ladies—Boone's Farm apple wine.

I went out with Paul one night and we bought a case of Mickey's Big Mouths, which we consumed several of before going to our friend Janet's, whose parents were away. I had about eight, and was pretty steamed when Paul told me to wait on the couch. He went into the kitchen, returning with two full ones a moment later. He had already removed the somewhat difficult pull tabs, which were a sobriety test in themselves. (If you didn't spill any beer on yourself, you needed more.) He handed me one, and holding his up to his lips, said,

"Chug!" I tossed about half of mine back before slamming it on the table and coughing,

"You fucker, this ain't Mickey's, this is brandy!"

"That ain't brandy," Paul laughed, "It's JD." Jack Daniels, the man who commands such high respect amongst those who feel a raspy-throated quality enhances their mature persona, had found a way to refill my beer. I glared that "I'll show you who's fucked up" glare at him before I threw back the remainder of the bottle. I can't recall whether it was head bangin to Pat Travers' "Heat in the Street" or doing the Watusi to Wild Cherry's "Play That Funky Music White Boy" that expropriated the contents of my gastric tube, but I swear I did make it to the toilet. Janet got in trouble when her parents returned because there was puke in the bathtub, but I think her kid brother had snuck a few too many. Of course, the next morning my mom had the usual allotment of yard chores awaiting me, in the 90 degree Roseville sun. I somehow managed to slowly operate the shovel through the necrotic dullness of my brain and central nervous system, but the repetitive motion was too much for my gut, so I eventually puked some more into the flower beds I was turning. No problem, just cover it up and let it compost itself.

I had algebra class with Clay that fall, and there was this foreign exchange student from Denmark in it, Arnie. We used to try to get him high, but he was always afraid that he'd get sent back home in disgrace. Arnie's exchange parents did allow him to drink a couple Tuborgs after school though, since he had been drinking them in Denmark from age ten. He took a winter trip to Cal Davis to get a look at university life and stayed in the dorms with some guy who was growing pot in his closet. When he came back he wanted to get high all the time. It was amazing what a fiend he became. So algebra became weed, and a notebook was a bong. "We have to get together and do some algebra, bring the notebook." It's kind of a worrisome trait in people. You think getting them high will be fun, then they just want to hog all your dope. But Arnie was a good laugh, and he had a few Danish sayings I'll never forget. "You guys and your wergins, give me a 40 year old woman with a loose juicy poosy."

Ahh pussy. It had to come up eventually. But for me, jerkin off was coming up a lot more frequently. I think I was just tooo weird for the girls there. None of the ones I could get close to were thinking along the same lines I was sexually, and certainly no one was thinking along the same lines I was in general. When I was in junior high I had found a book called The Whole Sex Catalog, by Al Goldstein and "Screw" magazine. Between that and hanging with Pam I was by far the best-educated pervert in the eighth grade. But I found that thirteen-year-old girls weren't responding very well to my desire to felch them, so I cooled out on my vile descriptions of dreamt of sex acts when I moved to Roseville. Strangely enough, high school girls seemed to be more interested in pervy guys, but not necessarily freaks like me, so it looked like highness was the only realm left to explore.

My parent let me visit Ivan at USC over Easter break, I think they were definitely seeing the advantages in separate vacations. They must have known that I was going to some huge rock concert, but Ivan was a responsible chaperone, and I had been good, (or hadn't been caught being bad) so it was no problem. The concert was the California World Music Festival, LA's answer to Day on the Green. Aerosmith, Foreigner, Cheap Trick, UFO, Van Halen, Ted, The Outlaws. It was a pretty monster show, although without BÖC it wasn't quite as good as the Day on the Green I went to. Hanging out at Ivan's apartment was very cool. It was kinda sleazy, in that post collegiate "I never clean or do laundry" sort of way.

Ivan had this pipe I really dug. It was an old Dunlop tennis racquet that had been drilled out, which was a little cumbersome, but I loved smokin dope outta that thing. It reminded me of my youth, admiring my brothers on the tennis team. It was actually a fraternity pledge paddle from his little brother. I was slamming brews pretty hard to keep up with Ivan, who at 21 could simply walk over to the beer store and get all he wanted. He tried to warn me about how drinking beer and smoking dope together would make me throw up, but I didn't know what the fuck he was talking about. That was all we did in Roseville. I think the problem was this nasty little water pipe he had. It had apparently never been cleaned, and the hose went too far into it so you got hits of the filthy water, which was enough to make you puke by itself. I spent my days there getting high, reading porns, and going out for tacos or burgers when Ivan had lunch. Wandering around LA was not too high on my list of thing to do. I wasn't afraid of its immensity or dangers, but what is there to do in Central Los Angeles besides get lost in a bad neighborhood? Just being with Ivan was good enough for me.

In one of our conversations he asked me, "Have you gotten laid yet?" I had to admit that I was only vainly attempting.

"Do you want to?" I wasn't sure if he wanted to buy me a hooker or what, but it didn't matter that much.

"Yeah, but who?"

"You know I had sex with Dave's girlfriend Lucinda, right?"

"Yeah."

"Well, I'll talk to Caroline." She was his girlfriend at the time.

"Fuck yeah!" I think Ivan really wanted to get the jump on Dave this time. Since he had moved to LA, he kept coming home to find their mutual decisions to get me high or give me acid had already been implemented. Ivan and I had always been closer, and I think he felt left out of the formative process of my character development. So the next night Caroline came over, we all had a drink, and Ivan took off to go hang with his buddies. She asked me if I had ever had sex before, and I replied that I hadn't really, but I wanted to. Thank God, I was finally up to the task. She took me into the bedroom. "Take off my clothes," she told me. She was about 24, a little older than Ivan, with dark brown hair and a friendly yet mischievous smile. I unbuttoned her blouse and she became the first woman to help me wrestle through the learning curve of bra removal. "Suck my tits." They were soft and warm, not too big, but upright on her chest. I put everything Pam had taught me to use, sucking her hard nipples like a big baby. Her nipples weren't the only thing getting hard at this point, so I proceeded to remove her skirt and expose her beaver. "Touch it." I spread it open to get my first exposure to Freud's guiding principle, and began to put all my years of pornographic reading into effect. I jerked her off and licked her nub while she sucked my dick and we fucked again and again every way we could think of. She was hot. She told me I was great, which I appreciated, but it had this feeling behind it, like she had enjoyed sex with me more than with my brother. That worried me a little, but I certainly had to thank him for the fact that I went back to Roseville a man.

9

Of course, this experience wasn't getting me any closer to getting laid or knowing how to get laid at home. It was only heaven tossing the dog a bone. So I went back to my life of getting high. And I started to feel sort of weird. Here my best friend was working 3 or 4 nights a week bussing tables so he could buy pot and smoke it all with me. I know he really enjoyed my company, but I started to feel kinda like a leech. Yeah, I was doing and sayin crazy shit all the time, which kept everyone entertained, but that was just who I was. I didn't feel like it was covering all the dope that I was being turned on to, and it bugged me. In my youth I had been big on entrepreneurship, but Roseville was kind of depressed for that, and I was kind of depressed to be in Roseville. My parents were too broke to give me an allowance so there really wasn't much I could do to restore my esteem in this regard. I worked that summer as a Bobby Sox scorekeeper, but other than the benefit of serious scoping of thirteen-year-old booty, it didn't pay very much. There had to be some way to get weed, but even with money the guy who was selling the Santa Marta Red had graduated and disappeared.

Clay and I decided to take some seeds out of the Santa Marta he had and try to grow them. There was a pretty decent spot out behind his garage, so I did all the homework by reading my mom's old issues of Organic Gardening. The plants were getting to be about four feet tall when I read about the fabulous fertilizing qualities of fish emulsion. We bought a pint, and in my junior science dude way, I decided we should apply it to the leaves, since the plants could absorb nutrients in this way. It would have been nice to realize that the dilution strength would be different for foliar feeding than root feeding, but it was my first crop. By the next day the weed started to seize up, like an old dog that accidentally swallowed a red rubber ball and couldn't breathe. We hosed them down and watered the hell out them, but after three days they were all turning yellow and brown, so we decided to go for the early harvest. Smoking that leaf was probably the worst thing I'd ever done to myself. It was like cramming a wad of old dead fish guts and napalm into the bottom of my lungs. It gave me a headache to boot. Now I was really bummed. I had completely fucked up my one chance to redeem myself and provide some weed. After a month of this misery it finally dawned on me, Hey! I have better connections than anybody back in Berkeley! Of course, without any money there wasn't much I could do.

I had a friend from the debate team, Ben Brainerd, who worked in a bank. He was always studying the stock market & shit, and had several hundred in a savings account, so I said to him,

"Look, you've got your money in a savings account at what, 5 percent or something? I could make you 25 percent a year."

"Doing what?"

"Selling drugs." He didn't smoke pot, so he was reticent at first, but the allure of real capitalism tied to my solid business plan won him over. Basically, he trusted me. He knew I was smart, had things figured out, and could keep my mouth shut. So around Thanksgiving I borrowed 300 bucks in cash. My parents let me take my vacation down to Berkeley, which they recognized for the educational Mecca that it was, (although they may have just wanted to get rid of me), and I met Dave at Barrington. He brought me up to see his friend Stymie, whose room was entirely painted like the cover of Dark Side of the Moon. I had met him before, but not under these circumstances. He was definitely leery of selling dope to a high school kid, and I could respect that. But I was Dave's kid brother, and had been partying there for years without getting busted or doing anything stupid, soooo I was allowed to shop at Barrington, the supermarket of dope. This was just about the time that Humboldt County put itself on the map, and there was orange bud and red bud and gold bud and the occasional purple bud all for the taking. Stymie had everything. So I bought a couple ounces of this beautiful pot, which was only $140 an ounce, and proceeded to get high. I went down to the Avenue and bought myself a funky little postal scale, the kind you clip your bag to and hang, got some baggies, and when I took the bus back home I was a businessman again.

Of course, my weekend was not without its introductory lesson in dope dealing ethics. You see, the folks at Barrington had a pretty well developed science of dope dealing. Pink Cloud, the ancient hippie, who I had bought my first lid from when I was in eighth grade, made sure that everyone knew the score. "Keep it cool! Simple as that. Don't sell drugs to people you don't know! Don't buy drugs from people you don't know! Don't hang out places looking to sell dope. Don't sell dope to people who ask you on the street. Just sell dope to your friends and things will take care of themselves." Fortunately, I was starting to make more friends, and things were pretty cool. I remember going to the Madison Square 4 with some buddies to see Midnight Express. We were in the parking lot pulling a Cheech and Chong, where you roll up the windows and smoke so much dope you can hardly see each other, right up until the movie started. We wander into the darkness to the only four seats left, in the corner of the front row. Here's this skinny kid, sweatin bullets, strappin on the fat load and trying to get out of Turkey. He's fuckin up! We're so high the tension is just bleeding off the screen and I'm half expecting to turn around and see that the theater's full of cops. We're crouching down while some 20 foot Turk is screaming at us "Bu dar hashish?" and beating our fucking asses with a billy club! This shit is fucked up scary! Ya ain't catchin me getting my butt stabbed in some Turkish prison. I'm staying right here at home with rule number one, Keep It Cool!

Competition was okay, but you didn't want to cut in on other people's markets in some sleazy way. There were basically two levels of operation at Roseville. The guys who hung out in the parking lot and sold joints of shitty Mexican and nickel bags of Lumbo, and a few guys who had the occasional quarter oz of Santa Marta, which was now more difficult to obtain. It was clear from the beginning that I was starting a whole new market, Killer Green Bud! I only sold nickel and dime bags, which were all evenly and honestly weighed, from tennis ball cans I kept in my locker. It's just so much cooler doing business out in the open. People come over, look in your can, pick a bag, drop a ten in your binder and go to class. Simple. And honest. I made sure there was enough margin for me to get a quarter oz and some cash, but I was doing everybody right. And we got high! I remember coming back from Berkeley, showing Clay all this beautiful pot and bonging out radically to Dark Side of the Moon, lying on the floor in the dark, just sailing away on the waves of "Breathe" and "Time." He had this hidden closet inside his closet, so I stashed my dope there, for a certain fee, which allowed me to give him some weed back, and everything began to feel right again.

I put the word out, to my friends, and the market started. The more we partied, the more people I met, and they were pretty much all cool, so eventually I was selling pot to a calculable percentage of the student body. The bright yellow can with the red Wilson lettering became a trademark for quality product. I started carrying my tennis ball cans with me wherever I went, to the arcade, parties, movies, because people would always be hittin me up, and I was committed to satisfying my customers' needs. Clay lived about a block from school, so every morning a bunch of our friends would come over before class, score, and bong out to Pink Floyd until the bell rang.

Can we talk about Bonging out?

It was certainly easier than rolling a joint, it was economical, athletic, ritualistic. I had come a long way since my first bong experience, and was determined to become an expert. Clay bought this green ceramic bong, there was something very aesthetically pleasing about it. Maybe it's just that everything gains such texture when you're high, but the stem had little finger notches so you could grab it just so, and lift your pinkie to carb it. It had a little depression around the bowl to put your weed. It was just fucking cool! But it was hard to clean, and ceramic, so it finally met it's demise when it fell out the door of the Hashmobile into a parking lot. I think that's when we got the first US Bong. Those were the best. You could see through em, clean em, reload the one-hit bowls instantly, or have a couple so the next guy would have his loaded already, bong after bong after bong. After a while we formed what we called the OH club, cuz we were so into doing one-hitters. The six shooter bowls were cool too, where you could load it up and have one guy after another do a bong, but eventually we'd compete and see how many of the six bowls you could do at once. That was Serious Lunging. It is something of an athletic event, seeing how big a bong hit you can take. Firing it all down as the cloud of smoke fills up the chamber and then carbing it to the rushing sound of water and air. And then, can you hold it? Is it the expando weed that blows you apart and leaves you drooling on yourself, eyes instantly bloodshot? You may try to avoid it, but there's something extra buzzifying about coughing your guts out, compressing all the blood vessels in the head. All the serious swimmers I've ever known maintained bonging as part of their workout schedule. It not only gets you totally wasted, it's great exercise!

We made bongs out of whatever was available too. The tennis ball-can was quickly converted into a bong with a nail and a stem. Jackson made this bamboo bong, but it had a stem that was way too long. You could burn your face if you weren't careful lighting it. I had really long curly hair at the time, so a bunch of it fell forward as I was lighting this hit and erupted in a ball of flame on my head. Boy did that crack everyone up. I went home later, my hair still all char stinking, and amazingly, my parents never noticed. I should've kept a log of things my parents never noticed.

"Dear, our son smells like he's on fire."

"Not at all."

Where to bong was another question. We used to go out to this housing development after they got water running and sit in the empty houses bonging out. A construction guy drove up one time and caught us there, but he had just come back for some tools so we gave him a bong hit and he split. I was stunned to find these guys smoking pot in the bathroom closest to the school office, but they had a cool plan. One guy would go in a stall and do a bong while the other two worked as lookouts to hold the bathroom door shut and watch the hallways. You'd do your bong, flush the toilet, and blow the smoke down. If anyone ever came the hall monitor knocked and you split just as they walked in. My favorite was the bong hit in the locker. You open your locker, stick your head in, fire down a bong, walk away and blow it into the bushes. Such an effective way to stimulate the mind between classes. Ever bong while you drive? Let your buddy steer until you're done coughing, or if you're a pro just have them light it for you.

Bonging through ice cubes, that was luxury, until the smoke expanded in your lungs. How about bongin through peppermint schnapps, Mmmm. I tried bonging through 2 Fingers tequila once, but you got such an alcohol fume buzz you couldn't even finish your hit. What about drinking bongwater, ever drink bongwater? I did, lots. If you have really good weed, and a clean bong, you could sort of liken it to wine tasting, if you need to rationalize the fact that you're completely ridiculously high. "Ooh, it imparts such a delicate flavour, a Mendocino '78." Of course, you have to trust that you're bonging with serious dopers, and that no one is drooling into your bong. Drooling into the bong should be punished by having bongwater poured all over your clothes and being sent directly home to your parents. It's far worse than peeing in the pool; it's like crapping on the sofa. It's defiling the ritual object. Of course, sometimes even that doesn't matter. We used to go drive off into the fields on the edge of the golf course to get high before we went somewhere, or to party all night. We drove out there one night after it had been raining, so it was pretty wet. Ed got out the bong and went off to go fill it. We fired up some rounds and I was totally high, so I raised my customary toast: "Drink, from the Firehorn!" Then I chugged a hit of the bong water. Clay just fell out laughing at me, he and Cleveland were both rolling in the mud while I stood there dumbfounded, like,

"What man???"

"Ed filled the bong out of a puddle!" Short term memory is the first thing to go.

Driving out to those boonies to party was the great thing about living in Roseville. We'd go to the edge of the seventeenth hole, where there was a high-tension tower. Jackson was probably the first to discover, adventurer that he was, that there was a way to climb it. Eventually we'd get high and race up it, and get higher. We'd smoke a doob and drink a beer, and just space out. It's pretty incredible up on top of a tower, with the power lines buzzin, scoping everything on the horizon. I loved racing up there, to be the highest, above the world with my friends. You read about the guy who broke up with his girlfriend and they found his body about 150 feet from a tower with his dick all charred? They found a bunch of empty beer cans and figured that he drank a six pack, climbed up, took a leak, and pissed onto the wire. Yow! I can't remember how many times my friends and I peed off those things. But I think you've got know enough to pee downwind. I eventually found another kind of tower, the sort of "X" shaped ones. I was the only person I know to climb it, since you had to go fifty feet out a peg ladder at a 45-degree angle. When you got to the end though, you were only three or four feet from these giga-volt wires, and they'd make all the hair on your body stand on end. It was a wicked buzz.

The towers were great, but Jackson figured out the next craziest form of entertainment. There was a railroad trestle bridge about a mile out the highway from town. It was just a cement structure, wide enough for a single train to pass over. He was dickin around out there when he found a trap door on the tracks that led to a little corridor for maintenance. Eventually, a whole bunch of us snuck out there at the scheduled time of night, popped the hatch, and entered this little crawl space. We sat on the planking that overlooked the highway and smoked a joint. From within the bridge, the railroad tracks were about one foot overhead, so pretty soon after we got high we began to feel the rumbling. It grew and grew as the train approached from an unknown distance, so much so that a couple guys wanted to run for it. But there was no way anybody was going to crawl out on to the tracks in the dark all high to find out just how close it was. That train was still highballing when it hit the bridge, and it sent the most overwhelming rumbling vibration imaginable right through you. It made you feel like your teeth would fall out, but it was absolute bone jarring fun.

Somewhere in that fog I earned my longest lasting nickname: Space-man. It fit, and it was good for business. "You try that 'space bud' man? It's some killer shit." I went out to get high with Paul one night. I brought some of this bud I had, and we drove to what he told me was "fag" park, in Sacramento. It was a gay cruising spot, a fun place to get high and watch men climb in and out of each other's vans. We took a few bong hits of this dope and were so high, it was like we were on another planet. There were no lights in the parking lot, so all you could see were the out-lines of the trees that framed the expanse of darkened lawn. Across the park, maybe a quarter mile a way, the colored lights of the Dairy Queen provided a depth of field pairing to the pulsing green illumination from the stereo. Our minds sank through the grunge of Black Sabbath and into the inky darkness of the park until, at 10 P.M., in Del Paso Heights Park, the sun erupted out of the night. The trees, the lawn, our faces all became completely apparent while the dim background lights disappeared. "Fuckin A!" I screamed at Paul, "The sun's come out in the middle of night!" Everything besides my thinking was as clear as day in that moment, I was simply thrust into hysterical wonderment. Not knowing what to do, or realizing I was leaning against it, I pulled on the handle of my door, which opened abruptly, spilling me out of the truck to the gravel below. It was so bright out as I fell to the ground that I repeated myself in free falling delirium, "The sun is out in the middle of the night!" But as I lay on my back in the parking lot I looked up to see a police helicopter with its searchlight combing for perverts, which I probably resembled. I bounded back up into the truck, yelling, "It's the fuckin cops!" which instantly achieved greater import than the miracle I thought I had witnessed. Paul fired up the truck, threw it in reverse, and spit gravel as we got the hell out of there. I must admit though, I liked being that high. Like I was on LSD.

1⑥

Several people knew that I had taken acid a few times by then, and wanted to try it. So on one of my runs I scored a hundred hits of JFK from some people who shall remain nameless, understanding at the time that it was a serious federal offense for them to sell me acid. Even though they were probably only 20 at the time, selling to a minor is an instant 10-year stretch. I had my brother to think about too, who might be incriminated for hooking me up, so I had to be extra careful. There were still plenty of straight kids at my school, and a large contingent of Mormons. I was pretty well known, both scholastically and as a high brain, but most of the kids who knew what was going on were my friends. I think they understood that although it was scary to their sense of propriety or danger level of adolescent choices, I was pretty together, and my product would be too. As much as I felt responsible for providing the LSD, the fact was that a bunch of people wanted to try it. It's always scary to take the leap into frying, though. You hear such terrifying stories about Art Linkletter's daughter and chromosome damage and going insane and seeing God and drowning in an inch of water; there isn't a lot of clear information out there. Not like today: "Hey there's AIDS out there so wear a condom." It would have been nice if there was a public awareness campaign; something like "Hey, if you're gonna dose, do it somewhere cool. Avoid stressful encounters. Avoid your parents." I used to be real afraid of drowning in an inch of water. I wouldn't go near it when I was dosed. One day I came home from school tooo high, so I took a shower to get away from my mom. I just couldn't deal with her. I was afraid I'd die like a turkey or something with the water running up my nose, but I got in the shower and it was like, Whoaa, this is cool! There's thousands of little droplets all hitting my skin, one at a time, but very quickly. Man, what is all this horseshit people have been feeding us about drugs? I'm dosing and going whitewater tubing!

What started out as a handful of people risking their sanity grew into a serious market as everyone else found out that their friends hadn't gone insane. I was the only source, which was definitely good for business, and hits were cool in themselves. The JFK sheets had lifted his portrait from the postage stamp, but his eyes were missing and there was a galaxy behind the holes. I'd always sell the rest of the sheet and eat the eyes myself. At first it was only on Friday that I'd bring it to school, so people had time to do it and recover over the weekend, but eventually some of us got more daring, and FRY-day took hold. A bunch of us would dose before first period and get together at lunch to exchange bizarre stories. I remember one kid who dosed for the first time and everybody found out by lunch, so everyone in his English class got together and when he walked in late the whole class started swiveling their heads back and forth. Needless to say, he bailed.

I myself would take acid every day it rained, it was just so beautiful! There's something about the rain that insulates you from everyone, as if there's a fuzzy screen going on between you, so you don't get too paranoid. But to stand in it and feel it pelting you, tickling your face and forming rivulets like a living force from the sky, is simply the best. The really best thing about it, for those who begin to understand how to use mirrors to see the world, is that the puddles everywhere reflect the sky and the trees. I could go to the park and stand under trees for hours, just looking at how different their canopies were in a reflection, and how the clouds sailed by in a puddle in the grass; just like that MC Escher print, but etched on your nervous system. Frying, for me, became an intellectual pursuit, one where I could drop the smallness of my usual perspective and watch the universe flow by. I really did feel that this was expanding my consciousness. I was always searching for intellectual horizons, and here was experience at its finest.

Clay and I drove to Berkeley once, and I dosed before we left home. By the time we got to Dixon, with its miles of sunflower fields, I was fryin pretty hard. As far as you could see were sunflowers, looking like a million eyes, all staring at me. But it didn't feel weird, just like I was in touch with something big.

"Hey man," Clay slipped into my reverie, "I'm getting tired. You wanna drive?"

"Dude," I responded, "I'm high!" as if his suggestion were ludicrous.

"It's okay, just space out on the road." I don't think I had ever felt anyone trust in me quite so much; not just with his life, but his car! We pulled over and switched, and in a minute I was spacing on the road, and it flowed. Cars moved on and off smoothly, glinting in the sun, colored metal exoskeletons blinking their drivers' intent. I just held my space while the river moved around me, and before I knew it I was there, and found parking! That taught me more about trusting myself, and the universe, while totally high, than anything else ever had. Clay and I used to have a little ritual when we'd go out at night, just to acknowledge that we were pushing the limits. I got it from watching Little Big Man, where before a battle he says, "It is a good day to die." So whenever we got in the car to go get ripped at night, knowing it was a risk, we'd say, "It is a good night to die." I didn't really expect to, but I trusted that it would be okay if I did. That level of trust in what I was doing, particularly in my friendship with Clay, was implicit.

In all that time though, I never once considered that there were any spiritual implications involved in my quest. I hadn't gotten a look at comparisons of drug use to Eastern practices yet, (another omission of small town libraries), not that I would have paid any attention to them. I was still pretty locked into my anti-religion mode at that time. Religion was slavery and God did not exist. I had discovered a copy of Anton LaVey's Satanic Bible in Berkeley, and decided I was a Satanist, but I didn't liken it to religion. Great stuff, that Satanism; no turning the other cheek. "If a man smite thee, smite him three times," stuff like that. Do whatever you want, have sex with whomever you want, the kind of stuff you want to hear when you're seventeen. The actually useful tenet I do remember is rather universalistic, "Positive thought and positive action yield positive results," but hey, it's hard to write your own religion. There was no one around for me to practice with, but just having my Satanic Bible made me all the more terrifying to the Christian freaks and Mormons at school. For me, religion was bullshit, spirituality didn't exist, and drugs were strictly a mental exercise. Things were pretty much black and white that way. It's funny to think of how much you heard the old "I took LSD and saw God" expression, cuz even if you have some sort of revelatory experience, chances are that God is gonna turn out to be an oil slick on the pavement in the rain, or one of your stereo speakers.

I did score some mescaline once though, just a fat tab for myself, and it was a very different trip. I always had to test my products before marketing them, to maintain my integrity, and to make sure that everyone could handle them. I was out driving with Clay and everything was all puffy pastels, breathing billowing clouds, soft. We were listening to A Quick One, by The Who, which had come to the end, with its rounds of "You are forgiven." I noticed these clouds above us parting, and I could feel this energy—like a giant hand, reach down through the windshield and grab me by my heart. It started pulling, and pulling, and I was— whelmed. Townshend was screaming "forgiven forgiven forgiven forgiven forgiven forgiven forgiven forgiven" and I felt like this hand was gonna pull me right out through the windshield if I didn't do something. I was struggling against this force, being lifted out of my seat, and panicking over what to do, and I didn't want to be forgiven, so I punched the tape deck and it spit out the tape and… I… was… **straight.** Clay looked over at me, "Dude, are you trippin?"

"Uhhh… Not anymore." I was totally straight, but I was experiencing some new questions, like, "Where the fuck did that come from?" There was nothing in my life that had ever related to any sort of religious consciousness, but I was just about to have an audience with God. I had no idea what this shit was about, and I didn't want one. Besides, being ripped out of myh body or torn through the windshield like that would've made a big fuckin mess and we can't be having that. So I didn't bother trying to cop any more mescaline. It was too hard to judge what effects it might have had. Acid was much easier to score anyway, and it was more…geometric in the way it disassembled and rearranged the universe. And that was safe.

Safety was important, considering my situation, and I took what precautions I thought were necessary. It wasn't so hard to be cool at school, "A" student, Captain of the Debate team, Head Photographer for the newspaper, I put up a good front. But I could never figure out how my parents remained so oblivious. I guess the fact that I was always high made me seem normal, but maybe they really didn't want to know. My father took me from school to the orthodontist one day, and Paul was in the faculty parking lot, doing bong hits, which is where I would have been if my father wasn't there. When Paul saw us in his mirror he yelled out his window, "Like father like son." I cringed, but my dad looked sort of proud, never realizing that Paul was referring to the pipe he was constantly puffing on.

One night my mom asked me what it was that my friends and I did 'til so late at night, since we never came home before four in the morning. I told her,

"Mom, I didn't want to tell you this, but you know where the "K" street mall is in downtown Sacramento? Well, we all go down there and score heroin, then we shoot up and lay around with the winos."

"Hahahahaha, son," she laughed, "you're so funny." Really mom, we all take acid and smoke pot and drink kegs and have bonfires and climb high tension towers and just go crazy! If anything, dealing with my parents developed my impromptu speaking skills, because I would go off on some bizarre tangent about any subject that came up and not get lost. Try maintaining a conversation with your parents over a spaghetti dinner while on LSD, or mushrooms.

I was so impressed with the effects of these fungi that I purchased a book about cultivating them, which had an address to mail to for spores.

I wasn't sure how I could pull it off in my bedroom, but months later I realized it would be a cool project for the Westinghouse Science Talent Search. I could get high and get a scholarship! Thinking he'd be helpful, I told my biology teacher I wanted to do a time lapse photographic study of fungal growth. I knew I needed to get some special agar, the bacterial kind, not the fungal, because psilocybin mushrooms are a higher life form. (Ever read Ray Bradbury's, "Boys, Grow Giant Mushrooms in Your Basement?") When I told him what kind of agar I wanted him to order, he said,

"You don't want that, that's for bacteria. The only fungus you can grow on that is psilocybin mushrooms." How the fuck did he know! Here's a guy who was too embarrassed and Catholic to answer the question, "Can you get pregnant from oral sex," in our sex education class. I couldn't believe that he'd tripped, or knew about growing mushrooms, but I played it cool.

"Grow what?" I responded.

"Oh nothing." So I let him get me the mycelial agar, which produced an exciting array of mold filled petri dishes in the sterile box I had built in my room. No prize for me. But reading that book did settle my mind on the idea that mushroom eating cultures liked to hang out in caves when they tripped, for the visual effects, and that a 165 pound man should eat 5 grams, which is a pretty good buzz. It also clued me into the fact that indigenous peoples throughout South America had been ritually using psychedelic plants for centuries, which returned me to my childhood interest in magic, and the desire to study the anthropology of drug use in "primitive" cultures.

I may not have won the Westinghouse Science prize, but I was developing my own research facility in drug use and human behavior. I was becoming something of a musicologist at the same time, trying to determine my career path. I wanted to study drugs, and anthropology, but I was into entertainment, film, TV, music, ways to reach people. I wanted to take people somewhere, through sound or images, to places they hadn't been before, places in the mind of the world. Nowhere did I find a better cohesion of my career ideas than my visit to Dave's for the Grateful Dead's New Year's show. I remember meeting one of his friends, Art, and watching him prepare. Art had a sack of peyote buttons from which he was meticulously scraping the white mesh that covers the surface.

"See this white stuff," he said, pointing it out to me, "it has these micro thorns that stick to your stomach lining and make you throw up."

"I thought it just tasted like shit," I replied.

"It does, that's why I chop it up and put it into gel caps. But these fibers would still make you puke." I was impressed with his research and methodology, hoping to apply myself honorably in the science of getting high. It seemed like everyone at the show was trying to get as high as I was, gyrating within the pulsing psychedelic symphony. There was a great sense of camaraderie, joy, love, and judging by the vibe of the people I met through Dave, who were earnest and intelligent, I would be proud to be a member of their community.

I kept up the product quality and the range of substances, getting a different friend to drive me to Berkeley every couple weeks. I also kept an eye on everyone I sold to, because I felt responsible for everyone that took my drugs. Yes, everyone is taking drugs to prove to themselves that they're responsible for themselves and their experience, but I knew that any real fuck up would come back to me, so I had to have some control over things. I did sell a hit to a girl once, when I knew I shouldn't have. I had this vocational television/radio class, where I'd go to Sacramento for half a day to produce TV shows and radio spots. The teacher's son, Jeff, and I got along great. We'd get high every day or dose sometimes, and run the studio, which was hell of fun. There were kids from every school in the region, and this girl, Paula Green, was one of the geekier ones. She kept beggin me to sell her some acid, even though she didn't really even smoke pot, and my buddy Jeff was like, "C'mon man, sell her a hit." So I did. The next day she came to class acting like a textbook psych case. She told us she had taken it before she went to bed, and spent the whole night up tweakin because her parents were hiding in her closet and talking! She kept twitchin, with this weird tic, where she'd shrug and blink. You know how if you walk around all day shrugging and blinking cuz you decided it would be weird, you just can't stop? It was like that. Everybody just wanted to slap her and say "get over it," but instead we abused her. We were filming the courtroom scene from To Kill A Mockingbird that day, she was playing the rich white girl, and I was the poor black guy Tom. I was really milking how she wanted me to "**Come**… up on the porch, and chop up de chiffarobe." (I still have no fucking idea what a "chiffarobe" is) I was pointing at her and getting everybody to stare at her, and when she was on the stand we got the whole studio whispering, "whore whore whore," while she continued to blink and twitch. Ahh, the cruelty of youth. But it made me ever more circumspect in who I dealt to.

Which is not to say I didn't have other close calls here and there. We were young and high, and perhaps my friends weren't quite as sharp as I like to think I was. My parents let me take the old '65 Fury III out on a Friday night, and we were bongin out in the parking lot by the arcade when I see the cops pull in the other side of the lot. Now, I always park facing out, so I just crank it and pull away. I cruise over behind the Mormon church, start throwing all our beers and dope down the speaker holes into the trunk, and boom, the cops! I didn't know how the fuck they saw us, but I hadn't spent any time behind the Mormon church, which was apparently a straight sight line. I figure, Cool, everything's stashed. So they get us all out of the car, and walk around it, and this cop reaches along the passenger seat, where Mackie was, and pulls out a bong! "Well, well, what have we here?" I look at him like, Mackie! What the fuck? And he's mumbling, "Uh, sorry Norberger." And then this cop looks on the armrest of the door, and right there is this little bud that Mackie was gonna fire up. The cop takes the bong and brings this bud over, and says, "So what do you guys do with this? You put this in here, like this?" And he takes this bud, crams it in the bowl, and fuckin packs it in there with his thumb, like a totally experienced bonger. "Well I don't know what I'm gonna do with you boys." But it looks like he's gonna let us off when Mackie notices these kids walking down the street and says,

"Hey officer, aren't those kids a little young to be out this late?"

"Yes, and looking at your IDs I see that you are, too," so he writes us all curfew tickets. Of course, mine mentions that he confiscated a bong from my car. Thanks Mack. I simply explained to my parents that it wasn't my bong, and it was cool. They probably didn't know what a bong was. When I went to my juvenile hearing and the judge pulled out the bong as evidence, I noticed that the weed, which had been ever so tightly packed in that bowl, had been reduced to ash. Cops!

11

Getting away seemed to be my forte, and I think I learned that if out-right escape wasn't possible, and lying didn't work, then grace would inter-vene, the grace of Onggh Yaangh. In Barrington someone had invented a faith for a Spiritual Anthropology class or something and called it Onngh Yaangh. Onggh Yaangh had all the necessary requirements for a religion, and icon, a mudra, a tenet, a comic book and a T-shirt. It had it's vaguely cultish feel, based simply on the nature of its devotees, who were Barringtonian freaks, but it was more of a simple faith, based on the tenet, "Those who know don't tell, those who tell don't know." I eventually realized that this idea was lifted pretty directly from the Tao Te Ching, and is about as simple a truth as the world holds, but it held an essen-tial quality for a community of dope dealers. OY was also a respectable looking icon, a flat headed alien looking dude who first appeared in the comic strip that described his origin. Flashing the Onngh Yaangh sign and repeating his name just gave you the sense that everything would be cool, which it was. I was sitting in my room one night, studying, when my dad came in.

"I want to look at your eyes."

"Huh?"

"Let me look at your eyes."

"What for?"

"I want to see if you've been doing any drugs." He took this flashlight and shined it in my eyes, searching for some reaction that he probably wasn't really aware of. Oddly enough he picked the rare night that I wasn't high, so I just acted resentful, and by the grace of Onggh Yaangh, things pretty much went on as they had.

Until Dick showed up. Dick started out as Clay's mom's boyfriend, and he was pretty cool. He wasn't really around while we were party-ing, but he seemed okay with it. One time he asked me to baby-sit his son while he took Clay's mom out. I kind of hedged until he offered me five bucks and a 6 pack. I figured—Cool! Clay's aunt showed up after an hour and offered to relieve me, so I just went out partying. At some point though, Dick moved in to Clay's house. Perhaps it was Clay's mom's house, but at the time it was hard to see it that way. I helped Dick move out of his apartment and when we were cleaning out his desk I found a pipe and some papers so I thought, Right on! This guy's one of us. But it wasn't very long after he moved in that he sort of pulled the Jeckyl/Hyde,

"I'm the responsible man around here," routine. That's how he earned his nickname. "Dick!" Everyone had felt so connected to that family that we all felt like the men of the house. We'd have killed anyone who fucked with Clay's mom, who was still superfine at 36. I suppose we all wanted to fuck her ourselves. I know I did. But she needed a man, and Dick felt it was now his responsibility to treat us like kids. The problem was that we weren't kids, and we were used to partying at what he now considered his house. Fortunately he'd be gone in the mornings, when we'd have our serious sessions to warm up for school, but people would go over to the garage or the old trailer in the driveway at lunch and he occasionally came home and busted them. Eventually both Clay and his kid brother had to kick Dick's ass, just to remind him what was up, but that didn't stop him from vibing everyone out. All you could do was say, "Hey DICK! Howzit hangin?" We still partied, but the garage, which had been a raging dope center for years, was off limits, since we had to be a little wary of Dick!

That was the spring of 1980, my senior year, and our basketball team was on fire. We had a new coach and he had swung a couple of black kids from Sacramento into school to play hoop for us. We had a pretty good team anyway, but that really made it. Ed led the cheering section in its intense derision of opponents and refs. "Ref sucks dick! Ref sucks dick!" was one familiar chant of our rooters. Me, I was on the floor taking pictures, and selling acid. Hoop is a great sport on acid. At the peak of the season there'd be at least a dozen guys frying at a game. Once or twice my buddy Ingalls, who was a reserve forward, would fry too, and we'd be in the zone together. And the team kept winning. They won the state title. But it was the regional title game that I remember. It was at the Fieldhouse at Cal Davis, a pretty big place, and there were a couple other games so I was in the stands before ours started.

Someone told me that Bennett wanted some hits. I see him there, way up in the stands, and I go up and sit next to him. I look around, see the rooters with their signs, who's on the left, the cheerleaders bouncing up and down, who's on the right, the vice principals down below us in the next section, and cool, I whip out my little bag. I used to carry my hits in the little rubber band bags for my braces. They had little animals on them to denote the strength of the bands, and consequently, the acid. So I cut out some hits for Bennett and his girlfriend, pass 'em over, and he hands me the cash. I go to stash my shit in my pocket and have this funny feeling in the back of my head, like someone's hammering a mountaineering bolt into it, and I turn around and there's DICK! He was sitting right behind us, watching the whole thing. Fuuuuck! This was not good. So the next day I went over to see Clay and DICK informs me that he doesn't want any "pushers" in his house. I just looked at him with that, "What the fuck are you talking about" stare, since I had never "pushed" anything on anyone, but there was no getting around it. My home was no longer my home, and I'd have to start using my own closet. He didn't narc me out, Onggh Yaaangh, which I guess I should've been thankful for, but being outlawed where I felt safest wasn't easy either. I knew that it put more pressure on Clay, too. But we were pretty autonomous by then, and things were drawing to a close with our high school career. Of course, this meant that pranks needed creation.

I had realized how plebeian the administrators at my high school were in my freshman year, when I returned from Xmas vacation wearing the shirt Ivan had given me, which was popular at USC. It had a box of Trojans on the front and back. Nowadays kids would be applauded for wearing such a thing, but my PE teacher sent me to the office and after conferring, the principals decided to suspend me for a day. They wanted to suspend me for saying "fart" at a pep rally once, but my mother informed them that she could also say fart in public, amongst other things. Stuffing the ballot box with Ed Darrow was a definite move toward expulsion. Especially when the vice principal, Mr. Rolletti, a guy too short to be a cop and carrying a big chip over it, demanded that I tell him who was this student that we were trying to get elected. "I can't find any Frank Zappa enrolled here!" But the best stunt was the final issue of our school paper. There was a column called Heap of the Month, where we ran a photo and description of somebody's hot rod, and I took the photos. I met with my buddy Johnny out behind the auto shop where he had his classic Willy's jeep. A few of our other friends were there too. So I take some pictures of the engine with the hood open, then I ask Johnny to close it and get inside, but he doesn't want to be in the picture. So Golden Boy, the quarterback, forward, left fielder, "A" student, all around good guy says,

"Hey, I'll get in there." I tell him,

"How about if you get in and shoot a BA?" So he gets in the back and puts this moon right between the headrests of the bucket seats, and I take the picture. It turns out that with the reflection of the windshield, Golden Boy's ass is practically subliminal. A little psychology allows my journalism advisor to think that she picked the right photo, and it runs in the paper. About halfway through lunch, word has gotten out, everyone is tearing the papers away from each other to see it, and some fuckhead points it out to the principal, to whose office I was immediately summoned. Oh, how disappointed they were, a top student abusing his position and responsibility. It was impossible to deny it, and it earned me a few days of home study, but at least I refused to tell them that the model was their own Golden Boy.

When I wasn't thrashing too hard, I'd just hang out with Don. Play chess and bong out. Don was really uptight about his dad busting him for pot when he first got high. His dad was pretty hardcore about the lawn and chores and shit, but he had been a biker when he was young. He had a chopper trike in the garage, so I always suspected he was cool. One day he took Don out to the garage and told him that if he wanted to get high, to do it out there. Don was blown away. So we'd sit back behind the woodpiles, where I could hear my mom if she called me but we couldn't be seen, and catch a buzz. Don had worked his way up to be manager of Foster's Freeze, so he bought a car and we would go to all the midnight movies, Pink Floyd, ELP, The Kids Are Alright, Song Remains the Same, 200 Motels. I could always provide dope, but Don got his own scam going. Instead of just raiding the till, like Wails had at Taco Bell, he'd trade burgers and shakes for dope. Fosters' was down by the pool hall, so all the loadies with their shitty lumbo would be coming in all the time, and Don would end up with a fat roll of shitty joints every weekend. I didn't know how he could smoke that shit, since I had all the green bud, but it was a good deal for him. We'd get high, read comics, or the porn mags we were starting to buy at his uncle's liquor store, and listen to music. Don was getting a pretty huge collection of records together by now. He had taken to trading his books back at a profit, collecting whole series' of different authors to make them more valuable, and using his profits to expand his record collection. I was in the problem mode of having total black market income, so I couldn't really buy stuff or my parents would suspect, but I aspired to be a DJ, and Don made me listen to a lot of cool shit.

As I said before, my father had put us on the classical train from day one, and we were all in band, which introduced us to jazz as well. But when I was about ten, Ivan joined the Columbia record club and got Led Zeppelin II. So when the folks were away it was "Whole Lotta Love" and "Ramble On." I wasn't ever that into Zeppelin, but after he bought Magical Mystery Tour I did become pretty obsessed with "I am the Walrus," (smoke pot smoke pot everybody smoke pot) and ended up on a serious Beatles binge for years. Despite being an out of it eight year old, it was no secret that those guys were talking about getting high. Even the pop stuff on the radio was full of reference to drugs and sex, because it was the language of our culture. According to the tests, I was reading at a college level (whatever that was) by the seventh grade, but it was hard to find collegiate reading material in my high school library. Now, I'll admit, Shakespeare pretty much says it all, but when you're looking for Henry Miller or Charles Bukowski, or someone to give you a flavor of the experience of adulthood, or at least adultery, your high school librarian's not going to help you out. Sure Moby Dick is a great tale of experience, but there are no more barrels of sperm to wring out on a starlit South Pacific night. "We want the world and we want it now!" And music is all about now. Sure there are marketing guys trying to cleverly aim it at the ideals of now, but the real stuff tells you what people are doing and thinking and feeling as young adults, and derelicts, now.

My mom made me read a bunch of books the summer after my junior year, cuz she thought I wasn't reading enough, which I wasn't. She made me read this one book, The Magnificent Obsession, about a young guy who gets drunk and kills this great doctor in a boating accident, so he invests his life in becoming a great surgeon. Gets the daughter. Very inspiring, very claptrap. I'm sorry, but I've been told these inspiring stories of courage and honor since I was a kid, and I'm tired. The president is a peanut farmer with a drunken brother. He's replaced an idiot who's replaced a criminal who's supporting a hack "B" movie star for the next election. Where's the inspiration here in America? Where's the experience? We're watching The Deer Hunter, we're watching Apocalypse Now, but a guy can't even take acid and kill for his country anymore, so give me… give me… Give me experience with overpowering, synasthesiac, transcendent, deafening sound! We needed a soundtrack for our lives, and while the drugs set the tone, the music colored it Deep Purple, and Blue Öyster Cult and Pink Floyd!

After The Magnificent Obsession I decided I could no longer read for entertainment, I had my own magnificent obsession. I wanted to be an electronic media maven anyway, so I'd just dose and listen to rock and roll. Take your Tolkien, I've got Rush, Proust, Quadrophenia, Orwell, or "Welcome to the Machine." The music told us who we were and where we lived. I remember trying to listen to Jimi Hendrix when my brothers got Are You Experienced? It gave me a headache. But after I took LSD, it opened up that circuit, and I became. And you couldn't understand the one without the other. Maybe we were too young at the time to really grasp the anger and melancholy of Pink Floyd, but who's going to argue with the sheer pick you up and transport you to another dimension beauty? For most of my generation, listening to Pink Floyd was eleusis. You could carry church with you on 8 track or cassette. I was talking to some college kids about Floyd recently, and they were telling me how great The Wall was, and I asked one of them if he ever listened to the secret message?

"What do you mean man, it's full of secret messages," he replied.

"Theee secret message?" I asked him, and he was dumbfounded. You see, now you can only get it on CD, so you miss the most important song, but Mackie and I had played it backwards on my dad's old hi-fi turntable and figured it out. If I have any real regret over high school, it's that I didn't run away to see The Wall in LA. I probably would've been beaten by the cops, like everyone else was, but I'd have been there.

12

I'll never forget Grad Nite, our Senior Class trip to Disneyland. Things were going great; I had been accepted to UCLA, full ride, I was pulling straight A's, made it to state tournament in speech again, and thought I had a chance to win this time. I even had a midnight DJ shift on the public radio station booked for the summer. The girl who had done all the planning for the trip was this really nice, albeit totally straight, Mormon girl, Terry Von. She had always been pretty cool, but had that kind of "well meaning concern for our best interests" that influenced her choice of chaperones. She had let everyone sign up for the bus they wanted to ride on, and the entire OH club was on bus number two. I came to school that morning with all kinds of drugs, but I sold everything by 8:15 and had to run home for my whole stash. We were lined up next to the buses, ready to bong the whole way to Anaheim, when Terry introduced our chaperones and let them say a few words.

"Good morning gentlemen. Terry asked us as fellow church members if we would chaperone you on your trip to Disneyland, which sounded like fun. But I want you to know that we are off duty Sacramento police officers. So let's get this straight, we don't want you bringing any of those kinky drugs with you on this trip. And by the way, Terry has told us a little bit about you. You must be Ed Darrow. Didn't you get into a fight with officer Oates and get maced? Aren't you Garry Jackson? You drove your '36 Ford Coupe off the road and had to get cut out of it, didn't you?"

He went right down the line, matching everybody to some prior offense. But when he looked at me, he sort of stopped, like he hadn't seen my picture or anything. Terry was cool enough not to tell him who I was! I ended up sitting right behind these two cops on the bus. I was nervous as hell, since guys kept waving at me to sell them shit. But after awhile I broke it out and sold twenty hits of acid, right under these cops' noses. I went into the bathroom and stashed dime bags of pot and got the money passed back in a comic book. I didn't bong out in the bathroom, but Sammy did and got away with it.

We finally got to Disneyland and while I got into my suit, cuz you had to wear a suit, I ate my 6 grams of shrooms. It was then that I realized that I had forgotten my dress shoes. I tried to walk in nonchalantly but a guard saw me before I was even in line and sent me to a trailer. I was freaked cuz I had so much stash on me, and I thought it was security, but inside it was a giant wardrobe department. They fit me into a pair of extremely lame shoes, little capsized boats made of cheap Paraguayan leather, and sent me back into line. I was getting paranoid, since security guys were frisking everyone, but I got a little old man who just waved me by. The Magic Kingdom.

I went right to Spaaaaaaaaaaaace Mountain, my namesake, and screamed through it about four times. We figured out that we could smoke joints in the boat ride, since no one was on it, and we could steer the boats off into the reeds to be discrete. The security inside was bizarre. There were these guys dressed like Japanese businessmen, talking in Japanese, but with little plugs in their ears. It was so unreal, the perfect place to dose. Cleveland was standing around eating some popcorn and spilled some, and this little guy with a broom comes and whisks it away. So he spills some more, and the guy comes right back. So we buy some more, and we're chowing it and dumping it, and this guy is sweeping all around us and between us, never saying a word while we're throwing it at each other and shit, too high. A bunch of guys went to the Main Street Restaurant and dined & dashed, then went back a few hours later and did it again. We stole everything that wasn't nailed down. Just taking flowers and giving them to girls. I met this girl who told me she really wanted a Dumbo, so I just strolled on up to a concession booth, picked up this giant fuckin Dumbo, walked away and gave it her. I could hear the guy yelling, "Hey! Hey!" but I just kept walkin.

At midnight I ate the remainder of my acid, which was down to a few hits, but enough to keep me trippin until dawn. I remember running into this girl I liked, Felicity, near Fantasyland, and she wanted to go there. I told her "Fantasyland is for kids," but she really wanted to take the Peter Pan ride. I was like, Fuck that! but she insisted, and you know what? When you're trippin that hard you realize, "We can fly!" We went over to "It's a Small World" after that, which really had me worried, but it was so ridiculous, all these tiny Zambians singing at you. I took off my tie clip, pulled out the little bag from inside my tie, and fired up a huge Thai weed hash oil bomber. It burned on and on and on and I was getting kind of paranoid, but the little Israelis and Arabs and Indians and Pakistanis and Turks and Greeks and Serbs and Croats and Tutsis and Hutus kept right on singing until we reached the big banner proclaiming that "The Small World was brought to you by Bank of America," at which point we were totally stoned. By then the bomber was just a roach, which I tossed in the river. They pretty much had to sweep us out of the park at dawn, and I had to run back and return my shoes before the bus left without me. We had a great time though, and it was mostly due to the drugs.

I had really been looking forward to getting out of school, I mean, I dug my friends, and I dug partying, but I felt that going to college would give me the opportunity to actually do something with my mind. I was planning on doing the Film/Television program at UCLA, with a double major in speech, so I knew I could meet some cool people and do some cool shit. I could check out ethnobotany on the sociological level, but it wouldn't be about doing drugs anymore. I felt like I had pretty much done all the drugs I could, and gotten away with it. I was going to quit drugs completely, go where no one would know me, reinvent myself as a serious student, be creative, and become a famous filmmaker. I was pretty excited about that. But I had a whole summer ahead of me, so I partied, going up to the American River, eating mushrooms or taking acid, cliff diving and tubing, smoking fatties in a power hitter while we floated downstream.

At the end of July my parents went away for a weekend somewhere, so I got Ed to drive me to Berkeley. I scored all kinds of dope, the usual summer staples of Thai sticks and black Afghani hash, some mushrooms, acid, and just for me, a stick of the original Buddha Thai. This was not some street corner "Buddha Thai" drek on a big piece of wood, but the real deal. The original, a sweet half-ounce bud wrapped around a reed that weighed half a gram, a bud unreplicated to this day. Two hits of it would paralyze you. Ed and I stopped by the Shortstop for some beers on the way home and there was this total southern boy in a cowboy hat and boots, who asked Ed if he knew where to get any weed. I'm like, No way, this is too coincidental. This guy must be a narc. But Ed starts talking to him and lookin back at me like, "Hey! Sell this guy some dope." The dude says he's staying with his cousin, so Ed agrees to follow him over there to check it out, and gets in the car. I'm thinkin, The bust meter has gone through the roof here, but Ed's tellin me "It's cool." So we follow this dude to his cousin's, and Ed knew somebody who knew him, so we all did some bongs and it was okay, and this guy whips out a ton of cash and wants to buy everything we can get. So I go out to the car and bring in like a pound of dope and some shrooms and acid and he buys it all, full retail. So we turn around and drive back to Berkeley and do it again, and still get back in time to have some folks over while my parents are out. I was feelin kind of burnt the next day, and they were coming home, so I stashed everything and went to the river.

It was the usual baking summer day driving up to Lake Clementine, where we could park and hike our inner tubes down to the North Fork of the American River. Ed and Clay and I ate a bunch of shrooms and splashed our way into the totally mellow, slow, warm water of the deep ravine. It was always beautiful there, sunny and hot, amazing serpentine rocks, great places for cliff diving, and Blackberry Island, a sandbar overgrown with totally ripe blackberries. It was heavenly. We beached our tubes there and gorged ourselves like bears. Our destination was Paradise, the nude beach farther down after the confluence with the Middle Fork. The Middle Fork is gnarly, huge crazy whitewater shit. When they come together it's a wild ass ride. You will be sucked under and you must hold your tube. Ed lost his once and almost bought it right there, and other people surely have. Now they have a fence through the river and signs forbidding anyone to ride through; a $250 ticket if the rangers catch you.

Just about the time we got there it got real cloudy, which was weird for up there, and not what you want because the Middle Fork is about 15 or 20 degrees colder than the North Fork. You know how when you're high and don't really feel in control of your body temperature and are probably pushing hypothermia, you feel kind of nervous? Well, I started feelin kind of nervous. I hit those rapids anyway, out to the middle, through the "man-eater" and held on and held my breath and held on some more until I popped up and whew, survived again. Everybody made it, and we all floated down to Paradise. But I still felt funny. The gray wasn't lifting, and we were pretty cold, so a couple guys split to get the trucks we left at Clementine. We had to hang there another hour or so though, and I began to get that cold, drained, pit in the stomach feeling. My newest attempt to keep my weed dry hadn't worked either, which was a bummer. The guys got back and we loaded up and went to Foster's Freeze for some hot grease, but it didn't make me feel any better. Something was buggin me and I didn't know what, so I shifted around on the hot metal of the truck bed, silently agitated during the drive back to Roseville.

13

I got home, slipped in the back door, changed into some dry clothes and put on my good son persona.

"Hey mom, what's for dinner?"

"I don't think you're going to have much of an appetite." What the hell was that supposed to mean? I wondered. I walked into the kitchen and sat down at the table, where they had already finished their martinis.

"Son," my dad says, reaching behind him and pulling out a QP slab of hash and slapping it on the table with a thwack, "what's this?" I stared at it for a moment, as my mind raced through the possibilities: Maybe that's all they found. You could say you were holding it for someone. BE COOL!

"That's a quarter pound of black Afghani hash, dad."

"And this?" He pulled out one of my film cans, the kind for 100 foot rolls, which was packed with foil wrapped grams and quarter ounces I'd already carved out.

"That's more." He took out a piece and unwrapped it, and when the smell hit my nostrils I just wanted to grab it and eat it so I could survive this.

"And why are these wrapped up like this?"

"So I can sell 'em."

"So you can sell them," he calmly repeated.

"Yeah," I swallowed, as my ears started ringing and that numb, floating away feeling took over.

"And what about this?" He said, pulling out the half pound of Thai sticks that had been in the back of a drawer in my chest bed.

"That's Thai weed," I said, thinking, Not the record box, not the record box.

"And this?"

"That's another Thai stick, the really rare kind." Stay out of the closet, stay out of the closet.

"And these?"

"Those are mushrooms, dad."

"What do you do with them?"

"You eat them and they get you high."

"And this?"

"It's a bong, dad, you smoke pot through it." Not the bookcase not the bookcase notthebookcase!

"So you sell these drugs?"

"Yeah."

"From our house?"

"Yeah." My mother came over and slapped my face.

"Do you know how many times kids have told me, 'Mrs. Norberg, your son's a drug dealer. Your son sells heroin.' And I never believed them, I just thought they were trying to get my goat for being a substitute teacher. We trusted you, and this is how you pay us back?"

We all sat in silence until my father asked my mother for the phone.

"Well, I guess there's nothing else to do but call the police."

"WHAT?" I screamed, bursting into tears. "You're gonna throw away my future, now that I'm finally on the verge of getting out of this dump and doing something with my life? The whole reason I did drugs was because I was stuck here! There was never any challenge, any culture. Drugs were the most intellectual thing to do. You made us move here, and you hate it here too, don't lie!"

The venom I spit at the bullseye of my father's failed intellectual legacy hit its mark, leaving us submerged in silence. My father let go of the receiver, which recoiled and swung, thudding against the wall.

"Well, what should we do?"

"I owe a bunch of money for these drugs, and I have to pay it back."

"To whom?"

"I'd rather not say."

"We could just flush them down the toilet," my mother suggested.

"Ben Brainerd."

"Ben Brainerd sold you these drugs?" My mother responded in shock, knowing him to be a "good student."

"Hell no, he just loaned me the money."

"How much money?"

"300 dollars."

"And where did you get the drugs, your brother?"

"No. I know these guys in the Sacramento. You know, you might not be able to appreciate this, but I have a lot of integrity at this. This is all really high quality stuff and I have a very professional ethic. I need to pay him back, with interest."

"And how do you propose to do that?"

"You could let me sell it all, one deal."

"To whom?"

"I'll find somebody."

"Can't you take it back to the people you bought it from?"

"I don't think so." We sat for awhile in silence.

"What made you search my room, anyway?"

"Somebody called for you and hung up. You were just getting too popular."

"Hmm, can I be excused?"

"You know you're grounded."

"For how long?"

"Until you leave for college." Fuck, I thought, but at least they hadn't found my acid! Onggh Yaangh!

The next morning they had decided to let me go ahead and get rid of the shit, but I had to do it all under their supervision. I called a friend from my TV class in Sacramento, someone they'd never met and wouldn't know how to track down, and I pitched him the deal of the century. "Brian, my parents just busted me with over 1,000 bucks worth of killer shit, but they're gonna let me sell it to pay off my debts, so I'll let you have it for $400. Just get the cash however you can, believe me it's worth it." So the next afternoon my friend Brian comes over. He's a pretty jovial guy, but seeing my mom sitting there watching us made him kind of nervous.

"Uhh, hey."

"Hi Brian. I've got everything laid out on the table here, pretty good deal for 400 bucks, huh?"

"Fuck!" he said, staring at the pile. He had probably never even dreamed of that much dope. I was totally invested in letting my folks know what an ethical business guy I was, so I said to him,

"Look, I want you to be sure this is good shit, and I'm not trying to rip you off here."

"Oh no, man, I trust you."

"Yeah, well you better sample this shit anyway."

"Man, your mom is sitting right there," he whispers to me like I'm insane.

"Hey, I want you to be sure about what you're getting." So I went to the kitchen and filled up the bong, and broke off a chunk of hash and made him burn it.

"Cwhohouha-yeah, that's good," he coughed.

"Now you gotta try this Buddha Thai." He just gave me this –whatever– look and fired it up. When he slumped back in his chair I knew my product had proven its effectiveness once again, and that in some way I had proven my integrity. I packed it all up in a brown bag, slipping in the bonus sheet of acid my parents hadn't discovered, and walked him to his car, after collecting my $400 of course. I gave it to my mom to hold onto, still carrying an air of pride in my work. It was a little tougher on Ben, since my parents knew him from debate team, and he came over after dinner. They kind of eyeballed him remorsefully, but when he argued that I was overpaying him I demanded that I had gotten my use out of his money and he deserved his interest. Sheeit, I had quadrupled that money!

Time began to go by rather drearily, and I counted down each day as I edged toward my impending escape to UCLA. The oppressive feeling of my parents' distrust mingled with their sense of failure and very little was said. They had decided to get as much yard labor out of me as possible while I was around, and that got to feeling like I'se in da ole South. After about ten days I managed to get them to let me go to the library with Don, whom they thought was straight since he still dutifully mowed the lawn. We went to the bowling alley, scored some hash, and ran into Ed and Clay, so we all drove out behind the golf course. We had just broken it out and were about to bong some when we saw searchlights, so Ed and I started throwing our beers. We told Don to stash the bong and throw his hash. Clay and Ed chucked theirs, I put mine in my pocket. Don took the bong and put it behind a bush, then came back. So it's the cops, and they come down and ask us what we're doing, "Uh, nothing officers," the stock reply. So they walk over to the bush and come back with the bong. "Who does this belong to then?" We tried not to stare at Don, whose bong it actually was, but we were amazed that he put it somewhere so visible. "Gee officer, it must have been there." They look around for about five seconds with their flashlights and here's this foil wrapped gram of hash on the ground right next to us. Clay and Ed were doubly stunned. Theirs were 100 feet away in the bushes, where they had thrown them, but old Don hadn't ever dealt with the cops, so he was a little nervous, and just dropped his. We all denied ownership, but they had seen someone hiding the bong. Without a positive ID though, or admission of guilt, they decided to arrest all of us.

So we get cuffed and put in the car, and I'm thinking, How seriously are they gonna search me? I slid my hands under my feet and around to my front to get my hash out of my pocket, but Ed told me they search the cars, so I hid it in my crack, which was good because when we got to jail they removed the back seat looking for stuff. I was surprised they didn't just keep their own baggie back there to frame people with. They put us in cells, but Ed and I were only seventeen, so they called our parents. When he came down my dad started asking the cops "Is there any way I can leave him here for the night?" There wasn't, so he told Ed's mom, "It's okay, I know how to hurt him where it won't show." Ed was a little worried about me after that, but I think my father was just subconsciously referring to the emotional and psychological damage he would inflict. He gave me the usual third degree shit until we got home, then took out the kit he used to cut hair. He knew I had always prided myself on my defiantly curly hair, so he went about cutting it all off. "When you go to UCLA you're going to look straight, and you're going to **be** straight!"

Now, my dad's a pretty big guy, big enough that even filled with hate as I was, he'd kick my ass. So I just sat in the chair, boiling. I looked over at the kitchen counter, where sat the knife block. In that moment I could hear Mr. Freelove, my eighth grade social science teacher, conducting class from some hidden neuronal pathway in my brain. "Kids, if you ever want to kill your parents, I suggest that you do it now! I've had two students who've killed their parents. The worst one was a girl who shot her dad because he wouldn't let her borrow the car. She was back in class in six weeks." All the dope was gone, even if my mom told the cops about it there was no evidence. As each snip of the scissors dropped a feathery weight on to my shoulder, I gravitated toward the counter. "Sit still!" I ran through the scenarios of jail, not getting into college, and my father's severed head, which even then didn't have enough hair to hold it up in Shakespearean glory. I was still seventeen, young enough to kill and get away with it, but he had found my weakness, my vanity. So when the Wahl clippers clicked on, buzzing away my hair to expose my scalp, my resolve was broken, and I was as weak as Samson himself. My father threatened that if I did anything else he would destroy all my mail from UCLA, so we dragged out those final weeks bitterly, hating each other.

FIRE

What element follows Wood?" the emperor asked, when he had returned to his discussion with Chi Po.

"Think about wood," replied Chi Po, "what do you do with it?"

"Build and burn," was Huang Ti's direct analysis.

"Yes indeed, Wood is the mother of fire, and fire is a time of building. The Fire season is that of summer, when the sun reaches its apex, and all things grow to their fullness. The color of fire is red, and it is the season of youth.

"Cannot we prolong youth through attunement to the elements?" inquired Huang Ti.

"Youth in that sense, is a manner of spirit," Chi Po reminded him, "Attunement to the elements maintains the health and suppleness of the body, but attunement also means we accept the transitions that come in time."

"What of Fire in the body, how is it tended?"

"The heart is he organ of Fire, and it is by maintaining the heart that we keep the fire burning safely in the body."

"So sparring, which employs the heart, is key to Fire?" Huang Ti interrupted.

"Do not confuse the structure with the function, my liege. Yes, being active keeps the heart working, to pump the blood through its network of vessels, but keeping the heart clear is more important."

"Clear?" wondered Huang Ti.

"Yes. Are you not aware of the heavy feeling that forms in your heart as a result of deceit, or of ignoring your own truth, no matter what it may be."

"I have had occasion, in the management of the empire, to do things which gave me concern," Hang Ti said, thoughtfully.

"This unclarity of heart is a sign. It is the foundation of anxiety, a negative emotion which affects the heart."

"But love, love is an emotion of the heart. Is it curative?"

"Yes, love can heal anything, if applied in time. Oddly enough, the feeling of joy can have negative effects."

"Physician, you do cause me to wonder."

"An excess of joy, as difficult as it may be to find, can distract the heart from its function. Have you ever met someone who giggled constantly?"

"Ha! Like a woman?"

"Even a woman, if her heart has no room for serious thought, will have no strength. There are many women in your palace whose honor would not be respected and whose duty would not be accomplished if they were not strong. Could your great empire survive without the strength of these women?"

"No, you are right. But how does joy prevent the heart from its function?"

"The heart's function is to store the Spirit. We can measure this capacity when we look into a patient's eyes. Is the radiance of spirit there, making them shine, or are they a shuttered window? The spirit is responsible for many things; restful sleep, clear thinking, proper speech. When the spirit is muddled we see the effect in disturbed sleep, speech, and thought. Would you care for the joy that keeps that broken fool outside the Tower Gate giggling to himself all day?"

"Mmmm," muttered Huang Ti, through a rueful expression.

"It is by maintaining a clear heart that the spirit is given shelter, food, and rest. Look about you in the world of men, consider the heart, and draw your own conclusions."

1

Like a knight in shining armor, but actually in his white Cordoba with Corinthian leather, Ivan arrived, and drove me to LA. God, what a relief it was to get out of Roseville. We took 101, and Ivan sparked up a J when we reached the ocean. It was night already, the harbor lights were twinkling, and I was cruising into my new world. Ivan was living in a house with his old frat brother, Mike Gleason. It was a classic bachelor pad, albeit somewhat cleaner than the last. Ivan pointed to a stack by the couch as we walked in, "There's the porn mags," he told me. A dart board hung at the end of the living room, so you could throw regulation or 20' overhand from the front door, which was next to the kitchen's never ending beer supply. I suppose it ended, but it was a brief walk to the liquor store and the next 12 pack of Bud. Gleason was in law school at the time, so in deference to sobriety he was always drinking Amstel Light. This was before Lite beer's ubiquitous existence, so it seemed fairly exotic. My favorite thing about Ivan's was still that pledge paddle. I sat around tokin on it with Ivan for a few days, but soon enough my college orientation began.

Whenever I'm involved in any sort of orientation, I'm reminded of my ninth grade English teacher, Mr. Curtis, who discretely joked with me when he distributed our handbooks, "This is your handbook, it tells you how to give a hand job." I imagine that he had come to disdain the process as much as anyone. Orientation at UCLA was, if anything, stunningly masturbatory. The first least impressive thing was that our orienteers were serious geeks. I was used to hanging out with college kids at Cal, but they were mostly freaky independent types, the kind these geeks thought were geeks. Now I was faced with died in the wool preppie stiffs, who maybe had a wild streak on jello shots once, but certainly seemed uniform in thought and appearance. The only thing I remember about orientation was being taught the UCLA cheer, "Icky la boomba." This was intended to be some sort of preverbal slur on the matriarchy of your opponent. Here I'm thinking, Oh my God, this is college? I'm used to screaming "ref sucks dick" and "your mom eats shit," and these guys can't even yell "I wear Trojans on my dick" at their crosstown rivals. The other disturbing fact was that most of my contemporaries were similarly out of it, although there was one hip guy I flipped shit with. At the end of orientation they had a little party, and I asked the one cool looking counselor if he ever got high, so he took me up to his room and we bonged out. "I'm not supposed to be doing this with the new kids, but you looked like you needed it."

I moved into the dorms the next week, Sproul Hall. Phase one of your institutional experience is always cell assignment, finding out what the roommate lottery has done for you. I got Roger Ramjet, a serious Air Force ROTC jet pilot wannabe. He was an alright guy, just a little speed crazed. He drove like a fucking maniac. He had run his VW up some little old ladies car at 90 miles an hour and still had three years of potential lawsuit if she had any more health problems. He told me that he partied in high school and loved smokin pot, but he had forsworn any more drug consumption in order to one day fly the fastest things on the planet. Poor bastard. Turned out my friend from orientation lived right down the hall. He was a six-foot, sandy blonde, buff surfer from Santa Barbara. He was smart too, and he had the clearest ice blue eyes. Another golden boy, we took to calling him Bob Bitchin pretty quick. I think he got laid by the second night in the dorms. He was a Deadhead too, and since I had just seen them on New Year's, we got along great. We couldn't convince our roommates to swap, though, so we just hung out as much as we could.

On my first night in the dorms I got into a long chat about getting high with some girl down the hall. I explained to her that Hendrix's "Are You Experienced," wasn't about having sex, as she (in her desire to think of herself as experienced) had assumed, but about taking LSD. "You know, 'not necessarily stoned, but beautiful.'" About an hour after I left her room the RA comes banging on my door because she was freaking out and accusing me of slipping her some acid! I told him in no uncertain terms that I didn't do that kind of shit, nor did I have any acid with me. I think she was just having some panic attack from being away from home, but it did worry me that you couldn't even suggest to these suggestible people, anything that might disturb their tenuous grasp on reality.

I went through the usual bullshit of trying to get classes, figuring my way around campus, getting my money, and acquainting myself with dorm life. I ran into another guy from my orientation who asked me if I wanted to go to rush. I was like,

"Rush? Yeah, I had tickets to see them on the Hemispheres tour but I got strep throat."

"No, frat rush."

"What the hell is that?"

"They have parties every night to get people to join, free booze!"

"Okay, come by at 7." So this guy came over with his high school friend from the valley, Keith. It's a popular thing for high school kids to do, cruise frat rush and get drunk, and Keith was a partier. Now, to begin with, I really had no conception of fraternity life outside of watching Animal house. I hardly knew they still existed. I guess Ivan had been in one, but I never really thought about it. Roseville didn't have any preppies, or any kind of recruiting to that scene. So I was entirely unprepared for the masses of Polo shirted, Topsider shod clowns trying to put forth their social mirage. The first house we went to was huge, one of the biggest on campus. Some guy was telling us that 150 brothers lived there while a bunch had places in town. They had a big brick-lined courtyard full of people, so I followed the line up to the kegs. All these people were standing around disconsolately, bemoaning the fact that the keg was all foam. I walked up to it, lifted it, felt that it was still half full, and retapped it. Voila! Beer! I could not believe that no one could tap a keg in such a place. You couldn't get a high school diploma from Roseville without tapping a keg. I chugged one down, filled another and split.

"Hey, I've got some pot," Keith tells me, "let's go down the street to this house that's pretty cool and smoke it."

"Sounds good to me." So we walk over to some other house, where they're playing 1944 on the TV in the living room. We grab a beer, sit down on the couch, pack a bowl and start to fire up when this guy comes over and says,

"Hey, you can't smoke that in here." So we're like,

"Okay," and we go out on their balcony and fire it up. Some other guy comes over and says,

"Hey, you can't smoke that out here." So we go into the bathroom, start tokin, and another guy comes over and says,

"Hey, you can't smoke that in here."

"What kind of party is this?" I snapped. "We can't smoke pot in the living room, we can't smoke it on the balcony, we can't smoke it in the bathroom, where can we smoke it?"

"Not here, man."

"Okay, fuck this. Thanks Keith, but this shit blows. A bunch of geeks in suits running around drinking foam and telling me I can't party, I'm going back to the dorms."

"Wait man, there is this one other place, Zeta Xi, it's on the way back." So we went over there and walked up the stairs to the living room. There weren't very many people around. We went out onto the balcony and this guy came up with the straight Animal House line,

"Jared Tate, damned glad to meet you." But instead of some weak handshake like the rest of these assholes, he whips out a fifth of Jack Daniel's and hands it to me. I took a swig, handed it back, and said, "Thanks, but what I really want to know is, is there somewhere around here we can smoke some pot?" He gives me this real serious look and says,

"I think you'd better speak with the president." He takes us down the hall and knocks on a door, opens it, and says, "Phi, these young men want to smoke some pot."

"Well, show them in," the president replied. He introduced himself as Droz, the Phi, (Greek for president) and asked us to sit down. "Gentlemen, welcome to Zeta Xi. This is some weed we grew up in the attic, have a bong hit." And I was home.

I had planned to change my whole life when I went to LA; get straight, get straight A's, get into film school, and get famous. But most of the people there and its entire social milieu were so fucking lame that getting back in with the loadies was the only thing that made me feel sane. As much as I wanted to deny it, I was pretty emotionally torqued from that last month with my folks, and here was a safe haven for my delinquency. The next night I went back and they pledged me. I didn't really have any understanding of this whole fraternity deal, the mandatory wearing of the pledge pin at all times, the suit & tie Monday night dinners, initiation. The fact that there was any formality at all really chafed me. But most of the guys in the house seemed pretty cool, and my pledge brothers were too. Droz asked if I had any nicknames, so I told him, "Spaceman." And so it was that Sheldon Spaceman Norberg was pledged into the brotherhood of Zeta Xi.

It's a funny thing, joining a fraternity. There's a lot of stress on brotherhood, as if you're entering into some great big family. As Ivan told me later, "I realized that the one thing I had in common with all my frat brothers was that each of us was dumb enough on that night to join." It's true, there was something there that fulfilled some part of what you were looking for, so you let a bunch of drunken guys sell you the rest. My closest pledge brother was the Hawk. He was a boarder who did tile work for an alumnus, who got him a room at the Zete house. He was 25, down from Seattle, with no idea why he joined, but he was totally into BÖC. Nobody was quite sure how they pledged him, being as he had no academic affiliation to UCLA, but hey, what the hell! Guys were always bobbing in and out of academic probation, getting kicked out, having to take classes at Santa Monica College to get their grades up to get back in. Speck, the total preppie Jewboy cokehead from Pacific Palisades hadn't even gotten into UCLA yet, he was still going to SMC. But he was such a smack he thought he'd be our president someday. Chico was some sort of human tank, I remember him bum rushing this drunk at a party once and throwing him down an entire flight of stairs before he kicked him out the door and on to the street. Barry Benson was a bizarre one, he didn't drink or do drugs, I think the cheap rent in close proximity to campus was his selling point. He's probably a doctor now. Krajkowicz was your average schlab from Orange county, and Carson was a really bright guy from Carmel. We used to listen to Hendrix all the time. He had a sunburst Les Paul and a black Strat on which he taught me how to play guitar. Sharky played tuba in the marching band and had a passion for explosives. I think he was legally blind, he had to wear these totally dark coke bottle glasses all the time, but he was always up for fun. Until he dropped out again, there was Bam-Bam. Bam-Bam had pledged the year before with his buddy Dane Watson, and then bailed out, leaving Dane to go it alone. This left Bam-Bam with friends and enemies in the house, amongst whom Dane counted on both sides. Bam-Bam was a precocious eight-year-old in a 6'3" 220 pound body. One of those guys who can and will do anything. For a bunch of white guys we made an interestingly diverse mix.

I started my first quarter at school with Freshman English—which was intended to force you to write without using prepositions, French One—where the language of liberté, egalité and fraternitie is taught by the Vichy, and Astronomy, which I supposed would interest me enough to fulfill a science requirement. I signed up for a class on technological development through time with James Burke, whose PBS show "Connections" I had really enjoyed. But this turned out to be another James Burke, a truly boring one. I dropped that class after one hour. The killer bad timing mistake with UCLA was that they had an eminent LSD researcher teaching there. He was still using students in his experiments, so I was ready to sign up on day one, but that August he died in a hiking accident in Hawaii. The Speech major, which I intended to double with TV/Film, had also been cut, so just about everything I really wanted to do there was nonexistent. You can't get into any Fine Arts classes until you're accepted into the major, which depends on a year of B+ average, so I had some time to kill, which I was not happy about.

2

Back at the Zete house I had my pledgely duties to fulfill. We'd have to set up and clean after Monday night dinners, have our study sessions of Zete history, lore and dirty songs, and line up. Line up is where all the pledges get in line and get drilled on what they're supposed to know or be able to do. Kind of like the Boy Scouts with more screaming and enforced beer chugging. I always knew everything and I liked chugging beers, so it wasn't much of a problem. There are always gonna be some older members who want to torture you just cause they got it when they were pledges, but Droz was kind of taking me under his wing, so I didn't get fucked with too much. After the meetings and beatings were over it was time to party. The Hawk would always have some weed, usually some Mexican from his construction pals. We'd stay up drinking until 2 or 3 every Monday night, which was not good for my Tuesday morning Astronomy class.

Bob Bitchin had this beautiful girlfriend who'd drive down from Santa Barbara every couple weekends, and she'd bring him some pot, so we managed to stay high in the dorms too. But I was sort of back in my old place of brokeness, hanging out with guys who were either affluent or had jobs. My grant money covered my needs and nothing else. I started working in the Student Center as a dishwasher for minimum wage, but it totally sucked. Looking at the inconsistency of dope supply for the Zete house, which was it's own captive marketplace, the light bulb came on. My payments for the dorms and school were split into thirds, due every six weeks, so I took my second student aid disbursement and got a Greyhound to Berkeley, and I was back in biz. LA was more sophisticated than Roseville, but they really had no pipeline for serious bud. Most people were still getting Mexican, which made it very easy for me to implement my program. Of course, hauling my dope around on the 'hound was kind of risky, but I just calculated my duress into my profit margin. I didn't need a UCLA MBA to make a margin. There was some resistance to the $50 quarter at first, but once people smoked the bud I was getting they quit complaining. The first thing I did with my money was to go down to Licorice Pizza on Wilshire Blvd. It was a record store with a massive head shop. There I bought an Ohaus triple-beam scale, (the preferred tool of the professional dope dealer) and a 3-stage, red, white and blue US bong. God Bless America!

It wasn't much of a problem dealing in the dorms. The RA was never around, and he got high himself anyway, so I wasn't too worried. I was sitting in my room one day with the door open when a red haired guy walks up, knocks and looks in.

"Is Roger here?" he inquired.

"Well obviously not, it'd be pretty hard to hide him in one of these rooms," I joked. "Care for a bong hit?"

"Uhh, sure," He replied, "The name's Kipnis, but my friends call me Kip." I was developing great social skills in college. Kip and I became fast friends, bonging out with great regularity. He introduced me to the dice games that raged upstairs, a sporting event where one toed the line between drunken enjoyment and singing bile splattered arias into the toilet. It was a good game, and a pretty respectable crew of players. Chunk, the vomitmaster, pulled my head out of the bowl on the night I hit the bottom of the learning curve. Of course, it helps to smoke dope when you drink that much, so everyone wanted to buy some from me. I was opening up new markets wherever I went.

I didn't wait very long to introduce my new compatriots to LSD, either. Most of them hadn't ever had any, but everyone wanted to try it, and we were young adults, so no one's parents were going to find out. I first dosed with a few Zetes after a Monday night meeting, and we stayed up all night. I got into a wrestling match with Chico at about 3 in the morning. He was shorter than I was, so I tried to wrap around his head, push him down, grab his legs and pick him up for a piledriver. But he broke out of it and ran me into this guy's door, which blew off the hinges, landing us right in bed with him. It's hard enough to think of a greeting in that situation, but on acid all we could do was laugh.

My Astro class the next morning was not so funny. I kept seeing giant cobwebs growing across the room and realized that I was probably better off not attending, which is a bad sign in your first quarter. My English class wasn't going much better, although it was at a time that I was usually cognizant. I didn't know what they wanted out of me. I had been getting A's in English for years and my SAT's passed me straight into composition. Maybe I was just too geared toward writing speeches, but my teacher, who was just some grad student anyway, was really fucking with me. I wrote one essay on Pink Floyd and it was brilliant. (Yeah, yeah, I was 18!) Admittedly, I stayed up all night on speed typing it, which was the first and last time I'll ever do that. I felt like I was on a fishing boat, sort of rocking and rolling over the typewriter. I got a D, but I wish I still had it just so I could see how brilliant it was. At the time I was ready to engage my prof in a serious conversation about his need to overcome his esteem problems and stop inflicting his bloated intellectualism upon us, but it might have reflected poorly on my own, so I just envisioned breaking his nose. My French class was rapidly becoming un sac de merdre. It wasn't until about the tenth week that I realized I was supposed to be going to the language lab every day and practicing. Duuuh! I was incredibly behind, but I was having fun.

I made another friend, Rod, who knew some people on my dorm floor and used to visit a lot. He lived in an apartment somewhere, but I think he had purchased a dorm food contract, where you actually pay the dorms to feed you their regular meals, (perish the thought) so he was around and needed to get high. He was an incredible artist, and he played guitar, so we called him Rock-it Rod, since Rocket Rod Foster, UCLA's upcoming basketball hope, lived in Sproul too. On Halloween, Rod and Kip and Bob and I took some acid and went cruising around. There was a girl who lived upstairs, Wendy Hummel, that I was always teasing, cuz she was a hardcore Christian. She was this fabulously stacked, Germanic wide-eyed innocent, and she showed up in a full-on French maid outfit. You know how it is when girls are young enough to feign innocence about their real desire, but expose it so drastically you feel like eating them alive. Wendy was like that. "Wench, come back to my room. I have a few things that need dusting, and I have some cleaning fluid for you." I said wicked things to her that night, but she just wanted to save me. I'd be having none of that. I needed the real deal.

I came back to the dorms around three in the morning, still pretty high, and went to my room. Roger was asleep so I left the lights off, but when I looked at him lying on his bunk he looked like he was swimming in space. He was face down and his bed seemed like a big pool filled with vaguely reflective colored shapes. It was really tripping me out so I turned the light on and realized he had puked in his bed and was laying face down in it. I checked him out to make sure he was still breathing and went to sleep on a couch in the lounge.

Roger had to make up for the inanity of ROTC life somehow. He was actually living in fear of any other cadets or ROTC officials coming to our room. "Sheldon," he told me, "I don't care if you get high all the time, I'd smoke all your pot in a minute if I weren't going to be a pilot, but if they ever come here you've got to hide the bong! I'll never narc you out, just keep it cool for me, okay?" I figured it wasn't such a bad deal, I had to keep it cool for myself, and Roger was entertaining in his way. He used to wake me up in the middle of the night to watch him light his farts. One night he wakes me up, "Sheldon! Sheldon! Check this out!" He throws himself on his back with his knees up to his chest, lights up a match, and rips this huge fart. But he had been sleeping in his boxers, and they just exploded in a ball of fire. He was rolling around on the floor, "Aaah, Aaah! My ass is on fire!" Right out of Canterbury Tales. Who knows what the neighbors thought.

Ahh, the neighbors. We were arranged in a guy girl pattern all down the hall, and at least half the neighbors would've preferred to be somewhere else. Cindy Threadgill, or Thrillwell as we called her, was the very nice girl to our right. She was a transfer student out of JC somewhere in the Valley, where she had grown up. Blonde, blue eyed, a little short, but with a tremendous heart, she seemed comfortable with the idea of actually studying and finishing her degree, rather than exploring all the things that must be explored at that age. Perhaps she was just a little shy. She had never gotten high but she was always impressed by my misadventures, and quick with motherly advice. "You can't dooo that Sheldon. Someone might get hurt."

"Of course someone will get hurt, Cindy, that's what life's about! And speaking of hurt, when are you going to let me devirginate you?" The complete incongruity of the question made it safe to ask, since there was no question of it ever happening. Perhaps the relaxed friendship of our neighborliness made it alright, funny even, in expectation of her singsongy reply, "You are going to have to be more polite, Sheldon. I don't think any girls want to heeeear that."

On the other side of the wall was Gina Lolobrigida, a stunning, olive-skinned Italian girl with saucer sized brown eyes and a rapturous body. The kind of girl you'd hang yourself by the nose with a gaff hook to get a date with, if it wouldn't just make you look more pathetic. I'd occasionally pound on her wall at night, just to remind her that if I could break through it I'd crawl into her bunk and pound her. But I was still a little weird for the girls here, and Cindy was probably right that they didn't want to hear my deviant suggestions. Most of them were fairly straight, or motivated in the preppie direction, so life for me continued to be about getting high.

There was one girl on my floor who liked to smoke pot, although she had to keep it a secret from her roommate. Paula was an incredible cutie in a tiny package. She was there on a gymnastic scholarship, as was her roommate, which is why she was hush hush. Her long wavy brown hair framed sparkling eyes that lit up when she grinned, as she often did, usually revealing a well-worked piece of Juicy Fruit. She'd come over to sneak bong hits, "Just a little one," was all she wanted. It wasn't that she lacked lung strength, she had just stopped growing at about thirteen. I offered to be her slave, but she had left some other guy her parents disapproved of back home in Denver.

It wasn't long before Thanksgiving arrived, which meant you had to vacate the dorms. I was pretty happy about spending my celebratory first holiday away from home with Ivan. We had discussed going out to see our uncle's family in the valley, but naaahh. KTLA had a long running tradition of playing Twilight Zone all day long on Thanksgiving. I now see that this was an enlightened statement about what it meant to live in LA. I was pretty excited because I hadn't seen the Twilight Zone since I was very young. I had sworn for years to Ivan that there was some TV show that scared the hell out of me when I was about five, where William Shatner was on a plane while these monsters, "Gremlins-that's what they are!" kept looking in the window. He always told me I had dreamt it, but my dreams are my dreams. So we stocked up on Bud, (I had plenty of bud, but Ivan bought some Bud) sat down on the couch, and proceeded to Zone out. It wasn't too long before "Terror at 30,000 Feet" came on, vindicating me on the one hand while relieving me from a lifetime of monkey-suited William Shatner obsession.

We had planned to go to the store up the street for some BBQ, since Ivan had a little grill out back, but they were closed. We were in the Zone, and our commercial breaks didn't give us time for anything besides 12 packs at the corner, so that was lunch. Around five or six I was getting pretty hungry. I didn't want to miss any TZ, but it was Thanksgiving, so we decided it would be nice to go out for dinner. We got in the Cordoba, threw Captain Beefheart's The Spotlight Kid in the 8-track, cruised the midtown area, and found nothing open. So we headed over to the West Side. We drove out Wilshire to Santa Monica, back up Santa Monica Blvd to Westwood, back out Pico to the ocean, but we couldn't find anything. We took Olympic back to the 405 and north to the valley. Sherman Oaks was closed, Van Nuys was dead, it was night now. We took 101 back to Hollywood, La Brea, Fairfax, we were starving but there was nothing open in that whole endless expanse of pavement! It was about 11 o'clock when we finally pulled into a 7-11, which provided a Gino's frozen pizza with our 12 pack of Bud. We took it home to the oven, and shortly before midnight, as the instinctual heartwarming aroma of childhood winters filled my olfactory memory, the char smell of urban male isolation brought me back to the reality of the worst Thanksgiving dinner of my life. Thanks.

Zete was a good haven for me, but living in the dorms, I spent most of my time with my dorm friends. At the end of the semester Bob, Rod, a couple of his friends, Chuck and Eileen, Kip and I ate a bunch of shrooms and went out to the sculpture garden on the North end of campus. It's a fabulous little environment to trip in, rolling patches of lawn, and some amazing sculpture, all strangely illuminated by the lighting they had wired up into the trees. Trees as a light source, Very LA. It was great for Frisbee golf though, or splitting up and spacing off in the corners. I was lying down in the middle of the lawn for awhile when I completely lost awareness of my body. I found myself floating in space, looking back at the earth. It didn't feel bad to be hovering out there, in fact it was quite peaceful. I felt like I could let go of life, move on, and still love all my friends back on earth. Eventually though, I returned to my body, which was almost glued to the ground. I was still very high. My standard dose of mushrooms then was five grams, while most of my friends ate a couple. It does take some insane desire to eat that much mushroom, eeaagh! But that was the dosage a 165 pound Indian would take in their cave dwelling ceremonies, so it seemed right to me.

When I got up I was impelled to go to the art building, and when I walked around on the plaza for a minute I found a photo laying on the ground. I can't remember what it was of, but it was interesting, and I stared at it so long that everyone came over. Then I spotted another, and another, and another making a trail that went into a doorway and down some stairs, which were covered in photos. The stairs led into a room, in which every surface, the floors, walls, ceilings, counters, desks, everything was covered with photos. People's parents, children, homes, lawns, dogs, cars, parties, weddings, the whole world of experience, human, natural and inanimate, trees, buildings, beaches, trains were all right there in someone's art project. And no one was there but us. We just groveled in the images, each one a glossy or matte moment in time that you could see right into with your high brained vision, traveling the world. There was a little alcove behind a counter and sure enough, hundreds of naked pictures were back there. Wives and girlfriends, sultry and bored, excited and mutely subservient to men's desire for silver nitrate representations of their genitals. Guys holding their cocks and grinning, never knowing that the scraggly kid working at the Fotomat was duplicating all their pictures for his thesis. After a while some other people came in and it began to feel a little weird. A: for being so high in front of anyone who wasn't, and B: for indulging our deepest voyeuristic impulses in front of strangers. We were too high to stay, but it was glorious while it lasted.

3

I was pretty excited to be done with the quarter, figuring I had eked C's out of my classes somehow, and having scored tickets to see the Dead that weekend. I knew Hell Week was starting that Friday night, but I figured No biggee, I'm going to the show. Droz was cool, and what were we gonna do anyway, mop the house or something. I had collected my necessary items: marshmallows, maxi-pads, athletic tape, a ball of twine, a brick, a jock strap, a white t shirt and a painters hat, a can of air freshener, 2 cases of Coors talls, I can't remember the rest of the shit but I'm sure it was all necessary. They lined us all up about 6 o'clock and Droz starts in,

"Welcome to Hell Week gentlemen, is there anything I should know before we begin?"

"Yeah I have tickets to see the Dead tonight so I hope this doesn't take long." They just went off. The Blade, who was a senior, and kind of a dickhead, started railing on me.

"What do you mean, pledge? You can't just walk out of here, this is Hell Week! You have no rights!" Droz was a little calmer.

"Spaceman, this is it. No one goes anywhere, no one does anything, unless we tell them to."

"How primitive," I replied. I ended up eating my tickets, which should have tipped me off to the fact that I had other destinies to fulfill. But then it began.

"Does anyone have any weed?" the Phi asked. This was the sort of thing which usually earned you pledge points, kind of a scorecard for obsequious activities. Krajkowicz whipped out a baggie.

"Aha," the Blade stripped it away from him, "none of you are allowed to get high."

"I want each of you to count out your pledge points, and you better have at least 500," proclaimed Droz. I had earned mine doling out bong hits, but Speck had thousands from running errands, dispensing lines of blow, shining shoes, he was the proud leader by far.

"Now throw all that shit in the fireplace," the Phi commanded. Speck was crestfallen, and the brothers chuckled as all our efforts were revealed to be worthless. "Now everyone get out your T-shirts, hats and El Marcos. Write Zeta Xi on your hats and put them on. Now take off your pledge pins. You are no longer pledges, you are now scuts! A scut is lower than whale shit at the bottom of the ocean! A scut speaks only when spoken to, and calls his betters sir! Do you understand?"

"Yes Sir!"

"Each of you scuts has a name, you will respond to your scut names only, understand?"

"Yes Sir!"

"Now write your scut names on your T-shirts." Speck carried on the tradition of the fraternity ass kisser and became Sammy Sperm Slurper. Sharky became Dan Drippy Dick, Carson was Harry Whore Humper, the Hawk was Pete Pimple Prick, Krajkowicz became Scott Scrotum Scratcher, Chico was Bob Beaver Biter, Benson was Thomas Tea Totaller, and I became Rasty Roland Road Apple. Each name had a vulgar rhyme that went with it, which you would have to recite whenever asked, or suffer the consequences, usually push-ups, beer chugging, or something gross. Then they lined us up out on the balcony.

You see, the hazing rituals of Hell Week, the most sacred acts of fraternity life, are designed to create a sense of trust and unity amongst the new brothers. You may never trust the older brothers again, but many do show their humanity in between bouts of torturing you. I'm not sure why, but it's important that everyone keep up the appearance of being a vicious slave owner. Perhaps it reinforces the idea that they're really cutting you slack when they do. So they line us up and begin going over everything we were supposed to have learned, and when anyone makes a mistake, everyone drinks a beer, in 10 seconds. Anyone with beer left pours it over his head. After six or eight people make mistakes it starts getting a little tougher, except for Thomas Tea Totaller, cuz he's nonalcoholic, so they just keep pouring beers over his head. "Don't you feel bad for your brothers, Thomas?" After the first guy blows chow they put us to work, scrubbing the kitchen floor with toothbrushes. A couple of overseers hang out to make sure we're not enjoying ourselves or talking too much, and about 3 A.M. they switch us over to cleaning the bathrooms. They rotate overseers, we clean, they quiz us, we learn more dirty limericks, they make us drink.

It wasn't until about four the next morning that they actually let us go to sleep, for 45 minutes. Then it was exercise time! Marching up and down the neighborhood until the sun came up finally earned us breakfast! We hadn't eaten for a couple days at this point, so the green oat meal with Tabasco and curry seemed pretty good. Mmmmmm. Now, some of us had heard things through our big brothers about preparing for Hell Week and hidden weed around the house, but it was pretty hard to sneak off and smoke it without getting caught. Fortunately I had stashed some with my big brother, Ken, and his roommate Wyck, who was cool enough to dole me out a little. They knew it would pay off in the long run to get me high, so I didn't suffer too badly.

Your big brother was sort of in charge of teaching you your scut name, the Ode to the Moose, and various things, so between slave shifts you'd have little opportunities to study where they'd sneak you some food and a bong hit. I was elected "Keeper of the Glade," which brought me the extra responsibility of both having a can with me at all times to dispel the noxious odors of scut, and memorizing every word printed on it. I remember Brother Wyck giving me a bong hit, hearing the Phi coming up the stairs and screaming at me in his crazed Texan drawl, "Okay scut, Ode to the Moose!" I dropped down on my knees and whipped out a perfect recitation, impressing the alumni Droz had in tow. Droz grabbed my Glade can and sprayed it around to dispel the various odors, and, as the ritual went, I had to deliver a complete ingredient list at the same time. It was sort of funny, since Droz was secretly feeding me bongs too. Perhaps everyone knew what everyone else was secretly doing, but maintaining the illusion is half the fun.

By the fourth night we were getting pretty grungy, we had scrubbed every dirty greasy grimy moldy puke-stained part of the house, then poured beer on ourselves and puked there again, so they finally decided to let us rest. We all piled into an empty room and started whispering our plots for revenge. "Hey, shut up in there!" Most of us passed out pretty quickly, but Scott Scrotum Scratcher climbed out a window, went down to the front yard, and hosed himself off. The light came on,

"Scuts! How many of you are there?"

"Eight Sir."

"I only see seven! What the fuck are you doing? You lost one of your scut brothers! Line up!" We staggered drag ass out to the balcony and there was Scott Scrotum Scratcher. They had been watching him the whole time from up there. "You guys have to learn to act together! How could you let Scott go off by himself?" We had no answer, so the Phi went on exasperatedly. "Scott Scrotum Scratcher, why did you leave your scut brothers?"

"I wanted to take a shower."

"Would the rest of you like to take a shower?"

"Yes sir!"

"Well Scott already did that for you." The Blade came out from the kitchen with a mixing bowl full of grenadine, molasses, eggs, vinegar, dog food, oats, and whatever other nasty shit he could find in there, then began to paint each of us with it. Then they made Scott paint us. They rubbed it in our hair, on our chests, all over our clothes, and it stunk. "Now to make sure that none of you gets any bright idea about cleaning up, you're all gonna put on your jock straps." We got into our jocks and they painted our legs too, so there was stench coming of all parts of us, then they tied each of our jocks together with twine. Now if anybody moved out of line, everybody knew about it. Then they sent us back to our room, and we quickly learned to maneuver single file.

Even with the windows open we stunk. We whispered about mutiny in the dark. The fact was that the eight of us made up a third of the house, without our dues they'd probably go bankrupt. We had pretty much proven in the pledge active football game that we wouldn't be intimidated, even thought the older alums were laying on some pretty good hits. The question was whether there was more value in sticking it out, to show them up, and potentially change things with our youthful political optimism. For three hours we slept on it. The next day was a total exercise in concentration. Every work detail had to be completely synchronized. If one scut needed to stand up, he had to tell you. If someone had to pee, you all had to pee. If a brother yelled at a scut and he had to stand at attention, everybody knew that they had to stand as well. There is probably no more cosmically unifying principal than "Move in the direction your testicles are being pulled. Now!"

As the day wore on we became more of a unit, determined, single mindedly, to stick it out. More beers, running in line, push ups, egg smashing over the head, singing, cleaning, recitation, "scuts stand on your hands!" We were doing pretty well; enough that they eventually removed the "collars of obedience," if only so they could play Marshmallow Duckpins. In this leisurely entertainment scuts walk back and forth in staggered rows while brothers hurl marshmallows at them. Sort of carnival game for vicious young adults. When you get hit you have to yell "bing!' and fall down. Occasionally someone's eye gets put out, but hey, that's why it's called hazing. It's a form of visual impairment. On the fifth night, it's time for a little celebration. Each scut is given a bottle of a Japanese plum wine, to go with the five-pound wheel of Brie we already had. The objective is to drink all your wine and eat all your cheese, the combination of which is sure to induce vomiting. Since Thomas didn't drink, the brothers got creative and tied a five-gallon bucket around his neck with some twine. "Okay Thomas Tea Totaller, since you're not going to join your fellow scuts in a drink, you'll have to share in a puke. All of you scuts drink until you puke in Thomas Tea Totaller's bucket." I'll never forget Bob Beaver Biter, trying to be polite as he hurled, "Sorry Thomas, blarrggh."

As Hell Week winds down we find every surface clean, the scuts a drunken but trim unit, all songs, limericks, rhymes and lore memorized, all beers consumed, the Glade an empty can, the true exercises of trust beginning. Do you trust that these exercises will make you a better person, that the brothers truly have your interests in mind, that they won't do some ridiculous shit that accidentally causes your death, that there is some point to this besides some bastards getting their jollies by enslaving you? That's nice.

"Take out your maxi-pad scut. Get your brick and your tape and cut twelve feet of twine. Now walk out on the veranda. Say hello to Brother Jared, scut."

"Hello Brother Jared, sir!"

"Ssshello, sshccutt. Ssshow y' doin."

"Fine, sir."

"Do you trust your brother, scut?"

"Tssshokay scut, I gotscha covered."

"Do you trust your brother, scut?" Fifteen feet below me stands a man I have seen drink beers all day, run from a bus stopped in traffic into a liquor store, return with a pint of JD and drink half in one swig, and still appear sober, and now **he's drunk.**

"Do you trust your brother, scut?"

"Yes sir!"

"Good. Put your maxi-pad over your eyes and wrap it with athletic tape. Can you see anything?"

"No."

"No, what?"

"No Sir!"

"Ya lyin scut! Wrap some more tape around there, cover that gap. Okay, now get out your dick and tie the twine around it. C'mon, c'mon, you don't need anybody to help you, do you?"

"No sir."

"Now I'm gonna tug on that twine, to make sure it's tight." Yoink! "Lookin good scut. Now take the other end and tie it around this brick. Make sure it's on there good. Okay now, do you trust your brothers, scut?"

"Yes sir."

"Good, cause you've got a dozen feet of line and it's fifteen feet to the ground. When I count to three your gonna throw this brick down to brother Jared and he's gonna catch it, aren't you Jared?"

"Shyoubetscha."

"One."

"I gotscha covered sshhcutt." Fuck.

"Two."

"Jess aim for my voische" Fuck!

"Threee!" Fuuuuuuck! Needless to say the string yanked pretty hard about the time the brick hit the pavement. Some guys screamed about it, but no one went to the hospital. "Good work, scut, you've proven that you trust your brothers. You can take the string off now, but leave your blindfold on, it's time for you to enter the chamber of darkness."

Right about this time I'm thinking, My dick's still on, I wonder if I'm gonna have to fuck a sheep now? They led me into a room, sat me down on the floor and told me not to say anything. Eventually all the scuts were led in and the Phi started. "I'm really proud of all of you, you've shown me that you can work together, trust each other, and trust your brothers. Now you must remain in darkness until you're deemed ready for initiation. No one may speak, no one may sleep. We will be watching and listening." When he turned out the lights, he switched the record player on to a song I now know to be "The Heavenly Music Corporation," from Fripp & Eno's No Pussyfooting, which, if you've never heard it, is 20 minutes of elongated, rubberized, electronic droning likely to cause either an out of body experience or nausea, or both. We all sat there quietly with our heads bound in maxi pads while the entire album side repeated, and repeated, and repeated for an unknown duration. On occasion you could hear the door open and close, so you knew people were taking turns observing us in the dark.

Eventually the Phi returned and began to question us. "What have you learned this week? Do you trust your brothers? What is the meaning of brotherhood?" Pretty heavy existential questions considering we were on about 12 hours of sleep for the last six days and were locked in a sensory deprivation chamber. The album was switched to Beethoven's Ninth Symphony, and we were left to ponder that for a few more hours. Having read and watched A Clockwork Orange a few times by then I felt completely resolved to sit through Ludwig van's glorious Ninth as many times as necessary, but it was getting kind of emotional. When we thought no one was there we began whispering again, about whether we could take any more of this. Should we stick it out or quit as a group? That would be showing them some brotherhood. I remember when Pete Pimple Prick started crying about how much he connected to each of us, which definitely shocked me. Not the sort of thing you expect from a 25-year-old construction worker. I think the brothers were listening some of the time, and not saying anything, sometimes they'd make their presence known if we spoke. If you nodded off someone would push you until you woke up again. This went on for what I imagined to be 24-30 hours, endless repetitions of "Ode to Joy" and "The Heavenly Music Corporation" during which I swore, I will never listen to whoever recorded this music! (Oddly enough, Fripp is now my favorite musician.) I had done a lot of drugs up to this point, so perhaps I was a little more prepared than most, but I certainly learned something about the nature of sensory deprivation and what it brings up for people, especially when applied as a form of torture. We decided to stick it out, all holding each other's hands in a circle in the dark, knowing that we could count on each other.

Eventually they loaded us into a van and drove up into the canyons for the initiation. Still in darkness, we were each put through our ordeal alone, as a final test of our trust. I have sworn an oath on pain of death, which I took very seriously for a long time, never to reveal any of what I've written here, so I'm not gonna tell you about how we were buried alive or branded with the Zete emblem, but simply that taking off that damn maxi-pad was quite a relief. After celebratory beers, escaping the park rangers, and returning to the house for some hour long showers and huge bong hits, we rolled down to Westwood for a Tiny Naylor's Lumberjack Breakfast.

4

Most of us went home for Christmas, which seemed like a pretty good idea since the dorms were closed and my T-day with Ivan was such a depressing event. I took my bong with me, just to defy my folks now that I was an adult. I'd sit out on the back porch and do some hits with Don, or go back behind his dad's woodpile like we used to. After I was there about a week my mom asked me what my bong was. Classically, she had assumed it was a vase of some kind. She was somewhat shocked when I told her, which made me realize I probably could have been bonging out in the laundry room all that time and she never would have known. Spending my vacation sitting around their house getting high didn't agree with the folks too much, so I split down to Berkeley. Dave was living with his girlfriend Rachel and Stymie in a nondescript little gray house on Colby Street, on the border of Berkeley near Rockridge. Between those three there was nothing to do but lay around and smoke dope, although seeing the Dead every night was mandatory.

The shows were pretty cool, I dosed or ate shrooms for all of them, (it's good to alternate so you don't build up too much tolerance) and found myself beginning to feel somehow attached to this amazing carnival cult. I felt like an outsider, for sure, but I was with Dave, and certainly ripe for another initiation. The feeling of total abandon that grasped the crowd, sending them gyrating, screaming, spinning down the halls on a blissed out wave that rolled from the stage out to the parking lot started to grab me too. It had scary moments of dark power, lamenting ballads of life gone awry, searing passion, and unadulterated fun, all within a framework of some caring, heartfelt feeling of good will. Maybe I was just high, but I felt safe there. Everyone was so happy to be there, it made me wonder if it wasn't some sort of secret religion.

New Year's Eve was always the biggest event, one you had to prepare for. Stymie asked me if I wanted to roll up some pot for the show.

"Well," I replied, "one of the reasons I like bonging out so much is that Dave taught me to roll joints. You've seen his joints right? Mine aren't much better."

"Here," he handed me some bud and went on in his fatherly tone, "The first secret to rolling joints is to have good pot. You have to break it all up so there's no clumps left." He went on as I attempted to roll. "Break it up a little in the middle so it doesn't get all lumpy. Now tuck the paper and roll it up with your thumbs."

"There's no glue on these papers," I complained.

"They're Modianos, man. You want to smoke pot, or glue? Just get a bunch of spit on there." After rolling about ten practice doobies for the master I had developed a reasonable skill level. Now we were ready for the show. I took my US bong with me anyway. It felt like a very Uncle Sam kinda thing to hand out red white & blue bong hits to whomever I met.

We drove over in their friend Manny's LTD. I can't remember too much about the show. After Art showed up with a couple quarts of orange juice that had been seriously dosed, things just took off. I do recall that when we where hanging around at the end of the show, we were all laughing at this one guy who was wandering around screaming, "I want my brain back!" It seemed pretty funny at the time. When we made it back home we discovered that Dave had spaced-out his sweater, with the keys, and they had decided to have only one person carry keys. (You don't want to be tweaking about your keys if you don't have to.) So we head back to the old Oakland Auditorium, and Stymie fires up a fat one for the ride. It's three in the morning on January first, so of course we have the windows up. It's not a long ride to the Aud, but by the time we get there we've totally Chonged out the car, and there are no less than a dozen cop cars out in front of the building. Manny just pulls into the main access road, right up toward the front steps, and throws it in park. About a half dozen cops start walking toward us while we all look around at each other to see who is going to do something. I'm holding this huge, still burning roach as the cops approach my door so I just eat it! Manny rolls down his window, which releases this cloud of smoke in this cop's face.

"Uh, excuse me officer, my friend left his keys in the show." The cop just stares at us, then replies,

"Try the lost and found." Dave bolts up there and we begin waiting, while these cops just stare at us. Amazingly, they had already stacked up all the lost articles and he picked his sweater right out, returning almost instantly. The cops just told us to drive safely. Onnggh Yaaangh! There must be some kind of strange secret society going on around here for us to get away with this, I thought to myself, but it hardly mattered, since we were headed back home to the whippet stash.

Raise your hand if you know what a whippet is, and raise an eyebrow if you don't. A whippet is a Nitrous Oxide cartridge. They look just like CO_2 cartridges, the kind for seltzer bottles and BB guns, but Nitrous Oxide is used to pressurize whipped cream, because it has a sweet taste. In case your wondering why anyone would inhale whip cream propellant, which is hardly a question in a society where teenagers regularly huff down butane lighters, secretaries catch a buzz on correction fluid, and the first lady imbibes nail polish remover, nitrous is generally referred to as laughing gas. Thus the Whippet, whippet good. If pot opens your mind, and LSD shows you the patterns of the universe, nitrous, particularly in combination with LSD, lets you fall between the stitches of the weave and into another dimension.

I was pretty impressed with my discovery of nitrous until Brother Wyck, who was a philosophy major, showed me a paragraph written in 1896, from William James' Varieties of Religious Experience: "Nitrous oxide... when sufficiently diluted with air, stimulates the mystical consciousness in an extraordinary degree. Depth beyond depth of truth seems revealed to the inhaler. This truth fades out, however, or escapes, at the moment of coming to; and if any words remain over in which it seemed to clothe itself, they prove to be the veriest nonsense. Nevertheless, a sense of profound meaning having been there persists; and I know more than one person who is persuaded that in the nitrous oxide trance we have a genuine metaphysical revelation." (Hey, so do I!) "Some years ago I made some observations on this aspect of nitrous oxide intoxication..." (heh heh heh) "One conclusion was forced upon my mind at that time... It is that our normal waking consciousness, rational consciousness as we call it, is but one special type of consciousness, whilst all about it, parted by the filmiest of screens, there lie potential forms of consciousness entirely different." I hadn't yet embarked on such philosophical approaches to these states of consciousness, but if there was some profoundly elevated state to be reached from sucking down little pressurized gas containers, I was gonna explore it. Of course, as is the way with these metaphysical realizations, as soon as the decision to go farther is reached, you've run out of whippets.

5

Back at school I was advised by an older brother, Merle, to get a job at Audio-Visual Services. This was the slack-all job, our official employee title was "slug." Job Description: Hang around the AVS lounge goofin off until it's time to cruise into the film library for a pickup, wrestle a movie projector into your truck, preferably the four speed, drive like a maniac until you cut up on to the pedestrian walkways that head straight for the building and park it in front, pretending you're some sort of university official, set up your film or whatever, and go get high. It was the perfect gig. There was usually a little booth in the back of the lecture hall so you could hang out and read graffiti unperturbed, but there were times you wanted to join the class. Showing Fellini movies to Italian cinema classes was a fairly regular gig, but there were some rare winners like taping surgeries, or neuropsychiatric interviews, or showing porn movies to human sexuality classes. Of course, whenever anybody showed a porn movie the whole AVS staff would review it back in the slug lounge. AVS was a good gig for me, an income stabilizer that allowed me to spend my grant money on drugs as soon as school started.

Assuming I had passed French One, which was a bit of an assumption, I signed up for French Two. I was shocked when I finally got my grade card, since I had never received less than a B since my second grade cutting and pasting debacle. Here I had flunked all my classes, shit! Academic probation. The Zete brothers were very helpful in this regard, since they had all been down that road at some time, and I got a schedule that I could rebound with. The real bummer was that without passing a foreign language I couldn't get into the College of Fine Arts, my whole reason for being there. With the Speech major cancelled I had no choice but to enter the undeclared nebula, which definitely gives one a sense of purposelessness. On the good side, Kip and I had both enrolled in Psych 10 and Modern Art History, which was quite evocative. Our professor was so engrossed, not only in styles and social influences, but in the emotional impact of events on various painters, that he once broke down sobbing in front of 500 students, overcome by the travails of some painter whose mother had died. The lecture hall turned quiet while a girl in the front went on stage and offered him a Kleenex. Art being art, the class was held right there next to the sculpture garden. Kip and I would meet and bong out every morning at eight, so as to get the full potential of staring at these masterworks. I took Astro again, and a Humanities class, and had brothers in each of them, which proved to be beneficial. It's always good to have someone you know in a class to help cover your ass, particularly when all you really want to do is party.

Which I did. At home, school, work, Zete, there was nothing I didn't do stoned, and my grades were improving. I got high before my art midterm (I had been high in every class so I figured it was consistent) and got an "A." My excesses earned me another nickname during this period, which came from my study of psychology. One of the first psychological categorization methods developed was the Sheldonian Theory of Body Types. It's the division into endomorph, ectomorph, and mesomorph. We were reviewing the diagram in Kip's book, when he decided to cross it out and replace 'body' with 'Bud.' The Sheldonian Theory of Bud Types described the Indica, Sativa and Cross. From that snickering defacement I became known in the dorms as "The Theory."

It didn't take long to get kicked out of the dorms, however, which was really silly. I was in the lounge with Bob and Roger, just sitting around and throwing shit at each other when Roger bet me I couldn't throw his shoe behind my back across the lounge and out the one open window. Whht—it was gone! Throwing shit was always a reflex action for me. So like a nice guy I agree to go downstairs and retrieve it from the second floor roof, where I was seen by an RA. I understood why they didn't want people on the roof, but it really wasn't a big deal to be out on the second floor. They didn't see it that way, so my contract was revoked. I was reminded of Alex, (from *A Clockwork Orange*), "I felt bad leaving the old staja…" but I figured I was moving up. We had a party first though, Roger and I. We snuck a keg in and put it in the maintenance closet across the hall, got one of those ginormous bags of popcorn, and proceeded to get drunk, pour beers on the floor, and crush popcorn into it. Roger was good like that, even if he had to live with some bizarre stench for the rest of the year, he'd abandon himself to a beer soaked frenzy.

Fortunately there was an opening at the Zete house. There was probably always an opening at the Zete house, or you could sleep on the couch until a boarder could be evicted or driven away. The departure of Jefe had left an opening. Jefe was the grandson of an African chief, who lived in Beverly Hills. He was a cool guy. He liked to wake up early in the morning and take acid, then go back to sleep so when he got up he didn't know if he was dreaming or awake. I liked that! Wyck moved into Jefe's room and I moved in with my big brother Ken, who was a nerdy Italian kid from San Diego. Ken had been pretty good to me during my pledge period so I felt fine about it. I did notice when I moved in however, that he had a cross over the door, so I turned it upside down. "Shel, you can't dooo that," he pleaded, which led to my realization that he actually was a Catholic. So I took the top bunk, which meant if God were to strike me dead it wouldn't wake Ken. I used to like to taunt him that way, y'know, "Hey Ken, Fuck Jesus! Fuck you God, strike me dead!" I probably should have had more respect for his aberration, but it was fun.

There wasn't too much cooking around the Zete house, we only had two pledges that spring, Rock-it Rod and The Reamer. Reamer was his real name, which I found endlessly funny. He was another boarder who got talked into joining. He used to let me borrow his car for pledge points. It was an MGB GT, which despite its non-convertibility was a pretty cool ride. Rod had moved in, so I saw a fair amount of him. We had a little sister party to which he invited these two high school girls from Bel Air, Terry and Mina. They were both a little too nice to be inducted as Zete little sisters, at least under Droz's reign, during which little sisters vowed to mandatory tubesteak injections. Terry had started going out with Rod though, and Mina tagged along, so they began to join in our forays to the sculpture garden. With six or eight of us going, it got to be a regular escapade.

Bob wasn't too into the Zete scene though. He was pretty clear about the fact that most of the older guys were assholes, and he didn't need that shit. He was right, so I would go back to the dorms fairly often to hang out with him. After I moved out, my buddy from down the hall, Bill, moved in with Roger. He had been stuck at the end of the hall with this kid we called "Fast Eddy." Fast Eddy was going premed. He studied with the radio playing static. He called his mom every day. He had no friends. He was, quite simply, a loser. So he got the new guy on the block, Craig. Paula introduced me to Craig, who had heard of my exploits and wanted to meet me. He was a skinny Jewish kid from the valley, good sense of humor, vulgar, incredibly sharp. He had already finished a year of college although he was still only seventeen. He too was going premed, but at the time he mostly wanted to get high and kill Eddy. I respected these ideals and gave him a whippet. He told me he knew lots of people in the valley and whatnot and thought he could sell some pot for me. It turned out he and I shared the same birthday, albeit a year apart. Not knowing much about astrology, or my own grandiosity, I assumed he might have enough of my characteristics to develop him into a protégé.

Sharky had set up a cool deal for himself that semester. He had a condo in Santa Monica, so he didn't want to move into the house, but he bought a truck with a big camper on it, which he kept parked across the street on top of Lot 8. I don't remember if he was legal to drive it with his visual impairment, or whether he got other people to ferry it back and forth to campus, but he'd live in it during the week and then retire to his condo. He was dabbling in coke at the time, so the camper became a sort of weigh station. We'd go up there and have these endless blackjack games, snort lines, smoke pot, drink beers, do whippets, whatever. That quarter played through, although it was a little hectic in the end. Someone reported the camper, or the Unicops stumbled on to him living there. They investigated while there was coke on the table of course, so he got busted. They didn't send him to jail or anything, but there was some sort of academic disapproval, which his dad wasn't too happy about. I had bagged on my reading of Crime and Punishment, so I had to rely on Merle's notes to get me through our Humanities final, but he was together so I got a B. BM was in as much trouble in Astro as I was, so we went dumpster diving for the final, a la Animal House. We came up with a winner so I passed out of that. For Art I just got high, which resulted in my first collegiate A. I had brought some whippets to the final lecture, which made the people sitting around me very curious. Kip explained that the bottle was my iron lung. Jackson Pollack's Dynamism of a Cyclist, on a whippet, mmmmm!

Hell week was rather tame, with only two pledges there was only so much punishment you could dish out, although it was nice to be on the dishing end. I agreed to meet Sharky at his dad's houseboat, out on Lake Mead. He left me the keys to his dad's Oldsmobile so I could get out there and drive him back, which was a bonus deal. I guess the old man had forgiven him his youthful excess, being well into his adult excess it only seemed fitting. I packed some acid, mushrooms, weed, and a few boxes of whippets in with my shorts and a t-shirt, but it was burning hot so I wanted to wait until night to drive out there. Since scuts aren't allowed any possessions, I took the Reamer's car keys from where we kept them and drove off to Terry's mom's house in Bel Air. I liked Terry's mom. She was in her mid forties, with silver hair, and a somewhat aged quality that could easily have been brought on by the LA sun. Perhaps it was the tough divorce, or dealing with three totally stacked teenage daughters, but she had a good-humored sense of resignation by this point. We'd head up there to jacuzzi and hang in the swimming pool, ogle Terry's sisters, trade banter with mom, and watch LA pulse from the top of the hills. It was a splendid place to visit.

After relaxing the afternoon away, I motored back down the winding roads of Bel Air in Reamer's MGB, feeling pretty cool. I was looking forward to some water ski adventure when I hit a patch of oil in the road. The back wheels slid out so I was angling sideways in both lanes coming around a curve. I tried steering back against the skid but no dice. I came around the curve and my door was heading straight into the corner of a two-foot high brick planter wall on the far side of this guy's driveway. With complete cognition of my impending paralysis or death, my perception sped up into that glassy slo-mo state. I popped the clutch in second and threw the wheel hard to the left, whipped a one-eighty, hit the dip in front of the driveway, jumped the whole car up onto the wall and slid down ten feet. It was an amazing sight, the front end perched over this guy's yard while the back stuck out over the road, and me, unharmed, balanced in the middle. It was apparent that there would be no quick and easy getaway from this, particularly when the old dude who lived there came out screaming. "The Chancellor is a personal friend of mine, I'm going to have you suspended until you pay for this damage! You young punks driving like mad up here, look what you've done to my home!" Considering that the wall had kept me out of his living room, I felt his home was in pretty good shape. We went in to call a tow truck, and the cops, so I phoned the house. Merle answered.

"Hey man, you've got to get your ass up here now, I just wrecked the Reamer's car, right at the West Gate of Bell Air, hurry!" It only took him five minutes on his Honda, an excellent emergency response time.

"Oh my fucking God! How the hell did you do that?!"

"This is the kind of thing that happens to me when I'm straight."

"You are lucky to be alive."

"Yeah, well I won't be so lucky if the cops show up and search my backpack, so why don't you get it the hell outta here?"

"What's in it?"

"The usual. Just don't need the cops to know what stashes I carry around with me." Merle shot me a look that read "You incredible scamming bastard," and rode off just as the tow guy pulled up. He was quite impressed with the graceful landing I had made, but implied that it would be rather messy pulling the car off, and that the frame already looked bent. I didn't feel like waiting for the cops to arrive, so I just walked away and left the old man screaming. I wasn't that far from campus, and a walk through the sculpture garden gave me a chance to compose myself.

It's a pretty wicked buzz being in a situation like that, and I was straight when it happened. I was responsible though, so I went back to the Zete house and found the Reamer.

"Scut, I have to ask you something, do you trust your brother?"

"Yes sir!"

"Good. I just wrecked your car."

"What?"

"That's What? SIR!"

"What? Sir!" he managed."

"I just wrecked your car. Don't worry, I'll pay for the repairs. I have a thousand dollars here which I'll give you when you're initiated, and I'll pay the rest off this summer. Good luck, scut." In the trauma of Hell Week he probably thought I was lying, but after some other brothers drove over to check it out, it was obvious that I wasn't. I had Wyck drive me over to Sharky's place, hopped in the Olds, and spent all night thinking about how badly I had fucked up while flyin like a madman at 100 mph across the desert. I pulled into the parking lot at dawn and passed out, but it was over 100 degrees by 8:30 so I didn't get much sleep. Sharky pulled in to gas up the ski boat and buy beers so we found each other and cracked one. I explained where I had been in the last 24 hours and he suggested I get drunk and engage in water sports until siesta time, which sounded like a good idea. Nothing like drinking six in the hot sun and being dragged behind a boat to make you feel like napping. And there at Lake Mead, you just pull up a tube and sleep half submerged.

They were laughing at me the next morning because I had never risen from my siesta and had slept in that position all night. We skied pretty maniacally the next day and dosed that night. Sharky's older brother knew this spot out by some coves where the rocks had caves you could snorkel down into. The moon was incredible, just glowing, and even at night the water was about 80 degrees so we kept diving in. I had brought some whippets, so I tried doing one, a double actually, and when I started getting high I threw myself off the boat and sank down. I have no idea how deep I sank before I regained consciousness, but when I looked up I could see the moon magnified ten times by the water, just hovering there, on the undulating surface. As I floated closer and closer to it I felt like I would fly right through it and twsh, I broke through the surface and could see it clear as day. It seemed like a pretty fuckin crazy thing to be doin, but I really had no fear of dying. Either those guys would have pulled me out or I'd have a great death, so we took turns at it until all the whippets were gone.

The next day Sharky's brother left, so he and I went out alone that night. We ate the last hits of acid and the shrooms, and roared over to the Arizona side of the lake where we could drink in the dockside bar. The bartender finally threw us out at closing, I think he was having trouble with our giggling, so we ventured back onto the boat. The moon had disappeared by this time and the boat had no running lights, so Sharky, being visually impaired, asked me if I wanted to drive. "No problem," I told him. I throttled out of the docks, opened it up, and we were flying. This was a pretty powerful boat, which hummed along the surface of the water like an endless rock skim. It felt like flying, really, with the still warm desert air blowin by us. Sharky helped me set a course for some lights in the distance, but pretty soon they disappeared into the mirrored image of the galaxy that sat upon the endless water. I was no longer just high, I was flying a rocket through the center of the universe! Lake Mead is pretty damned big, so I had no idea how long I'd been flying or where I was, but I knew who I was. I was the Spaceman! Flying through my universe! And then it hit.

Ghhkzzhunyunchkkrrnnhhnn!!! Sharky flew out over the prow and broke a rib while I hit the steering wheel.

"Turn it off!" Sharky was screaming as the prop continued grating on rock.

"Ohhh Fuck!" I said, thinking my fun license would surely be revoked. I hopped out and helped him get up, but that didn't make him feel any better. In my rocketship fantasy I had steered the boat up onto some sort of island. It was really just an outcropping of big boulders, which happened to lie at exactly the right angle for us to have planed up on them and fifteen feet out of the water. Lucky.

"My dad's gonna kill me." Sharky groaned, "I just got busted for coke and now this."

"I can't believe this shit either man, I just totaled Reamer's car three days ago. I can't pay for this. Fuck, man, I'm sorry." We sat there, each bemoaning our miserable fates, when I told him, "Hey, I've got two whippets left. We can each swim out of here, do a whippet, sink down and never come up again… Or we can just lay in the water and do 'em." He opted to survive our whippets, which I felt was honorable, so we did.

Morning greeted us with an incredible sight. Not only were we stuck on an island of boulders that hadn't killed us, our apparent course had put us within 20 feet of a rock point that stood out of the water ready to cut the boat in half. About a hundred feet away some little family had their rented houseboat moored to the island. I could just see the headline, "Vacationing Family Killed in Boat Collision." They said they thought they heard something in the night but couldn't believe it and went back to sleep. The boat was definitely fucked up. The prop was all chewed, and the hull was missing a few thousand dollars worth of fiberglass. We got it back in the water and managed to get it back to the launch, bailing furiously all the while. Then we packed up the houseboat and headed back to LA. I tried to drive safely, but that only left us more depressed. I agreed with Sharky that the best thing to do would be to let him take the rap, tell his dad that he was driving, so as to keep it in the family. That way it looked more like just a fuck up than being irresponsible and a fuck up. A couple days later we drove out to Joshua Tree for Rod & Reamer's initiation, which was a reminder of just how much I had survived that year. I found out that I had bent the frame on Reamer's car, leaving it irreparable, so I coughed up a thousand of the two it was worth and told him to hold on to it and buy a new one. I swore I'd make the rest of it by fall.

7

Meanwhile it looked like I had a room of my own. Ken had fallen in love with this girl named Sandy. She was from some sorority, I think it was ZTA, zits, tits and ass. She dated him once or twice and that was about it, but he had been pining after her all semester. "If only I could get Sandy to understand…" We had her sorority over for a mixer and Ken took some acid (smart move) thinking he could Rasputinize her into the sack. When she took off he proceeded to sit at the top of the stairs screaming, "SANDEE!" It was kind of a sad ordeal, after which Ken was somewhat unstable. I felt sort of bad, having sold him the acid, but he had been tweaking on her for months. Hell, he was my roommate, I had to trust him. When we were at Joshua Tree for Rod & Reamer's initiation Ken dosed again, wandered out into the desert, and took off all his clothes. Somewhere out there he left his family ring, which was the final straw. It was that "object with which you become so identified that your self conception is vague without it," and there was no way we were ever going to find it, so he became kind of lost himself. He went back to his parent's after that and didn't return for awhile. When he did it was only to pick up his stuff. He left the Chef Boyardee pizza-in-a-box on the food shelf, which I kept untouched in his memory.

This was the first time I had a room to myself since I lived in the garage in seventh grade. My rent doubled, but I didn't have to worry about anybody else's trip. I had made some pretty good money in the spring, enough to pay the Reamer and still have a wad to buy dope with. Things usually thin out a little in summer, but I had made several connections in other frats, Craig was moving shit into the valley, and I had a job. I had better weed than anyone else, too. I was still getting green when no one else could. I got better Thai and hash than most, so my market kept up. I hardly knew anyone else who dealt anything but blow. UCLA was Blow City. We were a small frat and four guys dealt. Sharky and Droz were always trying to give me some, to get me to realize how cool it was. Craig thought it was pretty exciting, too. Speck just fiended. It was an interesting dynamic to watch. People indebting themselves for powder amplified time which, at the end of the bindle, only created the vacuum-headed desire for more. Only when you come to the end of your credit are you faced with your inability to sleep. Weed certainly wasn't like that. No one was hiding their weed from their friends. Okay, to some extent they were, but not because they were going into the closet to smoke it all. It was a much more ritually shared substance. And while acid may keep you up until sunrise, and have its own brain-compressing comedown, no one is beating on your door at 6 A.M. for more hits. So I steered away from powders. I still did some here and there, but it certainly wasn't a product that had any integrity, or identifiable quality, so it wasn't going into my portfolio.

Fourth of July came around and Terry invited the crew up to her house for a pool party. Dane (who I had been hanging out with more) and I decided to eat some hits. It was a luxurious feeling, lounging by the pool in Bel Air, scoping out Terry's sisters, frying. Terry's mom asked us in for lunch, so we acquiesced, although we weren't very hungry. She had made up a bunch of hot dogs, so Dane and I splashed them with various condiments until they were truly psychedelic. Inside the rec room everyone was watching Hair on video. It was a bit bizarre, since we were the only ones tripping, that this was the background event. Mom & Jennifer, the 16-year old platinum blonde 38D teen queen goddess, sat down next to us at the table, and that was when the trouble started. Dane and I were having a little difficulty with these dogs, not knowing if we'd chewed them enough to swallow, or if we could swallow at all, while attempting to be sociable. We kept eyeing each other in silent communication of this fact, since we didn't want to look ridiculous with our endless mastication. There we were, chewing on these metaphorical penises slathered in sauce on a bun while everyone was dancing around naked on the tube, singing about Mellow Yellow orgies and shit. Meanwhile Jennifer, who had been ladled into her bikini, was whining to her mother about how she, at 16, was "totally sexually unsatisfied." Dane and I practically asphyxiated trying to swallow that bite, and were faced with the choice of upending the table and raping her there on the floor, or having another. The civilized veneer held out. We each took another bite and chewed for-fucking-ever as this discussion went on, the hippies frolicked, Mom smiled at us, and we exchanged glances of mute terror. Somehow we managed to plough through those dogs, eyeballing each other our plan for escape. We really didn't want Mom to figure out we were frying, or get Terry in trouble for it, so we went back out to the Jacuzzi. Whew!

We were quite relieved to get away, agreeing that sex crimes would soon have been committed. We got in the Jaccuzzi, but there was no button to push for the bubbles, which we needed, so I went around the side of the house to where the controls were. It was a little confusing, but I certainly didn't want to admit I was completely fucked up by asking for help, so I turned some valve and pushed a button which got them on. We were sitting out there bubbling along when Dane noticed the water level going down. "I think it's some deal where the water has to filter out some before more hot water comes in," I told him, "it'll just take a minute." So we started sinking down, laying further into the water, scooting out off the bench and into the middle. Dane kept asking me, "Is it supposed to be doing this?" But I was high enough not to want to admit to doing something stupid, so we sank down until we were off the bench. All of the sudden the water level got below the jets and they started making this incredible grinding noise, grrsshhhhh, spraying us in the face so we couldn't even see. Terry's mom ran out screaming,

"What are you doing?" and turned them off.

"I guess I must've turned the wrong valve there," I stammered.

"Yeah, I guess," was her sarcastic reply. Watching Hair still seemed too crazy, so we had to stay in the pool, where we could do no damage. But Ma was still pretty cool about it so we figured we hadn't been detected. It wasn't until the next day that Terry told us that she had told her mom were going to be on acid, and she was totally cool about it. We were the only one's who didn't know!

Despite the first week, the summer was going pretty well overall, and I pursued a fantasy I had been carrying for years to its logical conclusion. I had decided long before that I should roll the $100 doobie some day, and after reading the High Times article on rolling a cigar with weed leaf, I figured out how. I bought a load of Thai sticks and got myself a gram of honey oil while I was in Berkeley. The Hawk was growing some skinny plants under fluorescent lights in his closet, so I had plenty of leaf. I took the nicest stick from a half-pound, then meticulously slathered honey oil over these leaves and rolled them around it. It wasn't easy, I had to wrap the leaf down with thread to keep it in place. Then I oiled it down and did another layer. It took me a couple hours to get through all the oil, but it was a beautiful creation, like a giant blunt, but brown inside and green outside, and all of it was the real. I let it dry for a couple days, waiting for the weekend, then got everyone in the house to come up and smoke this thing. We weren't even a third into it when everyone was blown away. The Hawk and I stayed on it, with anyone who'd show up, for the whole fucking weekend. When it got down about halfway, it got to be too hot too hold onto, so Hawk dug around in his toolbox for a pair of vise grips, which made the perfect roach clip. Sometime Sunday afternoon it got down to about a quarter, so I broke it up and rolled three roach bombers from that, and one more out of those three roaches. I swear to God, that thing got a dozen guys completely wasted for over two solid days. If nothing else, I was achieving my goals of highness.

Craig worked for his dad as a restaurant vendor so he knew where there was a big restaurant equipment store in the valley. We drove out there one day and bought our first case of whippets, 600 to be exact, and a new bottle. Now, there are a few different ways to do whippets, the idiot way, the lame way, and the bottle. Being a compressed gas, nitrous is a freezing liquid upon release. There are these little plastic casings you can buy that twist a pin into the whippet and release the gas whilly-nilly out one end. These are meant to be attached to a balloon, but some idiots will try to suck whippets straight out of them, thus freezing their tongues. The plastic tends to freeze too, so even dispensing it into a balloon gets pretty iffy. If you try to do more than two whippets you burn your hand, which is lame. So much for the idiot and lame ways, although I'm sure there are morons who've gone after whippets with a can opener or a nail. The bottle, however, is designed for restaurant usage. It has a heavy-duty plastic casing with steel threads that fit the whippet perfectly, and a one-way valve so you can remove it without losing any gas. If you get the large bottle (get the large bottle!) you can load two whippets: A Double! The bottle valve also allows you to release the gas at a comfortable rate, which makes it the only choice for discriminating substance abusers.

Over a period of time I developed a certain technique. I could pop the whippet into the casing, snap my wrist so the bottle spun around and punctured the whippet, snap it back the other way, eject the whippet, pop in another, snap, and dispense the gas, all in less than 12 seconds, "The Fastest Whippet in the West." This was good because nitrous has a certain anticipatory quality to it. You want to maintain each plateau and accelerate into the next as fast as possible. If you're partying with a bunch of people you don't want everyone to have to wait too long. Of course, there is the entertainment of watching each other say silly things during the recovery period. "The veriest nonsense." One night I decided to see how many whippets in a row I could do without stopping for air. I was in the Hawk's room at the very back of the third floor, sitting in his comfy chair, listening to some BÖC, which we did frequently. I opened a fresh box of whippets and popped one, twshss! Inhaled it, thhooo! Snapped my wrist, ejected it, popped in another and repeated the process. I got through 16 whippets this way before I blacked out. I found myself floating, once again, on the edge of the solar system, somewhere out beyond Saturn. I could make out the earth very clearly though, as I hung, surrounded by galaxies, in the deep blackness of space. I wanted to leave a mark, like some sort of extraterrestrial vandal, so that my friends would know that I had been here, but there was nothing to leave a mark with or on. "In space no one can hear you scream," I thought. Perhaps I'll just test that. So from the core of my being I yelled to my friends back on earth. Even without a body it made my chest hurt. It was a few minutes before I regained consciousness, but when I did I was surrounded by Zetes.

"Uh, did I do anything?" I asked, somewhat sheepishly.

"Yeah man," the Hawk flailed in his demonstratively excited way, "you let out this death scream so loud these guys heard you downstairs and across the street and came running over here!"

"Cool, you got the message." It was a little difficult to explain what the message was, but I was thrilled that I had gotten it across the dimensions. I wondered what I could do with more nitrous.

Having all these spent whippets lying around did leave room for mischief. One thing I liked to do with them was shoot them out of my wrist rocket. I'd go into the back yard, the basketball court, put one in the web and stretch that thing back as far as it could possibly go, then release it into the night. I'd usually aim pretty straight up, with enough arc to deposit them on the parking structure across the street or onto another block. We'd listen for a ping, from somewhere, a sign that contact had been made. I probably dented a few cars, but it seemed very unlikely that anyone would get hurt, or that I'd be caught. Sharky, on the other hand, was more dangerously inventive. He would collect my spent whippets and make bombs out of them. We shared our back fence with Lambda Chi, whom we didn't particularly like, but we didn't particularly like any of the fraternities around us. Some guys from Lambda Chi were talking shit to a couple brothers while they played basketball one afternoon, so our guys started huckin beer bottles up there. Strategically speaking, we were in really bad position for that sort of thing. Lambda Chi was uphill looking down on our flank, and they responded with a rain of bottles onto the cement. Our guys ran inside while everyone started yelling, bottles were flying, but Sharky sensibly strolled up to his closet, whipped out a couple of bombs and tossed them back along the fence. End of story. I never heard another peep out of Lambda Chi.

I believe it was in retaliation for the coal incident that we threw a Sharky-bomb in Phi Psi's back yard. They had a big, walled-in court, which echoed like fuck, so they too learned to respect superior firepower. They had been barbecuing on their roof when someone tossed a coal on ours. We had an old wood shake roof, so after smoldering for a bit it caught on fire. We never would have noticed it, but the Phi Psi's were decent enough to call the fire department. They claimed that some sparks had floated over to our house, but hey, if we had thrown a coal on their roof we probably would have let the place burn. The Zete house was a pretty old wood structure, and the Fire Marshal wanted to impress upon us the seriousness of the event, in his self-important way. "This place is one big tinder box," he said. "You have a real fire here and one of you boys will be coming out in a green bag." We accepted the gravity of his statement as if he'd been any other old geezer in a position of authority, That's funny, everybody seems to come out with a bag of green!

Despite the fact that he had dropped out of our pledge class, Bam-Bam moved in with Dane down the hall from me. Between the Hawk and his buddy Lou, who had moved down from Seattle, Bam-Bam, Dane and Wyck, there was always someone to party with. Bam-Bam was always into some sort of sporting activity, so he pushed the limits of athletic bonging. First there was the inverted bong, where you did a handstand while your trainer lit the bong for you. It is a little tougher not to drool while you're upside down, and you have to be careful not to cough so hard you collapse into a cervical fracture. The effect wasn't all that unusual however. Marathon bonging was the real deal. It probably started with just seeing who could hold their hit in the longest, but Bam-Bam upped the ante. For a marathon bong you'd take your hit, run down the hall to the veranda, out to the back hill, down the side of the building, back in the front door, up the stairs, down the hall, up the stairs and back into the room, then exhale. Now that gave you a head rush. If you're trying to conserve your weed by maximizing every hit, do a marathon bong.

I was not too concerned with weed frugality, I was smokin and gettin paid for it. By the end of summer I paid my last installment to the Reamer. I asked him what kind of car he was going to get, but he had never really had that much cash in hand before so he drank it all in a summer of bar hopping. Maybe I was too frugal, but I just couldn't imagine blowing that kind of money on drink. I had saved some money to blow on seeing the Grateful Dead, however. I got in line early when they announced they were playing on my birthday. I had managed to wangle some floor seats, which I assumed were pretty good, but in LA if you didn't pay a scalping agency at least a hundred bucks a seat, they weren't that great. Most of the crew came to the show, Craig, Kip, Rod and Terry and Mina, Bob was still back home in SB. In the same way I had wanted to spread the amazement of taking drugs, I wanted all my friends to see the Dead.

I had gone the night before, which was pretty good, but I was extra excited about my birthday, a magic night. I decided to take a moderate dose, four grams of shrooms, which was starting to hit me when I met a friend of Dave's from Barrington, Bill Crooks. ("A friend of the Devil is a friend of mine.") When I told him it was my birthday he responded by whipping out a sheet of green gels. "Happy Birthday! Have some acid!" He broke off four for me, and that was it. I had taken doses that size several times, I had eaten that many mushrooms several times, but I had never done them together. Even at Mead, flying across the galaxy, I was on maybe a couple hits and a few grams. It was my night, I was getting higher than ever, and the boys played it. The show was wailing! Jack Straw, cowboy tunes, Althea, insanely brilliant Weather Report, China Rider like that Northbound train was rollin right through you, I began to see what was really going on. They still had a fairly huge speaker system, which not only vibrated your body at whatever frequencies they played, but in the dimension I was in it emitted fat waves of sound, in color, like barrels rollin off Waimea. You could position yourself to surf right down 'em.

By the time they opened the second set with Shakedown Street I was swimming in sensation. Aware enough to know that the song was about getting off your ass and making the effort to look for a girl, I began wondering if I should poke around. But Long Beach is not the kind of place where you leave your seat looking for action, unless your idea of action is getting your head busted open by psychopathic security dudes. In any case, I was too self-conscious and tooo high to be making any such efforts. Picking up girls had never been my forte, to the point that I had almost given up on the idea. The few I'd had always seemed to be gifts of the universe. As the show rolled on though, telling me the story of my life, (and probably doing the same for countless others, I now realize) I felt like something was happening on my behest. Secret wheels were moving to grant me what I was too lame to get for myself. My position in the grand scheme was being acknowledged, they were playing it! It was my birthday, some girl must be there to be sacrificed to my grandiosity. It was all I wanted, and I was high enough that I knew it must be true. I certainly couldn't ask anyone, no one was going to tell me, that was all part of the game, but it must be true. It must be that Mina, the beautiful 17 year old virgin, the China Doll Asian Princess, will be mine tonight. Happy Birthday to me!

("Maybe you had too much too fast, and just overplayed your part.") But what could I do? It was "One More Saturday Night." We made it back to the car and got on the Long Beach freeway, driving past the torchlit beacon of Cal Worthington Ford. I broke open a box of whippets and popped a couple, steeling myself for the ride home. In my extremely altered state it appeared that the asphalt of the freeway was nonexistent, merely an extension of the night's black expanse. The reflective lane markers looked as if they were strung in a swimming pool at night. As we flew through this blackness I could see we were approaching an overpass, which, in my state, I imagined we would collide with due to our altitude. "Bring it down, bring it down. We're too High!" I yelled, grabbing for the gear shift as if I could use ailerons to force us back down. Fortunately, Craig, who wasn't quite that high, held on to the stick during my outburst, thus preventing a potentially serious fuck-up. I can't help but chuckle at how perceptive I really was at the time, "We're too high!" Maybe it was just me.

We went back to Mina's house, where they had a birthday cake for me. Her mom went to bed so we were able to hang out pretty late. I kept waiting for the cue that everyone would leave so I could claim my prize, but it never arrived. Eventually I, me! Sheldon, was told that it was time to leave. I walked home, thinking Okay, this isn't working out quite right, but it had still felt good just to be with my friends. I let my despondence drift away into the night, coming down in the darkness between whippet fueled updrafts. I was still the highest, and now I had a calling in seeing the Dead. I phoned Craig the next morning, "Dude, they're playing in Vegas tomorrow night, we gotta go!"

℘

I had a great aunt in Las Vegas, so I called her up and asked if I could visit that afternoon, to which she replied with a gracious offer to take me to dinner. Craig and I got on the 10 and buzzed across the desert in his Prelude, tape deck and A/C blasting. We were sort of torched by the time we got there, so we took a nap. "We can go out for dinner around five," my aunt Dorothy told me. "Your cousin Duane is coming into town and has to be somewhere tonight." I was not prepared for that. This was actually my father's cousin, one of a chain of lawyers and doctors sprung from the loins of my Jewish relatives in Chicago. I wasn't tooo freaky looking, but I wasn't sure how I'd handle a conversation with a 40-ish lawyer. I took a nap though, and slept on it. It was still only 3:30 or so when I woke up, so Craig and I scanned the phone book for a restaurant supply place. We told Dorothy we had to run an errand, and picked up a load of whippets. When I returned, my cousin and his wife were already there, chatting with Dorothy. They asked what brought us to Vegas, so, assuming they were out of it, I told them,

"I'm here to see this band, The Grateful Dead?"

"Really?" Duane replied, "I've been seeing them since Purdue '68."

"No way!" I half laughed, astonished that there were freaks in my family before my particular branch bent. We had dinner, dropped Dorothy off, and headed over to the Aladdin, where Duane had a room. We went up and he broke out some hash he had brought, so I got out some weed and rolled a family affair. When it was about time to head down for the show I got out my edibles for the evening. I had decided to go into this show looking for a high water mark, so I ate five grams of shrooms and five hits to start with.

The Aladdin had a beautiful theater, plush, round, chandelier lighted, deeply carpeted with that casino style, "follow me" paisley. You had to take your shoes off, it was just so nice to dance on. There's something about certain theaters, the round ones that aren't too big, where security's not too tight, that when the lights go down and the show starts cookin, your mind starts melting and you feel like you've taken off on a spaceship, so you can just toss your watch, cuz it won't tell you anything out here. You're on the mother ship, with whoever you're with, humans or aliens, believing, or hoping, that they're your people. I had a feeling that night that something was gonna happen, something unexpected. So I wandered the floor, dancing along my elastic Dead boogie, scoping the freaks while they scoped me in the psychedelic robe of paisley patterned towels that my mother had sewn for me while I was in high school. It had a certain regal quality to it that I loved, a weight and feel that made me stand out and feel secure.

As first twitches of Scarlet Begonias rang out, I started stepping gradually down the big center aisle toward the front, knowing something was waiting for me there. About halfway down it I was amazed by a couple having sex right there on the floor. This was a free zone! I limited my voyeurism to gaining certainty that I wasn't just imagining things, before proceeding down the steps. As certain as I had felt some magnetic draw I ran into Dave and Rachel, bouncing along to candy coated sounds. Having had no idea either of us would be there we jumped up and down hugging, then Dave whipped a spliff from his overall pocket to sweeten the pot. Soon came my first joyful encounter with the song that would become the most significant for me, "Fire on the Mountain." "Fire!" if you weren't around to abbreviate it's title, had some of the fattest enveloping of any Jerry song. The envelope filter was Jerry's trademark, the effect that gives notes an incredibly expanded wwWOWww sound, which he commanded to stretch notes into giant bubbles. They stretched your brain right along with 'em, as you rode the soundsurf until Phil's bass rumblings swallowed you in the tube and you were crushed. Those boys had mastered the dynamics of volume, or so I thought at the time. They could certainly take you for a ride, but their lyrical ambiguity always left me feeling that I was still on the edge of some big secret. I spent that evening dancing with my brother in our warm fuzzy spaceship, then told him that Duane was there, so we could meet up at his room later.

When the show got out we made Hunter Thompson's Vegas look pale. 3,000 tripping freaks cruising through the casino, taking over the slots, roulette wheels, crap tables, and the bars, making a tie-dye splattered interface to gold-ring-fingered fat-belt-buckled snakeskin cowboys with their Dolly Parton wannabe wives and blue-haired sequin-gowned mothers-in-law. As all your senses collided in the inseparability of acid, every aspect of the casino vied for attention. The slithering purple and gold anaconda of carpet led us through the pulsing lights and spinning wheels of glitter that melted into the soundscape of gearing and crashing and bell ringing and change raining, and "SEVEN! WHOOOO!" while the friendly voice over the intercom paged Jack Straw or Mr. Charlie or Delilah Jones to the white courtesy phone. We were all high as fuck, and there were No Cops! I was somewhat on edge to begin with, since the laws in Nevada are pretty strict, but I guessed that some deal had been struck, as if we were just another set of rowdy conventioneers with our own particular rituals who should be left alone to promote commerce. I went outside to try to gather my head for a second, the miles of the strip seeming slightly less overwhelming than the casino floor, but there was no escape. The Stardust was right next door, you may have seen their sign on Vega$. It lit up all pink, then flushed out in purple. Twinkling stars emerged, harmonically oscillating my every neuron into its pattern until my whole body was a quivering pulsation of pink, purple, and stars. Overcome by this energy exchange, I was clutched by some sort of neon orgasm. I could see then why people would live in Vegas.

Craig got our whippets out of the car and we were ready for another foray into the casino, which was somewhat more tolerable now that I had been neon tuned. We followed the carpet back to the elevators just as Bob & Brent were coming out.

"Hey Bobby, want a whippet?" I asked.

"Uhh, no thanks," he replied. As they walked past us, Brent, who was the new kid at that time, asked Bob quizzically,

"What's a whippet?" I had to laugh, This guy's in the Grateful Dead and doesn't even know what a whippet is? I realize now that Bob was probably trying to steer him right before he could become another heroin casualty keyboardist. We went upstairs to deliver whippets to Craig's friend Spin, and his connection, BT, a big acid maker who wanted a bunch. He had a huge suite with a serious taper scene going, a dozen D5s rolling tapes from the show, piles of blow, dope, booze. We did a bunch of whippets, tweaking on the Lite Brite vibrating view of the strip from his room, then rolled on down the hall. I was hoping to get up to the next floor and party with Jerry, as every Deadhead dreams, but I didn't have the invite. We just went around getting everybody as high as we could, then met back up with the family to cruise the strip.

As twisted as I might have been, as trippy looking as we were, there's nothing like wandering Vegas to make you feel normal. The mere fact that all those people are there partaking in the mass delusion without being on drugs is enough to scare you straight. After being greeted by a chariot of toga-wearing muscle men and bronze skinned beauties in front of Caesar's Palace, it was hard not to imagine an Orgy Room waiting inside, at least with my imagination. I wanted to be fed grapes while getting a blowjob, all while watching Billy Graham be disemboweled on big screen TV, but Vegas doesn't really deliver what it advertises. Beneath the veneer of "name your fantasy" design and big time stage shows, it's just a dead end for manic gambling businessmen to risk the mortgage and Midwestern geezers to be plied into penury with free drinks and games of chance. We wandered. I never slept. No one sleeps in Vegas. Night's deep black serenity had all but been erased by excessive power consumption. You just grab your "All you can eat breakfast for $2.99" at dawn and get outta town.

9

With my uneven first year grades (perhaps shitty is a more appropriate term) some of my grant monies were revoked, which made things look dismal on the financial front. The summer's excesses had left me in need of fresh capitalization, which I expected at the school year's beginning. Fortunately the groovy people at financial aid convinced me that I should just acquire some debt, like everyone else. Voila! Now I had twice as much money as I had received in any of my previous disbursements. Of course, I had agreed that I would spend it on nothing other than room, board, and tuition. But if the government went around prosecuting people for misspent loans our prisons would be overcrowded with middle class white college-educated types, rather than impoverished minorities. School was still another week away, so I picked a ride off the ride board and headed up to Berkeley, where the Dead were playing the Greek Theater. Dave and Rachel had moved to a place up in the hills that they shared with Bagel and some other freaks. I got there about 3 o'clock, when the preparations for that night's show were getting underway. Stymie was there, taking a break from his new venture of dope growing, the results of which were pretty amazing.

That first set of Dead shows at the Greek were unlike any other, mainly because Berkeley was the town were the freaks meet to tweak. Adding the Dead to this was like pouring vinegar on baking soda. Bill Graham was still running everything himself, so the security was very mellow. In fact, the cops were not allowed inside. The Greek was such a great atmosphere, with a dirt pit for flailing in, a terraced level for standing, a large stone arc of seats, and a lawn above. From the lawn you could look out onto the bay, while the sun set behind the Golden Gate. The band had a tie dyed backdrop that the whole stage melted into. (I don't think a lot of people wearing tie-dyes from Macy's understand that a tie dye is a signature of having taken acid. A person's tie dyed clothing ultimately expresses their existence. They no longer have a body, per se. If you're dosed, you recognize that people are all just splatters of color, and I don't know if your granma wants some trippin hippie flashing on her.)

I took a quarter ounce of mushrooms for the first night, which sort of debilitated me. I was standing there with Stymie and Dave and their friends, trying to roll a joint when these two beautiful girls walked up. Here was my heaven sent gift from the Dead, but I was so buzzed I couldn't imagine them actually stopping to talk to me, nor could I actually speak at the moment, so I just sat down on the cement. I decided they wanted to talk to Stymie, since he was such a cool guy (although in truth he was much geekier than I) but they just stood there, looking at me. I finished rolling and fired it up, handing it up to Stymie as the first person in the chain of honor. I looked up at them and they were still there, smiling at me, so I went back to staring at the cement. They took a hit, but eventually left. Who knows what they thought, but some of my mushroom gut queasiness went away with them. It's amazing how hard it is to grasp what you want when you're too high. I sat through most of the second set, although I was in the standing terrace. It was easier to look through the forest of legs. I recall them weaving in and out of "Uncle John's Band" before playing "Morning Dew," which is what caused the city ordinance about the decibel level for Greek shows to be written. Phil was simply shaking the Berkeley hills. People called in to report an earthquake. I didn't yet make any connection between that song and nuclear war, I was just rent by the vibrations.

The second day I was in a little better shape. I slept in, had a big breakfast, and got stoned. Rachel's younger sister Ruth came up. She had come to New Year's also, but now I could see what a perfect picture this made, Dave and Rachel, Me and Ruth, hmmm. She was a bubbly dark haired Jewess, with a sense of humor, who liked to smoke pot and see the Dead, perfect. This was before personal ads so you just had to imagine the possibilities from what you were looking at. I decided I'd be extra cool that day and see what happened. There was going to be a party at Dave's house after the show that night, not that every night's not a party, but some are more intentional. Various folks had crashed there the night before, but more were showing up all day. One of Dave's connections delivered a bottle of acid from a batch that had been made up that morning, especially for the night's show. We took it with us. We set up a blanket near the top of the lawn and pulled out our various stashes. Everyone in the place was pulling out stashes, There were big dope deals going on right on the lawn. Being one of the first big years of Humboldt dope growing it was a sort of convention for dealers hawking their wares. Dave broke out the bot and dropped four drops into the indentation on the webbing between his outstretched thumb and forefinger.

"Wanna dose?" he asked me. "Made fresh today!"

"I just ate three gels, so just give me three drops," was my rather tame reply. He did, so I diligently licked the spot clean. I was reminded of Dave's agreement to dose with me when I turned 21, but I was still only 19. Besides, dosing at the show isn't the same as dosing with a person.

When the music started we wandered off into the pulse, jellying our way about the crowd. After a few songs Dave turns to me and says, "Here, take this." He pulls off his backpack, hands it to me, pops the clips off his overalls, drops 'em, whips off his shirt and disappears toward the trees. I figured, Right on! This place is so fuckin cool you can just get naked! I didn't particularly feel like carrying his shit around though, so I went back to the blanket. I was starting to get kinda high myself, but I figured everything was okay, so I dropped Dave's pack and his clothes while Rachel sort of stared at me.

"Where's Dave?" she asked.

"Oh, he's wandering in the back somewhere, he gave me his clothes to bring back here."

"He took off his clothes?" she said, astonished.

"Yeah, I figured it was okay here, right?" I asked hopefully.

"Oh no," she laughingly trembled, "we better find him." Hmmm, maybe my judgment is a little off. It wasn't too hard to find the naked man trundling about the trees, so Rachel coerced him into returning to the blanket where we thrust his rags back on him. We were pretty happy that I had gotten the pack, at least, since it was full of killer bud, LSD, the keys again, what have you. We puffed one and things seemed copacetic, so I set off again to see what I could see.

I was feeling pretty fine when I finished walking a circuit, so I stopped at the top of the lawn to admire the view. They were playing Bird Song when two swallows flew up, chasing each other in figure eights all around the stage before disappearing into the sunset. It was a classic Dead moment. I turned around to find Dave right behind me, agog with the splendor of it all. He went from looking into the distance with a glazed joy to staring at my face and smiling.

"Ivan, Ivan, I'm so glad you're here, I love you man." I must have responded with a slight recoil, since the only person to call me Ivan was my mother, when she was so flustered with anger that she could only remember its primary cause. Dave's expression now took on a tenor of fear, as his eyes looked straight through me, "Dad... Dad...."

"Hey Dave, it's me," but there was no contact, nor was there a process this time. All his clothes hit the ground that second, while his naked form descended into the crowd. I was vaguely concerned, although more miffed at having to drag his clothes back and report this to Rachel, who did not take it very calmly at all. I was entirely prepared to have a good time there. I didn't want to believe that this was a problem, nor did I want to fall victim to fear, since everyone knows that fear and acid don't mix. But we decided to begin an immediate search. Now I began to wonder,

If Dave took 4 hits of liquid and I took 3 and 3 gels, what's gonna happen to me? I'm high, but not **that** high. But what if this is all a test? Some way that the Dead and their whole secret society could see what I'm made of, how I'll react, if I'll freak out. Is Dave really freaking out? Maybe the liquid was just placebo. Whatever was happening I had to stay cool, responsible, clearheaded, on six hits!

We found Dave lying at the bottom of the lawn. Fortunately he had wiped out there before jumping off the wall to the next level, which the people there said he was headed for. A mere six foot jump onto concrete, but perhaps it was not the best thing for a blown-away barefoot naked man. We escorted him back up to the blanket, but he was delirious, grabbing whoever was close enough and screaming how he loved them before swooning into whatever dimension he was really in. I knew he loved me, but I wasn't sure if that meant I should spend the evening wrestling with his naked, flailing body. I wanted to do what was best for him, but I also needed to be sure that I was reacting correctly if this was a test. Somebody noticed the Haight Ashbury Rock Medicine tent in the very back by the trees so we carried him back there. It was the first time I had ever seen them, possibly their first shows, but I was glad they were there. They laid him down on the ground with enough room to roll around while he tweaked, then stepped back. Manny attempted to talk him down, but there was no down from his out, so we went back to the show. I tried to get back into things but everyone I met would either ask where Dave was or if I knew he had lost it. "Hey I hear your brother's rolling around naked in the leaves up there screamin," Bagel mocked. The show pounded on as we made our rounds to the Rock Med tent to check in on him. He kept going through this cycle of erupting with the few words that still held meaning at whatever level of consciousness he was, timed to the peaks of the intensity of the music. "LOVE! WHIP-PETS! ACQUIRE! GRATEFUL DEAD!"

He was so loud that the cops, who weren't inside the show but dutifully posted themselves along the fence to peer in on the inhabitants, kept asking, "What's going on with that guy? Hey, this is the police, what's going on over there?" It was sort of freaking me out, but the Rock Med guys just ignored them. Then one of them started a conversation with me.

"Friend of yours?"

"My brother."

"Hmm, you guys take some acid?" Now I was tweakin, Should I tell this guy, or is it a bust? The cops were right outside the fence trying to scope us with flashlights.

"Yeah," I nervously admitted.

"How much?"

"He took four drops?"

"Liquid?"

"Yeah."

"I've heard there's a batch out today that's pretty strong."

"Mmhm"

"You take any?"

"Three and three gels."

"Hmmmm" Dave started getting wild again so this Med guy, I never got his name, hops on top of his chest and grabs his arms. "Dave, Dave, it's all right, just stay calm buddy, just keep it cool," he coaxed. Dave went limp again, so the guy let go of him, trying to soothe him with words. Then Dave, Mr. Hippie Peace Love Groovy Dude, comes up from out of nowhere with a right, straight up into the Rock Med guy's jaw, that lifted his body half a foot. I helped the guy up, and at this point he decided that leaving Dave to tumble in the leaves and scream was probably the best idea. For a while I watched as Dave pounded it out to the tempo of the show, but I had to get back to the music myself, back to "Fire on the Mountain."

It was a starry night, balmy, a perfect time to be enjoying the show, but I was analyzing every thought. Is it okay to leave Dave back up there? Am I breaking a tribal law? Why aren't I that high? Is the acid fake? **Is** Dave **that** high? Am **I** that high? The pounding gave way to Black Peter, a dirge about lying on one's deathbed, at which time I could no longer stay away. Everybody seemed to come by and check on him, it was such good song for visiting your tweaking friend. The show was winding down, but Dave was definitely not. "LOOOVE!" ACQUIRE! WHIPPETSSS!" The Med guy told me "Look, the show's gonna end soon and you're gonna have to get him outta here. The cops are already trying to get his name and stuff so I suggest you let me shoot him up with Valium so you can at least move him. All you have to do is sign this form." I really didn't like the options. I couldn't leave him there, nor could I get him out in the shape he was in, but I was looking at signing a form that said we had both taken LSD and that I, as nearest relative, gave my permission to shoot him up. The incrimination factor was really freaking me out, but I didn't have a lot of options. I scrawled. Manny and I held him down while the Med guy injected him. I could tell Dave was beyond feeling it, but as the Med guy pushed the plunger I felt like I was getting a cardiac needle right in the heart. I thought I was having a coronary as Dave slumped into his trans-dimensional delirium.

The cops were still going off with their "What's going on over there," rap, but a couple of Dave's friends were able to carry him out without them finding him. Back at the pad they put Dave to bed while the party started rolling. All these dudes had brought down fresh bud from Humboldt. One guy whipped out a shopping bag that had a bud in it as big as his forearm. Various people were running off to the closet to do their blow, since there were too many people to share that with, but we smoked until four in the morning, when the twenty people left passed out on the living room floor. I was still too fried to sleep. I wanted to crash in Dave's room, where I thought Ruth would too, but Rachel didn't want Dave to be disturbed. I thought about trying to get Ruth to come over to my bag when everyone was asleep, but when she thought everyone was asleep she crawled into one of Dave's friend's bags and had sex with him while I watched, motionless. What a night!

Dave was still pretty drugged out when I got up. He was half limp, half-fried, and completely unable to talk from screaming so much. He seemed like he'd recover, but there was no way he was going to the show that day, which was soon. The Dead played this staggered schedule there, starting the shows two hours earlier each day. You got more night to party with bonus sleep deprivation to burn you out. It was a slow Sunday in the park, but it was the first show in the bay area that I went to without Dave. From the time I started hanging in Barrington I had always been Dave's kid brother. It made sense, he was eight years older than me. That had been my identity when I was there, but now I was elsewhere, and things were changing. Some of Dave's behaviors had already reflected negatively on me, as people expected his style of eccentricity from me, but I was developing my own eccentricity. As Dave's kid brother I had always looked up to his friends, creating my career from their beneficent risk. I wanted to impress them, to hang out with them, to be cool enough to be experiencing what they were. My entering into the legions of the Dead was certainly an activity that I followed them into. Like any tag-along kid brother, I wanted to share in the experience of people older than me, thinking that I'd be that much more mature then. But you can't really tag along into other people's maturation processes, you need to attend to your own, which don't proceed any faster or easier because you're with older people. I was going through a very different process than they probably had, one that now demanded I change my relationship to them by thinking of myself as myself, Sheldon or Spaceman or whoever I might be, since Dave wasn't around.

Assessing who I was in this context was not easy. It was always a very Berkeley type of scene at the show, freaky tie-dyed grubby hairy naked unwashed screaming free free free people. But I had my own scenes, in

Roseville, and now LA, which was not a very freaky atmosphere. I was trying to recreate this utopian Berkeleyan ideal of drug experience and freedom, but it was entirely within my little feudal empire. The original ideals of psychedelia, that the world would be a better place if everyone could experience LSD, drop their restrictive social values, and ascend, certainly seemed worth upholding. At the same time however, it was a business, in which I distributed enlightenment for $4 a hit. Since I had always had the lock on distribution, I controlled access to this enlightenment. As much as I wanted it to be, it could never be a completely free scene, for that very reason. It also fell under the weight of the fact that I wanted a certain level of acknowledgment from people for what I was doing, what I was risking for them. I wanted it from the universe as much as from anyone. But of course, the universe doesn't really work that way. I hadn't figured that out yet, though, so after the show I copped a big load from Dave, who had recovered enough to let me weigh out my selection, and caught a ride back to LA.

Despite the paranoid microanalysis of my weekend, my description of the shows to my friends in LA was only in terms of superlatives. If I found any reason to describe the Dave event at all I'm sure it sounded like a great heroic adventure of LSD excess. What really mattered was that I was back, I had the dope, I was in charge. With the new quarter kicking in, my biz took off. All my old people were back on line, the frats that took drugs would come buy me out. I only had to reserve enough stash so that the gang could trip on a Saturday night. With things moving that fast though, my haphazard modes of transport were no longer functional. I began to fly World Airways from LA to Oakland every couple weeks. It was before anyone knew that the government was flying all their cocaine the same way, they just had cheap flights. I'd usually get Wyck to drive me to LAX, since he had a car. I'd pick up a cab in Oakland, head into Berkeley to score my dope from Dave, or Stymie's partner Ben, maybe spend the night, turn around and fly back home. I was pretty paranoid when I first started doing it, with good reason. The weed back then was stinky! I'd have my backpack stuffed full of it, with some shrooms 'n hits to boot, so I was a walking bust beacon. World had their own terminal though, away from the rest of LAX, probably so they could unload their kilos of blow discretely. I'd try to have Wyck waiting when I got there, so that anyone who noticed that I reeked up the plane wouldn't be able to check me out for long. It was always a celebration to return with the herb du jour, but soon enough it would fly out the door, followed shortly thereafter by myself.

1◎

We had a real mix of pledges that fall. Kip joined, but otherwise it was a freak, a geek, and a couple dweebs. There was one kid from Tennessee though, Carl, who was kind of hard to place. Dane took a shine to him right away. My natural inclination was to assume that he was just some redneck Okie, but he was pretty smart. Since he was Dane's little brother I saw him pretty often. I don't think he had ever smoked dope before, but he was of a mind to try. How he could bong with that plug of chaw in his mouth I'll never know, but it was impressive, so I invited him to take some shrooms with us. Carl had a certain likeability, a joviality paired with a quick wit, but when he first ate shrooms he was like an animal. We were all wandering back from the garden, crossing the street before we got to the house, when Carl just dove up on to the hood of this car that was stopped at the intersection. He lay there staring through their windshield as if their car were a fish tank. With some coaxing we were able to get him off, but I wonder what those people thought. Back at the house he tried to do a flip over the railing of the stairway and land standing, but he misjudged it, landing on his back and thumping his way down the stairs. We were a little worried about him, so I sat with him on the stairs for awhile.

"Carl, do you want to come down?"

"I don't know."

"I can make you a sandwich, that'll probably bring you down some."

"Maybe if I just lay here, I'll be okay."

"Okay Carl, I'll be right here." After fifteen minutes or so he was able to move again, which was quite a relief, but the utter sense of abandon with which he approached every situation really excited me, so he became a crew member.

Kip had a job as a waiter at pretty nice restaurant in Westwood, the Brasserie. He was a pretty responsible guy, so they had him closing the restaurant half the time. He'd come home with a backpack full of turkey slices and German beers to share with us. On occasion he'd have us come down to the restaurant when everyone left. We'd sit there in a darkened booth, drinking St. Pauli Girls and watching UCLA girls walking by outside. Then we'd fill all our backpacks with brews and split. This was how I developed my taste for expensive beers. I already considered myself a connoisseur of drugs, so it was no wonder that the fine beers appealed to me too. I started heading out to the expensive liquor store on Santa Monica Blvd to get Oranjeboom and Swiss Lowenbrau whenever I could. Maybe my taste buds have changed, but I swear those beers tasted much better than they do today. Six bucks a six was pretty astronomical then, so perhaps they produced a smaller quantity. With the heightened perceptions experienced on LSD, weed and nitrous, it was worth the added outlay to rinse everything down in style. I was making a killing in business at this point anyway, so I could afford to. I was taking a sizable risk, so I felt I deserved to, but even after my overhead I was probably making 100 percent profit. With the bud I was getting though, the complaints were rare.

After a few months, I finally had enough money to afford my dream, the killer stereo. I had hooked up with an audiophile friend from the dorms who was able to get some awesome equipment. I bought a Nakamichi 700ZX tape deck and a 35 pound marble-based Kenwood turntable, (with the Infinity Black Widow tonearm) ran them into a 300 watt Apt Holman power amp and out through Infinity Reference 2 speakers, and transformed my room into a pure diamond of sound. People wondered how I could spend five grand on a stereo instead of buying a car, until they listened to it. Craig got some great board tapes from our birthday show, and we would just relive it right there on the carpet. Now when we returned from our evening's drug excursion, we could blast all night in my room. We'd crank up the tunes and sit around doing whippets, which was fun, but it got to be a lot of work, particularly for someone with as much control orientation as myself. Since I had such incredible skill with the bottle I felt it was my obligation to prep everyone's whippets. Of course, I had to roll joints, mix the tunes, and oversee the fun, which was getting to be a job. I enjoyed it, but I still wanted the next level of personal exploration.

AVS had its routine, school had its dullness, I pretty much lived to deal and party in my sound chamber. Bob had moved off campus, so I didn't see him too often, but Kip moved into the Zete house, Carl was around a lot, and if no one was home I just had to get high by myself. I fell into a routine of watching The Twilight Zone, which played from twelve to one, day and night. It was a marker in time. We'd sit on the couch in the living room obsessing on the details of Serling's morality plays, but only applying the ones we could appreciate to our own lives. We understood that "There will be consequences," but they were meant for some greedy pawnbroker, while "You've got to play kick the can!" was meant entirely for us. Getting high was what made us young again, it would keep us from ever getting dull and crotchety. Who knew that "To Serve Man"

was more than a cookbook, but a statement about blindly trusting what served your fantasies, or that despite is melodramatic goofiness, "22" was a clear example of the prophetic power of dreams. I think it takes more than a few years of school to begin to notice the deep metaphoric content of things, and much more to apply it to your life. So rather than wait for "Four O'clock," I just went about my career, "Something for you, sir?"

We had this amazing dog as our house mascot, Rho Phi. We called him Rhoph for short. He was a big black lab scam artist. I had never had a dog before, my father disallowed pets because of his allergies. Rhoph was a great beer drinking dog, who had been through a lot in his few years. His graying muzzle and the white crest on his chest gave him an air of distinction, while his huge weathered gray balls gave him the sexually mature bearing that you hoped you'd one day have. Sure you could rag on him for licking his cock in public, but he'd just look at you like, You poor jealous bastard, and go right back to it. My first year in the Zete house I usually just tortured Rhoph, in the prescribed manner. He had this way of sleeping flat on his back, with all his legs up in the air, twitching when he'd dream. Sometimes he'd be passed out in the middle of the hallway like that, so I'd get an ice cold beer and pour it right on those leathery balls. He would kip up in mid air, land on his feet already hauling ass, and be gone. It was cruel, but fun. The more I got to know Rhoph, however, the more I respected him. He went to more classes than any student ever did. He'd just wander into a building, follow people down the hall and head into a room that looked good. Then he'd search out someone he knew and sit by them. When it came to scamming he was a devil dog. You'd see him out at the food court begging lunch off sorority girls all the time, but what was even better was if they got up to pet him he'd just cram his snout up under their skirts. I'm not sure if he was getting dessert or just a sniff, but I saw him do it on several occasions.

Rhoph had been smoking pot for awhile before I showed up, so he liked my room. He'd just shoulder into the door and trundle in, expecting someone to blow dope smoke in his face. Sometimes we'd take a bong hit without carbing it, then hold the bong up to his snout and blow the rest of the hit in his face. It wasn't like we were forcing him or anything, he was one of us. Dane used to say that if Rhoph had opposable thumbs he'd do his own bong hits. If he had lip muscles, he'd smoke joints. Bereft as he was of such appurtenances, it was our duty as brothers to help him out. It used to annoy me somewhat though, that he would get high and then lay against my speakers. I was always telling him not to touch the speakers, because he was dampening the acoustics, but he loved that deep bass too, I guess. One night I was weighing out some shrooms and one fell on the floor, so Rhoph walked over, sniffed it, and proceeded to eat it. I told him, "Rhoph, that's gonna get you pretty high, but if you like it, you can eat whatever shrooms fall off my scale." We had an amazing trip that night, and Rhoph was right there leading the way. He was communicating with us, telepathically I guess, showing us things from a dog's eye view, running and jumping and saying, Isn't this cool? I gained incredible respect for him, and he always ate the shrooms I made sure to spill for him after that.

11

Craig called me one day to tell me that he had a motorhead friend with a nitrous tank for sale. I had no idea of this, but much like it mixes with oxygen to catalyze brain activity, nitrous is used in racecars for bursts of speed. Here was the ticket to top fuel brain dragging, so we bought it. The only problem was, we had to get the guys at the performance shop to fill it for us. Two guys who never had a day of auto shop trying to tell some fifty-year-old mechanics that they had a midget racer, yeauhuh. The guys in that industry must hear all kinds of stories. They filled it though, 20 pounds of nitrous ready for abuse. Trouble was, we were right back to the lame way. I got a bag of balloons, which fit okay over the nozzle, but this wasn't just a whippet screaming out. This was a pressurized cylinder of liquefied nitrous oxide. If you turned the nozzle too fast you'd pop your balloon and send freezing liquid spewing onto your friends. Or the neck of the balloon would just freeze to the nozzle and the rest would break off and fly away. This made for some entertainment as people chased it around the room inhaling its wake. Puncho balls seemed to work the best of anything, but with the added consideration of freezing your fingertips getting them on and off, the tank was kind of a bust. I was as determined as Tennessee Tuxedo to make it work, however, so I considered the professor and his three-dimensional drawing board. I had heard of people hooking up hoses to tanks, and quite obviously that's what dentists did, but there was always the issue of pressure. The hoses that were made for racing tanks were braided aluminum aircraft injector hoses, which were obviously no good since they allowed the nitrous to stay in a pressurized state. The valve on a racing tank isn't the same as the valve on a medical tank, so there wasn't a regulator to fit it. What we needed was a new kind of system; a hose that went to an unpressurized storage system, or a storage system that the hose was part of—something, like a big ass industrial balloon. So it was that I invented "The Bag." The bag was simply a heavy-duty garbage bag with a three-foot section of ¾" interior diameter clear plastic hose duct taped into it. These were structurally modified, through intensive duct taping, to withstand the rigors of hardcore nitrous fiending, and an era was born.

With the whippet you got your lungful, maybe more with a double, which was usually enough to give you some trajectory if you were on acid. But the bag gave you 30 gallons of sweet, cool, nitrous, with which to apply your own rate of inhalation until you heard the wa wa wha Wha

WHA WHA WHA—like a sonic boom that simply evicted from your body. That is the point at which the term "laughing gas," comes into play, because people do the most amazing things while they're out of control. First, of course, come convulsions, which is why a lot of people won't do nitrous. They see other people convulsing and worry that if they try some they'll become epileptic. (In truth, they're simply afraid they'll look bad.) Of course, it doesn't take much to get over that. As my junkie friend TB would tell me years later, "I fear nitrous more than any other drug. People will run from heroin cuz they know it's evil, but you can give a nun some nitrous and she'll turn into a raving fiend in 15 seconds." (I'm sure this is true, but I've always wanted to test it out anyway.)

People's convulsions tell a lot about them. Most people believe they're still doing nitrous. They'll be inhaling at some imaginary nozzle while their whole body shimmies around. A lot of guys will appear to be having sex with the bag, squeezing all the nitrous out and sucking on the hose, which goes limp after awhile because it's no longer frozen. This causes interesting autonomic nervous response, a sort of embarrassed look, implying that "my dick has melted!" Some people crash. They just fall down. Most people will fall down if they're standing, but some people will fall down even if they're lying down. This gets to be a bit of a predicament. Sharky came up for a bag once, knowing that he tended to twitch out and fall, but he had devised a system to protect himself. He would stay in the hallway leaning against the wall, sliding downward inch by inch until he was sitting on the floor. He did a whole bag like that, slowly, inch by inch, squatting down against the wall. He finished the bag just about the time he reached the floor, blacking out in perfect timing. This hydraulic motion must have created some stored energy though, for at that moment his legs sprung out from under him, sending his body three feet up in the air and stretched out flat as a board, then landing on the floor with a skull cracking thwack. There was just no escaping it. I didn't go into this to watch my friends injure themselves though, so I developed a new heroic diversion. I'd have my eye on everyone in the room, so that the minute they departed their body I'd fly out of my chair and gently lay them on the ground. It was a chore I could afford.

Some people appear to be able to avoid the spastic collapse of the body, only to perform amazing deeds. I learned to be very careful about this once when Wild Bill came over. He was an incredibly drunken fool that I knew from dorm dice games. After we named him Wild Bill he started to think of himself as Wild Bill HiCOCK, so we started calling him Wild Bill He's-a-cunt, or simply the Cunt. The Cunt arrived to buy some pot and saw that I had the tank out. He beseeched me for a bag, which I denied him, knowing the dangers of an out-of-body cunt. He begged and pleaded and offered enough money that I figured I could handle it, if he swore to leave immediately afterward, which he did. I wouldn't let him sit in a chair. I knew the kind of damage he was capable of. He had to start out on the floor. He paid me for a bag, then set about sucking it down in his spastically fiendish manner. When he had finished the bag he was down on his knees, sort of hunched over. He began to make this "rrrr" noise, like a child pretending to drive a car. Then he proceeded to push himself across the room, while keeping his face down on the carpet. When I realized how far he was going with this I jumped up, but it was too late. He wiped out my coffee table, spilling bong, beers and everything else on the floor, before he came to a halt against the far wall, still rrring. As he recovered I physically threw him into the hall, locking the door after him. I did notice, however, that he seemed to have lost part of the end of his nose. We determined from the blister and scab he developed the next day that he had given himself a friction burn. I'm not sure if the humor outweighed the grottiness of Wild Bill's cellular matter imbedded in my carpet, but it was good to know his idiocy did not go unpunished.

Of course laughing at these physical manifestations is the lower end of the scale of nitrous humor. The gyrations of the mind are far more entertaining. It's like comparing the Three Stooges with Monty Python. It seems that when you are in the peak of your nitrous experience, beyond the veil as it were, you are, shall we say, conversing with God. It may be symbolic, visual, sensory, auditory or any combination, but you quite often feel that you are being exposed to the core truth of existence. The Big Game is to relay that truth back to your friends in the mundane world before the curtain falls, thrusting you back into your body, out of the reach of the divine radiance. "CHIERFLAGWHUNUNASMUS-MAAAH!" The whippetee will scream, a moment before finally coming to, at which point he'll look around excitedly as if he actually made some coherent statement of cosmic relevance. This can be extremely funny. I was certain that on one particular occasion I was speaking backward in a foreign language. If only I could have translated some of it.

It also seemed that there was a cyclical role-playing going on. It was as if we were channeling some medieval court. As each person went in and out of the nitrousphere, they would be displaced by the next person-age in the court, who would say something revelatory about their character, to which the fool of the moment would reply brilliantly, cracking everyone up. Then it would rotate and start over. I always meant to tape our sessions so we could divine the cosmic thread from what people were saying, but it was too much of a hassle. We didn't have the tank all the time, either. It would have been a bit much to pretend we were racing that often, but we tripped almost every weekend. You don't necessarily need nitrous to be thoroughly entertained however; there's something universal about simply being on drugs with a group of people. An idea will flash across the general consciousness, in reaction to something that happened, which everyone will relate to. I always seemed to be able to grab that idea first, but Carl amazed me. The second that you were opening your mouth to say whatever it was, he was speaking the exact same thing. I took to calling him "Quick Carl," from the old Marathon candy bar ads, because he did everything so quickly.

12

Carl and Kip's Hell Week was much less punishing than mine, perhaps because I was doing the punishing. It is a real eye opener to see just how far you'll push your friends through the same crap you considered doing away with a year before. Devising torments appealed to my devilish streak, which was coming out more and more at that time. I was high score at Marshmallow Duckpins, and I threw hard. I dealt out a good number of bong hits, but after getting scut Sewer to beg for "a hit of the green, Sir," I whipped a fistful of old salad in his face and cried laughing. I developed the practice of making a scut stand on the basketball court and drink a beer that I poured from up on the veranda. Carl was so amazing that he actually got most of it down before I steered it up his nose. Oh I was evil. Who more insanely fucked up than I for the brick toss? We didn't do anything too bad, nothing that really risked physical injury. The university was cracking down anyway. They were all irate about the Beta pledge hazing scandal, where my friend Marcus was left, passed-out drunk in his underwear, in the prestigious Rolling Hills community. He was discovered there by a housewife who was jogging by at dawn. She called the cops. This focused a lot of attention on fraternity hazing. It wasn't as if these exercises hadn't been going on all along, guys were often left cuffed to a toilet in LAX in their underwear; they just never got caught. The Betas should have realized that they were dealing with Marcus, "The Sproul Leaper," Cannetti, who had fallen five floors while drunkenly peeing out of his dorm room window during his freshman year. He had gotten busted before that for swiping a car out of the dorm parking lot and running over an old lady. The guy was hella fun, but not the kind of person you risked getting caught with.

Around the end of Hell Week Cindy Thrillwell had a Christmas party. She had moved off campus with another girl from our dorm floor. I told her I'd be there, since I hadn't seen much of her or the dorm crowd that semester. She had been going out with some guy she met in one of her classes. I met him once, he seemed pretty good for her, a normal guy. The party was on a Friday night, so I had to deal a bunch, hang around, do whatever I did until 11, when my parties got started. When I got there Cindy answered the door, saw me, and ran crying into her room. There was no one there. They had all left, her roommate Elaine explained, although Cindy had told them I would be there and several of them wanted to see me. Cindy had also very much wanted me to be there, Elaine said, so I had better go talk to her. I sat down on the bed next to her and tried to explain.

"Hey, I'm sorry, I just got caught up doin stuff, I didn't mean to be this late. I thought it would still be going. I brought you a present and everything. What's the matter?" She kept her face buried in her pillow, sobbing while she spoke.

"You know I've always really liked you Sheldon. I really wanted to go out with you but I couldn't bring myself to ask. That's why I went out with Steve, but we broke up months ago. I never had sex before I was with him, but the first time we did it all I could think about was you." (**Hello!** Ready for the brick through the windshield of your consciousness?) "The reason I had this party was so you'd come over, so I could give myself to you for Christmas." I was totally unprepared for this admission. Sure I had been cooking up every deluded fantasy I could about getting laid, to no effect, but here was someone who was actually in love with me, wanting to give it up. That's what made it tough. I really cared about her, but I couldn't quite see her as girlfriend material. She was just too nice, edgeless, what would I tell my friends? They'd be in shock. I was way too freaky. But there she was, soft, crying, looking at me like I had the power to make her world. So I did. I vaguely remember candles and Love's Baby Soft. I had to return Wyck's car though, so I crept out at four o'clock, promising I'd call her soon.

Being Christmas time, I had to take off after that. Christmas in LA is not a pretty sight. I wasn't headed home, I didn't have much interest in seeing my parents. I was going to my home away from home, The Oakland Auditorium, where the Dead would play their five-night stand again. I had been pretty excited to take my bong to the show the year before, but now I had a serious plan, I would sneak in the tank. The shows were pretty good, but New Year's was always the heavily anticipated event. Was everyone excited about seeing Bill Graham dressed as Father Time, flying across the building on some bizarre contraption, or was it the free breakfast he served up on the steps afterward? That had degraded somewhat since my first show, when they were serving up fried eggs and biscuits and juice. Perhaps the "this is your brain on drugs," inference wasn't what people wanted to see when they came out of show frying. It eventually came down to a box full of stale bagels and green oranges, but that was the eighties. Social services were taking a beating in every sector. Perhaps people really dug New Year's because they had made it through another year without getting busted. Okay, okay, I'm just jaded now, it really was the biggest, most fun show you've ever been to. The

Neville Brothers opened that year and the boys played four sets. 10,000 tie-dyed freaks with noisemakers and glitter also made for a reasonable backdrop to the huge sounds.

We had a bunch of seat upstairs, which seemed safer than being on the floor. It appeared that like those chambers in Dune that give birth to stars, the whole room was a swirling cavity of cosmos that you could accidentally fall into. The physical restriction of the seats was helpful. There wasn't much room to fill the bags though, which made things extremely funny. Right in front of me was this old bald dude with his wife and two teenage kids, who had encouraged him to come to the show. Every time I filled a bag, its freezing, steaming surface would swell up against this guy's chrome dome until it looked like his head was smoking, but he never turned around or said anything. Finally Manny, being a goodwill ambassador of highness, tried to converse with him.

"Hello sir, hope we're not bothering you."

"Oh no, I just came here with my kids."

"In case you're wondering, this is laughing gas, wanna try some?"

"No, that's okay, you have a good time though." We went ahead with his advice. When it got around midnight I filled all the bags and we carried them down the winding ramps to the floor. When they started the countdown we started gassing out whoever we came into contact with, as well as ourselves, which made the spectacle of Bill's explosive entry with it's tonnage of glitter confetti all the more spectacular. We ran the tank out before their "Dark Star" encore, but you could hardly complain about being semi-coherent for that long awaited gem. I felt I had arrived, as a Deadhead as well as in the sense of establishing my mastery of partiness. Now that I had the tank, I wasn't really Dave's kid brother any more. I was my own entity, Sheldon.

13

My next quarter of school showed some promise, although Soc 1 looked like it would be pretty boring. Why can't they teach Socialism as an introductory requirement instead of sociology? The first day the teacher asked how many students knew that the average opiate addict of the late 1800's was a middle class housewife. I was the only person to raise my hand. I took a basic Music class, which was mostly beating out 4/4 rhythms on a wood block and playing pentatonic scales on piano, but I did manage to get into the History of Rock &Roll class, which was always packed. It was taught by Dr. Robert Louis Stevenson, a direct descendant of the author, who I am distantly related to as well. I had met the Doc in the dorms, where he was faculty in residence. Story was that his family had died in a house fire, which left him a little unstable. He was always cool to me though.

Gleason moved in with his girlfriend, so Ivan had to find a new place. Wyck had moved down to the room behind the kitchen, so I got Ivan to move across the hall into room 33. It was pretty cool to have Ivan there, along with all my buddies, but I began to recognize just how much he did drink. We all drank, and liked to get completely fucked up, but we had occasional nights of sobriety, for whatever reason. Ivan, however, was always moving on to the next 12. I think the development of the 12-pack may have caused some upward spiraling in America's alcoholism. It used to be you just got a sixer, or a case if you were seriously invested, but everything was organized into units of six. With the advent of the 12-pack you could go all the way to twelve without stopping, and that's a pretty good load. If you stopped around ten you knew that you needed another 12 to start up again, so you got another 12. I was concerned about Ivan's consumption, but it didn't really worry me. I figured he'd get over it or through it, depending on the circumstance. It only started to amaze me when Ivan's boss would call me, at 9:30 or 10:00 in the morning, since Ivan didn't have a phone, and ask me if he was there. This guy would beg me to wake Ivan up and send him to work. Apparently, Ivan was so fuck-ing good at what he did that they couldn't fire him. They threatened, they told me to threaten him, but they couldn't do it. A lot of his job was telling major LA contractors that they had fucked up and making them do their jobs over. To be done with any tact at all required serious drinking bouts, and Ivan was a professional. The night I finally realized that he was out of control I came home to find him in his room, where he seized upon the idea of explaining some complicated subject to me. I don't remember what it was, or how complicated it actually may have been, but he went on and on and round and round, babbling incoherently until I finally had to stop him and say, "Ivan, I took two hits of acid tonight, and you're more fucked up than I am!" That cooled him out a bit, but not me.

I had stumbled on to the fact that the Fox Venice was having a double feature of Pink Floyd movies, More and The Valley, neither of which I had seen. Craig, Kip, Dane and I went. Carl, who was getting political for some reason, was concerned about that night's big rush event and stayed at the house. The rest of us ate a fistful of green gels, crammed the tank along with a couple bags into a duffel, and waltzed it right through the front door of the theater. The Fox Venice was one of the last of the old Fox Theaters. A monument to the art deco architecture of Hollywood's heyday, it was now a fading rep house. It had a glassed in room in the back of the theater, a cry room, where the ushers watched the movie privately, only disturbing patrons when they required admonition. We took over a row about two thirds back. It was the afternoon matinee so it wasn't very crowded.

More is an interesting film. I believe it's adapted from the stories of Paul Bowles. Accompanied by a Floyd soundtrack, two young lovers travel to Morocco, discover hashish, take LSD, have affairs, and wind up heroin addicts. As the drug explorations of the movie progressed, so did ours. I was trying to keep a low profile, because the usher's room was about ten rows directly behind us. I slowly filled the bags, trying not to blast any louder than the movie, but it had some rather quiet sections. Oddly enough, no one ever seemed to notice. When the music was really cranked, I'd let it rip, filling the bags in the space between rows. I brought along my gas mask, which I swiped from the UCLA Med Center. It was just a facemask with a rubber seal that you could fit to a hose, but it did fit perfectly. When people got too whipped out and started breathing back into the bags it would pop off in their hand. It was extremely entertaining to see your buddy clutching the mask to his face and fiending on air while you inhaled the bag you had stolen from him. By the time More was over, we were pretty high. I was impressed that no one had complained. Most of the audience filed out to the lobby, so we tried to look cool, with these hosebags laying in our laps.

I had always had pretty amazing pot, but this was the beginning of the unbelievable Humboldt bud, the shit that not only reeked incredibly but tasted like apple pie in the sky. I rolled a joint of the Tutti-Frutti, an aptly named superweed that I had scored, lit it, and took the first hit. It was like smoking fruit flavored rock sugar! Oooohhhhhh! Fuck! That shit was good! You have to understand, this is the Fox Venice, the coolest rep house in LA. In a matinee of stoner movies, who's gonna give a fuck? I pass the joint down and look up to see a sort of geeky looking guy in a vest, an usher. "You can't smoke that in here." Oh fuck, we're busted. "You can't smoke that in here," he repeats in a somewhat adenoidal monotone. I look down at the gas mask in my lap, the empty bags in my friend's laps, the tank, I'm looking at Dane like what the fuck, is this invisible? "There's no smoking in the theater," he tells us, "You can smoke in the lobby though." Cooool! We were pretty high by now, but this was cool. He either didn't notice all our nitrous gear or didn't care, so we just cruised into the lobby, which was packed. Everyone had gone there to smoke cigarettes. I hate cigarette smoke, so we just stood in the corner by the theater door and rekindled this bomber. It didn't get around once before every person in the lobby was staring at us. This shit reeked so much that it cut through fifty people smoking Camels in fifteen seconds. My mouth was watering for another hit, but the fact that everyone in the theater was staring at us and wanting a hit too was a bit much, so we went back to our seats. We kept hitting on this log of pure pleasure though, until the usher showed up again with "You can't smoke that in here." AAAAAAAAAHHHH! All our nitrous shit is right there and he's hassling us over a joint! Of course, at that moment the joint had assumed greater importance to us as well. I was just flabbergasted. Unable to face the lobby again, however, I relinquished this gigantic roach, a third of the joint, to the usher. I bet he was thrilled.

Finally the second feature began, The Valley, Obscured by Clouds. Have you ever heard the album, Obscured by Clouds? Pretty fuckin cool, huh? Ever seen the movie? I didn't think so. There is a reason no one has seen the movie. It's tooooo fuckin hiiiigh! It's probably illegal in several states. It's basically the story of this ambassador's wife, who hangs out in New Guinea buying rare bird feathers to smuggle back home to her fashion friends in Paris. She runs into this hippie guy, who lures her with the promise of the rarest feathers if she'll accompany him to the Valley, which has never been mapped owing to its obscuration by clouds. In the hero's journey, the hero must endure amazing travails, which fortify his sense of self for the return home. In the highbrain's journey, one's ideas of self disintegrate, leaving the stark questions of existence, when one realizes that there is no return home. We had lost all compunction about being highbrained at the Fox Venice. The ushers were obviously going to ignore our insanity, so I let it rip. Loud. I was just blasting bags full whether there was loud music or not.

I thought this movie was getting pretty high in the scenes where she was talking French and being subtitled in English, while the Englishman she's talking to is being subtitled in French, until they both are being subtitled in Dutch, and start speaking Spanish, but by the time they got high with the aborigines, it was getting to be too much. I was wailing out nitrous and no one in the theater seemed to notice. I began to believe that they must have all been tripping too. Why not? This was certainly the movie for it. But how could we be getting away with this? We had our bags hanging over into the row in front of us while we reclined and huffed. The tank was screaming! I just couldn't fuckin believe what was going on. When our protagonists decided to make the final trek, into the Valley, I couldn't take it anymore. I had to leave. We stuffed the bags into the duffel, grabbed the tank and carried it out through the lobby, which amazed the snack bar people. The harsh winter light on Venice Blvd stunned our eyes, which had been acclimated to the jungle floor by then, but we had to go. Craig and Kip and Dane were feeling too high too, it was just one of those insane events. (I finally was able to track down a copy of The Valley on videotape a few years ago when I was living with Dane again. We wanted to see if it was really that insane. We smoked a J beforehand, and I swear to God, we agreed to shut it off during the same scene that made us leave the theater, it was just toooo hiiigh!)

We drove back to Westwood for some Tacos al Carbon. Driving across LA on acid was a piece of cake compared to watching that movie. We headed back to Zete, where there was a major rush party going on. The national president, Pete Jensen, was there, glad-handing and trying to indoctrinate us with fraternal propaganda. We had met the year before, when he noticed me as a bright guy with good potential. Fortunately I downed a beer or two before he spotted me.

"Sheldon, how are you?" he asked, giving me the Zete handshake.

"Pretty good Pete," just frying like hell.

"You know Sheldon, I've got to talk to you about this bong thing. You're a pretty smart guy, and I see you're popular here, but you can't be getting these rushees high all the time, it's not good."

"But Pete, we like getting high, so do they."

"Well that's okay, but you shouldn't be rushing guys with the bong."

"Well what do you suggest? I'm only painting a clear picture of how we have fun here."

"These guys are pretty young though, you should rush 'em with a beer."

"Pete, this is California. Weed isn't even a crime here. If a guy's 18 and wants to get high, we can get high together, no problem. But what you're telling me is that I should give these guys beers, even though the drinking age is 21, which makes it a crime. I don't mind giving guys beers, but I think it's more of a bust than smoking pot with them, which I prefer." He thought about that for awhile.

"Gee Sheldon, I was worried that you were heading in the wrong direction, but what you said makes a lot of sense. I'm glad we've got you here."

"So am I, Pete, so am I." I had to run upstairs after that. "Dane, I'm so high I just talked Jensen into thinking smoking dope was good for rush week! Woohoo!"

14

By this point I had become the Tank Master, and there was no more pretense of normalcy. After Vegas my cousin Duane had taken to calling me Whippet King, but Tank Master had a grander sense of aristocracy, which appealed to me. I got bag-filling down from a tremulously long period of cold flow to a momentary high-pressure burst. FfffwWhopp! "Your bag sir." I'd have a few bags rotating so that everyone was indulging, tweaking, recovering, and laughing at whoever else was tweaking. I'd have the Craig chop the dope, which I'd roll into joints or have Kip load bongs. I ran the tank and the room, but most importantly, I made sure everyone was safe. No one ever hit the floor while I was running things. I'd fly out of my chair the moment I perceived someone taking leave of their body, grab them, and lay them down. Eventually I also developed a certain cruel skill of snatching the bag from anyone who had departed, which often left their body grasping at the air, clutching for the bag which they no longer had any real need for. To run this entire operation, while dosing harder than anyone and huffing as much nitrous as I could, was the ultimate exercise in control. Although I always encouraged people to increase their doses, I oversaw everyone's substance intake, their access to altered states through the nitrous flow, and the music. I controlled everything, protected everyone from injury, and came to feel that they were my charges, while I tried to be their guru. (Hey, have another hit off that crackpipe dustmaster! On second thought, maybe that gas is plenty.) There were times when I would massage everyone's feet, obedient to my ideals of service. But as much as I wanted everyone to experience fantastic heights of consciousness and pleasure, I was losing my own freedom, or my ability to really seek that out in the company of my friends. There began to be separations between us.

I think it was Art who pointed out to me that I had something of a thralldom going. He had moved down to the LA Zen Center to get his shit together for a while. Art was a pretty astute student of human behavior, who I respected very much, so I had to take his counsel fairly seriously. Without any competition in the marketplace, or other directional leadership in getting high, people had to accede to whatever behaviors I set in place. This is not to say I didn't notice any of this myself, but the paranoid rankling of my mind was dismissible when I was in an ordinary state of consciousness. On the other hand, they weren't admissible when I wasn't. I began to notice that there was something of an uneven quality in the way certain people deferred to me. One night we ate a bunch of shrooms, which got me to some paranoid questioning of who my friends really were. Does anyone really go down to that core level with me, or do they just like me because I have all the drugs? They had all liked me before, but things were different now. I realized a good way to test this would be to judge their reactions to some odd behavior, so I decided to spit on everyone. Not in the face, not maliciously, but as if I were just completely spaced out. I was spitting up phlegm all the time anyway, so it just seemed like I had forgotten they were there. Ptuuh. Dane spit back on me, Jingles spit back on me, Carl looked at me funny, Rod whined, but most everyone just acted like nothing had happened, or they should just ignore my crazed behavior. Shit! Art was right! True, everyone assumed that I was higher than they were, because I was always dosing harder, so perhaps they didn't want to disturb whatever trip I was on. But the idea that they wouldn't just spit back on me had me a little worried.

I was developing a sincere delusion of grandeur, which people pretty willingly played into. I was probably able to mask it to some degree, with my lightning sense of humor, but there are always those places where your button gets hit, leaving you stalled in the brain fart of Can they really see me? panic. I was driving the bus, no question about that. Craig and Kip were my sergeants, assisting me in whatever needed doing to keep rolling. Rod, Terry, Mina, and our friends from the dorms, Chuck and Eileen, hung out together more on their own, and viewed our excursions as a fun social thing to do. Dane, Carl and Bam-Bam made up the "back of the bus." They'd actually sit out on the veranda and I would pass their bags through the window. They'd have their own running commentary about what going on inside, which was usually the funniest. I wished I could be out on the back of the bus with them, laughing about me in my delusion, but I had to drive. There was also the fact that I always had to dose harder than everyone else. Not that too many people were pushing the limits, but I always needed to. For me, taking drugs still had some search for ultimate truth. Yes, it was a scarifyingly crazy fun way to go, but I was compelled to push to new levels, thus the tunes, thus the tank, thus the Dead, thus whatever the next level was. Eventually I realized that my egomaniacal search for heights was all mine, and that most everyone else just wanted to have fun, which sort of bugged me. Perhaps I hadn't set a great example of what fun it was to be tooo fuckin high all the time. But I didn't really want to do it all alone.

Sometimes, in the dawn when everyone had gone home, I'd walk down to this pastry shop in Westwood that had these radical cherry Danishes. I'd take them back to my room and huff down a couple bags between bites of this sweet fruit pastry, until that wa wha Wha Wha WHA rush of nitrous transport would hit, turning me into a giant cherry Danish. It sure beat the hell out of being an Oscar Mayer wiener. I had originally developed this whippet-food transference idea with Wyck, who was from Texas. We'd eat jalapenos straight out of the jar while doing whippets, until our whole consciousness was just one big flaming ass hot pepper. Whew! That would make you sweat. But the cherry Danish was so sweet, it made you feel loved. Locked in my room in the early morning hours of LSD comedown, perhaps I could admit to needing this. I couldn't admit it to Cindy though, or admit to my friends that I was sneaking over to her house for occasional sex. I was keeping her separate from the whole scene, unable to be my two selves at one time, like Lazarus, from the old Star Trek, afraid of the collision of matter and antimatter worlds. She wanted me to smoke pot with her, since she hadn't yet and trusted me to guide her. In some respect it relates to the whole idea of losing one's virginity, that first drug experience. While I relished the idea of de-virginizing most people, Cindy's cherry somehow reminded of the Dave episode.

15

The phone. There's a way that the phone overtakes your consciousness when you're a dealer. In the days before the answering machine, the pager, or the cel, you had to answer the phone. You had to be in your room, waiting for it. The phone was money. Every missed call could be a hundred dollars, and you'd never know you missed it. Trying to be a flagrant young punk but having to sit by your phone like some love struck teenage girl gets to be a problem though, so I implemented a serious business strategy. I had earned the respect of my clients, and I recognized the value of my time, so I swiped an Office Hours card from some professor and tacked it on my door. Now I had a set schedule to deal, answer the phone, or feel free to be too high to deal at all. "Sorry man, it's after office hours, I'm tooo wasted." The "Sheldonian Theory of Democracy: No cash, No vote," was fully in effect. Arriving at the appointed hour, with cash in hand, assured friendly service. No checks, no fronts, no wasting my time. I'd get occasional complaints, like Chunk's, "Theory is burnt!" but these were largely ignorable.

After the quarter had been going a few weeks I got my final study list in the mail. This is the computer's final tally of your adding and dropping classes, your official class list with 72 hours to make any changes. I was enthused as I opened it, since I had the cool class schedule already verified, but after tearing along the perforated strip I removed the carbon printed page which read; Library Science — 8 units. I just about had a heart attack. What the fuck is this! To get classes in the first place you had to wait in line for six hours before jockeying with a computer terminal operator for another two hours of yes, no, maybe so, to see what kind of schedule you might get. Then you went to classes trying to get permission to add or whatever. It was a serious nightmare. Now I'd been dropped from all my classes, which had been substituted with fucking Library Science! What the fuck is Library Science anyway? Twelve hours a week of shelving books? The real kicker was that with only eight units I'd be below my required academic load, meaning I'd have to return my aid money. Fuck Fuck Fuck! Fortunately, I had my bong handy, which allow me to focus on a resolution.

I still had three days in which to add back all the classes I was already in, so I went to my torturously boring Sociology class and explained my problem to my professor, who understandingly signed my add form, as did my Music professor. I turned them in, thinking I'd get Doc Stephenson after class the next day. I was pretty excited about that class. It was project based, everyone had to make presentations on their favorite band after about a month of lecture and listening to roots music. I was going to do my project on Pink Floyd. At the end of the class a crowd of students descended on the Doc, as usual, to question him or try to get their own admission. I was standing toward the back of the crowd, patiently awaiting my turn when Rho Phi wandered in and sat down. Before I got my chance to talk to him, Doc Stephenson saw Rhoph and yelled,

"Who's dog is that?"

"Well he's not exactly my dog," I responded, "but he lives with me."

"Get him out of here!" he screamed.

"Okay, okay, but the computer dropped me so I need you to sign me back into class." Doc had just been staring at Rho Phi, fuming, and when he turned to me his face was a contorted mask of anger and distance.

"I will not!" he exclaimed, as if retaliating for being disgraced.

"But Doc, you've got to, it's not my fault."

"No! No, get out of here!" I didn't know what to think, he had completely tweaked. He turned away and wouldn't speak to me, so I took Rho Phi and left. I waited outside for him but he wouldn't even look at me. I figured that he must have had a dog before his house burned down, so that seeing Rhoph there just kicked it all up for him. I didn't know what to do, the computer had fucked me, the Doc freaked out on me, there was just no saving my ass. I only had eight units, so I expected the financial people to be demanding my money back. I still had it all, but without it I couldn't buy drugs, make money, or afford to live. The idea of being rat-fucked in such a way was truly disconcerting. I decided the best thing to do would be to stop attending classes altogether and eat LSD every other day. (One needs a day to recover between doses you know.)

Without any classes to attend I was in need of some diversion. At the suggestion of Rod and Carson, I decided to take up the bass. I had been noodling around the blues with them for awhile, but my fingers weren't really fine enough for guitar, and they needed someone to hold down the bottom end. Like your average stoned teenager, I got ripped off at Guitar Center, but I got what I wanted, a Fender Precision Bass. It was actually the aesthetic remembrance of watching David Gilmour play his Strat in the Pink Floyd movie, where the screen gets sliced into 64 little images of its smoothly curved royal blue body pressed up against his chest, that made me have to have it. The tone was okay though, and it gave me something to teach myself to play with, although my approach was rather half-assed. I'd dose and position myself in between my borrowed amp and my stereo speakers, blasting Pink Floyd's "Echoes" repeatedly while trying to play along. There was something comforting in being massaged by the fat, round tones, dreaming my rock star dreams, but it had little to do with how much discipline and daily practice it would take to actually play like Roger Waters.

The Dead announced shows for March of '82 at UCLA's Pauley Pavilion, my backyard. Cindy, who I was still surreptitiously seeing, wanted me to take her, but I just couldn't. She was waiting for me to bring her over to eat some acid, but I just kept seeing this nice suburban girl, perhaps wanting the same things I had wanted so long ago, but really unaware of whom she was dealing with. After the shows in San Diego I was getting pretty clear about the fact that I was fucked up. I wasn't saying anything to anyone, but the tank was talking to me, the band was talking to me, and I was having weird paranoid fantasies when I was dosed. I think it grew out of my trip with the tank, and controlling everything in that environment, but eventually it seemed that I must be some sort of royal personage, in whatever scene I was involved in. Perhaps it was the whole world, it seemed like everyone else knew something I didn't when I was tripping. They were all waiting for me to lead the way, like I was the Messiah, but it always had a black underside to it, since the fantasies I really wanted to fulfill were too scary for me to approach.

It's not that they were so out of the ordinary, just expecting to be tripping and having orgies, without having to expose myself emotionally or deal with what it would mean in relationship to my men friends, with whom I was always trying to define my place in the social order. But everything becomes suspect under the LSD microscope, and I kept my fantasies just under the surface, where I waited for everyone to telepathically concur, to give me the sign that I should act on them. If everyone knows what's going on around here, then I must be somebody really special, and they're all just waiting for me to do whatever I want. To really be having fun, I need to be tripping and having sex at the show. If I would just go for it, anybody would do it with me too. I began to see myself in that old Marvel comic, Son of Satan, where the son of Satan has all the powers of Satan but really wants to do good. It was a ridiculous good/evil behavioral dichotomy played out within the Jesus/Satan paradigm, which, despite my Satanic façade, I had really never had any belief in or understanding of. (Whether 'tis nobler in the mind to suffer the slings and arrows of outrageous dementia, or to act upon it and deal with the spears and clubs.)

About this time I started to have some strange body reactions when we'd trip too. I began to feel like I was no longer in an enclosed body space, but that I could feel everyone in the room. I'd drink incredible numbers of beers, but I couldn't tell if I had to piss. When I would go piss, I'd be paranoid that something would happen with the tank while I was out of my control position, or that my friends would be talking about me. This spinout would consume my mind to the point that I would be unable to remember how to pee. I'd just stand there, in the mephitic, bare-bulbed Zete bathroom, in front of the piss stained porcelain maw of the urinal, with my dick in my hand, trippin. When I'd finally make it back, pretending to be relieved, it seemed as if I were still aware of everyone else's bodies, and I felt like I needed to go pee for them too. I began to wonder (in my more lucid moments) if all that piss wasn't being magically recycled back into cold beers. Basically, I was getting weird, and not in a "weird is good," way. With all this shit going on, I just couldn't imagine dragging a neophyte chick from the valley into the fray.

I was pretty keyed up when the Dead finally came. I invited Stymie, Manny and Art to come down and stay over. Dave was elsewhere, but I felt like I could finally bring the guys around in whose honor I had conceived and built my empire, to visit it first hand. It was extremely important to me to impress them, despite their serious stance of "whatever." It was a strange meeting though, North and South, elder and younger, recreational fun seekers and a chasing after God knows what zealot. I had gotten to the point of taking the show as some divinatory form. Yes, they were talking to me, and the set list and quality of the show determined what they were saying. If I was having a really good time, they rocked. If I was tweaking, they were weird, or lame. They opened up the Pauley show with Shakedown again, meaning I had to get laid, but I was there with all my dude friends. As much as I wanted to explore the company of women, it had always been more important to me to party with the dudes. Maybe it was just safer for me, but this was my home turf, I had to party these guys out. None of them had girlfriends, a fact which they never seemed to consider. Maybe drugging was really an alternative to sex, despite the two being lumped together all the time with rock & roll. Maybe they had just gotten used to being spudly.

Between my American socialization and living in LA, I had some bent views of women to contend with anyway. Sure the Dead had a love groovy scene going on, so maybe I was looking for a hippie girl with flowers in her hair, but I was still thinking in terms of what I wanted a girl for. What I wanted to do to her. How hot and nasty she'd be. How close she'd come to the socially defined parameters of beauty. I certainly didn't want any sorority girls, which was fine with them, I'm sure, but beautiful with a wild mind I could handle. I was looking for someone to reflect how cool I thought I was, someone who liked to get high, someone—with a pussy. Whether she would, or could, be my equal, or foil, I wasn't sure was possible. Girls' minds always seemed to run a little counter to my own, so I focused on the sexual common ground that I hoped existed. It was almost as if knowing her as a person would ruin it, by humanizing her. The idea of we, or doing things with, was secondary to pounding sex and partying. I was running the scene, so why shouldn't I expect a chick to fall right in line?

That said, I was experiencing some mixed feelings. I had finally gotten laid, after a prolonged dry spell, by a girl who was totally in love with me, whom I liked, but who didn't quite fit into my scheme of expectations. The idea of being nice to someone or someone being nice to me hadn't really ever crossed my mind, I was far more concerned with fucking. Maybe I was too "LA" at the time to really be a Deadhead myself. It didn't really seem to matter, they had plenty of dude oriented songs, but my attitude was pretty much fuck this, fuck that, sort of a hippie Johnny Rotten. Just fuck it. Still, I kept wondering if a girl was out there for me. Tweeaakkk! The show became somewhat lackluster, as I analyzed everything, but Stymie and I managed to keep each other entertained. I did meet this girl I knew though. Sarah had formerly gone out with a guy I dealt to. I invited her to my house to party after the show. There was always the tank to look forward to.

We got back to the house and began raging. I had invited most everyone I knew, so every time I returned from whipping out I was looking at a different group of people, which was slightly more disorienting than usual. My Berkeley friends remained, however. Sarah arrived at some point in the festivities and joined the circle. She was really short, like 4' 11" or something, but pretty cute. Not that I was paying a whole lot of attention. I was thoroughly focused on getting obliterated with my pals. But it seemed that every time I returned from whipping out, someone would excuse himself and disappear. Sarah stayed, however, staring at me with her dark brown eyes. I began to wonder what sort of things I was saying under my nitrous spell. Was I telling my friends to leave so I could have sex with this girl? I really felt that I was more interested in the nether realms of nitrous than her nether regions, and besides, it would be bad hosting. (The Greek tradition and all) I began to suspect that she was telling them to leave while I was oblivious. Maybe that's what happens when you're oblivious. Despite my feeble protesting they all decided to go down the hall to Dane's room, where perhaps things were a little clearer. I made sure that they took the tank with them, as a final sign of my commitment to their highness, when I closed the door.

Sarah asked me to turn out the light. I didn't know what was going on. Perhaps if nitrous and acid existed thousands of years ago we'd never have reproduced.

"What do you want to do?" I asked.

"I want you to fuck me," she whispered. Confused as I was, I understood this. But I didn't understand the reasoning behind it, we hardly knew each other. Sure, that's how it worked in my mental exercise of meeting some hot babe and having sex with her, but it felt strange coming in this direction, particularly on acid. As vain as I was, the idea that I was attractive to someone else was too vulnerable an issue, so I wrapped it in my delusion. She must know who I secretly am! She's been sent for me. I guess this is it. With the music pounding, on the floor between the speakers, I slipped in and out of her tiny body until we had come and come down enough to carry her up to my loft and drift away. But my mind still wandered down the hall, wondering what I was missing with my friends.

16

I knew I had to deal with Cindy soon after that. I just couldn't risk her sanity. I was resolved that she no longer be involved with me, but I was worried that she'd want to come and trip even if I told her I couldn't be in a relationship with her. Fortunately, I had an idea that would quell that too. I invited her over one afternoon that week, when I knew no one would be around. When she showed up, her usual cheerful self, I told her, "Cindy, I want you to suck my dick." She smiled, in a nervously embarrassed way, then got down in front of me as I undid my jeans. She worked it as best she could, sucking my head and stroking the shaft until I squirted out a load that she valiantly tried to swallow. She looked up at me, with my come dripping on her lips, like a child looking for approval after a difficult task. That's when I told her, "Cindy, I've got a new girlfriend and I can't see you anymore. She's coming over right now, so you have to leave." The look on her face, like she had been hit by a train, barely disguised the feeling that she was going to vomit my spew all over me. She turned and fumbled with the door, hoping to hide the tears streaming down her face before she ran down the hall, but I could see them there. I could feel them too. But I was one cold, hard-ass motherfucker, if that's what I thought it took to do the right thing.

Sarah was actually pretty nice, although I still couldn't figure out what attracted her to me. She certainly liked to have sex. The first time I went over to her apartment I took a can of whipped cream with me. In an out of character move I painted her with it, rather than inhaling the gas, then licked it all off her. We had sex endlessly, but we didn't challenge each other too much with questions of why. I think she could tell that I was still somewhat introverted about it all. She really wanted to get me camping, so we could do it outside, which I understand now. At the time I preferred the security of my own space. I felt in enough control to allow for most anything. We were having sex on the floor in the dark one night when she heard a noise.

"What's that?" she asked, a little frightened.

"Oh that's just Rhoph, scratching."

"He's in here?" I turned on a lamp to see Rhoph lying there, watching us. She hadn't realized she was having sex in front of a dog.

"It's okay, he likes you."

Sarah started coming along on our excursions, which made me feel somewhat anxious. Since everything was a reflection on me, I was very concerned with how she appeared to the group. She had the interesting habit of vomiting after taking drugs, whether it was mushrooms, acid, or MDA. (I had worked that into the lineup now too) When she'd start coming on, she'd puke. She didn't seem to have any problem with it, "It's very cathartic," she told me. I was always worried about Hendrixing, so it kinda bugged me. She did weigh less than a hundred pounds though, so it was probably good for her to get things out of her system.

Without attending any classes I had plenty of free time for Dead tourism. I decided that we should go to Reno, Craig, Sarah and I. It was a pretty long drive, which is one of the ways you determine your ability to travel with people. It's hard to be specific at this point, but there was some sense of need that Sarah projected, perhaps it was just that she wasn't a guy. We found ourselves a hotel, got cleaned up, ate our doses, and cruised over to the show. Craig decided to try to tape the show on his walkman, which the security guys found on his hip.

"What's this? they asked.

"Uuhhh, that's my colostomy bag, sir," he replied. They visibly blanched before politely ushering him into the show. Centennial Hall was like a big fucking dumpster. The sound bounced off the back wall and worked its way around like yelling down a well. This was my first appearance at a show with a girlfriend, and it made me wonder, Will I be having sex with her? I never liked to feel bound to anyone at the show, so I left her during the break to wander the echodrome. Somewhere in the midst of a joint I ran into this biker chick who wanted a hit. She was stunning, in a biker chick way, leather pants, halter top, cowboy boots, incredibly cute. She looked ready for a pounding right there on the floor. We danced around a little but I had to keep moving. They opened the second set with "Feels Like a Stranger," which is the classic Crazy shit!-Do I belong here? tune. It does portend that something Strange will be happening, but the one line that stuck with me was "If this is love then how would I know."

My doses had kicked in fully, so when I found Sarah in the crowd my head was just spinning with the "should I or shouldn't I" question. The music would swell up enough that it seemed that no one would notice us having sex, but if I looked around it would slow down so I could see that everybody was watching me. It was much easier having sex in front of my dog than hundreds of freaks. By the time "Estimated Prophet" rolled along I was tweakin again. I had everything there in front of me to complete my fantasy, but was it right? In the greater Dead love groovy sense

I had killed a girl who was in love with me to be here with a girl I wasn't sure I even knew. If I had sex with her right there, would that mean I was bound for life, in some secret satanic pact? Tweeeak!

As the blackness took over I felt as if I was walking a tight rope through space, afraid of the fate on either side, only to navigate the insane lane down the center of being too high. Bobby began to talk to me. "No, no, don't worry 'bout me no no! Cuz I know where to go." Whoa! I knew I was lost. Scared! Any step could be the wrong one, so I just tried to stand my ground. "Gonna fly away! Ha! Hey!" Bobby continued, making me almost pray that I could do just that. Closing my eyes made it hard to stand up, but opening them let me see that all eyes were on me. I felt like I'd either collapse or explode. They toyed with playing "He's Gone," which really had me worried, but finally Jerry began the riffs that carried us back to "Eyes of the World." The return from madness to beauty was enough to make me cry, but the happier I became, the more certain I was that I should just go for it. Everyone around was all smiles, as if it was safe. As much as I wanted to, as much as I felt the Dead, whatever they were, wanted me to, I just couldn't. It wasn't like I had ever had a shred of "moral decency" in my entire life, I was just paralyzed.

I was far off into my head when they began jamming, but Phil laid it down so hard at the end that my body shook, and I heard popping sounds like balloons breaking all around me. It felt like I had done a big whippet, but even more like I had an orgasm. I thought that the popping sound had come from inside my head, and that everyone could hear it, which would explain why they were all staring at me. I was sure I had come in my pants too, but I didn't exactly want to check.

"Having fun?" Sarah yelled at me over the band.

"Oh yeah," I mustered. I still couldn't get over the idea that I should be having sex with her there, like it was some initiatory rite that every-one would feed off of. I had to wander again, it was too much contradic-tion to stay by her, but everybody in the place seemed to be watching me. Toward the end of the show I ran into the biker chick again, who now seemed even more insistent that I should dance with her. It was hard to avoid her seductiveness, which she seemed to want to take to its natural conclusion, but as my mouth watered this gnarly biker dude walked up. He was covered in tattoos, chains, leather, malice. Stepping right up to my face he growled,

"You talkin to my girlfriend?" He motioned to the buck knife he had managed to slide right past security, "You mess with my girlfriend I'll fuckin kill you."

"No, no. I was just heading into the show this way." Which I did, immediately.

Here were the twisted signals. Freaky chicks coming on to me so I can be murdered, the whole show seemingly indicating that I should be having sex with my incidental girlfriend, and me, unable to trust anything. Perhaps I was the innocent here, like the Wicker Man. I hadn't exactly chosen her, so how could she be mine? The show ended, finally, which was something of a relief, but I was still worried that the entertainment was me. When we tried to leave, they had closed the front doors and were ushering everyone back into the hall. I swear to God I got sent back in two or three times. I was high, yes, but I began to think that now I'd have to fuck Sarah in front of 10,000 heads who couldn't possibly be paying attention to the band. Even worse, I had to pee! With everyone watching me, in my mind at least, that would doubtlessly be impossible. Tweak! Tweak! Help Mr. Wizard, heeeelp!

The doors opened, I could feel the breeze coming in. I managed to escape, this time, Onggh Yaaangh. In the parking lot I saw biker chick again. Craig, who had been with me the first time I saw her noticed her too, but I told him "Don't even look over there man!" We went back to the hotel to settle down and I took a monster piss. I wanted to go out partying, but Sarah wasn't up for it. She did want to have sex though, perhaps she had the same thing going through her mind all night. I hadn't ever asked her, as usual, it had all been up to me. Craig went down to the casino while Sarah and I merged, but after finally fucking I had to leave her there alone. She didn't want to come along and it just felt too weird to be frying all night in the room with her. She and I got into some kind of argument on the way back, which made me think that travelling with a girl was not the greatest idea. Much simpler to see if you could meet someone at the show, providing they didn't get you killed.

17

Craig and I continued to have our diversions. One was dosing for gymnastic meets. Paula would be there, as would all the other gymnasts, in their sex suits, as I called the revealing unitards they wore. It was very entertaining watching them hurl their bodies around the unevens or the floor itself, while the trails of color from their sex suits burned into your brain. Paula was having some trouble in school though. Like most athletes she had tutors, but she was really there to compete, and gymnastics is pretty stressful. You're basically trying to work out hard enough to keep from growing. If you're really small you might still have a shot at the Olympics, but even that was a fading dream after Nadia came through and lowered the championship age to prepubescence. Gymnastics is really about prepubescence, which makes it hard on college girls, whose bodies are already cracking with hormones. This leads them into behaviors, things they think will help them hold on to their little girl's dream. I was shocked when Dianne told me that she had been suspended from competition for not eating. I had never heard of such a thing, how could you not eat?

"You know, you eat, but then you make yourself throw up," she told me.

"Oh my God, why would you do that?"

"I can't afford to gain any weight, I don't want to end up a fat old Greek woman like my aunts."

"What can I do?" I pleaded, powerless. "Is there anything I can do to help you?"

"I don't know. I have a counselor, but I don't know." I held her as she cried, this little girl whose body was fighting to break out of the oppressive dreams of her sport, but whose mind had carved out a twisted scheme to hold it in place.

I came home one day to find a letter from my mom on the front table. Despite being from my mom, it was pretty exciting, since I hadn't received any mail from anyone while at college. I went up to my room to savor reading it. First there were a few newspaper clippings, a couple of recipes that a college guy could probably whip out, and this incredible right wing propaganda about weed. I just had to laugh at their attempt to claim the usual brain damage, criminality, leads-to-hard-drugs bullshit. It was already the 1980's! Reading my mom's letter was even more tragicomic. "Son, your father and I are very hopeful that you've mended your ways and are making the most of your educational experience, but we do worry. I wanted to send you ten dollars for some food, but I'm afraid that you might spend it on drugs." Sheeit, Mom! I haven't spent ten dollars on drugs since eighth grade! I haven't spent less than 100 or 500 or 1,000 dollars on drugs in years! Ten dollars I could spend on food! I went to the campus store, bought ten dollars of crackers and cheese and salami, got some beers out of the machine and told everybody to come up for a joint and to read this letter. We had an incredible laugh at the expense of my poor deluded mother, who had no idea how much I was making of my educational experience.

It was around this time that Dane's mom died. I don't think any of us knew how to handle that. It wasn't the sort of thing that was supposed to happen at that age. No one was ready to open up the can of worms of how we might feel if we lost our own mom, (no matter how out of it she was) so we just sort of empathetically agreed with him in mute suffering. It's not part of the dynamic of what's communicable at that point, in that place. Without wanting to admit it, or delve into it, though, you still had to feel. Dane spent some time with his dad in New Mexico after that, returning with a strange gift for me. It was a little porcelain dish, about two inches square, with the New Mexico state emblem emblazoned on the cover. It was the sort of thing your aunt or grandma collected to keep who knows what in. I puzzled over it for a day or two. It was a gift that carried some real feeling with it, but had no real purpose. After smoking a joint, though, I realized it was the perfect size to put roaches in. I conferred upon it the title of New Mexican Refugee Holder, telling Dane that if he ever needed pot he could smoke whatever was in the dish. He had a driving job for the university, taking the Chancellor to the airport at 6 A.M. and such like. He'd come into my room very quietly before work to bong up a roach. If I woke up, he'd pack me one, holding the bong up to me in my loft so I could imitate Jefe by getting high and going back to sleep. In that situation it was the most acceptable way to acknowledge our caring for each other. It's kind of skewed, living in that all male environment, trying to outman each other, at an age where expressing yourself holds the potential for ridicule. I occasionally wondered what I was doing in a house full of men, with whom I shared extreme experiences, and loved. It just felt natural to be together in our boyish dereliction, but in the introspective uncertainty of acid, it sometimes worried me.

I worried too, that because I spent so much time with Craig, people thought we were queer for each other. Being queer was so derogatory, probably because we were all afraid of it, but I really wasn't looking for that, I just felt like Craig was a protégé/kid brother. Maybe he wanted to follow me because he thought I was cool. Maybe I really was cool. Most people seemed to think so. It was only my paranoid departures that made me doubt it. Craig and I dealt so much that we did everything together, ending up at this 24-hour place in Westwood pretty frequently. There were three girls working there that were pretty fun. Lauren, the hostess, was really nice, just looking for people to be nice to her. Jill, the bartender, was a little older, talked a blue streak, and served us free drinks even though we were under age. Natalie, the waitress, was beautiful. A perky blonde from Pennsylvania she had come to LA to find whatever people come to LA to find. She'd bring us our milkshakes in the steel cup, with the whipped cream can on the side, so we could suck down the nitrous. I had met several girls I wanted to fuck over the past year or two, but there was something about Natalie that you wanted to grab and hold on to. I was too lame to do it, but she was fun. Everything she did she made fun. It was a little hard on me, getting as jaded as I was, to watch someone have so much fun doing anything. I thought she liked being around me, but I was so caught up in my shit I played it safe by deciding that she wasn't on my intellectual level. Perhaps she wasn't, but I'd have partially lobotomized myself to even up the playing field. Everyone else liked her, so I invited her to join the crew and she and Lauren became fixtures around the house.

Bob came over to go out shrooming with us one night, but we were finding the garden to be too contrived. There is a clear difference between mushrooms and acid, as far as your desire to be in a natural setting. The sculpture garden, with its light-trees, reminded you that you were in a completely man made environment, a strange, oppressive artifice. Bob knew how to sneak into the Botanical Gardens, so we followed him over there. You could crawl into thick stands of bamboo or mingle under catalpas in the moonlight. There were no lights there either. Bob and I snuck away and hid in the bush for a long time, silently, while everyone else went about their trip. We were feeling pretty animal there, which I hoped everyone would be, so it annoyed me that they were just chatting away, even though they were almost out of earshot. We hid there even when they all started looking for us, yelling. I knew I felt better there, alone and quiet with Bob, than I would by going back, but I had my responsibility to think of. Just getting back on the cement path made me feel very disconnected. I had moved from a tiny strand of the living world back into the dead concrete megalith of LA. Eileen was berating me for hiding from them, which just added to my dissociated feeling. It was as if a rubber ball surrounded me, so that I couldn't feel anything, because it was all dead. I was living in a dead world, surrounded by people who really weren't going where I was going, and it was becoming claustrophobic. After that night, I decided that I'd only do mushrooms in the wilderness. The city's electric pulsation called for the twentith century chemical synthesis of LSD.

Chemically merging with that electric pulsation, I found myself at the video arcade every Friday, dosed in the darkness, while the sound effects created an auditory vista behind me. My consciousness was entirely focused on one thing, however, Centipedes. I never had much appreciation for video games. I played Pong when it first came out and find almost all video game formats to be just as boring. Centipedes was a different story. Every time you destroyed a level of invading bugs, the psychedelic colors got turned up a notch. Lying in a field of mushrooms, with spiders flying in and attacking as the centipede methodically winds its way toward you is full-scale high brain battle. The game was obviously designed by and for trippers. I was the first to break 100,000 points, after which the screen turns black with flaming purple bugs that simply scorch your brain pan. I proudly left a long string of high scores, with the initials LSD. It was always a good way to start the weekend.

Whatever your religious preference, LSD does create access to what can be valuable states of altered consciousness. I agreed to take Wyck to the airport in exchange for his car, which was a sweet deal, so I spliffed him out on the way. I was driving back down Sepulveda, totally high when I came to this long downhill stretch. I wasn't exactly paying attention, so the forced right at the bottom of the hill took me by surprise. I didn't want to get off Sepulveda into Inglewood so I cranked it into the Chevron station that still afforded me a few feet of driveway to duck into. Right then I heard screaming and a thud and I turned my head to see these two kids on a moped laying it down right into my passenger door; Wyck's passenger door. I was tweaking, I hadn't seen them at all. I threw it in park and ran around to help them up. The kid whose moped it was started calling me a motherfucker and trying to swing on me. His buddy yelled at him to cool out. They were both pretty scraped up, so I helped them get their bike up and off the street. I told them I didn't have any insurance, and that it wasn't my car, but I'd try to help them out. I didn't want to fuck them over, or get sued, or talk to the cops! We checked out the kid's bike when he calmed down. It was a little fucked up, but he figured it was fixable. I gave him a fifty, which was all I had, but I gave him my address too, in case it cost more. Then I slipped him the giant roach from the bomber I had just smoked, the supreme sedative, and I never heard from him again.

That night, however, I took some acid. It was a mellow evening, some Frisbee golf with Dane and Carl, no big deal. When I went to bed though,

I fell into this totally real dream state. I was driving down Sepulveda when I came to this long downhill stretch. I wasn't exactly paying attention, so the forced right at the bottom of the hill took me by surprise. I cranked it into the Chevron station that still afforded me a few feet of driveway to duck into. Right then I heard screaming and a thud and I turned my head to see Me! on a moped, laying it down right into my passenger door. Then I was on the moped, taking it hard into my door and going down on the pavement, and I woke up. Whoa fuck! That was hairy! I went back to sleep, and I was driving down Sepulveda. The forced right at the bottom of the hill took me by surprise, so I cranked it into the Chevron station that still afforded me a few feet of driveway to duck into. Right then I heard screaming and a thud and I turned my head to see Me! on a moped laying it down right into my passenger door. Then I was on the moped, taking it hard into my door and going down on the pavement, and I woke up. Fuck. Again. Fuck. Again. Fuck. I was looking right into my eyes as I carelessly took the right than ran me over. I could feel the thud on the door as I bounced back and laid it down. The pavement was chewing up my leg and then my arm as I slid. Fuuuuuuck! I replayed this sequence about ten times before I drifted off to sleep. You've never been to any traffic school that made you a more aware driver.

What some people wanted to do with their psychedelic experiences though, truly amazed me. Maybe skypiloting adventures aren't compulsory for everyone, but I was worried by some of my clients' search for the zenith of mundanity. I sold drugs fairly regularly to a guy from Phi Psi. He asked me if I could sell him a quarter-pound of mushrooms, which was the largest order I had received by far.

"No problem," I told him, "you gonna start dealing?"

"No we're gonna have a party."

"Cool," I replied, all in favor of large psychedelic parties.

"Yeah, the royal wedding is going to be on TV Saturday morning at 4 A.M., so we're gonna have a party and eat mushrooms at three."

"The Royal Wedding?" I asked, unaware that such a thing still existed.

"Yeah, Prince Charles and Lady Diana, it's gonna be cool." Now I can see the veracity in wanting to be drugged if you had to watch the royal wedding, but we're fucking Americans! Why the fuck would you? If then Quaaludes, certainly not mushrooms. At least take acid, which is a much better drug for staring at the TV. I let my personal prejudice get the better of me, gouging him for a reduced retail rather than wholesale rate. That's one of the great things about dealing, you can change the prices based on your appreciation, or depreciation of each of your clients.

18

As much as I realized that I wanted to blow off Sarah for Natalie, I was still trapped in my own vagueness, so I convinced Craig to ask her out. I don't think too much convincing was necessary. She was pretty cute, and the simple allowance that I wasn't going to make a move made her a good choice. Sarah lived over toward Santa Monica, and she was a chem major, so I didn't see her more than a couple nights a week, but Craig moved into the house so he and I and Natalie would party most every night. When the Dead announced shows at the Greek again we all decided to go. Kip wanted to come too. I don't know how we all fit in Craig's Prelude, but that's the glory of Dead tour. Dave & Rachel had moved down to a little place off College Ave in Elmwood. It was nice, but it didn't have a lot of room for crashers. I rented a room at a hotel in downtown Berkeley in which all five of us stayed.

The shows started out pretty intensely, for me that is. I was somewhat uncertain in my relationship state, and being with all my LA friends on the turf where I most wanted to be accepted, made me a little nervous. Jerry opened with "Bertha," the "I've got to get away from this woman," song. Both Bobby and Brent said "fuck" during a song. I'd never heard them use expletives to intensify things, so it came as a bit of a shock. I had my usual time twitching through the first night, but nothing that wasn't getting to be fairly ordinary. The next morning we were all laying around in the hotel, so I decided it would be good to surreptitiously have sex with Sarah while watching cartoons and talking with those guys. She was tiny enough that I could put her beside me and ease in and out of her while watching Yogi Bear and discussing the merits of the previous night's show. Eventually I wrapped her in the blankets and dragged her off the bed and into the shower, where I could pound her. I'm not sure if we were as surreptitious as I thought we were, but no one said anything. I only wished it could be that easy at the show.

Dave and I had decided to cook up some treats for Saturday night. We baked up a pan of brownies with a quarter-ounce of black Afghani hash, and having decided that the Greek was a "natural" setting, made a giant salad with about an ounce and a half of mushrooms. It probably would have been delicious if the mushrooms were fresh, but they weren't, so while everyone with us had a bunch of salad, they put most of the shrooms back in the bowl. This left it up to Dave and I to finish them. "If you don't eat your meat, you can't have any pudding!" I'd estimate that we ate a half-ounce of mushrooms each, just so we could give ourselves permission to have a brownie. "Cassidy," "Lazy Lightning," "Deal," the first set kicked in pretty good. So did the shrooms. I thought I was getting pretty high, until Dave took it upon himself to, uhh, try to have sex with everyone. Perhaps my tweak was a common theme, or simply common to my family, but Dave started trying to tongue the ears of just about everyone in a twenty-foot radius. Men or women, it didn't matter. (The Pansexual is loose! The Pansexual is loose!) If he could get some tongue in return, so much the better. Most people simply tried to act unaroused. Not that you'd be aroused by some tweaking freak such as Dave licking your ear, or maybe you would, but hopefully you'd try to discourage him without seeming too hostile.

This was starting to throw me for a loop. Here I was, a big freaky dope dealer, starting to think I was gonna have to kill myself if I didn't manage to have sex at the show, tweakingly repressed into a fucking pinnacle of virtue while my (theoretically more experienced) older brother is groping and tonguing 50 people he's never met. The worst part of it was that he did it to me too! Having sex with my brother at the show was not what I had in mind. Rachel couldn't take another scene like this so she just bailed. I was left in the embarrassing predicament of having my brother groping everyone while trying to maintain a respectably cool front to my friends, on half an ounce of shrooms. As darkness fell I began to feel very animal. The show deteriorated into some sick Bobby fest that seemed like catcalls against my puritan behavior. I couldn't go around licking everyone, I was too tweaked to even try to have sex with my girlfriend. I was beginning to lose my body boundaries again too, so everything became a swirling daze.

Dave took to laying on people while saying, "Love me." Hell, it was what I wanted, what we all wanted I'm sure, but perhaps not quite like that. As things got weirder I began to feel the division between myself, the Dead, the crowd, my friends, and my brother. I really couldn't handle being with him, it embarrassed me in front of my LA friends. I didn't feel like I could leave him there; once again it felt like it betrayed the most basic trust. I couldn't do what it appeared the Dead were telling me to do, what it seemed the whole crowd, the whole vibe of the evening was telling me, to rut there in the grass under the stars. The more animalistic I felt, the more it seemed that the crowd was too. With all the howling that goes on at a show, I began to realize that these people, these Deadheads, this cult to which I wanted initiation, was one of lycanthropy. I had certainly studied it enough as a kid, no wonder I was drawn to it. There's always some edge of insanity running in the families of werewolves. Now that I was becoming an adult, it was coming out. Everyone now seemed hairy, dogfaced, exposing their fangs in grins that acknowledged their understanding of my need to mate this dark haired Dead girl, or die. If I was gonna do that, I'd have to take a pee first. But my boundaries were so twisted I couldn't tell whose body I was in. Every eye was on me, all knew my purpose, even if I didn't, or only imagined it's grand design. But in the grottiness of the head, knowing that everyone was waiting for the outcome, I couldn't pee. Knowing that whoever was standing in the stall next to me, hearing nothing, was signaling the crowd that I was incapable of having fun, was killing me. If there had been a way to hang myself right there, I'd have done it, rather than face them all. But I had to sneak back and pretend I was ready. ("Ready for love," as Dim said.) I was far more prepared for a one size fits all white coat, but that would be escapist.

Dave had managed to lose his clothes again as he crawled about the lawn, so I had something to take my mind of my immediate trauma. Sarah was probably getting bored of all this when they played "Good Love," to which I was unable to respond in the manner I assumed I should. By the time the show came to a close, I felt as though my behavior had pissed off several thousand werewolves who were waiting to feed off the energy my sexual exhibition would create. My brother was completely incapacitated, but my friends wanted to go back to town. Every time I got Dave aware enough to sit up, he'd pull me down on him, crying, "Love me." Once again I felt that to leave him there would be a betrayal of the faith, but I really needed to go with my friends to preserve my image. The werewolves all around gave me a sense of impending doom were I to break the code of brotherhood, whether or not I'd already blown my ritual task. I was feeling pretty wimpy, but I knew that if I had to kill a bunch of people to get out, I would, which didn't make me a whole lot happier. Truth is, it scared the hell out of me. Eventually they started kicking everyone out. Craig really wanted to take off, but I couldn't leave Dave there. I felt that I was responsible, through my youthful pledge that I would never abandon him or Ivan, no matter what the cost personally. That cost was rising. When the Bill Graham guy came by with a little electronic sign that flashed, "The party's over," I knew we had to go. I tried to get Dave to go with me, but every time we took a step he'd collapse on me, looking for "love." Fortunately, Manny, who's a pretty big guy, and Willy Went, who's not, agreed to heft Dave out of there. This allowed me to escape, although I had to run the gauntlet of angry werewolves, which kept me ready at any moment to fight to the death.

Of course, nothing ever came of it, just another tweaked out Saturday night on too much drugs. The next day was the usual Sunday recovery, great set list, but sort of slow and slack. I think Dave stayed home again. I received the usual number of taunts and well wishing inquiries about him, but no one asked about me. They all knew what was up with me, it was just a secret. Dave was some sort of operative of the consciousness that I had been struggling so hard with. It wasn't that I was any less high than he was, I just couldn't expose it. I was still waiting to be recognized for my impenetrable exterior, or be able to take the go ahead to enact my twisted interior. The Dead knew it. Maybe I hadn't lived up to my potential, maybe I hadn't been able to step up to my dark messiahhood, but I still had to have another chance. Maybe things weren't quite right yet. There had to be more opportunities. Maybe with a different girl, in a different place, I'd be able to make it all happen. While I could imagine that I might be going crazy from all this shit, the idea that it was only happening in my head was beyond me. Nor could I accept the fact that this wasn't fun. What could be more fun than what I was doing?

19

Since mushrooms were now out of the question, I began relying more on MDA, the Love Drug. The first couple MDA trips were pretty fun, except for the fact that I would mix it in water, which made dosing seem like drinking a fish tank. MDA heightens your sensory awareness; taste, touch, hearing, all senses become amplified. And it gives you occasional total body rushes of shivering pleasure. It does in some sense make you feel like you could love everyone, so our sessions got very lay around massaging, but never turned into the orgies I hoped for. Perhaps if I weren't "in charge." There is nothing like smoking pot on MDA though, especially my pot. It's as if the warm sweetness is flushed through your lungs and out to every cell, and chasing it with a bag is pretty delightful too, although not brain catapulting as it is with LSD. We had an all night ultimate Frisbee game on top of the parking lot once, a brilliant suggestion from the back of the bus. The sensory ability and agility of the body under MDA made it truly impressive. The only problem was that, being a speed derivative, it dried your body out so much that the next day was cramp city. I ended up puking from that one.

One night Mina OD'd on it. She was pretty light, so the standard dose was probably a little much for her. She started shaking uncontrollably, sweating, having heart palpitations. It made me really worried. I called my connection up in Berkeley, Dr Space. He told me that alcohol should flush out some of the high, but that the speed would take awhile. So we spent most of the night taking turns holding her, playing mellow tunes so she could come down. After that episode she was unable to drink water. I felt bad about it for years, but she seemed to prefer Coca-Cola, and LA water was toxic anyway. Still, I was a little wary of taking MDA at the show. The idea that a drug could make me love people I didn't even know worried me. How would I know who to be suspicious of? I preferred the delusion that everyone was an agent of Satan, which made the stark terror of LSD much more homey.

I still had a few bouts with cocaine left though. One night Carl and I were sitting around when Wolfie showed up. He was dealing coke, but wasn't a serious business guy about it. He asked us if we wanted to have some, and laid out a few lines. We began having this marvelous conversation, listening to music, drinking beers, just hanging out. We were having such a great time that Wolfie kept laying out lines. I rolled up a couple doobies in the course of the evening, but whenever the talk would start to die down, Wolfie would lay out some more lines. Carl and I later agreed that we hadn't really talked about anything of any importance whatsoever, but we were there talking when the sun rose. Soon after that we dusted Wolfie's bindle, to which he replied with amazement, "That was an eighth!" He was cool about it, he didn't want to charge us, but it shocked me that we had each snorted up over a hundred bucks worth of coke. Fuck! Trying to get to sleep after that was murder. I can see why people would just keep snorting until they collapsed. Coming down off coke is like being an aluminum can that's getting crushed in super slo-mo. Craig was selling more blow by that time too, so we'd stay up and do lines with Natalie. He bought one of those melt point testers, the device that showed you what percentage of what cut was in your stomped on bag. We melted this reputedly great blow that gave a completely indecipherable temperature reading. We could not figure out what was in it! That was one thing helped to sour me on the whole coke craze. The other was basing.

I had done some base once with Droz, who was getting pretty heavily into it, but it seemed too twisted. Sure I controlled the tank, but I was trying to distribute as much as possible all the time. Basing was this weird "one for you, one for me" deal, when there were five people waiting, jonesing for hits. Craig and I decided to do up some quantity, so he and Natalie and I could smoke it all. Prepping it was exciting. Instead of just buying a vial on a corner somewhere in the ghetto, you had to actually throw your coke into a bunch of baking soda with the vain hope there would be something left when you were done. We didn't have a base pipe, so we constructed the "Baseface," which was the gas mask I had for nitrous attached to the glass from a hurricane lamp with a big coke screen in the other end. You had to hit it once to get the hit burnt, then suck it down, but it worked. It's a peculiar buzz, as if some arctic wind has sucked your brain out, leaving your sweating body clenched, benumbed in accelerated pleasure, if that's pleasure. Personally, I enjoy having a brain. The idea of my heart pounding furiously while my mind is sucked out holds very little interest for me, particularly at that price.

No, I preferred dosing. Dosing, tanking, driving to Canter's at three in the morning for a kreplach and a knish. Visually inhaling the dazzling procession of neon light prostitutes that once lined Sunset Blvd. Costumes that beat out Broadway or Studio 54, crying "your fantasy, realized," for 50 bucks. Equally lurid but somewhat less interesting were the tank topped muscle boys on Santa Monica, the gauchos, ready to do the same job of sword swallowing, but for a different clientele. The most telling experiences of Sunset were driving in almost at dawn, when the respectable hookers had closed their legs for the night, but the girls who still needed a fix, and looked like it, were left hunting. We drove by a thrashed looking old gal one night, makeup smeared, clothes hanging off her, not a pretty sight. We slowed down as she thrust out her crotch, but even with the windows up I could read her lips saying, "You want it?" Eeeuuugh!

I was tooling around Westwood one day when I saw a poster for The Wall outside the lobby of some theater. This excited me more than whatever torturous Dead show I was gearing up for next. As much as I had given my life up to the Dead, I was born to Pink Floyd. The movie was still a few months away, but I knew I'd be first in line. After a few days of seeing this poster, I had to have it. It was mounted on a sandwich board that was lightly chained to the door, so I walked up, in broad daylight, broke the chain, and walked away with the whole stand. I put my Wall poster up where I could see it from anywhere in the room, which was covered with rock & roll posters by this point. I was fixated on it, hoping it might answer the question of the Secret Message, *"What Shall We Do Now?"*

The quarter came to a close without the financial people ever figuring out that I had slipped, but in my manic frying I had lapsed into more serious paranoia. Word was that UCLA had started an undercover program to go into the frats to bust coke dealers. Although we had our share, I suspected that the more moneyed houses had more. I wasn't looking forward to them stumbling onto the fact that I was the only psychedelic dealer around though, a fact that would've been obvious with very little research. But with Ronald McDonald Reagan in office, it was pretty clear that the nukes would be flying pretty soon anyway. I began keeping the last 20 hits of a bottle stashed in my drawer, as preparation for when the air raid sirens went off. I was fully expecting to take a massive dose and come on in time to see the atomic fireball expand overhead. I'd have my Vuarnet's on, of course. I didn't go anywhere without my Vuarnet's on. I was dosing so often that I couldn't. Being out in the sun would cause trails from passing cars even when I wasn't high. I was definitely building the wall, behind shades, drugs, and enough volume on my stereo to make the world disappear. I finally managed to ditch Sarah. I don't recall saying anything in particular to her, I just refused to talk to her anymore. I hadn't been able to say anything to her in the first place. Other than The Wall, I was simply waiting for the end.

2⑥

Carl, Dane and Bam-Bam had an interesting program that summer. I had watched them go through their periods of quitting this or that drug, only to fall back into usage at a later date, with a beaten feeling. I was far too smart to ever make any claim to quitting. I knew there might be some point at which I might not use, but the idea of enforced stoppage is just a trick, luring you to eventually feel that you have no control. For a certain period, though, they decided to do a different drug every day. I vaguely regretted not doing ether with them, but at the time it seemed like a pretty lowbrow high. They did the whole cycle, coke, weed, acid, chaw, speed, tequila, 'ludes, ether, shrooms, beer, nitrous, MDA. It would have been nice to have them compile a report, but that wasn't the point. The point was to have fun! Which is what they did, by and large. Getting high with those guys was just fun. Carl and I went to the beach one day, carrying a watermelon along with the beers in our ice chest. We didn't really have any way to cut it open, so after playing rugby with it for awhile I smashed it over my head, which split it pretty cleanly in two. We devoured our halves by smashing our faces into them, scraping out the fruit like woodpeckers. Then we put the rinds on our heads like helmets, so that we were protected when we resumed our rugby game.

I think it was Bam-Bam who discovered the hot tub behind the apartment building up the street. They didn't even lock the gate, so you could cruise through to Jacuzz. We decided to have a little party there one night, Bam-Bam, Dane, Carl and I, and being summer it required a watermelon. We did a little cleaner job of dividing it, but eating soon devolved into reenacting the dining hall scene from Alien. This was accomplished by convulsing a few times before forcing a bunch of the red melon out between your teeth, as if your guts were being rent and forcing you to barf up blood. Then you let it roll all down your face and chest before collapsing into the water. This degraded further into spitting seeds and eventually melon in each other's faces, until we smashed the rind over ourselves in a frenzy. Needless to say, the Jacuzzi was sounding kind of fucked up by that time, so we decided to get biblical and made our exodus from the red sea. After that, the gate was locked. It hardly mattered though, since the Jacuzzi was permanently closed for repairs. I loved those guys, Bam-Bam and Dane and Carl, the "back of the bus." They were always having fun, and I wanted to venture off with them all the time, since they always seemed free enough to do anything. But I was so caught up in being me that I couldn't be one of them, and that bugged me.

I was noticing how paranoid I had gotten by this time. I was used to it when I was dosed, but with the whole purported undercover thing, every day was worry. The fucking idiot Ben Kirk, who had been elected VP, rented room 33 to a couple of grungy biker dudes after Ivan moved out. It was a known rule that only brothers and their friends could live on the third floor. That, plus the fact that I was dealing, made it sheer lunacy to have put them there. But Ben was young and clueless. The way he denounced us and tried to rally his scut brothers into quitting while in his night of darkness almost forced us to give him the boot then and there, which perhaps we should've. It was pretty hard to conceal the fact that we were partying wildly, but I made every effort not to speak with these biker dudes, who were now stationed right across the hall. We had a couple of really cute boarder chicks that summer too. The one I really liked was around the corner at the top of the stairs, but not quite where the main part of the third floor was. I would occasionally meet up with her or the other girl downstairs, but as much as I wanted to ask them for a date, my paranoia kept me silent. They were friendly and all, but inviting them to party might be a total bust. My only option was to scope them out through the hole in the first floor shower.

There was another boarder who lived on the first floor that had me worried for a while, but I realized that not even a narc could degrade himself as much as Steve Blowhead did. Steve Blowhead, what a fucking idiot. He was older than any of us, maybe 28, and claimed to be from Beverly Hills. His mom had finally kicked him out of the house, I guess, for being such a derelict. He was always hunting down the next bindle, preferably of stuff that had been well cut. For a guy who did coke all the time, he had the strangely narcotized appearance of someone who was falling asleep. His eyes were always half shut. You couldn't tell if he was actually talking to you or conversing with his eyelids, which was just as well, given the scintillating nature of his discourse. He would pontificate endlessly, however poorly informed on the matter at hand, which made him more a source of amusement than argument, since you could practically laugh in his face without his noticing behind those half masted eyelids. He claimed to be a connoisseur of everything, and was always either complementing me on whatever I was drinking or smoking, or contrasting it against something he had once had that was better. Dane and Carl let him hang around because he was always buying more blow, even though Speck kept a stash of extra cut dust just for him.

Dane had lived with Bam-Bam before Carl moved in, so some of the "never clean the room first" competition, where you just let the filth build up until the other guy cracks and has to clean, remained. Their table was always covered with old beer bottles & such. Wyck had been up there one night, and being a fan of nasty German white wines, he left the dregs of a bottle of Schwartzkatz on the table. Blowhead came in foraging afterward, did a bong, spied the wine bottle, and chased his hit down with it. Arching his eyebrow without actually opening his eye, he sighed poetically,

"The wine at the end of the bottle always has more flavor," and departed.

"Particularly wine that has two cigarette butts in it," we guffawed, as they were no longer floating in the now empty bottle. But old Steve Blowhead never noticed.

It was a terribly dangerous room to be picking up old bottles in, because Carl, Dane and Bam-Bam all chewed Copenhagen. One evening Blowhead imagined he was sneaking a free swig off of an unfinished Bud bottle, and actually chugged the whole thing before we started laughing. But even his cultured palate could not mistake the fact, that in his search for ambrosia, he had guzzled a mouthful of chaw spit. I think that was the only time I ever saw his eyes wide open. The look of slack-jawed stunned terror that overwhelmed him before he ran to the bathroom to begin his half-hour of retching could have illustrated a volume of Poe. We had to turn up the stereo to cover his grotesque gagging noises, as well as our own gut wrenching laughter.

21

The Dead were slated to play Red Rocks at the end of July. Red Rocks was something of a hallowed place on the Deadhead's map of the stars. A beautiful amphitheater, carved in the giant red rock cliffs somewhere outside Denver, it was home to a fantastic set of shows in 1978. I had a tape from one of those shows that was killer. Stories from the first Red Rocks were tour legend. There was the guy so deep in the crowd that the cops couldn't get near him as he waved thousand hit sheets of Green Dot in the air before tossing them up for grabs, and the well known tragedy of the kid who fell off the rocks. He had been up on freebie hill when the cops started chasing him. The band went on the PA, asking them to cool out, but they continued to chase him until he fell to his death. (Here's the bad place to insert the Grateful "Dead" joke) It had been four years, so things seemed to have cooled off enough. Craig, Natalie and I flew out together. We had spent most every night that summer together, and Natalie had moved in with Craig at the beginning of the month. The flight was a blast. A red-eye to Denver, it took off at about 10 P.M., packed with Dead heads. We kept taking turns going to the bathroom to smoke pot, but eventually some guy locked himself in there for a while. The smoke was coming out the door so the stewardess started pounding on it, yelling, "This is not your private party room!" Deciding we should just go for it, I twisted one up on the flip down tray and sparked it right in the middle of the plane. Pretty soon we were puffing wildly, while the stewardesses retired for the evening. As usual, it was totally cool. No sky marshals awaited our arrival.

The next morning we called Paula's house, hoping we could visit her for lunch or something, but she had gotten worse. Her parent's had put her in a mental hospital that had a special program for anorexics. This was not what we wanted to hear, but we bought some flowers and went to see her. When we got to the hospital the receptionist told us she was on the third floor, but that she wasn't allowed visitors. She said she'd give her the flowers, but I was already halfway to the elevator. When Craig and I got out on the third floor, a nurse was already waiting to tell us we couldn't be there, but she was easily pushed aside. I began to feel like McMurphy, expecting to be thumped and Thorazined by some big orderly, but I proceeded to find Paula's room. She was just a skeleton of herself, on IV's & some gnarly thoracic feeding tube shit. She was so happy to see us but so embarrassed by her state that she broke down crying.

"I haven't been eating, so my parent's sent me here," She croaked. "I don't want to be here." The nurse interrupted us.

"You are going to have to leave, we've called security."

"They're so mean to me," Paula cried.

"Hey, we love you, you've gotta be strong," I told her, holding her now even tinier body. Craig gave her the flowers and told her to do what they said, because we wanted her to be well again. A guard arrived to conclude our visiting time, so we left as Paula cried. On the way down in the elevator I started having this feeling, like a piece of metal pipe, hard, cold, unfeeling, with the wind whistling a little bit right through me. It was a new sensation, the broken distance of thinking I'd never see someone alive again.

Natalie, who we'd left in the lobby, wanted to know what had happened, but we didn't feel like talking about it. We needed the decompression of our next errand, a stop at Denver Restaurant Supply to stock up on whippets. From there we drove out to Chief Hosa State Park campground, where we met up with Dave & Rachel and Stymie, Manny, Willy Went, & Bill Crooks. They had advised us to meet them and camp there, since it was only 15 miles from the show, and the park's namesake would soon be converted to the more sagacious Chief Dosa. This is where you really got to see the heart of Dead tour. Old hippies were coming out of the woodwork like Tom Joad's people escaping the dustbowl; in a funky old truck with all their possessions hanging off of it. It brought you back to that core question of heart vs. head; "Are we all really that similar that we can share a good time here, or am I really so fucked up that I belong with these weirdos?"

Red Rocks, however, is a truly stunning place to see a show. The towering slabs of rock create an almost prehistoric feeling, while the lights of Denver twinkle in the distance behind the stage. The really amazing thing is not the incredible expanse of starry sky on a midsummer night, but the endless rain that prevents you from seeing it. It wasn't very cold, but before long we were soaked, soaked and dosed. Security there is incredibly tight; not for any particular reason, they're just a bunch of fucking pigs. They would shove you around for dancing in the aisles, or get really militant if you were trying to move down into a different section. By the second set the place was so wet that boys were backing upstage in order not to get shocked, so the show ran a little short. You had to walk about a mile up these steps to get into the show, but they really felt treacherous on the way out, wet, with security packing 5,000 high heads down 'em. Back at Dosa we hung around the campfire doing whippets. It's a little difficult to do whippets in the rain because the cylinders freeze when the gas is released, then they freeze to your wet hands. Ahh, the price of fun! I wandered the campground, talking to various freaks. I remember this older hippie woman talking about how she had orgasms whenever Phil hit the right notes, reason enough to stay on tour all the time. It made me very concerned about whether I was a necessary sexual element to the show at all, or if I were missing the proper response to the music myself. Despite my experiences in Nevada, neither of which had actually made a mess, I hadn't decided that following the Dead was about hoping to come in my pants.

The second night they opened with Shakedown. They were talking to me and I was searching. It was raining like hell, so they had backed all their stuff upstage 10 feet to begin with. I had dosed pretty hard, knowing that this was the place for something to happen. The first set was hot, in that Dead synchronous way. They played Lazy Lightning and there was lightning. But Natalie, whom I associated with that song for some reason, was with Craig and, by my own ruling, off limits. She probably would have been up for a threesome, but I was at the show to prove myself, not get more confused. At some point Craig and I split to another section for a better view.

Now, at the show, you have your various divisions of people. There are the twirlers, who fill the halls spinning with their peasant skirts centrifugally expanded, the tapers, filling the center section with the black bug swarm of microphones and telling everyone around to shut up, the screamers, who just have to scream and don't mix well with tapers, the folks who have to pack the front, the people just grooving and dancing on the floor, the Jerry freaks, the Bobby freaks, the Phil freaks, they're discrete separations, but they exist. Somewhere into the second set, which started off pretty hot but had wound it's way down, I found myself in a section I had never been in before. It seemed that it was all guys, guys with mustaches wearing dolphin shorts. I had never imagined it's existence, but Craig and I were in the middle of the fag section! What does this mean?

I kept looking over at Craig, being reminded of some of his more anal behaviors, his orderliness, the occasional ambiguity caused by his one lazy eye. Oh my God, I couldn't get it together to have sex with any girls at the show and now I have to be a fag! The terror of this thought compounded my need to piss, so I wedged my way through the sea of wet hairy mustachioed men with a panic driven fervor. I headed up the steps to the top where the bathrooms were, but the rain had flooded them out.

From fifty yards back it was all six inches deep in raw sewage. Judging by the olfactory sensations, there was no heading any farther. If I thought I could have peed right there, I would've, but I assumed that with the crowd right behind me, and various people coming up every second to share in my discovery, there was not a good chance.

I went back to try to get back into the front section, but the security thugs weren't letting anyone down, and pushed me back into the fag section. I found Craig and waited for the end of the show in mute paranoid terror. I considered peeing my pants, since I was already completely soaked, but even that would have been too liberating. I waded through the rest of the show, awaiting the final buzzer for my escape. The security guys seemed particularly vicious that night, and in my projection of self-loathing I feared they would beat me up for being in the fag section. It was more than just paranoia, however. They threw a guy down a whole flight of cement steps right in front of me, and from what I saw he hadn't done anything. He stood up, with difficulty, flipped them off, and spitting blood, screamed, "Fuck You, Motherfuckers!" The crowd was too huge for them to catch up to him again, we were churning to get out, and it was pouring rain. I was still higher than shit, and when I finally escaped to the parking lot I went the wrong way.

I followed this trail around to where I saw a spaceship, with its door open. There were a bunch of bikers, on super chromed out choppers, escorting Jerry into a custom van that was waiting to take him up into the saucer. Whhoooaaaaa! I wanted to run over and go with him, but I was feeling pretty unworthy. If the bikers didn't kick my ass, the aliens wouldn't have a male humanoid urinal on their craft either, or they'd just probe me. I ditched down behind some cars to secretly make my way back. Somehow I found Craig again, with Bill Crooks. Natalie had gone back with Dave and Rachel, so the three of us split together. Unfortunately, Craig was pretty high himself, so I drove. Now I was really worried. Colorado highways didn't have the little reflector bumps that California highways did, so in the rain I was just sloshing through the unknown. After awhile it occurred to me that I was going the wrong way, although when you have no sense of time or distance it's easy to deny it. We pulled over at a HoJo's, where I ordered a milkshake, sans whippet, and took an incredible piss. It was draining out of my eyeballs. Only my good fortune of having grown up in Roseville, where I learned to drink eight beers before peeing, had allowed me to survive. We were so high we almost let Crooks drive, but he was an unlicensed street freak, so Craig managed it. Having driven 20 miles in the wrong direction already, I was satisfied with not dying.

Back at Dosa, tripping campfire parties were raging. We went back to Craig's tent for the whippet stash. As too totally high as you may be from dosing, (read paranoid) which may be cumulatively increased by nitrous, the moments of escape into the nitrousphere are still highly motivating. So we whipped out in the tent until our combined vibes of wanting to commit acts with Natalie were too much, at which point I sublimated mine and departed. I wandered off until I found a clearing in the woods, where I sat on an old stump, and cried. I really didn't want to be so fucked up. I didn't want to be fucked up at all! I just wanted to be high, to have fun, and to share that with all my friends. I was rapidly becoming a freaked out twisted cripple. There are times, late at night, when you're on LSD, when you really have to worry that you'll never be sane again. If you aren't already insane in your normal waking state, perhaps you'll just never come down. Or maybe the weird conceptions that you've formed while tripping will stay with you.

The cumulative tweak of the last five months was killing me. With each step I had tried to escape it, but, like quicksand, I only mired myself further. A man and woman came out of the woods and began talking to me. They were very short, but cheerful, and wise looking. They seemed to understand that I was having a hard time, being alone there in my torment. They reassured me that things would work out, and told me I should go back to camp. After they disappeared back into the woods I realized that they were elves! I wandered through the campgrounds all night and never saw them again. I did run into Natalie though. She had left Craig with the whippets because he was getting too weird on her. Having sex while on LSD can be a strange proposition, but she told me that he wanted to put a whippet inside her, which wasn't all that exciting for her. We wandered back to the clearing, where we sat talking about the whole scene. I apologized for anything that might have gone wrong, since everything was my responsibility. We watched the sunrise in this little meadow. With the mist clearing the grass and flowers took on their acid comedown halo of brilliance. We were pretty burnt out though, so we went back to our tents and crashed.

Sunday we were all fried. Saturday's tweaking had taken its toll. Craig seemed somewhat suspicious of me, and I of him. He had gotten all bent on Natalie when she returned in the morning, maybe he felt he was losing his hold on her. I was tired of being rained on, but not enough to have broken down and bought the 5 dollar plastic poncho that parking lot people were making their fortunes on. The rain made it hard to smoke pot though, which was a drag. You had to wait for the correct moment of dryness or your doobie would fall apart. The Dead were probably about as burnt as the rest of us, so they threw out a couple of gems in an otherwise mediocre effort. We all headed back to Denver after the show, to get a motel and a shower. I was planning on going back home with Dave. He and Rachel drove her Camaro while Stymie took the rest of the crew in his old Toyota truck. We were all heading back via Yellowstone, Craters of the Moon, and the Tetons to do some hiking. Craig was going to fly back to LA. We spent the day getting camping supplies and food, and decided to have one last serious meal at the restaurant near our hotel.

Natalie and Craig had been arguing all day. She wanted to leave with us to meet some friends up in Boulder, but Craig wanted her to go back to LA with him. She was getting tired of his possessiveness and she really just wanted to see her friends. Rachel had offered to take her there, since it was on our way to Yellowstone anyway. This really upset Craig, the idea that Natalie was using my cool friends to escape him. When we got together at the motel to go to dinner, he refused to let her come to dinner with us. This behavior was embarrassing me greatly, especially now that I was in front of all my Berkeley people. Not that it wouldn't have anywhere, my protégé, freaking out, on another person! Not too cool. Rachel stepped in and reaffirmed Natalie's right as a human to do what she wanted, so she came with us to dinner while Craig remained at the motel, stewing.

The restaurant across the parking lot from the motel was not an IHOP. It was a very fancy prime rib place, but we had no idea how fancy until we went in. It was all sort of Elizabethan inside, the servers were in period costume, and we had two waitresses for our table. It was expensive, too. But we were dope dealers on tour! A week before I had left LA I sent Dave three grand I owed him by Western Union, which they paid him twice! So we were financially solvent. It was a pretty weird setting, eight hippies sitting in this very upscale, for Denver, restaurant. We decided we would just ignore Craig and take Natalie to Boulder on our way. Our salads had just arrived when I saw Craig enter the foyer. He spotted us and came straight to the table.

"Natalie I've got to talk to you!" he insisted.

"I'm having dinner," she replied.

"Hey man," I said, "can't you just let it wait."

"This is none of your business," he fumed as he grabbed her by the neck, yelling "You're coming with me!" In a second I was around the table, wrapping him up as Dave and I pushed him back to the front door.

"You're trying to steal her way from me!"

"Dude, you are blowing it," I discretely reminded him in a forceful hush. We got him out to the foyer before he ran out the door. The manager was there when we turned around,

"Would you like me to call the police?" (Just what every dope dealer wants to hear.)

"Uhh, no thanks, he's just a little upset."

I went back to my salad, looked up at Natalie, who was recovering from her brief strangulation, and managed a smile. I could feel my heart beating in my throat as I chewed the delicious ranch dressing covered shreds of crispy iceberg lettuce, which were becoming somewhat difficult to eat. There is nothing that stands between me and my food, but my appetite had completely disappeared. The salad wasn't getting it. The freshly baked rolls, which were delish, weren't getting it. I was forcing myself to chew them enough to swallow, but I needed water to get it down. By the time my platter of prime rib arrived my sympathetic nervous system had completely taken over. My senses were so keyed up I could feel people breathing from across the restaurant. The pit in my stomach was not for want of food, but from intuitive knowledge of imminent violence. To which I reacted, the moment I saw Craig come back through the door. He was practically running toward Natalie, yelling

"You're coming with mhha," when I shouldered into his chest. I carried him straight out from there. Out the foyer, out the front door, out to the parking lot, where he met the pavement as hard as anyone I had ever body slammed.

"You are fuckin up!" I yelled, picking him up in a chokehold. My body was overwhelmed with rage, pure brute power. "I could fuckin kill you," I screamed, feeling how simple it would be to snap his neck right there. "They want to call the fuckin cops on us!" With his eyes popping out of his crimson face, it was apparent I was going to get no response, so I threw him down again. My fury was hoping he'd get up so I could hit him in the fucking face, but he caught his breath and screamed,

"You're trying to steal her from me."

"Dude, we're just letting her do what she wants to."

"You're always trying to take her away from me."

"What are you talking about?"

"You're always staying up with us so I can never have sex with her."

"What? I thought we were having fun!" I insisted, never having considered that another paranoid perspective might be compounding my own.

"Where did you go last night?"

"We went for a walk. If you hadn't tweaked out on her maybe it wouldn't be a problem. Now don't try this shit again, or I will fuck-you-up!" I left him there sobbing in the parking lot, only to fend off another query from the manager as to the need for police assistance. "No, no, he won't be a problem. Thanks though." My roast beast lost more degrees in Fahrenheit than I had gained in appetite, but I sliced each piece, swathed it in horseradish and masticated it brutally before sending down my gullet to the seething acids that awaited. Despite the further increase in apprehension at our table, mine had gone down considerably, indicating that Craig was not going to risk a return. He was that smart.

That incident taught me a few things. First, how dangerously powerful anger could be. Like my father, I considered myself to be nonviolent. I had always talked my way out of anything I insulted my way into. The full bore fear that I would have to kill someone at the Greek was nothing compared to having the adrenaline raging through me, knowing that I could kill someone, my friend, and having to back down from wanting to. That was scary. Second was that Craig's emotional state had made him completely wig out. Sure I was tweaking all the time, but I didn't take it out on anyone but myself. I might have been cruel to some girls, but I wasn't violent. Most importantly though, was that this emotional reaction had risked a serious blow it. I'm sure the Denver cops would have loved to interview all of us, but professionalism should have argued for avoiding that risk. Perhaps Craig wasn't the professional that I reasoned myself to be. I saw it almost as axiomatic that these intense emotional states brought on dangerously high risk behaviors, ones which threatened the safety of our enterprise. Of course, so did taking huge doses, but that was what we were there for. That was the Acid Test! It couldn't be helped. I was left to ponder this as we drove to Yellowstone.

The problem with Natalie's plan was that she hadn't been able to reach her friends in Boulder, who were undoubtedly partying after the shows. When we drove through town she called them again, but there was no answer, so she came with us. We got to Yellowstone late that night, so after our hooter we took some slugs off the brandy we brought, and crashed. We awoke to find that even with a zillion tourists around, and driving from place to place, Yellowstone is amazing. We had to keep it somewhat cool, not get high in front of the rangers or anyone, but the place was still awesome. I was particularly taken with the sulfur pools that formed endless tiers of built up salt sediments. It looked like cell structures of blue bubbling water with yellow white rims. It probably would have been more fun to trip there than at Red Rocks, but it was just fine being straight. I was able to hang out with Natalie while we walked around, but there wasn't much room for privacy. She was her usual giddy self, excited by the flowers and trees and animals. She was such fun to be with, a child in a young woman's body. Perhaps it was only my sense of incredible oldness that drew that line, as our chronological ages were the same. We spent a day touring the park, but we couldn't get a backcountry permit, or a camp space, so we had to split. I called Dane from a payphone, to tell him not to let Craig into my room when he got back.

"Dude, he went in there as soon as he got back and trashed all Natalie's stuff. I think he took a bunch of your tapes."

"Oh fuck. Why didn't you stop him?"

"I thought you guys were friends. What happened? He's telling everybody you fucked Natalie and ran off with her."

"Shit. Sorry man. I should have known. He just wigged out, and no, I didn't fuck Natalie. I'll be back in a week, I'll see ya then." The aftershocks weren't over yet. I told Natalie what happened,

"Oh fuck, I knew it. He trashed my stuff?"

"Yeah, apparently he took all your clothes and piled them up in my room before pouring Clorox on them."

"Oh no! Everything I own was in his room! Fuck. That asshole."

"Sorry Nat." We climbed in the back of Stymie's truck together and finally held each other, having shared in our losses of trust.

We drove up into Montana and had dinner in Bozeman, before proceeding into the vastness. We pulled over in a likely spot, a wooded patch between two big hills. We figured we could crash in the dirt somewhere there. I wandered off with Natalie until we found this huge bolder, which we climbed on top of. The stars were brilliant, and the night was warm. I finally somehow admitted to her that I had maybe loved her all along, but didn't know how to deal with it. She replied, to my usual stupefaction, that she liked me too, and went out with Craig partly because she thought she could be closer to me. She expected that we'd be having a threesome or something anyway. A couple frat guys in LA, who knows? But we both felt relieved to finally be together alone. So we made it, on top of that rock, in Montana. It wasn't a grudge thing, like "Craig trashed our shit so we're gonna do it." We were just far enough from everything that we could be real, without tripping on who was who or what meant what. It wasn't anything great, for her I'm sure. I probably lasted about two minutes. (Okay okay, a minute twenty-five) But the relief of having gone through what we had to be together, holding each other, under the stars, was overwhelming. Still, we didn't make any commitments, we were just on tour.

One thing made sense to me though, and that was that the only way to be safe from dangerous behavioral shifts was to avoid any intense emotional situations. I just didn't think it was a good career move to be at the mercy of incredible anger, or a love that drove you to violent acts of jealousy. The idea of being possessed by anyone, or manipulated based on your relationship, seemed ludicrous, especially when the potential danger existed of someone narcing you out over their tweak. It was risky enough tripping your ass off, but not to control this dangerously unpredictable side of the mind was too much. I decided that I would cease to have emotions from that point on. I was always kind of Spock like to begin with, I would simply shut off my emotional processing unit. I knew I'd always love the people I was supposed to, in some universalistic way, but sex and love had already been disjointed enough that I wasn't concerned about lacking one for the other.

Shutting myself off in this way probably made my return to LA a little easier. I flew back in the simple mental process of wondering just what the fuck I was going to do. I got back to my room, where Craig had dumped all of Natalie's clothes and poured Clorox on them, but Carl had cleaned things up. Craig also had the combination to my stereo closet, so he had taken all my Dead tapes and copied them. My possessiveness made me consider taking all his copies and breaking them, but my new detachment prevailed. I was still in a quandary about confronting him anyway. Should I kick his ass? What for? He had told everyone that I had stolen Natalie and fucked her, which was not the case, but why should I care anyway? They all thought my stealing Natalie was either cool, since stealing women was part of the Zete creed, and the subject of the Dead's own "Minglewood Blues," ("My number one occupation, is stealing women from their men.") or totally confusing, because they thought the three of us were having sex together anyway. I went down to Craig's room that evening.

"So, did you fuck her?" he sneered.

"Yeah I fucked her, on top of a rock, in Montana." We glared at each other, having lost all love or respect. There was nothing more to say. I considered having him thrown out of the house, since he was just a slimy boarder now, but I didn't think he'd stay much longer.

As for myself, I had no idea what to do. Although I hadn't heard anything from the U, I assumed I owed a bunch of money on top of flunking out. I didn't think there was any going back, since I could never get into my major now. All they'd done was fuck me over anyway. I hadn't learned anything there yet. But I couldn't go home. I didn't have a car and

I threw out the boxes for my speakers, which were too valuable to move improperly. What would my parents say if I showed up with a 5,000 dollar stereo? I couldn't go through the whole drug dealer thing with them again. Maybe I could move to Berkeley, but Dave didn't really have any room. But I'd be losing my AVS job as soon as they found out I wasn't a student. Maybe, if I'm lucky, Reagan'll just push the buttons tonight, toasting us all in a high wattage display of Technicolor atomic intensity. Maybe, if I'm lucky.

There was one thing left, though, The Wall. It was opening soon, Friday the 13th of August, in three theaters, London, New York, and down the street in Westwood. As high as I had built the wall around me, I would be the first in line. But time only crawled as I pondered the question of my future. Besides my no home, no education situation, I was acutely aware of my degraded mental state. I certainly was paranoid, and I didn't seem to be thinking as quickly as I had before. It's hard to make witty, off-the-cuff remarks when you have to analyze them to see if they reveal some vulnerability. After what happened at Red Rocks, I began to wonder about tripping itself. Maybe I just shouldn't trip anymore. But I was too afraid to be afraid. I knew that if fear made me back down from what I felt was right, I'd have lost. How could I ever resolve my insanity without taking more acid, since it was obviously the key.

Friday the 13th! An event for which I had ritually eaten acid for three years. Perhaps I should try staying straight and see what happened. I pondered this tumultuous decision until that Thursday evening. Could I actually go the whole Friday the 13th, attending the opening of the Wall, without taking acid? Laying between the speakers on my floor, listening to Quadrophenia, I decided I must. The most awaited day of my life I would navigate in consensus reality, or as close to it as my current mental state allowed. I lay on the floor in the dark, drifting toward sleep, listening to the rain and the ocean as Jimmy came down off his pills, took his boat out to feel the power of the rock, and let love reign. "I need to get back home, to cool, cool rain."

22

"Dude, wake up! Wake up! Wake up, man!" I looked up and I was staring into my own face, and I was dead serious. I grabbed myself by the collar and slapped my face. "Dude, you've got to wake up!" I couldn't believe this was happening, I was in a dream, with myself, in full color, and I wasn't fuckin around. I slapped myself again, forehand and backhand like Doctor Mbenga slapped Spock, yelling **"Wake up man! Wake Up!"** I opened my eyes. I was in my room, on the floor, the clock shone through the darkness, 3:15 A.M. What the fuck? Why the hell am I waking myself up at three in the morning? I did have to take a piss though, and I wasn't on acid, so I got up to go down the hall to the head. When I opened my door I saw it, and I knew this was it. The biker dude was staggering half drunk/dressed/asleep into the hall from room 33, which was now a small inferno. I could hear the Fire Marshal, "You have a real fire here and one of you boys will be coming out in a green bag," so I bolted down to Dane and Carl's room and kicked the door off the hinges, **"FIIIIRE!** This is it! Get out!" I ran back down the hall screaming FIRE! past the empty clip for an extinguisher, down to the second floor, past the empty clip for an extinguisher, down to the first floor where there wasn't even an empty clip for an extinguisher, and over to the Phi Psi house next door. I grabbed an extinguisher from their lobby, (they were good frat boys) and ran back upstairs. When I turned the corner the wall of 33 was already collapsing. The flames blew me back down on my ass. I couldn't even see a crawl space to get to my room and save my shit. It was a pure wall of flame. I didn't have time to run through the whole scenario of my world being destroyed or how I might save it before I realized I was burning! Fuck! I dropped the extinguisher, turned the corner, and leapt down the stairs. Everyone was out in the hall by now, but I ran to the living room screaming for Carl and Dane. Thank God they had escaped. I grabbed Carl, sputtering about losing everything,

"I was just up there and it blew me away, there was nothing I could do."

"Hey, at least you got us out man, you saved our lives." Carl was pretty happy about that, but he had run out naked when he realized what was going on, since their room was right up against the fire. Dane had at least been sleeping in sweats, so he had some clothes on. I ran out to the basketball court to see if I could get up to the veranda and into my room, but it was already engulfed. The windows were exploding as the black smoke poured out. Everything was being reduced to ash, and I was starting to feel nothingness in its place.

Kip gave Carl some clothes, and we went down to the front lawn, waiting for the fire department with baited breath. It seemed like forever before they arrived, every second devouring our memories. We all crowded the sidewalk as they ran hoses up through the house and began pumping. Dane was worried about Rho Phi, "I haven't seen him! Have you? He doesn't like fire, he must have run to campus. RHOPHI!" But Rhoph's deep, resonant barking was not to be heard. The fire guys were blasting and chopping, mostly working to contain the fire to the upstairs, where it was already unstoppable. We stood there in our varying states of undress, watching the flames shoot up into the night, black smoke and steam from the hosing erupting from every blown out window and hole in the roof. After an hour or so, when the third floor appeared to be mostly charred steaming rubble, and the fireman were cutting it apart and throwing it into the basketball court, the fire captain came down.

"Did one of you have a dog?" Dane looked up, stricken,

"Rho Phi?"

"I'm sorry son, looks like he got trapped under someone's bed."

"NooooooOOOOO!" Dane just ran, across the street, through the bushes, into Lot 8, and on until the echo of his anguished scream disappeared. Rho Phi had been sleeping beneath his bed. Buck. Sleeth. The gray-balled wonder. Gone.

"The smoke probably got him while he slept," consoled the fire captain.

"How did it start?" we all wanted to know.

"It looks like someone was smoking in bed, or on their couch upstairs." We all turned to look at the biker dudes, who really had no possessions to begin with so they hadn't lost much.

"Let's fuckin kill 'em," Ben Kirk hissed, ironically. But the cops were already there, and the two of them got on their shitty black chopper and rode off into the night, never to return. The fire guys upped the pace of chopping the place up and hurling everything out the windows. As dawn broke the crowd of half-naked Zetes was swollen by onlookers and more cops. We were anxious to get back in, since the fire seemed to be out, but these cops wouldn't let us. They started telling us that they had to protect the place against looters.

"I'm so sure, officer, like anyone we don't know is gonna walk past us into our burning house to steal some shit?"

"Those are our orders."

185

Out of nowhere the Cordoba rolled up, and Ivan toggled down the window.

"You alright, brohammer?"

"Fuckin A man, how'd you find out?"

"It was on the news, so I came right over. You need anything?"

"Yeah, get me outta here, to a liquor store." We rolled down to 7-11, which had just opened the beer fridge again, bought a case of Bud and a fifth of Johnny Walker Black, drove back to the house and parked. I took the first of what would be many swigs that day, and chased it with a chug of Bud. "Fuck." I went back to the sidewalk, passed the fifth around, and started handing out beers. After a couple beers the fire guys were pretty much done, but the cops were still "protecting" the house. We started giving them shit. This lady cop starts hassling Wyck about having a beer.

"Do you have an ID?"

"No, it's in my wallet upstairs. Mind if I get it?"

"You know I can write you up for that open container?"

"Oh yeah, pig! Give me a ticket for drinkin on my front lawn why don't ya?" She stepped back and put her hand on her revolver. "Oh yeah, pig," Wyck screamed, "why don't you shoot me? C'mon and shoot me, pig!" She backed down, moving off to the periphery, but it wasn't a good sign. I took the bottle and a twelve down the street to Mina's house, where her mom graciously allowed us to shoot and chug in rotation as we waited to get back into our home. Ivan had to split for work, but he promised he'd return.

They didn't let us back into the house until the firemen had cut out every charred piece of wood, hosed it down, and thrown it in the back yard. They also tossed every ghost piece of furniture, or remnant of anything. That was their job. The TV news guys and campus reporters were all over it, interviewing Dane & Carl for the paper. "'We're homeless and missed dying by minutes," they said simultaneously. That was a good joke for awhile. They'd get together and say it in unison. When we finally got back in we went straight upstairs, into a veritable coal mine, all black and wet. But the big excitement was in the backyard, where all the charred debris was. "Sheldon! C'mere!" Merle yelled. My speakers, which were pretty heavy oak panels, were still in one piece, albeit completely charred. My stereo cabinet, with its thousands of dollars of components, half melted into slag, lay there amongst the broken two by fours. There was my scale, only recognizable by the shape of the lump of metal. I was hoping to find my wallet, since it was pretty fat, and they say compressed stuff doesn't burn. It had the picture of Dave and Ive, all high on acid and crammed into a photo booth, an irrevocable link to my childhood, but it was nowhere. "Hey man, check this out!" Carl came from the far side of the pile with my bass. The case had been burnt off it, but the bass itself was only lightly charred. Here was a symbol of all my dreams of spaced-out glory, tangible, in its denial. If there had been any place for that broken dream to hurt, I'd have cried, but it just waved around in the hollow of my chest. They had put Rhoph in a body bag and left it out in the triangle, the little plot of dirt at the top of the property. We all sat and stared at it for awhile, knowing it could have been one of us. "In a green bag." This was what happened when you didn't take acid on Friday the 13th.

By afternoon most of the alumni had heard and stopped by, as well as UCLA officials, promising assistance come Monday. The alumni wanted to take us all to dinner, so it was decided that instead of seeing the Wall, we would have a wake for Rho Phi. We went to the restaurant where Kip worked, the Brasserie, although he was with us that night. Dinner there was good, and we had a few beers, but every one of us bought a fifth of whiskey to take back to the Zete house. We lined up all the tables in the living room and sat around them, a bottle in front of each of us. Everyone was there, Natalie was back, with Lauren, Ivan, Dane, Carl, Kip, Merle, Slappy, Sharky, Bam-Bam, Wolfie, Speck, Wyck, Droz, Caleb, The Blade, Chico, Too Tall, Krajkz, RX, Chunk, Doc, the Sewer, Rod & Terry and Mina and Chuck and Eileen. The Hawk had been home in Seattle, but sent his regards, now that he nothing to return to. Craig, who had disappeared in the morning, had gone home and borrowed six hundred bucks from his dad to pay me off; there was still some honor beneath our hatred. We told commemorative tales of Rho Phi, and drank. Dane opened.

"We all knew what the Fire Marshal said, that if had a real fire, one of us was coming out in a green bag. Rhoph knew it, and I think he sacrificed himself, like a brother, so that we could all make it out. I think that was his good deed, so he could be reborn as a human. RHOPHI!" We went around the room, toasting.

"To the many magazine subscriptions of Rufus Rowphi! Drink!"

"Rhoph in class! Drink!"

"Rhoph's fake limp that got him picked up on Wilshire by some rich family that we had to take him back from, and his attempt to pretend he didn't know us when we got there! Drink!"

"Rhoph playing Frisbee! Drink!"

"On the beach! Drink!"

"Scamming babes for food! Drink!"

"Smoking pot! Drink!"

"Jumping through the window! Drink!"

"Watching me have sex! Drink!"

I knew that in my heart, whatever or wherever that was, I loved that dog and these people, but I felt nothing. I'd felt nothing for days and now I only felt more nothing. I knew that I was supposed to feel pain now, that it was allowable. But pain would have been something, and there was nothing. So I decided I would make sure I felt pain. I would drink until I hurt, or until I died, which was fine with me at that point. So I drank, until I was crawling. We had agreed to bury Rhoph in the triangle at midnight, but I was so fucked up by then I could hardly crawl up there. They were all taking turns shoveling, but I couldn't even stand up. I scooped some dirt out with my hands. I was laying there in the dirt, shivering and twitching, but I had to be there. Ivan asked me if I wanted to go back down to the couch, but I had to be there. When they got the hole done and put Rhoph's body bag in it, I puked in the hole. Then I lay there, face in the dirt with one eye open, while they covered him.

They got me back to Kip's room, where I slept on the couch. I seemed to remember puking radically, but when I woke up I was clean. I felt pretty good too. When Kip told me he thought he heard me puking I looked behind the couch, where there was this huge loaf of meat and whiskey. It was almost solid, like a soufflé. It cleaned right up, and I was ready for breakfast. The primary event of the day was, of course, seeing The Wall. I did have the good fortune of leaving all my T-shirts in the first floor dryer the night of the fire, so with the pair of scrubs that Chunk gave me I had some semblance of a wardrobe. The real problem was that we had no weed. I got someone to take me to another dealer down frat row. It was appalling for me to pay $50 a quarter for Thai weed, particularly with my knowledge of its worth. I had to buy it though, no courier service was delivering me a load today, and I needed to get **stoned**. We smoked it up and headed down to Westwood for the matinee. The line was fairly long, but it didn't matter as long as I got in. We made it up to the door, filing in one by one, but as I entered the usher stopped me,

"You can't come in without shoes."

"I don't have any shoes."

"Sorry, you'll have to go home and get some."

"Hey, my house burned down the other night, and I don't have any shoes. So can I just see the movie?" The manager had come over since we were holding up the line by now.

"Sorry sir, we can't let you in without shoes." I was about to go ballistic on these two guys, when Mina came out of the theater with a pair of shoes, which fit perfectly. The usher and manager looked at me in wonder as I put them on, sarcastically saying, "Excuse me," as I walked by them. Dane and I had discovered at some point that we could trade shoes, and boy was that handy.

"The Wall" was "The Wall." Pink was receding from his emotions into his private Idaho, loveless, having sex with whoever bought his persona, watching TV, drugging enough to keep the world at bay. How shall I complete the wall? The message was not particularly uplifting, and while the ones who really love you may march up and down outside the wall, it's up to you to come out. This is a process in itself. But no one tells you that. How to build it, perhaps, but how to get out is your own problem.

23

But now I was free. There was nothing holding me in LA. I could move back in with my parents, whoopee! I slept on the couch in the living room with Natalie. Craig would stare at us when he came by, but I didn't care. I was most concerned, in my still paranoid state, with the fact that someone had been sneaking in every night and pouring some syrup on the back of my head, which I discovered every morning. Who would do such a thing? Craig, maybe, but without waking me or Natalie? How? After a few days of tweaking about it I discovered there was a blister on the back of my head that matched the one on my nose, only bigger and pus oozing. I was pretty close to the fire when the wall collapsed, and the heat had left its mark. (Carl and Dane and I went down to DMV for new licenses, and I had a blistered nose license photo for years.) UCLA offered us all big emergency loans, which I took and never repaid, but I also got a retroactive withdrawal from my completely flunked quarter. I suppose I could have gotten one even without the fire, if I had told them what kind of psychological duress I was under, but I couldn't imagine doing that. I just accepted the slip of paper that would give me some leeway should I ever want to take up my academic career again. I took my remaining money and bought a killer pack and sleeping bag, not knowing where I'd end up. There were no more strings. In my stumbling tweaking way I had snatched the pebble from the master's hand, and it was time for me to leave. Realistically, I had just been booted out. I said good-bye to my friends, my brothers, took my new pack, my retroactive withdrawal, my tie dyed T-shirts, a ten-pound tank I had left in Craig's room, my charred guitar wrapped in a garbage bag, and Natalie, and drove up to Berkeley in her Honda. "Strike another match…"

We slept on the floor in Dave and Rachel's living room for a few days, but that next Saturday was my 20th birthday, and the Dead were playing in Oregon. This was how it was meant to be. My 20th show, on my 20th birthday, at the Country Fair, with all my Berkeley friends, and Natalie. No tank, no one from LA, I decided that it would be the first show I didn't dose for. I really had to see if they were talking to me or if I was just high. Even in my sobriety, I Know You Rider made me think I should get down with Natalie in the grass whilst surrounded by freaks , but I was still too tweaked. In the second set they broke out a new song, the first new thing they had written in a few years. Then I knew, whatever happened, wherever I went, whatever I did, however much I dosed or didn't, that they were talking to me. "West LA Fade Away" was all about selling drugs in West LA, just renting time in a little room to do some deals, until "The place burned down." I couldn't imagine who else they could have been talking about, two weeks after the fact, which made me about as certain of my mysterious position as if I had been dosed. "Nobody else around here, you must be talkin to me!"

We had a party back at the hotel, where a dozen people crashed in our room, but it had a sort of anteroom that Natalie and I were able to crawl off to, alone. I really dug that girl, but I was still pretty distant from myself. If anything had gotten through my denial of having emotion, I didn't know how to feel it anyway. We drove back to Berkeley, but I wasn't set up to have her live with me. I wasn't even set up to live. So we held each other another night, then let go again, as she went back to LA. Now I could digest the fullness of my loss. I really had nothing. Sure my brother loved me, so I had a floor to crash on, but my prospects were only as vast as my mind was functional. It's hard to go from being the wheel to having a job, any job, unless it's really fuckin cool. But to go from being a bright, collegiate, world-is-your-oyster wheel to a warehouse job, or being a busboy, it's unthinkable. It would be more dignified to claim insanity and go on SSI. Dave told me that it was getting about time when Stymie would need people to trim pot for him, and Stymie had invited me up there while I was in Oregon, so I was leaning that way.

The Dead were gonna be playing on Labor Day at the PUS Festival though, which was looking like the new Woodstock. All my friends in LA were expecting me, and a bunch of my high school friends were going too. I didn't know if I could hack it, and I wasn't particularly excited about going out to smoggy San Bernardino with a million people who wanted to see Fleetwood Mac. I knew I could get a ride if I wanted, but when I opened Friday's paper there was a big picture of downtown LA on the front page. It was barely visible through the smog. The headline read, "LA Fades Away." (Deadheads at the Chronicle?) I packed my pack, got a ride over to Golden Gate Park with Dave and Rachel, said good-bye, and put my thumb out, heading North.

EARTH

What element is left when the coals have died out, physician?" asked Huang Ti, as their conference resumed.

"The ash that is left from bonfires is spread out as fertilizer, and becomes Earth, as do we all. Earth is the center to which we align ourselves. Food, water, shelter, the things that sustain life all come from Earth. It is the conduit for the transformation of chi."

"How does Earth appear then, in the cycles of man and nature?"

"Earth is the time of transition from one season to another, and also of late summer, when things are in fullness but harvest is not yet begun. In men, it is the time of adulthood, when one settles into living his life."

"As emperor, I found that to be a time of much work. Tell me how the Earth element relates to one's responsibility."

"The emotions associated with the Earth organs are pensiveness and worry. As one takes on responsibilities there is often much cause for thought, but to wallow endlessly in thinking produces no result. Action must be taken, and when action is taken on the basis of mind and heart, the world moves in its course, leaving no room for worry."

"And where does worry affect the body?"

"Where does it affect you, emperor?"

"I find it disturbs my appetite," Huang Ti laughed.

"Indeed, as the organs of the Earth are the stomach and spleen. These break down the raw matter of food and transform it into chi. The spleen shows itself in the mouth and lips, which conduct the pleasure of eating to the body. In the flesh, the muscles and fat, the character of the Earth element in the body may be seen also."

"So my fat subjects have an abundance of Earth?"

"Excess or deficiency, it is relative to the balance of all elements. We are each born with a different elemental balance, so one's excess may be constitutional. For a time it may even protect him from damaging that organ with his behavior."

"How can one maintain a balanced quality of Earth?"

"By remaining in the body, in touch with the ground."

"In the body?" quizzed Huang Ti, eyebrows raised.

"Yes, this is the danger of too much thinking. We find occasion to leave our bodies and enter the imagined world of possibilities. The further we travel into the realm of the mind, the less attention we pay to the body, to breathing, to feeling our emotions, or our connection with the earth. This can cause serious injury, and distort the mechanism that maintains the body, hunger. When we eat without being in our body, we are never sated, and when we worry or think too much, we are never hungry. Remember what you are doing while you eat, you are feeding your body. Also remember that while you are consumed with thought you have a body which needs to be fed. When we begin to lose our digestive capacity we realize the importance of returning Earth to balance. I have found however, that in all illness, if there is hunger, then cure is possible."

1

In my happy-hippy hitchhiking naiveté, I hung around the bandshell in Golden Gate Park, asking people if they would give me a ride north. Who the fuck was going to give me a ride from Golden Gate Park to Humboldt I don't know, but my brain wasn't fully operational. Amazingly, some guy actually offered me a ride. I didn't know quite where he was going, but it was 101 North. He was in his late thirties, kinda pudgy, wearing dark wire rimmed glasses. We walked over to his car, a dirty white early 70's AMC, a step below the Gremlin, and drove off. Once again, I was heading into a new world. Passing over the Golden Gate Bridge into Marin County, my driver put his hand on my thigh. It seemed absentminded, like he was used to resting his hand there when he drove, so I sort of shifted and brushed it away. It wasn't too long before he did it again though, and that I wasn't ready for. I fell back to thinking what I had always thought I should do if faced with this situation. The highway was clear, we were in the left lane, there would be no problem. All I had to do was smash his trachea with a hard left chop, grab the wheel to keep us on course, reach across his choking corpulence to open the door handle, and stuff his fat fucking faggot body out onto the unforgiving belt sander of 60 mph pavement. The one thing, the only thing that prevented me from this, was the fact that I would have to drive his piece of shit AMC myself. (I guess I was still hyper-reactive after Red Rocks.) I demanded that he let me out, and after some "don't you want to come back to my place for a massage" bullshit, I found myself in San Rafael. Okay, I thought, I've made it through the first leg, 15 of 300 miles, Onnghh Yaangh.

It didn't take too long to get picked up in that swinging burg, and I was spared the butt lust, despite the fact that my next ride was from an Englishman. He was driving a pretty new Chrysler, and seemed rather a bon vivant.

"How's it goin, mate? Like something to drink?"

"Sure," I replied, although I hadn't reached anything resembling a state of road parch.

"There's an ice chest in the back seat, and make me one while you're in there." I was considering what that meant when he went on, "You like screwdrivers, eh?" I had leapt from the frying pan into the fire this time. His cheap Styrofoam cooler was loaded with ice, a half-gallon of orange juice, and a fifth of Smirnov. Not wanting to seem impolite, I poured us each a good one, and resumed my position in the front seat. This was not his first drink of the afternoon, so I figured I might as well loosen myself up in case of accident. My erstwhile chauffeur was heading to Santa Rosa to visit his sister. "She's really a fabulous girl, you should come with me to meet her, we'll have dinner." It seemed like a delightful proposal, but he kept mentioning her in a sort of wink wink, nudge nudge way that made me wonder whether they had an incestuous thing going on, or whether he thought I should fuck her while he watched, or both. In the 45 miles we covered to get to Santa Rosa he killed off three off my finely wrought screwdrivers, so I figured it might not be perceived as too ungrateful of me to claim necessity of furtherance and part company. I have occasionally wondered what that night might have held in store, but I've met enough snaggle toothed British girls not to worry about it.

Santa Rosa was like a lot of places. Sunny, surrounded by rolling brown hills, it soon gave way to the vineyards, whose ripeness lent a sweet flavor to the evening air. My next ride had me winding through the drive through town of Cloverdale, where citizens ambled up to authentic 50's burger joints for a root beer, and I began to notice that time and technology had slowed. Heading past the Russian River's rock carving on the Mendocino border and on into the tiny hamlet of Hopland, whose brewery didn't yet exist, geography began. The features start to take shape beyond Ukiah, (where I slept the night in a pear orchard) forming the ridges that surround and outline the town. Winding over Willits Hill, a feeling of ascension takes hold. Hills eventually give way to staggering cliffside vistas of densely wooded valleys. (Densely wooded due to being totally logged out years ago, and filling in with every tree that joined the race to survive.)

The winding strip of road rolls past rock slides and ramshackle homesteads, expanses of fir forest, white oak, tan oak, stunning red trunked madrones with their green gold leaves glinting in the sun, occasional pines, scrub patches of manzanita and ravines that cut deep into the rumpled layers of the mountains. Onward and upward toward Humboldt, where the mountains cracked open to give birth to the Redwoods. Even from a car I could feel the majesty of the redwoods. Those so huge that they've been left in place, with the pavement curving around them, bear the scars of cars that missed the curve; grill metal reminders of the lives lost imbedded in the trunks that didn't budge. To stick your head out the window and stare up to the top of the spires, living cathedrals blocking out the sun, bringing their own sense of life down from the sky, gives you a sense of the planetwisdom. Moreover, leaving it out long enough to have it almost reduced to a bark stain reminds you of your own insignificance. Humboldt seems more alive than anywhere else, bigger, although you can't really tell, since the road is just a groove between walls of forest.

I made my way to the junction for the Lone Star Highway, at Gerber, which is little more than a sign and an in-and-out-of-business redneck roadside cafe. It was pretty slow for hitching, so I walked the few miles up the hill to the next town, Lawson, which acts as a junction between the Lone Star and the next town north of Gerber, Barneveld. Lawson was a flat expanse at the top of the hill, with little box houses on cleanly mowed acre plots. It featured a little market with a gas pump that looked like it had been there since the forties, and a little service station up the road that looked like it had been there since the '30s. The station had a real air of country authenticity, so I walked past it and stood with my thumb out. It wasn't very long before some redneck old logger pulled in, gassed up, and eyeballed me. He was your average old coot for these parts, in a Chevy pickup with a gun rack that held a 30/30. I was somewhat stunned when he pulled out of the station and right up to me, asking "Need a ride?" "Billy, we fucked up," instantly sprang to mind, as I imagined this old redneck taking me down the road, blowing my brains out, and dumping me in a culvert. "Throw your pack in the back," he commanded, before I had a chance to reply. I heaved my pack into the bed and nervously climbed into the cab. We got about a hundred yards down the road when he turns to me and in a vaguely Walter Brennan summation says,

"You headed out to visit your weedgrower friends?"

"Uhh, no," I stammered back, shocked that he had read me that easily, and worried about his intentions.

"Aahh come on, everybody out here grows weed. I used to be a logger, but the timber companies have been cutting back for years. My friend's son showed me how to grow a weed plant and it's great. The wife wants a new washing machine, I grow me a weed plant. I want to take a fishing trip, I grow me a weed plant."

"No shit! You grow weed?"

"Everybody does it out here."

"Cool!"

He gave me a ride all the way to Cross Creek, the next junction of roads going hither and yon, and from there I got a ride to the mile marker where the road for Caldwell Buttes began. It was pretty remote out there, so I wasn't expecting to get another ride, and I began the five-mile hike my directions said would take me to the private road. The Bureau of Land Management maintains most of the roads out here because they lead to government owned land. At a certain point, by the description given me, I found the turn up, (you went much more up than off) and began heading that way.

It was incredibly peaceful crunching along the dirt road, surrounded by forest, listening to birds chirp and watching squirrels run up and down in the canopy. I came to the gate, stepped around it rather than opening the lock by dialing 1492, and wondered what I would discover on my voyage to this new land. I also wondered just how many locks out here used that same memorable combination. When the road crested you turned away from the mountain's edge and onto a flat, which quickly displayed a beautiful lake and views of the surrounding mountains. This is it! I walked around the lake and came to the cabin, which had been built there some years before by a family that attempted homesteading. I walked up to the cabin to find a woman inside, Katrina, who told me that Stymie was working on the shed. She pointed down the driveway, which I followed back to the road, and then down to another clearing.

"Hey maaaaan," I called out, causing them to pause from their construction.

"Duuuuude," Stymie replied, "howzit goin?"

"Better, I think, now that I'm here."

"FucknA, let's smoke a doobie." He climbed down from where he was working on the rafters of the new shed. It was a two story 20'x20' structure, rough framed with plywood walls. They were still working on the roof, trying to get it together in time to haul in the years crop, which they fully expected to exceed the capacity of the cabin, which served as general living quarters as well. Stymie twisted one up, introduced me to his partner, Mulehorn, and Manny joined us too. Manny had been working for Stymie that year, growing and doing construction, stuff that needed doing. I knew that Ben was a partner too, since I bought weed from him while I was at UCLA and Stymie was growing. He came up to the ranch whenever there was a major project going on. Their other partner, Bernard, whom I had never met, greeted me with a "Hey," and a querulous look of appraisal. We smoked a tube and I was invited to grab a hammer and start on fitting the tongue and groove together and nailing it into position on the second floor.

I could hardly recall having done a day's construction work, and it felt good. Over a regular ranch dinner of spaghetti we discussed my plan, or lack thereof. I assumed there would be some weed trimming to do, and other than that I expected to volunteer myself for whatever work needed doing. Those guys were all cool with that, except Bernard, who seemed a little standoffish about having other people around his weed. They grew together as a communal effort, splitting the finished product in shares after all was said and done. Stymie showed me a couple of weed patches, just to display his handiwork to an awestruck novice, but I didn't spend any time tending them. I mostly worked on the shed, which I started crashing in once it got roofed. In the shape I was in, getting fed and having a roof over my head was enough to make any efforts worthwhile, and killer weed was an executive perquisite. Bernard and Katrina lived in the cabin, as did Stymie, Manny crashed in his tent and Mulehorn inhabited Ben's trailer. Empty bare wood suited me fine, it was good just to have a space to be in. It wasn't long before the place was in decent shape, but by then the buds had peaked, and they began filling it with plants.

2

Weed production is both an art and a science. Coming in on the back end of the season, I first learned about drying, trimming and curing. Drying is incredibly important, and it takes awhile for weed to dry. You can't just cut it down and trim it. With weed that valuable you sure aren't going to throw it in the microwave like some high school kid. Of course, a microwave was out of the question anyway. This was before these guys even had a generator. Living in the woods, you have a woodstove. If you run the woodstove too hot, you dry your weed too fast, which gives it a harsh, brackish taste. You need to move the plants around, to maintain even heating and airflow, but at the same time, a plant that dries too slowly can mold. Humboldt's great growing attributes pose serious difficulties for those trying to finish their weed properly. The fog that feeds the redwoods can start a bud molding while it's still on the plant, and around harvest time the rain starts too.

The rain in Humboldt is legendary. 60-80 mph winds are not uncommon in the mountains, with endless buckets cascading from the sky. Sitting inside the shed, facing windward, you see nothing but a sheet of water washing the windows. But outside, in the creeks and on the roads and on the hillsides torn from logging, erosion redefines the landscape. Trees fall, boulders roll, rivers flood and roads wash away, while the dedicated, the stoned, trim. To gather your plants when you awaken to a thunderstorm can be terrifying. Hoping for an extra day of sunshine, which could increase your weed weight by as much as fifty bucks a plant, you find the broken limbs laying in the mud, already halfway to molding, and if you're clever enough to cut them off for a $200 loss, you may avoid losing the whole plant or those hanging next to it in the shed. Mold can wipe out two to five thousand dollars of bud in 36 hours, if left unchecked. So the wet weed gets closest position to the stove, until it's okay, and hopefully not burnt. After four or five days of rotating and drying, the stems of the plants, which are where all the moisture goes, come closer to being dry. Before that point the leaves are still too moist to cut properly. When the plant's ready to be trimmed, you take it down, cut the branches off, and go to work.

Bud is basically the female sex organ, and yes, we are perverts, spending all our time trimming the bushes of, and ogling plantpussy. As you get out toward the top of a plant, or the tip of some branches, an unending bud will form; the cola. In the days of big weed, colas weighing more than an ounce and even as big as your forearm were not uncommon. A nice quarter oz spear was fine though, assuming your plant has enough branches to rack up a pound. Because those guys had sold so much pot over the years, they had collected a wide variety of seeds, which translated to a great variety of weed. There were mostly indicas, with their broad, deep green leaves, and a couple sativas, with their thin many fingered leaves, the classically portrayed weed leaf of media imagery. Crosses of various types abounded, as well as location oriented strains of Afghani, purple Kush, and Thai.

Each plant was a miracle of its own device, from the color of the bud, to the radiance of its hairs, to the crystalline schmint deposits. The shapes of each plant differed enough to make trimming an exercise in the proper exposure of its features. When it came to trimming, I was devoted to complete exposure, cutting away every leaf that hid the pockets of schmint from view. Manny had a hand microscope with a built in light so we could examine the structure of the crystal, which varied depending on the plant and it's maturity. That was serious Bud Science! Stymie was also certain that curing your weed, leaving it bagged in buckets for at least three months, was essential to leeching out the chlorophyll and allowing the taste to fill out. It's difficult for a lot of people to do this, because by harvest time they are so clutching for dough that they will sell the shit the minute it's picked. In a cyclical economy, with black market risks over your head at all times, many people lack the capacity to give their weed its due. Stymie's was always superb.

Each bud had its characteristic odor, even when fresh, which varied from potpourri to grape concentrate. Of course, tasting was a major activity. People got excited about the $100 a pound rate for trimming weed, but the serious smokers trim for the tasting. Joint after joint is rolled and smoked in an attempt to define and appreciate the attributes of each plant. As many joints as I have smoked in the short four or five hours of a Dead show, it's nothing like trimming. By the end of the day your THC level is so high that a joint can hardly affect you, you can't even get high, you just taste. But this sad fact is overcome by the incomparably rare fruit of weed trimming, scissors hash! Scissors hash is the concentrated resin that collects in your scissors blades from hours of cutting through the schminty appendages of a weed plant. You can trim all day and acquire only enough hash from your scissors and fingertips to make a tiny ball, but it is the freshest, strongest hash you will ever smoke in your life. Each toke will hit you as hard as if you had concentrated the 20 joints of the day into it. It's paralysingly good!

I wasn't a particularly fast trimmer, I was committed to my aesthetic of bud appearance, and I was still kind of brain dead after the whole Zete affair. Various other friends of Stymie and Bernard showed up during the weeks of trimming, in their various mental states. Another guy who had burned himself out, possibly by taking too many shrooms at Barrington, was Joe Palumbo. Joe P. never spoke to anyone the whole time he was there, and he lived exclusively on raw yams. We each wrote our names on our bags, brown shopping bags from Safeway that we used to collect our trimmed buds, but Joe's self concept was pretty far gone. He labeled his bags Joe Pizza, Pre-man. It made me feel saner to have him around, but a little more worried about what the liabilities of tripping might be. Stymie pointed out to me one day though, that "It's not the people in your life who take a bunch of drugs that will go crazy, it's the people who are going to go crazy that go crazy." I imagined I had escaped with my sanity to some level, I was still pretty astute, clear, fast, funny, but I was not altogether well either. It wasn't like I was particularly paranoid of anyone or anything, but being high all the time was exacerbating my inability to pee. It was survivable, there, in the pouring rain. With no bathroom you had to stand outside in the wind and water anyway, which could be viewed as a stoned out nature commune, but it didn't bode well.

Trim and huff, huff and trim, never know your life's purpose. The days went on, sitting in the green, looking out into the gray. I felt kind of lame noticing that Bagel had trimmed twice as much weed as I did in one weekend, but my brain atrophy was probably less time consuming than my perfectionist trimming style. Some folks like to simply shave the outside leaf down, which does protect the inner crystal, but it leaves the bud looking more like something they'll complain about buying later. It does allow you to make a lotta dough and smoke a lotta dope at the same time however. I just plodded along, knowing that it was a grand thing just to be there, working for Stymie.

Stymie was really a great guy, smart, funny, and pretty goofy too. I can still picture him, in threadbare jeans held up by a belt of green jute twine, with his weedleaf covered pullover sweater or his gold and red plaid lumberjack shirt obscuring the hair that grew from every pore of his body. He was double jointed, so he could wrap his arms around the back of his head and cradle it in his hands. No matter what you felt like, seeing Stymie's troll like head being carried around like this, as if he could pop it off and stick it back on, was sure to make you laugh. Despite his bearded, longhaired, hippie freakness, he had grown up pretty straight, and was a super nerd, so he was used to being an outcast. He had taken up dope smoking at Cal and began his career selling the hash he kept stashed in the back of a transistor radio that he carried with him to the park in his home town. I think moving into Barrington did a lot for him, allowing him to be who he was in a segment of society that could respect him. He was the mellowest guy, nothing ever phased his composure, and if something fucked-up happened it was just cause for another doobie. He never complained, except for various tirades against the government or right wing pigs or religious idiots, but never carping about petty shit, or seriously demeaning people. He was the kind of dope fiend you could respect.

After six weeks in the woods he took me to town. We ate dinner at the best Italian place in Eureka, and stayed at the motel that had the "sauna" showers, so we could bake the crust off ourselves. That was probably the best shower of my life, at least since the end of hell week. We were each in there for an hour. They even had the luxury of TV, which isn't much in a county that boasts two stations; right wing and moderate republican. The amazing thing about that motel, and apparently every one like it on the strip of highway that ran through town, is that every big rig gearing down sounds like it's coming right through the wall. It was a big change from the woods, and I must have woken up 20 times with the room shaking like it was gonna fly apart. But those log trucks have to keep rolling, either to wipe the economy out or to uphold it, depending on who you listen to. Humboldt presented an interesting dichotomy in that sense. It was still fairly redneck in outward appearance, but the mills weren't keeping things alive. The chainsaw shops were selling more generators, and the motorcycle business was picking up, particularly with the advent of the three-wheeler. People who would jump back from your hippie freak ass if you knocked on their front door gladly accepted your cash from behind the register, knowing that it was weed or welfare for everyone. We picked up all the supplies and a bunch of food, and cruised back to the mountain in Stymie's orange Toyota SR5.

By the time I was done I had cut my way through fifteen pounds, and decided to take it all in the purple bud I had trimmed, which was far more valuable than cash, Freewheeling Franklin and all. I thanked Stymie profusely for providing me with a place to get my head together, dope, money, and most of all his friendship. He politely deferred, maintaining that it was just what we do, but I let him know that if he ever needed me for anything I would always be ready. I snagged a ride back to town with Manny, who had traded his LTD for a Datsun pickup. It was mid November when I returned to the couch at Dave and Rachel's, but this time I had a stash.

3

I stumbled across Craig's buddy, Spin, living around the corner with a bunch of other heads on College Avenue. They made it easy to start dealing again, since they were all hooked up to BT or Mex, for whom they mailed hits around the country and did acid deals on tour. Spin introduced me to Dennis the Menace, who was a hard core partier, and extremely funny guy. Interestingly, we had all been involved in brutal romantic entanglements on tour. Spin had lost his girlfriend to Phil, Dennis lost his to the Dead's sound guy, and I swiped mine from my best friend, then almost killed him. In the world of taking innocent girls into the hurdy-gurdy of the Dead scene, or seducing them with piles of drugs, the rule seems to be that they'll move up toward bigger and better piles. I can't say I blame them. I started hanging out with those guys, meeting their friends, and running a few things around town.

Natalie came up for the shows that December and moved in with me on the couch for awhile, which was nice. We had a tank party with the usual crew after the New Year's show. Art was back, having disappeared from LA before the fire. He had married a woman he met at the Zen center, Mona, and I hadn't seen him since. They had a courthouse wedding and a shotgun divorce. They drove back to Kansas to see her family, but no one there was prepared to meet her longhair husband, so they all freaked out. I think they had her deprogrammed or something. Art said it was not exactly the high point of his relationship. He came back to LA alone, wound up working on a farm in Newhall, and eventually made it back to Berkeley. He had missed the whole ordeal of the fire, so now we had time to commiserate again.

The funny thing about having him there was that he was suffering immensely with an infected testicle. Art's the kind of guy who doesn't restrain himself from telling you about his most intimate details, and this one was overwhelming. I don't recommend taking acid when you have a physical condition like that, because you tend to focus your whole trip on it. Art's condition was also difficult for the rest of us, since acid does tend to dissolve your boundaries, leaving you indefensibly empathic. We were there on the couch, zoning out behind some bags, when Art, with his face scrunched up in wound contemplation, would say, straining over each syllable, "I-feel-like-my-nut-is-a-cushion-that-I-sat-on-through-the-whole-show." It was enormously funny, the way the sufferings of other people are enormously funny, but you couldn't help feeling it, in empathetically vicarious detail. The party went on, with Art drifting out into nitrous bliss himself, before returning to groaningly remind us of his testicle's status. "I-feel-like-someone-is-shoving-a-Stop-sign-up-my-butt!" Pain or humor, the poor bastard left me in tears.

I held a very interesting experiment the next morning, after everyone had split. There was still some nitrous left, so Natalie and I decided to have sex while whipping out. I must have gotten inside her before I started on my bag, but when I came out of my nitrous high my dick was limp and cold, as it was up against the bag that Natalie was now departed on. I got hard again pretty quickly, but it was difficult to fuck her, since she wasn't there anymore. I took the bag from her while she was passed out, refilled it, tried to stick my dick back inside her and started huffing again. We sort of went back and forth like that, each of us waking up from our nitrous buzz to find our partner was relatively uninvolved with the act that required mutual attention to derive pleasure from, trying to reinvoke some level of sexual interaction, and going back to our high. We eventually sought our pleasure as nature intended, however, lying beside each other and sucking the tank dry with our own individual bags.

Natalie liked Berkeley, there was always something going on. She was such a party girl, she'd meet people wherever she went, and of course, they all loved her. I didn't feel particularly insecure about letting her go off to do her thing, but she would introduce me to the people she'd met, and I really didn't want to know them. I was starting a dope scene again, and I didn't want to be involved with people that I didn't trust, or thought were a bust. Natalie trusted everyone, and amazingly never got screwed too bad for it, but I couldn't go there. She'd be hanging out with Dennis and this big acid dealer he knew, Mex, and guys she met through them, who would just pay her way. This got me kind of tweaked. I started worrying that she was gonna fuck this one guy, who I really didn't like, despite the fact that she told me she loved me. She really was just out having fun, but after awhile I couldn't take it, so we broke up and she went back to LA. Now I understood what worried Craig so much.

Not long after that Rachel decided to leave Dave, in one of those – "I need my space," sort of moves. He was pretty broke up over her. So in an effort to obtain some emotional support, we began making nightly forays to Bott's, Berkeley's long established ice cream parlor. It started out simply enough, a couple scoops of dark chocolate or toasted almond, but pretty soon we got inventive. I began having a cookie in a cup with two scoops covered in chocolate dip. I asked one of the friendly teens working there if they smoked pot, and ended up trading weed for ice cream on a nightly basis. Our creations got more depraved as Dave and I competed for the family crown of abdominal grotesquerie. Dave finally beat me though, by eating a creation at Bott's and following it with a sundae from the candy store down the street. It's amazing how much abuse you can pile upon yourself with the assistance of big reefers. Except for the pain, it's thoroughly enjoyable to degrade your intestinal lining, laying there in Romanesque fashion, inhaling appetite stimulator into the fraction of lung space that's left above your expanded gut.

Dave had actually turned me on to the premier experience of this nature, Shem's Palace, years before. I had mixed feelings about it at the time, since I was so burnt out when I first went there that I fell asleep on the table. Over time though, Shem's became ritual, and Shem himself, my buddy. Shem was an old Chinese doctor who had come to America to open a clinic, but wasn't recognized by the medical establishment in 1960. To avoid deportation he became Bill Cosby's private chef. Eventually he opened a health food Chinese restaurant that featured about 150 items of hippie weirdo veggie delight. In addition to his fabulous onion cakes and pot stickers, he served sea vegetables, gluten and soygluten balls, and everything else you'd expect at a Chinese restaurant, all available with extra ginger, garlic or a special "digestion sauce." It was a funky old house that he had converted into his restaurant, where his whole family now worked and lived.

The very cool thing about Shem's was that he had a smoking section upstairs, in the back. I'm not sure if he actually knew what was up legally, but pot smoking was entirely permitted. It was totally raged in; seven course meals with a palate cleansing doobie between each course. Over the years it got to be an incredible scene, like a stoner Chinese Passover, particularly after Dead shows. We'd get the back table and hold court for hours. They had a payphone in the entry, on which we'd take calls. I've actually sat there for lunch and dinner, rolling out a pound as various people dropped in for a meal and a deal. I think it's crossed everyone's mind that perhaps the food there wasn't so great, but we were so high it seemed like the Chinese Chez Panisse at the time. Shem was a wonderful man as well, one of the most humble people I've ever met. (Despite my total lack of humility, I am able to appreciate it in others.) The funny thing was that our benumbed concept of eating health food was extreme to the point of sickness. We'd eat and smoke until we couldn't breathe, and on particularly vicious nights we'd head up the street to McCallum's, another hand made ice cream shop which served up 12 scoop abominations for the young, stoned, and self-abusive.

4

When the spring semester started at Cal, Eileen, Terry, Mina, Bob and Chuck all transferred from UCLA in a mass exodus. I don't think they were following me, it just became pathetically boring there after I was gone. The girls moved into Barrington, my life's dream, while Bob and Chuck got an apartment a block away. It was strange now, as I tried to tag along and get reintroduced to Barrington, while they were on the path to their own individuation. They acted somewhat disdainful of me, like seniors to a freshman. Admittedly, I had rather blown things in LA, but I couldn't do what I had done there in Berkeley. I understood their need to create their own world, but it stung, being ostracized, particularly at Barrington, which they would never have heard of if not for me. I went over there one night and they had dosed, and the house manager, Derek, invited us to the hot tub up the street at Rochdale, a co-op a block away. We went there but they asked Derek's friend to tell me to leave, since they thought it would be too weird to flash back to LA. This bummed me out to no small degree, but I guess I was a reminder of the past they were moving away from. Of course, I assumed they were going to have an orgy with these guys instead, but it was only my tweak.

Eventually Dave and I moved out of his place, he into storage, and I into Barrington as a crasher. Eileen introduced me to a guy named Luigi, who after smoking one doobie together, became my lifelong friend. He was another Jewish half-breed, but unlike myself, he had an Italian mother. He invited me to crash in his room for as long as I needed. I was stunned by his charity, and did crash there for a while. I summed up the situation at Barrington pretty quickly, fronting Luigi some pot to sell and working my other Dead head connections. Stymie was living with Bagel, so I could always go get what I needed fronted to me. I eventually moved in with Manny, living on the balcony of his apartment, which he had boarded up so no one could see him doing Thai deals all day long. It was a convenient spot for my pack and sleeping bag, and I awoke every morning to a doobie of Manny's design.

I was starting to get it together when the Dead played Vegas again. I flew out to the show in Tempe the night before, where they played "Help on the Way," a great song that had been in mothballs for about five years. Needing help the way I did, and imagining it to be an indication that I'd be cured soon, it was inspiring to say the least. A bunch of folks from Barrington drove out and were going to Vegas too, so I planned a party at the Aladdin where I had reserved a room with Dave. I wasn't dealing any acid, so I told Luigi's roommate Gil to bring me some hits, but only if he could get liquid. I flew to Vegas and checked in early, so I could abuse my wallet in the casino, where I kept getting hassled by this one security guard who demanded that I wear shoes. I only had my work boots, which were rather cumbersome, and I took them off whenever I went to the pool. I knew I had to put them on to get to the show though, so I did. In the hallway between the casino and the show Gil finally tracked me down and gave me four blue gels. I really didn't want them, since it was pretty shitty acid, but I ate them anyway.

I took off my boots and danced my way through the first set, but by the second I was tweaking pretty hard. Eileen pointed out to me where Craig was sitting and righteously demanded in her new leftist Berkeley sentiment that I go bury the hatchet, so I was on full scale alert. I could see him there, sitting next to Jill, the bartender, and holding a nitrous bag. He had snuck in a five-pound tank. I maneuvered my way over and sat down in the row in front of him. Our eyes locked and through the tension I reached out my hand. He kept eyeing me, while hitting on a bag, but refused to shake. He tentatively filled a bag and handed it to me, so I started whipping out while we stared at each other. He passed his bag to his other friend and lit a joint, which I took a hit from and handed to his friend. We had neither looked away nor spoken when his friend, who was far less experienced in these matters, broke the buzz saw of energy flying between us by dropping the joint down the hose of the bag, which erupted in a ball of flame. I took this sign as an indicator of our relationship status and headed back to my side of the show. There was no going back, it appeared, but I was just as alienated going forward. The boys, as usual, read the bizarre energy and twisted the show even further. By the time it was over I was in a state of complete mental collapse.

When we left the theater the hallway that went back to the casino was blocked by a line of cops, who were demanding that everyone go out through the parking lot and around to the front. I just wanted to go back to my room and shrivel-up. I knew that everyone knew how freaked out I was and I couldn't take it anymore. I went straight up to the cops and yelled

"Arrest me! Arrest me! Just get it over with!"

"You have to go out through the parking lot sir," they replied.

"No, just follow me back to my room, that's where the drugs are, you can arrest me there!" I walked out into the parking lot but none of them followed. I suppose they thought I was another crazy practical joker. I followed the thousands of other heads around to the front entrance, still hoping to return to my room and be swarmed by feds. As I entered the front door I ran right into the security guard. Fuck! Isn't this guy off duty yet?

"Sir, you're going to have to put your shoes on."

"Okay! Okay!" I plaintively cried. Submitting to his authority, I stepped aside the throng entering the casino and knelt down by a slot machine. Taking my boots from around my neck, I undid the bow that held them together and put them on. By the time I laced them up, because you always miss an eyelet and punch your opposing hand as you attempt to tighten them, the digital task of tying the knots was far beyond me. I wanted to lie down on the floor, to be taken away on a stretcher, but I needed to make it back to my room so I could be arrested. With my shoelaces trailing 18 inches behind me, getting to my room was murder. Every step I took some freak was standing on them. It was jerk-fall-lift-stomp, jerk-fall-lift-stomp, every step of the way. The casino was its usual explosion of stimuli, which wasn't making the task any easier. I eventually found my way back to my room, but despite my being stunningly easy to follow, there were no feds! What now? I locked myself in the bathroom until I could pee, then lied on my bed while my mind swam. Eventually my friends began showing up. The cops apparently weren't coming so we started partying. I was feeling incredibly alien, however, and my party facade was nowhere to be found. I asked Eileen to take a walk with me and went to hide out in the stairwell.

Despite my problems with her on the bus, I had originally wanted to fuck Eileen. I wanted to fuck pretty much everybody, but when I met her she was a pushy New York Jew girl in tight pants and too much makeup that doubtlessly needed to be fucked. She was pretty smart, and laughed at my jokes, but she was hooking up with Chuck, so that never went anywhere. Now they had broken up, and she was trying to be a Berkeley hippie chick. Since she was the only girl there who knew my history, I hoped that she could understand. I dragged her up a few flights of stairs, sat down on the carpeted steps, and spilled my guts.

"I'm so freaked out. I don't think anyone likes me anymore. I'm afraid they never will." Eileen had never seen me with my guard down, let alone in this kind of admission, which somehow inspired her compassion.

"Hey, it's alright. People like you, it's just different than LA. You're not in charge anymore."

"I don't know what to do."

"Just be yourself."

"Will you hug me?"

"Okay." We sat there, hugging, in the stairwell of the Aladdin Hotel, for an acidically indeterminate amount of time. People walked up and down, but I was able to ignore them. I showed the security guys my room key three times, proving I wasn't some Deadhead trying to crash there in the stairwell, before they finally booted us.

"Will you sleep with me?" I asked her.

"No."

"Why not?"

"It's not like that." It really wasn't, but I had never exposed myself that much to anyone, so as high as I was, I felt I had crossed some serious line of intimacy. I had in fact, but it just wasn't like that. By the time I came back to the room everyone had left, which was a relief, but Eileen had a room elsewhere, which she returned to. I was still too high to sleep, so I cruised the casino, found Dennis the Menace in the bar, had a drink and hit the strip.

My hair had gotten somewhat unruly since the house burned, and living in the woods without a comb I had developed some huge knots. I had never been one for hair combing, since it would never hold a style other than its own. In fifth grade I was known as "The boy who never combs his hair." Sometimes I'd comb it straight up, to look freaky, but it made its own decisions. While I was wandering the strip, coming down in the dawn, this bird, lacking any natural structural materials in Vegas, decided my hair would make good nesting fodder. It was probably right, but it hurt! So right then I decided that no one could ever make me comb my hair again. I had been introduced to Bob Marley and Rastafari by now, so I decided I should just dread out. When I got back to Berkeley I shaved all my hair off, to get a clean start, and began my experiment.

5

Dave had taken over things in town when Stymie moved up to the ranch, and to keep things flowing he worked with The Face. I was staying with Eileen in Barrington at that time, driving her roommate Tonya insane with the sight of a naked hippie and the threat that we'd be doing it right there in front of her, young Christian that she was. Eileen was still averse to having sex with me though, so it wasn't really a problem. The problem was Tonya's presence, although I'd have been just as happy to erode the boundaries of polite society and get down with her there. Anyway, when Dave told me that The Face had offered him her house while she summered in the woods, I jumped to it.

I had established some things with people I knew from tour, and in Barrington, moving loads here and there to keep things rolling. Now that I had a place, Eileen finally relented and began to have sex with me. I was somewhat apathetic about being with her, since I saw her as more of a trustee than some dreamt of true love, but she gave me what I needed, a place to bury my bone and get a little understanding.

Stymie came down to town and told me he was gonna fix the shed to live in, so I volunteered as a laborer. This time, I drove up with him. His truck was a little more worn than when I had last seen it. He got snowed in and left it parked it up against a huge snowdrift for the winter. When he returned in the spring he found that neither the drift nor the truck were where he had last seen them. With the brake off, his truck had rolled downhill and into a tree as soon as the snow melted. No problem, every SR5 pickup has some funky body damage. It was more big adventure riding along with Stymie. He knew all the sights along the way, Gordancher's turkey ranch, where they bought all the turkey shit for growing weed, Friedman's lumber, which had everything imaginable, Garberville, weed capitol of the western world, the Cider Work's, the family run apple juice business in Barneveld, and Old Baldy's Cross Creek store. The only place for beers and canned beans for twenty miles, it was the last outpost of civilization, where old Baldy held court. "Howdy young feller," was his stock greeting, since there was no one left in those parts older than old Baldy. As you headed up out of Cross Creek you passed Richardson Rock, a giant lichen covered thumb poised on the side of the highway. The lichen would change from green to purplish brown during the course of the year, bringing life to its barren face. I came to see that rock as the gateway to my home, with Entwhistle's "The Rock," from Quadrophenia, pounding in my head every time I passed it on my way to Caldwell Buttes.

The Buttes were a prominent formation in the area, named for the fearsome indian killer, Caldwell. Caldwell would take parties as far north as Washington, just to kill injuns. Legend has it that he was so angry when they named the Dawson River after "that fool from the Bureau of Indian Affairs," instead of him, that he made his own political statement. On the day they held the commemoration picnic on the riverbank in Cross Creek, he went upstream, killed a band of indians, chopped up their bodies, men women and children, and sent them down the river on rafts he lashed together. It left quite an impression on the revelers at lunchtime. The Lizard Ranch sat near the top of Caldwell Buttes, from which you could see the ocean, 40 miles away. The property was part of a section that had been logged in the 50's, subdivided in the 60's and purchased by a family in the 70's. Hoping to get away from the rat race and live the country life, they built the cabin and the groovy Yellow Submarine painted shitter that stood near the lake. They had gotten into their family squabbles and headed for divorce one year. The husband decided he should winter up at the cabin, got snowed in, and ended up eating cat food for a month. After that he was never the same. His wife leased the place to a couple guys who tried to grow dope a few years before Stymie bought it, but one of them had gotten whacked out from living there too. Maybe it was the old dead Indian energy, but something made people go crazy up there, and apparently, it wasn't LSD.

I began working as a laborer, which was a good change of pace. Stymie bought a load of cedar siding that we paneled the exterior with. Ben came up to help and I learned a bunch about construction from him and Manny. I became a regular caulk bead expert. The place looked great when we were done, but it had been somewhat contentious with Bernard. He had put up his share to build the shed, which he wanted for drying, but Stymie and Mulehorn wanted to give him the old cabin, since he and Katrina already lived there. He wasn't paying for any of the improvements, but he liked to feel cheated, so he bugged them about it. When they would have their meetings I was asked to leave, since I was just a flunky of sorts, but Stymie would usually fill me in on the tenor of the situation. They had decided to grow separately that year, since the last year's split had caused some haranguing by Bernard about the superior quality of his effort, and the idea that he should receive a bigger cut. So Bernard grew with Katrina, Mulehorn grew with Ben, who helped prep everything for planting before returning to town, and Stymie grew with

Manny. I just did whatever was necessary, working all day on the cabin myself, or watering the patches they showed me. Near the shed there were the upper and lower patches, which sat in small cut out terraces down toward the creek. Across the road and way the hell down the ravine was the Armageddon. It was named for the end of the world task of hauling all the shit down there. There was the Gumby, the Lizard, and the plants up on Tweak Peak, where Manny also grew a few of his own. All in all it was 30-35 plants, but they were in full sun, so they expected a pound off each of them.

I began to sense the rhythm of the land. The oaks had filled in, the grasses were up, the wild flowers were blooming. There were beautiful wild irises everywhere, and little orange and red things, acting as wake up calls for the bees. Firs dominated, but the scrubby tan and white oaks filled in, and you could see the forest progression where the young fir groves made their way under the old oaks, and vice versa. The lake provided for several ducks, endlessly croaking frogs, and occasional geese on their migratory stopovers. The ranch was home to deer, porcupines, rabbits, squirrels, snakes, lizards, they called the place the Lizard Ranch for its preponderance of native species. The Blue-tailed skinks were amazing to see, their electric cobalt tails glinting as if you had dosed. Hawks commanded the air, while buzzards laid claim to the fallen. Woodpeckers drilled homes in the trees, where owls held the night sentry. To walk out in the meadow at the new moon was to see black like Mammoth Cave when they turn the lights out, except for the billion stars and dust trails of the Milky Way. You could see stars in Roseville, but not like this, and after a couple years of bloody red sunsets of fantastic LA, all my perceptual faculties were getting scrubbed clean.

I'd hike to the spring to get water, carrying a couple five-gallon jugs down the road to the old iron pipe sticking out of the hill. It was the cleanest, tastiest water I'd ever had, straight out of the earth. Sometimes I'd go down there just to drink straight from the pipe. It seems weird at first, drinking water out of the earth! Until you realize that that's where water comes from, and that you have a completely clean source, your civilized stupidity can really get the better of you. I was taking my turn at the two-burner propane stove to make spaghetti or chili a couple times a week, becoming a regular fixture. I began to meet the neighbors, who I had simply nodded to the previous fall, but were the denizens of the community in which I was now living.

The main guy was Dan, Danny Wine, the Cowboy. He had discovered this mountain years ago and directed all these guys to it. He was one of the original Freak Brothers, from the seminal weed ranch in Garberville. He had sold pot to Stymie for years, before breaking out of the Freak Brothers' ranch and moving up here with his wife, Lidya, the tattooed lady. Lidya was as hard core as she was beautiful, and she was beautiful. She had long, curly brown hair, falling about her smooth high-cheekboned face. Her crystal blue eyes shone with an intelligence that became obvious whenever she sat behind her piano or broke out a guitar, melding her dexterity with her songbird voice. She was the first woman I ever saw with a ring in her nose, a stud actually, but it belonged there. When she wasn't on her horse she was barefoot, in the dirt, growing things or having sex with her man. She was a wild woman of Humboldt County, running away from Haight Ashbury in her step van and landing it in Panther Gap, where everyone was wild. No one thought she'd ever marry, but Dan was about as tough as saddle leather hisself, and the two of them were quite a couple. To make up for being married, Lidya liked to fight, men, and she did pretty damn good, unless she was too drunk, and Dan would have to carry her home. Dan had run away too, from New Jersey, at 16. He met up with Taco Sauce and Beetle in LA, and together they decided to get back to nature and head up to Humboldt. By the time I met him he'd read every Louis L'Amour book and lived like a Sackett with a spool of bailing wire. He could start a fire by cussing at a wet piece of wood, fix a fuel injected Ferrari with a toothbrush and tweezers, and shoot a bear dead between the eyes and kill it with a pea shooter. He had two other partners on Hobo Camp, which is what he called the pond property down the hill.

Hoss was a good ole boy from down Mississippi somewhere that D&L met at the fiddle fest in Weezer. Grunt was, well, his name says a lot. I liked to believe that it was some sort of combination of the words "get" and "drunk," but it was a term as definitive of his character as anything else. Like Dan, Grunt had been through the wild years in Garberville, before anybody figured out how to grow pot, when they'd get all tanked on cheap wine, build bonfires and walk through 'em. "Fire walkin; fire talkin; burn the midnight oil." Grunt's fame was having fallen into the fire and not gotten out. Over the years I have seen a few people fall into the fire, but no one had the marks to prove it like Grunt. After I got to know him pretty well I quit calling him Grunt, and simply referred to him as "Uuuuuunnhh!!!" Down next to the pond property was Hector, who had been involved in the breeding of Hindu Kush and Mazar-al Sharif plants into the fabulous Heinz strain. Way off down the hill were the Tree People, who planted tens of thousands of trees in Panther Gap after the great forest fire took everything out in '77. They were serious back-to-earthers, who walked everywhere, which is why you never saw them. Other than that there were just the "Rocky fellers." Rocky had moved up from San Diego and brought up a huge crew to build his empire. His brother had a place and so did their friend, each one with a crew of guys trying to grow 300-400 plants. "Gotta make a million." I guess coming from San Diego you get used to seeing those truckloads of Mexican and think you can just do it yourself.

The days went on and I grew used to the country life. Our country life, that is. Wake up around 8:30, water some plants, have breakfast, get stoned, start work, at lunch have a peanut butter sandwich and a Pepsi, smoke a joint, go back to work, smoke a joint at sunset while the sky turns pink and green and purple, have dinner, get high, and maybe play a game of Acquire. Acquire is a bookshelf game that those guys had found scintillating. The board is a grid, 1-A through 12-I. You get a set of tiles and some cash, with the purpose of forming and merging hotel chains, crashing your buddy's and profiteering from your own. We changed some rules to suit our capitalistic tendencies, but the best change was playing for whippets. Every time you started a company or made a merger you got a whippet, but you had to do it before you bought stock, so you'd be more confused. It was Acquire that Dave was screaming about at that first Greek, I guess there's just something archetypal about it. Our goal was to one day have the real cash game, which would require everyone to put up 10 or 20 thousand, just for fun of course, but big fun.

You couldn't get enough cash to play real money Acquire by sitting around, though. Even growing dope was unlikely to make you a million-aire. It's a long term investment, March through November, to find out what your return is, and it's fraught with risk. The continuous influx of cash, or return on investment, is what makes dealing so attractive, and necessary, when you're carrying on other cash intensive projects, like building a house. We decided to head down to town to see some Dead shows, since it was possible to take breaks with things in place, and, our regular connections notwithstanding, the Dead was the hub of the drug dealing industry. Stymie had a pretty solid network in town, and I was building one, but having four or five thousand people craving dope in one focused area is definitely good for business.

I was working my way into Stymie's trust, not that I hadn't always had it, but I was working directly with him now, so he knew me better. Having sold off his entire weed crop from the prior year, he needed to score some more on the way down. We pulled off in Redway, the town adjacent to Garberville, the Western gateway to bud. The Briceland road weaves out of Redway past the Eel River, and on through the town it was named for to the ocean at Shelter Cove. As roads do in the country, it breaks down in slides, threatening those who abuse the one lane sections with death, or worse, no truck. (As the old cowboys say, "Taint nothin lower than bein left afoot.") Every cut away from it leads to some terrifying road up a ridge, but the one we finally turned on wasn't too bad. It led off to a valley where the growers had been prosperous enough to keep it maintained. It was fairly steep though, so in the freshly graveled sections you could spin out and slide backward, which is never a pleasing thought. When we crested the hill we passed a small cemetery of old dead rigs, turned right, and went straight down a driveway that appeared to have been cut by people getting their cars stuck in the mud at distances progressively further down the hill. At the one point wide enough to fit two cars, an old green step van had been retired. It still acted as an altar to the wild parties that had taken place in it, both while stationary and on the road. Coming to the bottom we parked and walked over to a handsome A frame cabin, the dwelling of the Freak Brothers.

The Freak Brothers had earned their ranch name by getting kicked out of a party at the Fuck Up's ranch, who told them, "Go get your own ranch, you freaky bastards." They had been many since Danny Wine, Taco Sauce, and Beetle formed it, but of them all only those two remained. TS and Beetle earned their nicknames for their early culinary developments. When they had all been living in tents, "and loving every minute of it," Taco Sauce had scored a case of his namesake at the Canned Food Store for cheap, and used it as his sole flavoring agent. Beetle had been something of a naturalist, and after reading up on protein sources of jungle natives, he decided to experiment with the local fare. They don't call it "back to nature" for nothing. Far more than being a couple of freaks, these two were hard core entrepreneurial businessmen. Long Island Jews who knew their way around the New York garment district, they could have been stock traders if they had been assigned to a duller life. They knew everybody in these woods, and had the clout that goes with a dignified corporate name such as the Freak Brothers.

I was a little nervous about meeting them, since they were pretty much at the pinnacle of dealing, unless you got into some bullshit industrial drugs, which I had never wanted. Of course, they were totally cool. They went off into the woods for awhile, returning with several buckets. They dumped them all out, keeping items separate by grower and price, and allowed us to peruse their wares. We wrangled up ten pounds of the finest weed available, after which they got out their triple beam and weighed every bag, all of which were over. It was the ethic in those days to throw in some extra bud for good measure, to counteract drying or merely to serve as a bonus. It was part of the job to have memorized the gram weights of every different kind of bag, ziplocs, garbage, and eventually turkey and freezer bags, which also differed by brand, so you could accurately weigh everything without dumping it out. We counted out the cash, the pounds going for a fraction of today's market rate. The Freaks were the friendliest most professional people you could ever want to do business with, and by being with Stymie I had immediately been accepted as one of the same. We puffed one to seal the deal, shook hands, and got back on the road, which in May was not so much of a problem. Neither mud nor the pigs (who wallow in it) were affecting the road.

6

The Dead played the Greek again that weekend, and I made several new connections. Bernard, in a move I've never understood, walked up to me and told me that I needed to meet this guy, Hogarth. We were practically standing next to each other, so it didn't take much. I had been hearing about him from various people, and vice versa. I'm glad Bernard never asked for a cut, because old Hogarth rolled out some pounds for me over the years. He also introduced me to a couple folks that were deep in the taping scene, so I began to deliver qps and run off tapes of the shows. I was always looking around for bottles, since I had determined that liquid was the cleanest way to get LSD, which I had a ready market for in Barrington. I could always go back to the gels, and I knew all of BT's people, so I could get Scrubbing Bubbles or whatever their hit du jour was, but it all seemed weak and funky. Those guys scored me bottles that were pretty fuckin good, and introduced me to Jan, who made them. He was an intense character, a serious vegan type, who only dealt with the purest quality product. His acid was always super clean; made from white separated crystal, it glowed bright under the blacklight. He was the only person who still went to the trouble of dealing liquid, which needed more care due to its unstable nature. He checked me out pretty hard, not wanting any fuckups in his scene, but I wasn't dosed at the time, so my stable exterior made me seem worthy. I also had the killer bud he craved, so it looked good on both ends. I took a few hundred hits to Luigi, in one-drop breath freshener bottles, and he quite happily fed them into Barrington.

Things were going well enough that Luigi and I and our girlfriends decided to go back east on tour. They were all from there, so they had people to see, and I figured I could just roll on tour. I brought only the finest seal-a-mealed stashes with me, stuff I had left from trimming and other collectibles I'd run into over the year. I didn't want to travel with very much weed, it wasn't in my game plan to be dealing on tour. I could take care of a couple friends, but no Turkish prison for me. We flew to NY and got a bus down to Maryland for the show. We had a stopover in DC that amazed me. We pulled off the freeway and onto some road that led through this gnarly ghetto. It was all old two-story houses, stilted up with stairways to the big porches where dozens of black folks were sitting around. It went on like this for what seemed like miles, depressed vacant poor people with nothing to do. Suddenly we came upon the station, and we were a straight shot to the Capitol. We could see all of the glory of our nation, glowing like a beacon of celebratory architecture that somehow ignored the fact that a swamp of poverty and despair surrounded it. Never let anyone tell you that Dead tour wasn't educational.

The bus dropped us off somewhere down the road from the Merriweather Post Pavilion, but we were still pretty early. There wasn't much of a crowd, since it was a reserve seat show, so the best we could do was stake a place on the lawn. The sky was getting pretty black though, so I was glad to be early because it allowed me to strip out some still clean garbage can liners to put all our stuff in. By the time the show started it was raining pretty hard, and it didn't stop. It was one of those rains that beat your face so hard you could barely keep your eyes open to watch the band. It came on harder than Red Rocks, and by the time the second set started everything was flooding. The center of the lawn, for about twenty yards across, had turned completely into mud. It was there that I began to realize what it meant to be "on tour."

Everyone perceives every show through their own filter of experience, gauging the brilliance or dullness of the performance according to their dose, and whatever other factors come into play, but I had never come close to understanding "Truckin," until that show. Soaked to the bone, miles from home, no ride, nowhere to hide, you damn sure better be high! They were blowing it out, and all you could do was surrender to it. We started jumping up and down in the mud, kickin it twenty feet up in the air and screaming, cuz we were in the heart of the tour now. Some guy got the bright idea to start sliding in the mud and we torched the whole center of the lawn section by running from the top and belly sliding all the way downhill. It was fantastically liberating!

As luck would have it we ran into Natalie, who had moved back to Pennsylvania and thought we could get a ride with her. The problem was that the whole place had flooded. The bridge that you crossed to get into the show was out, so everyone had to follow a line of cops with flares over the hills and around. Never the kind of thing you want to do on acid, I'd sooner have taken my chances in the creek with our bale of stuff. The parking lot was a lake, but we managed to cram nine people and our gear into someone's mom's Chevy and head out down the road. We got on some highway and began looking for a motel. There were no vacancies for twenty-five miles, but we finally found a place. I had cash, so I got them to drive around the back while I registered. We tried to be mellow, but it wasn't long before the manager came around to find that we were grossly exceeding his occupancy limit, and kicked us back into the black, wet night. We ended up driving to this guy's parent's house another hour away. I was stunned when his mother took us in at three in the morning, bringing down fresh towels so we could all shower.

I met Jan at the next show there, and sold him the ounce I had brought with me. He couldn't believe that was all I had, since there was a killing to be made in California weed, and thought it sort of silly of me, given the nature of his business, to be that paranoid about it. I still thought it was smarter to be less bustable than more wealthy. 10,000 hits you could carry on your person, without any kind of sign, but you could smell my bud a mile away. You never knew who was sniffing around, either. Slag told me that he had thrown an ounce of coke into the lake at the Saratoga show because he was so dosed he thought the feds were on to him. As far as anyone knew, the feds were anywhere and everywhere on tour. The word Fed eventually entered the vernacular as a description of anyone who was not cool, but at the time, nothing was as uncool as a Federal Agent. One thing about Jan though, he did run a pretty respectable scene. I had begun to figure out how the whole acid market worked, but he clued me in to a few of the more degrading aspects.

Acid making is a major bust, so to minimize the risk, the main guys would employ mules to cart the product around for them. This is pretty standard in criminal enterprises, but the only people who won't get busted with a bunch of acid are kids. Dead tour is rife with runaway teenagers, or kids whose parents are heads that don't mind them running off with someone else. The big dealers, BT and Mex, the only one's I knew personally, and rather peripherally at that, would coax these kids into hanging out with their extended family by giving them tix, drugs, meals, hotel rooms, whatever. They'd set them up with D5s so they could tape the shows, thus establishing them in the trip while gaining access to more clients. I'm sure it was an exciting deal for the kids, the ones I knew thought it was. They had tapes, trips, blow, dope, sex maybe, and no parents. They also dealt thousands of hits. Who could ask for more? It was a funny business. It reminded me of selling seeds in that they'd earn prizes for selling the most product. Slag had the original artwork from the Scrubbing Bubbles in the funky dive apartment he shared with Monkey in Berkeley. He probably moved a hundred thousand of those hits to get that. Sure, I was selling acid too, hundreds here and there, but nothing like the volume these guys were into, and they were mostly under 18. This is not to say that they weren't smart. I've met a lot of people who were too smart to bore themselves through school and chucked it for a self-made life. But when I think about how out of it I got, I wonder what delusions a fifteen-year-old who's carrying grams of crystal on tour suffers from.

After the City Island show, where the band was literally backdropped by the Three Mile Island nuclear plant, tour got kinda hairy, so I decided to hitchhike back. My first day I got picked up by an Ohio State Trooper, the kind with the funny hat. "Boy," he says to me, "the last guy we found out here hitchhiking got picked up by three crazies on the turnpike who left him with a screwdriver stuck in his neck." I wasn't quite sure how they determined he had been hitchhiking, they probably just thought that was a good way of explaining his death as a "victimless crime," so I decided not to argue. He pulled into a rest area and went on,

"If you get back on the turnpike, I'm gonna arrest ya, if you ask anybody for a ride, I'm gonna arrest ya, you're not carrying any drugs with you are ya?"

"No officer."

"Good, otherwise I'd have to search your pack and arrest ya. Now you call your folks and have 'em wire you some money so you can get the bus"

"Yes sir, thank you sir." Of course, there was no Western Union there, and the busses didn't stop at rest areas, so I hitched out with a guy wearing a Yale Ultimate Frisbee Team shirt, who I figured was safe.

He dropped me off near Chicago, where I had some breakfast at Denny's, went to the bathroom, and was entertained by the local graffiti. "Kill the niggermayor," the wall boldly exclaimed, only to be rebutted by "I kill me a honkie, I feel good all day." Hmmm, I thought, what a fun town. I managed to hitch from Denny's to the south side of Chicago with a very friendly black man. We got into talking about drugs, since I was getting pretty rastad out by then, and he told me about his fear of LSD. "Makes you crazy n'shit." Despite my problems with it, I had to disagree, and was rather shocked by his admission that he did occasionally enjoy PCP, which he found pleasantly euphoric. "Different Strokes..." At least we both dug weed. He dropped me at the train station, where I caught one into town. There weren't too many people on the train, so I didn't really pay much attention to the fact that I was only white guy on it. Taking the bus down to the lake, since my father had always told me to go to the Museum of Science and Industry, was more consciousness raising. The bus was packed, so it was impossible to ignore the fact that I was the only white guy on it, a freaky white guy no less, with dreads and a full pack. I was not spared this acknowledgment by the ten-year-old girl sitting across from me, who turned to ask me disdainfully,

"What the fuck you doin on the bus, white boy?"

"I really don't know myself," I had to tell her. Things seemed pretty bleak there, in the sweltering Windy City, so I caught the Greyhound back home, fortunately escaping the massive LSD sweep the feds pulled at the shows there that weekend.

7

I headed back to the ranch and began paneling the interior of the shed with redwood that Stymie bought, trying to match the grain from one panel to the next, and hammer lightly enough not to leave telltale dents in the soft wood. It was very aesthetically pleasing work, creating a psychedelic continuum from the wavy marbling of the grain, bringing warmth to the whole interior. Dealing was a trade I was proud of, and good at, but even when you select the best buds for yourself, they all get smoked. You may have grown the most amazing bud, and gotten thousands of people high, but it becomes a memory, or what's left of a memory when your memory's shot. The Deadhead shed and it's graffiti etched shitter are still standing though, a monument to the dope dollar and the stream of consciousness of the moment. Of course, as is the case throughout the Humboldt woods, and most of the expansive rural areas of America, the old junked cars you left will probably remain longer that anything you built yourself.

Mulehorn bought himself a three-wheeler that spring, since the Big Red was becoming the must-have item in Humboldt County. He would drive me around on the back of it, which was no less dangerous than being on the front. Three wheelers had the amazing steering mechanism of needing to slide. You could point the front wheel, but you had to slide the back to make the turn. There was no leaning, and God forbid you should put your foot down. The natural inclination on any kind of bike is to put your foot down for stability when you turn. The first time I rode on the back of that thing we went down Deadhead hill, the insanely steep section that heads down from Lizard to Hobo Camp. Being as steep as it was, it had acquired some huge ruts from the downhill neighbors spinning out endlessly in their attempts to ascend it and escape the mountain. We were bouncing down through the ruts, heading into a turn, when I put my foot down. No sooner than I made contact the huge knobby back tire grabbed the heel of my boot and began its ascent of my leg. There was certainly no reaction I could have made, even if there was time before the wheel ate up my leg, to avoid the startling chain of events. I was dragged down crotchwise under the bike, as it mistook me for the road. I sort of did a sideways splits until I was down on the ground and the fucking thing rode all the way up my ass and over my back. It tore my pants apart at the seam, leaving me dangling in a provocative manner. Oddly enough, it didn't hurt too badly, so I hopped back on and we motored off, wiser for the experience.

I eventually conned Horn into letting me tear off on the thing alone, which is how I discovered the real drawback of sliding to steer. I came around the curve into our meadow a little fast, it was dusty and the road leaned away on the outside. I couldn't corner by steering and flew off the road. I landed on my back, which seemed okay until I looked up, and saw the 300 pounds of vehicle following directly in my path, airborne. I was able to kick my feet up just in time to catch the pedals, grab the handle-bars, squat it and spring it off of me, but not before it broke a couple of my ribs. I denied it at the time, getting right back on and riding until I felt like I was gonna die, causing me to take up residence in the big black chair for about three days. After that I pretty much had a handle on it. I only put my foot down another couple of times.

After a few months my decision to grow dreadlocks had caught up with me. They had gotten to be a few inches long, long enough to fall right into my eyes. They weren't long enough to tie back in any way, and while I suppose I could have worn a hat, it wasn't my style. Besides, the only baseball cap I'd ever had, a Grateful Dead minstrel hat, burned up in the fire. It seemed irreplaceable. So my hair was in my eyes, all the time. It became a Zen exercise of sorts, to do everything with big fuzzy knots of hair hanging in my face. Learning to see through them, or around them, so I could have a conversation, was an interesting task. I persevered until they got down to my nose, at which point I could flip them up on top of my head. Of course, if I wanted to ignore the world, I could just hang them in my face like Cousin It. The neighbors loved it. "Hey look, it's Matt Head, the welcome mat." But I could hold my own with those boys, smokin, drinkin, wrasslin in the dirt, I was game for it all. There were enough trees I could usually hike off to take a piss if I needed to, so that wasn't too much of a problem. Living in the woods just allowed me to be the big kid I always wanted to be. Ben had left this BMX bike up there, it was too small for him, which made it way too small for me, but I used to love taking it to the top of the driveway, bombing down the hill and jumping the berm at the bottom. It made for awesome wipe-outs, since it was hard to control a bike that small, but I loved crashing. One of the great things about being in the dirt was that you could crash, get up, and do it all over again.

The summer was back and forth like that, up to the ranch, down to some shows, hang out with Eileen in Barrington, sell some pounds.

Whenever there was a set of shows in California, we went, and as it was, I always had to dose for at least one show out of a set, and things sort of maintained their weirdness when I did. Other than that, things were swell. Eileen moved into a single room that fall, so I moved in with her when I wasn't on the ranch. Dave had gotten very political after his episodes, (the transformative effects of psychedelics and all,) and he started disappearing to anti-nuclear protests. I took up the remainder of the clients, hiking bud across town, meeting people at their houses or in cars at bus stops or parks. I'd keep my weed stashed under Eileen's dirty clothes pile, which was usually fairly large, or in her closet. I wasn't too worried about rip-offs, since I kept it cool in my dealing. I'm sure a few people I didn't want to know knew what I was up to, but I wasn't doing deals downstairs or with anyone I didn't trust. I would disappear to Humboldt intermittently too, so I wasn't always apparent.

I had my 21st birthday up at the ranch. We had a little Q down at the Hobo Camp, me and Stymie, Mulehorn, D&L, and Hoss and Grunt. I pledged that I would drink no more alcohol, now that it was legal for me to do so, but that didn't last. The pond was nice, it was deeper than our lake and had fewer waterweeds, so you could see a little. It also had a little dock you could dive off. You could snorkel around into the reeds hunting frogs until a crawdad bit you. Grunt had his funky shed up a little loop driveway from there, and D&L had a cabin across the meadow right on the ridgeline. They weren't living there anymore, since they had bought the property at the bottom of the mountain, Sherwood, with Stymie and Bernard as partners. They liked the pond though, from the meadow next to it you could see the sun setting over the valley below Bell Mountain. It was as calm a birthday as I'd had in years, but that was okay, I didn't feel a whole lot of need to have a persona with these folks. They'd be breaking my balls no matter who I was, so I might as well just be me, having fun.

That fall's trimming season wasn't quite as intense as the year before, since the production had been split up. Most of Stymie's plants were at least a pound, he had the dopemaster touch. Mulehorn's plants, on the other hand, were always scrawny and suffering, owing to the fact he had been a botany major at Cal, and was using scientific precepts in what was an otherwise completely raw environment. Each plant was tagged with its owners tag, to avoid confusion about who trimmed what, but when they had finished packing the place with weed, it was hard to find the tags in the sea of green. Bernard had his usual level of harangue going on, but it was survivable. Art came up that year, he had moved back to Barrington as a crasher. Dave even showed up for awhile, which made for extreme Acquire festing. I was pretty thrilled about getting to help pick the weed, which was an event in itself, although '83 was not as good a year as '82. I eventually likened weedgrowing to the wine business. There are good years and there are bad years. Late frosts, rain, fog, any number of climactic and weather conditions could affect your crop. The weed was still pretty good, but not like the year before. Stymie did okay though, and he got a cut from the cowboy's work on Sherwood, so he made sure I was on a good footing when we went back to town.

The one memorable thing about that trimming season was that Bob Weir played a show with his band, the Midnights, at the bowling alley in Garberville. I had seen him play solo when I was at UCLA, and I must admit, I was something of a Bob head. As much of a glamour boy as he was, he did have songs about stealing women and being an insane visionary. I particularly liked one Merle Haggard cowboy song he played, Big Iron. It generally gave room for some crackling solos by his lead guitarist, Bobby Cochran. Actually, the band members were all quite talented. The band was one thing, but the fact was that everyone there was in the middle of trimming made it better than a Dead show. I was standing there with Stymie and Horn and the Freaks and Grunt, and four or five other guys I'd never met, when Stymie whips out a bud.

"Try this!" he exclaimed. Every guy in the circle followed suit.

"Well check this out."

"Puff."

"Smoke it and know it." Every time you lit a joint the guy next to you would too, it was a tasting extravaganza. Sometimes it's nice to take a breath between hits, but that just wasn't happening. It was all hit, pass, hit, pass, hit. Somehow I had enough throat left (I think my throat was more durable in my youth) to get up front and scream "Big Iron!" incessantly. They had played for a pretty long time before Bobby declaimed, "I'd like to dedicate this song to all the gays in the audience, because it's becoming more apparent." Then they launched into a ripping version of it, during which Bob's gestures alluded to the idea that the sheriff's big iron was between his hips rather than on the side. The typically paranoid side of me wanted to jump up on stage and scream at him, "Who are you callin a fag?" since I was high enough to take this as personally directed. Everyone knew that Bob was whatever Bob was, but I didn't think that just because I was enjoying the rugged life of men growing weed, that he should be casting aspersions. (Touchy!)

Maybe it was my own distorted sense of what relationship was or should be, but my deal with Eileen didn't make it any easier for me to feel defined. I wasn't really "in love" with her, although I felt that I did love her in that universal sense. We did abuse each other pretty heavily, verbally and emotionally, but somehow I still trusted her. She was the only person who had an inkling of what I had come through, seen me at my most tweaked, and didn't tell anyone about it. I think that she knew how afraid I was of exposing myself, and that kind of kept me her prisoner. As the fall quarter began, I felt sort of trapped by the fact that I was living with her while dozens of fresh faced hippie babes roamed the halls of Barrington. It seemed that everyone there was fucking everyone else, either in stints or short-term relationships. I didn't really want to blow my scene though, not with my pounds stashed in Eileen's closet and nowhere to go if she kicked me out. It's difficult to find a safe place to rent when you're a drop-into-town-dope-dealer. I really wanted to jam on the girls across the hall, a menage with the delicate Fred Burrhead and her punk roommate Manimal would have been thrilling, but I couldn't see asking them to let me move into their room. I got used to passing up some thrilling ideas to purportedly live others, which is not to say that I wasn't conflicted much of the time, but that certain fears got the best of me. I grudgingly rationalized my inability to be as free as I'd have liked as an expense of my work.

I spent most of that winter at the B, since some other people had come on line that year. I occasionally sold to Pete Reiner, the insane coke fiend, who was actually a very nice intelligent guy, when he wasn't tweaking. Oblio was the new kid, a transfer from some JC in LA, who was a little older than the rest of us. He had that sort of innocent quality of the kid from The Point, which earned him his nickname. Oblio's father was purportedly one of those bible thumping missionaries, who had him out selling the word and the book for most of his youth. Having grown up with Stripe, though, who had introduced Bernard to dealing, Oblio was certainly ripe to join the cynical establishment of proto-hippies at Barrington. He had probably never smoked pot before he got there, but was smart enough to recognize a market that would pay for his attraction to thick books.

Stymie was working with Ben to try to buy a house in town. Ben had been renting a pretty cool house for years, but Stymie had to float around whenever he came to town. He moved in with Bagel for the winter, in a place off University Avenue, but was itching to get his own digs. He called me up one day and told me to come over to discuss something.

"Dude, I'm out of weed and I'm supposed to be looking at property with the Realtor tomorrow. You think you could drive my truck up to the Freaks' and score ten pounds for me?" I probably busted a seam jumping out of my chair,

"Do I ever, gimme the keys!"

"It'd help if you drove a little mellower than you're acting right now."

"Okay, okay, I'll be cool."

"Yeah, well don't hurt yourself trying. Come over tomorrow morning early and pick up the truck." I was thrilled. This was about as much responsibility as I had ever undertaken. I was gonna be handed twenty thousand dollars and the keys, with a serious professional assignment to complete, what I was born for.

I got up early, for us, at around eight, and walked over to Stymie's. "Okay, if they haven't got enough of the good, just buy what good they have. Don't get anything funky. Look out for weed in white bags, there's always a ton of shake at the bottom. Weigh them all. Count this." He handed me a wad of stacks of 20-dollar bills, for the most part. They were rubber banded into thousands, fifty 20s, ten hundreds, or some odd number of hundreds, fifties, tens and twenties. I counted them as smoothly and surely as I had my own piles, knowing that I had a need for this skill. I took the keys, fired up the Toyota, flashed an Onnggh Yaaangh back at Stymie and headed down University for the freeway. I made my way across the blight of Richmond, over the bridge to Marin, and was sailing into the country. I drove nonstop until I got to Laytonville, where I had to gas up and get a Pepsi at the Park and Take It deli store. Then I drove the rest of the way to Redway, and out to the ridge. The road was still a washboard, and the rain had made it a muddy one, but at least it kept the dust down. I felt a little nervous as I headed down into the Freak's driveway, toward the biggest dope deal I had ever imagined. I got down to the cabin and TS was waiting for me with Beetle.

We joked around for a minute and they went off to fetch their loads. When they got back I was in heaven, cracking open bud and sniffing it, inspecting to see if there had been any trace of mold, (which is identifiable by softness and browning of the stems) going through my professional agenda. There were a few cheapers, some which seemed worthwhile and others that didn't fit our product criteria, so I bought everything that looked right and scaled it out while they counted.

"Hey, this pile's off twenty," Taco Sauce told me.

"No way, I counted them all, try it again." He recounted it and came up right,

"Hey Shel, you're okay." I couldn't help but grin. "Oh, and those red bud bags weigh 14.2 grams," he went on.

"Damn! I thought I had some serious overage here."

"Yeah, well, it was a tough year." Meanwhile, it had begun raining again, and it doesn't simply rain in these parts, it dumps.

"You better get out of here while you can" Beetle told me, so I thanked them both, loaded up my duffel and hopped in the truck. Their driveway had a sort of ledge that dropped you onto the inhabitable part of the property. It was just about impassible in normal conditions. You had to run your truck up it and keep going. I went up, spun out, and slid back down, went up, spun out, and slid back down. The truth was, I hadn't much dirt driving experience. I burned hell out of the driveway, hit the ledge, squealed it up into the next set of ruts, swung right, left, right, slammed into the hill, grabbed traction and dug it up to the next patch of gravel where I got enough speed up to slog through all the mud that was in my way. There were a couple more hairy spots toward the top, but I got over them, and I screamed like a fucking rodeo redneck when I got on to the main road. Weeeehaa!

It was an adventurous way to make a grand, since Stymie paid me $100 for every pound. I bought an old Datsun 510 from one of his motorhead high school buddies, who was now the weed guy for their home town. It was certainly a step up from walking around town, and it gave me the flexibility to move into winter residence with Stymie, Manny, and Dr. Space in a house they found up in the hills. I was pretty into breakfasting on wheat grass and carrot juice on Telegraph Avenue while living at Barrington, but Dr. Space was so health oriented he had his own lawns. He was always pounding down some Chinese herbs or elixir or ginseng or royal jelly or Zumbaforte to keep himself jacked up. He was totally into chiropractic, popping every vertebra in his body on a moment to moment basis. The guy was pretty tuned into the subtle energies of the universe—for someone who seemed to be completely off the planet most of the time. The rap on Doc was that he came from a wealthy East Coast family, and was a total highbrain to begin with. Hanging out at Barrington and dealing acid though, he developed a passion for inconceivably huge doses. He would drink an entire bottle of liquid before going to class. 100 hits! They say he held lively discourses with his professors, which I believe. "Could you watch my stuff for a few days, I'm going to Egypt," he once told Bagel, before popping the top off a bot and tossing it back. He was a pretty intelligent guy, but he was definitely operating on a slightly different plane. I thought about trying the 100 hit dose myself, to see where I'd end up, but I figured I was tweaked out enough in my own way already.

Christmas rolled by and the shows came again, but now they were moving to the SF Civic Center, which had a much more sterile quality than the Oakland Auditorium. Jerry had started getting pretty puffy, enough so that Bagel had taken to abusing him mercilessly with screams of "Slim-Fast Jerry! Metri-cal Jerry! Break Dance Jerry!" and shit like that. I went to Original Joe's before the show, which Bagel had always recommended as the place to eat a dosed burger before the show. It was a heathen experience, but I ordered a loaf of their gnarly garlic bread to go, and hurled it up to Jerry as a health recommendation. I figured it as a Stinking Rose bouquet, a compliment to all those regular roses people were constantly throwing at him. Before they came out at midnight they played a movie. The hall went dark and all of the sudden there were cop lights and sirens everywhere. The film started with a bunch of cop cars pulling up into an alley, blue lights flashing, scary enough to make the whole audience jump back. The chief got out, walked up, staring down at us through his cop shades, and said, "We've had our eyes on you for a long time, but now it's 1984, and your going to have to start looking after yourselves!" Those boys did have a sense of humor.

We went back to Barrington to party after the show, but Luigi had a 6 A.M. flight back to Boston. We were still tripping, but getting onto that late stage exhaustion. I rolled a gigantic bridge doobie, to uphold the tradition of smoking a joint when crossing water. It was some super sugar puff weed, and we were instantly tripping full bore again. I decided that it would be best to drive through the semi-trucks that were appearing to cross the bridge perpendicularly in front of me, which turned out to be smarter than trying to swerve out of the way. Despite my various hallucinations, we made it to the airport, and Chanukah-like, that reefer burned the whole way there!

9

Ben had stumbled onto a new connection that winter that started to change everything. The indoor guy was growing up in Oregon somewhere, in a totally professional setup. He had the buried generator feeding an underground room in a semi-rural house where no one was the wiser. He had gotten Northern Lights seeds from the Seed Bank, and was growing a 20 pound batch every few months under 1000 watt halides. I remember seeing the first load, it came in square 5-gallon buckets sealed with duct tape. The bags were all pressed flat, square in conformity with the bucket, making the bud look like a solid sheet. They didn't have their drying technique completely down, so the moisture content allowed it to press together. When you broke it apart the bud was sort of oddly stemmy, like it hadn't filled in all the way, but it was covered in shmint. Ridiculously covered in shmint. It was so schminty it looked like it had been dredged in cocaine. Being slightly wet it was hard to burn, and it tasted kind of chemically since it was hydroponic, but it had quite the distinctive buzz. It was as if someone had removed your brain and filled your head with bricks wrapped in cotton. I was not particularly attracted to this feeling, but I knew who would be.

My friends in LA were always hounding me to bring some weed down there, but no one really wanted the responsibility of dealing. I had met some of Bagel's LA friends on tour, so I called them, flew down with a bucket, and "Science Weed" was born. What more could you want in LA? It was perfect for bonging, which was about the only way to burn the shit, so the economic utility was clear, and two hits would totally numb you to the fact that you lived there. Everybody loved it. They were clamoring for it. It was easy for me too, I could just take my sealed bucket in a carry-on duffel bag. I did get stopped at the x-ray machine once though. The security guy looked at the screen and then pointed at my bag,

"What's this?," he asked, switching from bored automaton to quasi-authoritarian. I had packed a bunch of stuff that I hoped would make it look okay, but I really had no idea what he was seeing.

"Books," I said, unzipping my bag to show him.

"No, this," he said, pointing to the bucket, which I had wrapped in my wetsuit.

"That's my wetsuit," I replied nonchalantly.

"No, this!" he clarified, authoritatively smacking the bucket with his fist so that even through my wetsuit it thudded with a density I felt in my chest. I hadn't really expected things to go that far when I packed my bag, and wondered what x-ray images of feathery bud in plastic bags really looked like.

"Uhh, it's my custom windsurfer sail," I tried hopefully. He looked back at his screen,

"Oh. Okay. Have a nice flight."

"Thanks." I waited until I had gotten through the concourse to breathe, but I seemed to be able to. I had a beer and a whiskey as soon as we took off, after which I felt fine. I walked out past security at LAX and was headed to the escalator when a guard yelled out,

"Hey you!" I just kept walking, not wanting to find out if they wanted to talk to me. He ran up behind be, "Hey, stop right there, didn't you hear me?"

"Me, I just came off a flight," I said, looking bewildered.

"The head of security wants you." Fuck! Did they phone ahead to bust me? I thought about jumping down the escalator and into a taxi, but I figured I'd just brass ball it over to the chief.

"Here he is," he said, delivering my perturbed and questioning face to a blue uniformed Filipino woman.

"That's not him, I wanted the guy in the green jacket," she told him, which left me feeling better than if I had run, but still ready to explore different transportation options.

The train was much better, so laissez-faire. I'd just stash my luggage in the bin, and head to the bar car. I went with my buddy Wizard one time, we ended up smoking pot in the bar for half the ride. I think the attendant was nasally challenged by the ever-boiling coffee pot in her cubicle. Maybe she didn't care. There was this high school kid taking the train down from Oregon to visit his older sister in San Diego. He had taken acid for the first time, and was telling us about it.

"Yeah, I got this hit from my friend, it's 10,000 mics." Wiz and I were chuckling, knowing the "this shit's so strong," paradigm.

"Whoa, you must be really high. Try smokin this." It was obvious he wasn't on a Doc dose but it was fun to act like he was. "Wowowow, did-didiid youyouyou seeseesee thatatatat!" There was this old guy in the bar, so we asked him if he minded us smoking pot.

"Nah, I used to smoke reefer when I was your age. I don't anymore, but go ahead. I spent fifty years in the merchant marines, and I'll tell ya something," he went on, "I just went to San Francisco and all the good whores were gone. They used to have good whores there in the, the,"

"The tenderloin?," I interjected.

"Yeah, the tenderloin. Real nice girls. Now they're all beat up lookin. It's depressing."

"Can't argue that, can I get you a beer?"

"Sure, thanks." We went on having a good time until they closed the bar car, forcing us back to our seats, but it was transportation at its most civilized.

I liked taking my forays to LA, I got to go wild with my friends and live out my trip as a professional drug dealer. I'd move most of the weed to my Hollywood guys, then make these intricately designed packages to overnight my money back. I certainly didn't want to be wandering around LA with that kind of cash. A pocketful of weed and my crazy friends, okay. I'd front Kip a qp, to make sure that he and Bam-Bam and Carl could stay high. Fortunately, the Science Weed only came in every few months, so I had plenty of time to recover from being in LA.

10

It was during that winter that Art turned me on to a very valuable book, LSD Psychotherapy. LSD Psychotherapy was the definitive tome, the clinical experience of Stanislav Grof, the world's preeminent LSD researcher, and it gave me some hope for mental recovery. I had begun to worry that I was actually brain damaged. I no longer had any academic pursuits, and didn't feel that I could handle any. I still knew what I knew, and could figure things out, but I was too gelled to read much more than comics. Hanging out with my Barrington friends, who were wading through Lit Crit and politics, made me feel painfully inferior on the intellectual level, a condition that was entirely new to me. With my debilitating paranoid trips, my satanic conspiracy delusions, and my inability to pee, I knew that I needed more than just vocabulary development, I needed some help. I had vaguely considered therapy, but it was clear to me that despite being insane, I was still pretty functional. I didn't need anyone to tell me I was crazy, and I doubted that there were any therapists out there who had ever taken LSD and nitrous. How could anyone possibly understand my mental deviation, even begin to have a dialogue with me, without having experienced that place? I had never heard of Grof before, but he had begun psychiatric assessment of LSD in Prague in 1957, and continued until 1980, when the US government refused all researchers access to LSD. Having already conducted some 10,000 sessions, he seemed to know what he was talking about.

He theorized that LSD promotes recall of the birth experience, which cycles through four stages. The events of these stages vary from universal amniotic consciousness to being crushed to death. A successful trip allows one to move through the stages and integrate the symbolic material that is encountered. An unsuccessful trip may leave a person stuck in one of the four zones. It appeared to me that I was returning again and again to the hell-world level, and having difficulty releasing to a state of ego death. Reading about his experience with patients whose egos were so rigid that they were unresponsive to 2,500 mic injections, I decided that my best chance for positive resolution lay in upping my dosage. It seemed that Dave had gone through some sort of transformation in his LSD overdose, and now he was becoming involved in political action. All I wanted was to be able to forget the bizarre tangent that seemed to overwhelm my consciousness when I was dosed.

There's something about taking acid that reminds me of an episode of the Twilight Zone, the one where the astronauts come back from space and disappear one by one. No one remembers the last one except the guy who's next to go. Since you're in the middle of all of time while your dosed, it seems like the stuff that's in your mind is how the world will be when you come down. I was often worried that I would forget something, like a friend, and that when I got up the next day he'd be gone, with only a glimmer of a recollection. It could happen to anything, your family, your house, your life; if you forgot it, it would no longer exist. And I was never quite sure the next day that I hadn't forgotten something. My hope was that if I could forget my paranoia, forget who I had become, I could somehow come back to who I really was. Of course, there was no getting hold of Dr. Grof, so I had to test this theory on my own.

Barrington used to have wine dinner once every quarter. I think it started in the more innocent days, when drinking cases of wine constituted a party. As Barrington became a stronghold of psychedelia, electric Kool-Aid supplanted the wine as the beverage of choice. I don't recall the theme of that dinner, but acid was budgeted, and I sold them a bottle for the punch, which Luigi made from Tang. He told me it was exactly 100 cups, into which he dumped the whole bottle. Veterans, we each had a couple cups to start things off. It was only about fifteen minutes before I started coming on, hard. I looked around for Luigi, but couldn't find him. I went upstairs and finally tracked him down, but my body was already vibrating.

"Duuude." I was feeling like electric jello.

"Duuude," he mirrored back.

"This acid is more than 100 mics. I think it might be 250," I sputtered, against the stream of synaptic firings.

"I'm frying," he concurred.

"I think we'd better warn everybody." We nodded jerkily in mutual concern, since it was an effort to control our neck muscles. Our eyes were blown open, both from coming on and worry that anyone else had drunk more than one cup. We worked our way downstairs but it was already too late. The ritual had begun. The room was a pounding cacophony of pot beating. Every plate, pan, bowl and tray in the building was being beaten in a primal thunder. We went to the punchbowl but it was less than a quarter full, which meant that more than half the room was on the way out. Nothing to do but join the fray.

I grabbed a pot and started beating, despite the dark overtones my psyche was painting on the scene. My now hypersensitive nervous system was being assaulted by a cacophonous dishware orchestra. It crescendoed and decrescendoed a few times before finally breaking down, after which milling about commenced. I went back to Eileen's room, 107, to get some bud and clear my head, but I was swimming. I really wanted to hang out with Luigi, but I could hardly walk. Eileen found me there, looked at me once and laughed, "You're trippin, huh?" She could read me. She wanted to go upstairs to Mina and Terry's room, but I was too blown away to move. When I finally gathered enough resolve to head upstairs I walked past a group of punks on the stairs. They had obviously dosed, and were having their catharsis.

"I became a punk so I could be myself, and not belong to some fucked-up clique," a scrawny, spike-haired, chain wrapped girl cried.

"I don't want people to hate me just because I look different." It really struck me, in that moment, that everyone was crying for acceptance, no matter how bizarre and frightening they may look, everybody just wanted to fit in. I ascended the stairs, in my favorite purple velvet shirt, my fuzzy safety blanket. I found the girls chatting away delightedly, none of them having imbibed the punch. They decided that I needed decorative accessorization, which came in the form of a tinsel garland wrapped around my head. Looking at myself in the mirror, my dreads and beard melted through the centuries until I saw myself reflected, Jesus, being crowned with thorns.

I guess I wasn't crying blood, so the girls took no notice of my inner panic, as I staggered out into the hall to be scourged. Martyred for the sins of Barrington, how epic. I wandered down to Ruth's room. Rachel's younger sister, who I had fantasized about years before, now lived here too. She wasn't in, but her roommate Derek was. The champion lothario of Barrington, he enjoyed seducing whoever came through its doors, male or female. I think his sexual certainty scared me as much as his gender blurring, since I was often lost behind my haze of fear. To my abject horror, he was lying in bed and watching TV with none other than my brother Dave. They invited me to join them, which was probably harmless, but to my trip it was one more grievous sin for me to atone for. Luigi's door was locked and there was no response, perhaps because he was being molested by Lina Hosenman, the fright of which he recounted to me the next day. I spent some time on the roof, but it was too populated, so I went back down to the AK. The Alternative Kitchen, which was where vegetarian meals were prepared every night, had the most beautiful mural in Barrington. It was The Last Supper, with each of the character's heads a vegetable. Jesus was a carrot, Judas was a beet, the colors were so rich you could just have an epiphany and die there. I spent a long time looking at that mural the first time I took acid, and now it was finally realized, certainly I would be crucified that night.

I went back to 107 and hid. Eileen came in at some point and discovered me.

"There you are, come up and party."

"Mmmmmmnnnnnn."

"Not doing too good?"

"Mmmmnnnn." She took her clothes off and got in bed with me.

"Come here," she said, surrounding me in a mothering way, which she was good at. She seemed to take on a grotesque appearance, but merging with her flesh got me hard anyway. We started making out, and I tried feeling inside her, but it felt like I was probing an alien. When I tried to fuck her, I felt like I was cramming a rock between two other rocks, and it was hurting my dick. We had exchanged crystal necklaces at Christmas, amethyst points with garnets banded to them, pledged to our heart relationship, and to holding on to it. My dick was feeling like that jagged piece of crystal, like it might even snap off. Not being dosed, she was feeling just fine, but it was freaking me out. I got to thinking that she was an alien, trying to suck some jiz out of me, but I couldn't come. After recovering from that I went downstairs to see the band, Spacely Sprockets, playing to a sparse crowd. They weren't very good, and everyone had pretty much left. When they started packing up the lead singer complained, "I've taken plenty of acid, and these people can't handle it." He drank a Dixie cup and before the band could pack up he was crawling on the floor, "I'm looking for my keys," which is where he spent the rest of the night.

I was kind of bummed out the next day, not because I hadn't been crucified, but because I hadn't even seen Luigi, who it was my intention to trip with. As was his habit, he arrived in our bed, where I lay in recovery the next afternoon. He and I and Eileen would often lie there, carping about whatever, making fun of each other, smoking pot. Eileen didn't really smoke weed, but she thought it made me smell good. Luigi and I exchanged our tales of trauma while Eileen laughed at us. It was interesting how our trips paralleled each other, although he didn't get all Christy about his. Perhaps Jews have Moses trips, but I wasn't at all Christian myself, so maybe he was just okay. We decided we'd take another opportunity to trip together soon, and he went to get some breakfast. As was customary, Eileen and I got in some more fucking before we got up. That was how our days usually went. Party 'til late, fuck, crash, wake up, fuck, lay around, take visitors, fuck some more, get up around 11, noon, 2, and start the day. Eileen was of Slavic heritage, as am I, and she could take a serious pounding. Our suitemates used to beat on the wall occasionally when the bed would be slamming into it and keeping them awake. We were inspired by the cracks in the ceiling though, which were inscribed, "These cracks courtesy of Andrea 'Ka Thump' Ludlow." I guess she had been getting pounded upstairs at some point in the past. We were on the ground floor section of the building, so there was no such problem below. After getting some breakfast I perused the Sunday paper and found a good excuse to trip again, Ravi Shankar.

I had always been interested in Indian culture, having been initiated into TM at ten. But other than the Maharishi I had never really experienced any of it outside of George Harrison's sitar noodling on "Within Without You," and the Indian Import store on Telegraph Avenue, where I bought my first bong. When we got to the show I was surprised to find that there was such a large Indian community. We had to sit in the balcony. We had taken our doses while walking over and were coming on before the show started, now situating ourselves in a familiar but unfamiliar setting. Ravi came out, sat on his carpet, and as the drone began he seemed to turn inward and begin his journey. There really wasn't much to see from the balcony, so I closed my eyes for most of it, but there was no mistaking the crafting of a story in deliberate rhythms, chord structures, and bending tones which eventually built up to his meandering solos. By the time they took a break I was pretty high, but excited. I certainly didn't have to deal with any of my usual show paranoias, feds, heads, deals, dreamgirls. Hell, everyone there was an Indian! I went to the bathroom, which was full, and I noticed another guy who was taking a long time to start peeing. Finally, he began singing something Indian. I didn't know if it was a particularly focused Vedic chant to urination, or a pop song that relaxed his mind, but it worked for him. I realized that my trip was very much about sound too, if I could hear people or thought they could hear me peeing, I couldn't. Maybe singing will work! I thought. It seemed too weird to be singing into the urinal though, so I went into a stall where I could be alone.

When I came out I overheard the most amazing conversation.

"Did you hear the tape from Chicago? He played raga number 72 and it was incredible!"

"No no, can you make me a copy?"

Oh my God! I thought. These guys are brown-skinned chutney eating Deadheads! They're all computer programmers, too! They're all the same folks I from the Dead shows, **only they've changed their skin for Ravi!** It was more of the same, since any paranoid fantasy is a suspected possibility when you're high on LSD. I was starting to tweak by the time I came back and told Luigi. The second set was much more jamming that the first. The tabla player, Swapan Chaudhuri, was laying down more stretched out and spinning formations, forcing Ravi to jam over the top. Even more deadly than the Dead, their songs all went on for at least 20 minutes, if not 45. They took this raga through so many twists and turns and tweaks that I was beginning to get really freaked out. I was losing my sense of where I was, who I was, what was was! I thought to myself, I can't handle this anymore, if it doesn't end soon I'm gonna freak out! Ravi and Swapan were pounding out this exchange and just as that thought crossed my mind they both trilled on their instruments three times, prrrrrrrrrrring prrrrrrrrrrring prrrrrrrrring POP! and it was over. As soon as the tension was released I was okay again, and could have gone for another raga, but the show was over. It was obvious that my mental incapacity had caused them to stop, and I felt that the displeasure of the crowd would be focused on me for breaking the chain. Who knows what they were thinking, or saying to each other in Hindi, but I interpreted it as negative and practically ran out of there. Another exciting multicultural experience.

11

Ben and Stymie's search for a house had led them to one conclusion, mo' money. Real estate hadn't totally mushroomed out yet, but there were a lot of expenses rolled into it. One was hiring an accountant to dummy up a couple of years taxes so you could get financed. It did seem to be a heathen act, paying taxes, especially when then money lined the pockets of Ron Reagan's cronies, and what surplus there was went to busting you. But dope dealing is as much a part of the American Dream as anything, so it needed to be done. Ben had a separate piece of property next to Lizard, Garson Knoll, which he had bought with Bernard. It was the actual top of Caldwell Butte, but was too steep to be inhabitable. He knew he needed to grow some weed on it, but things were deteriorating with Bernard, who despite being partners with him on two properties, found that Ben's staying in town made him something of an outsider.

Although Ben usually worked several weeks of the year, he wasn't living there, exposed to the same risks. Not that Bernard couldn't find reasons to disdain everyone, it was just a good reason to disdain Ben. It also made it easier for Bernard to grow a bunch of his own weed there, which, since the split, Ben had no share in. Ben asked Stymie to grow on Garson for him, and split the take, assuming he'd help install the weeds to begin with. Garson offered terrific exposures at the highest altitude, which translates to killer bud, a driving force in Stymie's worldview. It was a big job though, and Manny had moved back to town to escape Bernard's abuse. As a non-partner, he had received more than his share of that. So, around March of '84, Stymie asked me if I wanted to be a partner. I wouldn't have a stake in the land, but if I worked all year I'd get a third of his weed. I had to think about it for all of a nanosecond.

After all that had gone down that winter I was psyched to get the hell out of town. I decided to drive the back way, up I-5, so I stopped in Red Bluff to get some groceries. My aunt Doris had been living in Red bluff for some years, and I hadn't seen her since I left Roseville. She was a rugged independent type, who had retired up there to hunt, fish and do some real estate deals with her second husband. I really had no intention of visiting, but it had been a while, so I looked up the phone number and gave a her call. She was insistent that I come out and have lunch, so I decided I'd go ahead. She could only freak out like the rest of my family. I pulled up and got out of my car, which was a heap of primer black and yellow, and Doris came out.

"What happened to all your beautiful hair?" she cried, since I always had the nicest curly hair in the family.

"Well Doris, it got to be full of knots, so I just left it that way." They were curious about what I was doing, so I figured I might as well tell them.

"You know, the folks haven't been talking to me for a couple years now, since I got in trouble for selling pot, so now I live in the woods and grow it, which is working pretty good for me." I was expecting a big harangue as my uncle launched in,

"If a man's putting food on the table and taking care of his own, who's to say he's doing wrong. The only problem I have is that I can't go out to my favorite hunting spots 'cause all them fellers are up there growing tea. They've got those no trespassing signs all out there, but other than that, I got no problem with it."

"There's been a lot of dropouts in our family Shelly, you're not the first," Doris went on, completely amazing me. "You know, we grew up before the depression, so we see things a little different than your mom does." It was true, she was 12 years older than my mom, old enough to see how things really were during the depression, and be a little more realistic about the world. I was speechless, that people from my family still loved and respected me as the person they'd always known, even when they knew the scary evil truth about me. What really blew my mind was my uncle's funeral, years later, when I discovered that he was a highly respected retired cop, the Chief of Police in El Cerrito. Fuckin A!

I met Stymie at the cabin and we proceeded to unwinterize it. We cleaned out the mouse shit, started the siphon line, checked the propane, got everything orderly. By that time it was already dark, so we unloaded the generator Stymie had bought and fired it up. Mulehorn got himself a VCR over the winter and taped a bunch of movies off cable. He brought up a little TV with it to usher us into the new level of luxury in weedgrower living. This was civilized end of our dichotomous rural existence, The Mulehorn Film Festival. The next day's trip to town found us in the less civilized task of our chosen reality, unloading truckloads of shit. It was a steamy, stinky, gritty job, shoveling all that shit into a pile that could be used as a staging point, or perhaps, army like, be shoveled back into the truck for movement to another staging point at a later date. As it was, several truckloads of shit were necessary, as well as a few of peat moss, and a rather large supply of blood and bone meals, which were purchased at the local tallow works. It's nasty shit, but it ain't no chemical fertilizer. Of course, some thousands of feet of black pipe, which comes in convenient 500' rolls, and the other necessities of a water system, clamps, joints, glue, helped fill out the runs to Eureka's burgeoning lumber and garden supply mecca.

The purchase of planter pots in graded sizes was no less a cause celebré, judging from the mountain on display there. That was the first project to take care of, fill some hundred pots with soil and start our weeds. We built a little shelter cum greenhouse to store them in, under the trees where it wouldn't get too hot, and started our other work. Ben had arranged with his indoor guy to try growing a load of clones outdoors, which, to the best of our knowledge, hadn't been done. His guy was the first serious indoor producer we'd seen on the market, and we covered a pretty wide market. Eventually, he brought down a couple dozen clones, which looked different than the rest of the weeds. We had several seeds from previous purple producers, as well as a fresh supply of the Heinz from Hector. The Heinz plants looked like little conifers, sturdy vertical stems with sets of two perfectly even branches set at 90 degrees to the next. The clones were sort of floppy. They were, after all, branches that had been cut off of a mother plant. Somehow they get the cellular information to move up the chain so a branch becomes a stem and so forth, but we wondered if they'd be able to survive outdoor life.

The first thing to do, obviously, was map out where we wanted to plant. Garson had 60 acres, but a lot of it fell to the backside away from Lizard, the road and the sun. The top was covered with manzanita, with a few madrones here and there. As you came down the slope there were some big firs, oaks, and open spaces, so we determined where we could run a water line along the trees, get some things in the open, and use the manzanita for cover on top. We began cutting our holes in on top, since they would be in the sun longer every day we waited. They were good training, being almost solid rock, and took two of us hours to dig. I got blisters on my blisters hefting the mattox, which was my personal favorite tool. It was so rocky that Stymie went to the hardware store and bought a Gnar bar, a twenty-pound breaker bar. I was smart enough to buy a pair of cushion handlebar grips for it, so you could whack rock and not feel like your elbows were shattering. We would smash rock every way possible, dig, smash, scrape and dig, until we got a hole big enough for a serious weed. Usually 4x4x4 feet did the trick.

We were traipsing around up top one afternoon, about to start digging a hole in a manzanita patch, when a rattlesnake went off right next to the spot. We all jumped back, since none of us had ever seen a rattler. It seemed like a good sign that it was by our hole, and it was pretty small, but Ben and Mulehorn started chucking rocks at it, which pissed it off, and I must embarrassedly admit that I got into the hurling of bigger and bigger ones to try to kill it. From what I knew they only had timber rattlers up there, which aren't that toxic, although baby snakes have difficulty controlling their venom and are quite dangerous. Now that I know there are Western Diamondbacks as well, I don't feel quite as bad.

Like snakes, the sheriffs were out there too, but they only had limited resources before the government's Campaign Against Marijuana Planters, CAMP, began. People had developed methods of camouflaging plants over the years, mostly by hanging army surplus camo nets on lines between trees where they could be hoisted if you were flown. Covering your trails with leaves, burying water lines, there were several techniques that people had developed in the more impacted areas. Caldwell was pretty remote, however, and we didn't feel particularly at risk. Lizard weed grew pretty much out in the open, although patches fell inside forest clearings, so they weren't glaring. Stymie just figured that he wasn't trying to grow a ton, so it shouldn't be a big deal. Paranoia was just a minor part of the job description, a career stress, which was alleviated for the most part by living in the wilderness. If it ever came up, Stymie would issue his stock reply, "Worry is the furthest thing from my mind," as if he were some sophisticated cartoon character. The busts we read about were for insane numbers of plants anyway. Either they were exaggerating wildly, or there were some dope growing fools out there, probably both. The flyovers began fairly early in the year, with spotter planes examining the ridges and valleys, taking photos of every square foot of the county. When the plane came buzzing along you tried to cover what you could, stay out of sight, and hope they decided that you were just small potatoes. What you really dreaded was hearing the choppers, which start coming out in midsummer to direct the ground crews to the plants. It got to be like MASH after awhile, where you'd hear 'em miles down the valley and start tweaking. "Choppers!" They'd usually be heading down the road somewhere, so it was just a good heart rate increase.

After digging about a dozen holes on top we worked down the side, which was a piece of cake, comparatively. I thought I was getting pretty buff from digging, but then came the other half, filling. We would drive a truck up to where our giant piles of shit, peat, greensand, (Ben liked greensand) and blood were, fill the truck with some vaguely proportioned mix, stir it about with our shovels, and drive it up to the staging area on Garson, which was still a quarter mile or more downhill from the patches. Then we'd fill five-gallon buckets and lug them up to the holes, which hold about thirty buckets each. That's a lotta fuckin trips up the hill lookin like Kwai Chang Cain covered in sweat and cow blood. As I got tougher I'd try to carry them iron cross as long as possible, which wasn't very long. When you've bucketed all your shit, you can carry the fifty pound sacks of bone meal and lime up to add to your holes. The lime helps cool down the high nitrogen levels so you don't burn the roots off your tender young transplants. We routed in water pipe, pounded in rebar and stretched fences where we could. This was work like I had never known work, sweating in filthy grime until every muscle ached. Thank God one of the other projects of the prior year was to build a shower.

When we got done we all went to the nearest restaurant, which was a hunting lodge about 25 miles out some road, the Fuckin A or something. Dan and Lidya came with us, so I took them in my Datsun, just to impress them with how I had come up in the world, and drive like a maniac. We had a great dinner, got completely wasted, and I sailed us back home, making sure to put on an impressive burst of squirrelliness when I got to the private road. We stayed up drinkin and watching movies, which was a rare treat for them, since they had lived out there year round for ages with no TV.

With Garson done and plumbed, Ben went back to town, while Stymie and I got to work. Although the holes were already dug, we had to refill Gumby, the Upper, Lower, Tweak Peak, Lizard, and Armageddon, which was insane. Lugging fifty pounds of dirt a third of a mile down a ravine is very different than lugging it uphill. Every time you wipe out you spill it all and have to go back up for more. We built a couple more holes tucked into the firs by the lake and things were looking pretty good. The starts were beefing up nicely, even the clones were looking a little more uniform, life was good. Of course, there were the usual hassles with rigging water. Some of the holes were spring fed, which needed checking frequently, other's were gravity flow out of the lake, and the ones at the top of Garson required that we buy a pump and bury a tank up there. Maintaining the tanks and lines and flow was a constant chore. If the feeder breaks the water's surface you lose your gravity flow, springs dry up or get dug into by animals, and the pump breaks down, it's always something. But it's real work, in an environment that makes you healthy, no matter how much dope you smoke.

I began having a rather odd problem after a couple of months though, which started to really bug me. I noticed a blister on the inside of my cheek, which I figured I had burned while eating pizza or something, but then they appeared inside my lips and on my tongue. I was worried that I had contracted some rare disease until I finally figured out that the heat from the ten or so bombers I was smoking every day was causing them. I was totally thrilled, then, to find a cherry flavored aloe vera juice in a health food store somewhere, and since I knew I'd be smoking a bunch for the next few months, or longer, I bought a gallon. Every time we smoked a J, I'd take a swig and swish it around in my mouth. Smart! The idea of cutting back just never occurred to me.

12

When the starts had all grown to being a foot and a half or so, it was time to introduce the next stage, sexing. The little shelter that we had built for them was easily adapted to this process, which merely required that we drape it with black plastic an hour before sunset and remove it after sunrise, increasing the increment of darkness every day for a week or two. The plants think the year is ending and that they had better reproduce, so they show their characteristics. The females make hairs and the males grow balls. As soon as a plant shows its sign it gets separated, so that it can get enough sun to revert to the growth stage if it's female, or be killed if it's a male. If it's a male of a valuable strain, it can be penned up somewhere to be used for breeding in the fall. As long as you remove it's balls regularly so it can't release any pollen without your control, it's okay. The really together people will hold on to seeds from every year, so they can back breed. If you find a weed from a particular year is really good and you have the parent seeds, you can grow them again for seed stock. The seeds from a really good plant may not be so hot, though, due to lapses between generations, which is what makes breeding such heavy weed science.

Once the girls snap back into their growth phase its time to plant. Obviously, the clones were known to be female, so we didn't have to run the sexing trip on them, and they got planted early. They needed it, because compared to the Heinz they still looked weak. We put them all on Garson, since they were Ben's product, then filled it in with other things we had. We built our little cages to keep out the deer, which will wipe out your crop faster than anything. They can eat the leaves right off of a young plant, which, unable to photosynthesize, will die the next day. In the fall the fuckers will eat your bud, which tastes gnarly. Then they'll jump right over your fences, bounding about the woods completely high. When a couple plants on Garson lost branches we put out rat traps too. The wood rats like to make their nests at your expense, but Stymie's peanut butter bait did away with several of those varmints.

After walking up and down Garson a couple dozen times, and watching Horn on his 3-wheeler, Stymie realized he needed some transport too, so he got himself a Yamaha XL 125. It was a street dirt/bike, but not for long. As much as he trusted me, however, he knew me too well, and refused to let me borrow it, unless I was specifically doing maintenance runs. Lidya's birthday was coming up, so they were gonna have a party for her down at the pond. We went into Barneveld to get a bunch of booze, and I discovered Meister Brau on sale for something like three bucks a 12. I stocked up on what became our year round standby, the friendly neighbor, Mister Brew. It was always handy when Grunt came over. We couldn't really find anything for Lidya gift wise though, what do you buy the toughest woman in the county "Where the men are men and the women are men." She already had a bowie knife. We had long been familiar with the phrase, "So tough she wore barbwire panties," though, so I decided to make her a pair. There's probably enough old barbwire lying on property lines in Humboldt County to reach to the moon and back, so it wasn't very hard to come by. I fashioned a good length of it into three loops, so you could step through the waist loop into the leg loops, and wrapped them up in a grocery bag, the closest I could get to a plain brown wrapper. Lidya was so excited to open her present, she couldn't imagine what we'd got for her. It was about the only time I ever saw her jaw drop; her eyes bulged out behind her granny glasses and she just started howling. Dan cracked up pretty hard too, being the old cowboy that he was.

"Put 'em on," I yelled at her, so she gingerly snuck them up over her jeans.

"Woooohaaaa!" she yelled.

"Girl, "Dan started in on his cowboy rant, "You make me harder than the times of '49."

We proceeded to get completely torched. Stymie and I rolled fatties while we poured down every consumable liquor on the premises. Dan had grown some opium poppies and harvested some goo already, which he prepared for doobage by boiling it and rubbing the tar all over the paper and weed. Willy Went, who was visiting at the time, was extra excited, being an abuser of all sorts of drugs. He took a massive toke off this joint, held it for a minute, and fell flat into the dirt. "No way," Stymie exclaimed, "It can't be that good!" He took a giant hit, started wobbling, and grabbed the picnic table for support. "Hun ya dee," he exhaled, and looking at Dan exclaimed, "My hero!" It was the kind of joint that took your high to new lows. When the fire had died down to coals without anyone throwing another log on, which meant we were completely hammered, Stymie stood up and announced, "I'm going home." With that he turned and walked right into the pond. It was a good thing we were already laying in the dirt because we all would have fallen down in it laughing. He dragged himself back out, "Shit fuckin A, I seem to have gone the wrong way." We were peeing ourselves already when he hopped on the motorcycle and took off up the hill. The road forks immediately when you leave the pond and it wasn't ten second before he had gone around the loop of Grunt's driveway and was back at the pond. "Huzzah, it is I!" He tried it again and came back once more, "Fuckin Aaaaa," trailed off behind him into the distance.

We could hear the bike winding up the road toward the extremely deeply rutted curve where we heard it crash, sputter and die. "Oh fuck, I better go up there," I mumbled, not too thrilled about dragging my own ass out of the dirt, but I could hear him trying to kick start it again so I knew he must be alive. It roared to life, wound out for a moment, and died again. This happened a few times before silence returned to the night. The coals were wheezing, the crickets were chirping, the frogs were croaking, and Stymie, wet, exhausted, and very wasted, staggered back to lay down in the dirt by the firepit and sleep.

"Stymie! You're totally shot, dude!" Dan laughed at him.

"Merely... mechanical... failure...," he groaned before passing out. When the sun had raked us to consciousness, but while the dirt still held its appeal for a place to be, the abuses of the evening caught up with Grunt, who erupted in his famous morning salute, **"Who Shit In My Mouth?"** After the night's Christening, the bike was missing its taillight and a turn signal, so Stymie felt a little better about letting me ride it. I soon bought myself a motocross mask, with the goggles attached to a facemask, and began roaring up and down the mountain with my dreads flying like something from a hippie Texas Chainsaw Massacre.

Despite my aborted attempt to get into UCLA Film School, I got a great film education from Mulehorn's VCR. He was a culture vulture when he was living in town, and it was the Mulehorn Film Festival all the time up at the ranch. We were heavily into film noir, the Mitchum noirs: His Kind of Woman, and Out of the Past. After all, Mitchum was an avowed dope smoker who had been arrested and served time for it. He shot several films in Mexico, so he could hang out and get high. We loved his disdainfulness, his rugged, "just living my life —don't fuck with me" attitude. But we watched them all, The Big Heat, The Big Sleep, the Big Steal, all those Big movies, The Killers, The Maltese Falcon, The Strange Loves of Martha Ivers, classics, classics, classics. We watched Kane again and again, the Magnificent Ambersons, Touch of Evil, anything Wells had a part of, and then we got into samurai. I've seen Seven Samurai so many times I know the lines in Japanese! The same goes for Yojimbo. We were in highbrain heaven. We'd invite the neighbors, make a pizza, crack a case of Mister Brew, spark a doob, and get lit by the glow of flickering images.

Grunt came over one night to watch a movie, so we got completely fucked up. After the second movie we were all passing out in our chairs, but Grunt snapped to.

"Fuck it's late, I'm outta here,"

"Just crash here, man," I told him, but he was already out the door. I could hear him thrashing through the woods, drunk as fuck, with no flashlight, and no moon. I heard him wipe out down the hill and called out to him, but there was no reply, only what sounded like a bear rustling through the woods. The next morning Dan came over. He told us he had gone by the Gruntstead and couldn't find him. He was in the greenhouse when Grunt came up, all crusted in mud and blood. After staggering down the hill from our place, wiping out in the creek, and cutting his head on a rock, he decided to sleep right there in the mud. That was what made Grunt Grunt. Perhaps there is something about living in nature that pushes you to extreme levels of thrashing, it's just hard to be a clean living primitive all the time.

Watching the plants grow had a way of rooting you into the reality of nature though. All your urban dreams were far away as you sat and admired the change from spindly start to bushy bush. The stems that started as smooth twigs had become rough, striated trunks of fiber, while the leaves went from palm size sprigs to baseball gloves angling to catch the sun. Seeing a plant go from it's sleepy early morning state to alertness as the first rays hit it was a window into plant consciousness. Stymie would take me out to patches where we'd sit and talk to the plants, telling them how good they would be, blowing the smoke of their ancestors on them so they could look to their future with pride. All the while the season slowly turning, the sun's position in the sky changing degree by degree, it's hour of appearance and disappearance elongating as the days of full mountain heat approached.

There is a lot of calculation to dope growing, as far as the sun's angle is concerned. If you could afford to grow in the sun, as we did in the days before the feds were draining the treasury to stop weed, you needed to make sure your patch was in the path of the sun throughout the season. Finding a place that looked sunny when scouted in July could cost you if you hadn't calculated the sun's angle in September, when the plant is flowering. Even misjudging the nearby trees could cut hours of direct sun out of your budding days. You want to give your plants the healthiest start you can, to beef up the trunks with bone meal and let them eat blood, or serious composted teas, to give them enough nitrogen and potassium to grow full and strong. In the fall, at budding time, they need phosphorous, which is what made Humboldt the cornerstone of the bat guano market. Sun can't be overstressed though, a small plant in good sun will produce more bud than a huge plant in the shade, so you had to be aware of direction and angles of descent. Even a really beefy plant can get into trouble when the bud gets big though, since the weight can break the branches off. You need to nail a bunch of stakes of rebar around it and tape the branches up with twine or green tape to support the weight. Then you're strapped in for big bud production. It's technology applied totally in support of nature.

I was out one morning, watering on the Lower patch as the sun was hitting it. Hanging entwined in the fence was a big garter snake, with a baby bird in its mouth. The bird must have fallen out of the nest, or perhaps it was kicked out, but it was too small to have tried to fly. This snake was trying to eat it, but wasn't big enough itself, so it just swallowed the head and hung itself there in the sunlight, trying to coax the bird down its throat. I guess it had been working on it for awhile, because the head was starting to digest a little bit, which garnered the attention of a yellowjacket. I sat there for a long time as I watered, watching this scene unfold. The yellowjacket kept buzzing up into the snake's face, trying to get a bite of the digested bird. The snake, which was beautifully colored, as was the little yellow bird, kept recoiling from the yellowjacket, which became more violent in its attack. It tagged the snake in the face again and again until the snake finally spat the bird out and dropped out of the fence. The birds head was all wet and half-digested, so the yellow-jacket took a nibble at it before flying off, at which point the snake came back, swallowed the head and crawled back into the fence. I felt like I was watching a nature program, but for real. Everything was a nature program out there.

On the nasty side of it, there were some unpleasant creatures too. The wood rats tried to tear up your plants for nesting materials, the mice ate your home and crapped everywhere, the yellowjackets buzzed your barbecues, although they were hardly as scary as the hornets, but by far the most insidious creature in the woods was the tick. We had a whole passel of dogs and one of our grooming chores was to pick all the ticks off them. We kept them all in a half-gallon mason jar, the Tick-jar, which we threatened to pour into anyone's sleeping bag who fucked with us. They really are heinous little benefactors of evolution. I had always imagined them to be bloodsuckers, but the truth is that they simply bore into you and let the capillary action of your body engorge them with blood. They make no effort. You get pretty used to checking yourself for ticks, wearing white underwear, and maintaining hypersensitivity toward skin sensations. Eventually I knew whenever a tick was on me, but it took me awhile to develop that awareness.

I was sitting in the house having lunch one day when I began to have this feeling, a hot, burning, stabbing pain, in my dick! You know how sometimes you'll get a little weird nerve twinge there, from being folded in your jeans or something, so I just adjusted it and waited for it to go away. But it didn't go away. It got worse, and worse, until my dick was screaming so loud it felt like The Tell-Tale Heart was in my pants. I could no longer nonchalantly gab at my friends, as I was about to scream "Can't you feel my dick!" I went out behind a tree, whipped it out, and my dreadlocks must have stood on end. Right behind the head of my dick, in the soft skin where it grows out of the shaft, a fucking tick was buried. Holy Shit! I held my cock in my left hand, grabbed that fucker with my right, twisted counter clockwise and ripped it out. "Aaaaaaaaahh!" I sawed that fucker in half with my fingernails before returning to the cabin.

"What the hell was that?" Stymie asked, "Get your dick caught in your zipper?"

"No, I had a tick in my dick head!"

"That'll teach you to try fucking those dogs," Horn laughed. I fired down a Mr. Brew and a doobie, went upstairs and lied face down on my bed, where I forced myself to sleep away the afternoon. Oh the Tick-jar would have been an unbelievable torture, one we reserved for Bernard himself.

13

Bernard used to complain about everything. Every situation was our fault, since he was the only "enlightened" one of us. The first most ridiculous incident was when he brought a dead lizard over to the shed, and proceeded, in his slow paced nasal whine, to tell us how we had killed it. "You guys... are driving your 3-wheelers... and killing the lizards. You need to get rid of your mechanical contrivances... and get back to nature... before you decimate the wildlife." We weren't happy about killing our beloved lizards, but Bernard totally ignored the fact that he was the only one of us with a four-wheel drive truck, which he took his own abuses with. At the time he complained about the dead lizard, his truck was stuck in ruts he churned up on Tweak Peak, while trying to carry a full load of turkey shit off the road and up a hill. He tore up lots of ground before he blew his U-joint and left the thing there for a month. For Bernard, our mere existence was much more grievous than any assault to the sanctity of the land, since he could never have complete dominion while we were there.

After hearing enough of the mutual complaints I asked Stymie where Bernard came from and why the fuck they had him as a partner. "Well," he began, "Bernard moved into Barrington in '78. He was a pretty smart guy, and he started seeing what was going on in Barrington. I don't think he had ever done drugs, but he went to high school with Stripe, who had been in Barrington for a year already, and knew the scene. So Bernard decided to start dealing. He didn't drop out or anything, nor was he that much of a partier, but he got really into the uh, business aspect. He was the first person to really break the rules, you know, 'Don't deal to anyone you don't know.' Bernard figured he could deal to anyone he wanted, people from the Avenue, guys who hung out in Durant Center and sold weed to whoever came to town, anyone from campus. Pretty soon people who had never been to Barrington would come in the front door and ask where Bernard's room was. He got so big that he ended up hiring other people to man the store. He set up a desk in a walk-in single, the rooms with the long hallway into a bedroom. The guy would sit behind the desk, with a scale in front of him, and sell anything people wanted. A gram of this, a quarter pound of that, whatever quantity, whatever product, to whoever wanted; and they wanted. People would be lined up out of his room and down the hall, and they weren't all your middle class collegiate kids. Dudes from Oakland and wherever would come to score, and see people doing deals for whatever quantities, so it became a target. They came up with guns to rip him off, but he was never there. They made all his roommates lay down on the floor at gunpoint and shit, took the money and drugs, but they never got him, and he always had more. I've got to admit, I made a lot of money off him early on, so did Ben, but then he broke the next rule, 'Don't jump the connection.'"

I hadn't any concern for that rule in my early days, I had pretty much started at the top of the ladder, but the business was based on connections. You make a connection and you make money selling down the line, the true origin of multi-level marketing! If someone below you gets bigger than you, and would be better served by knowing your connection, you can either sell the connection or collect a per unit fee, at most, fifty a pound. "I introduced Bernard to the Freak Brothers," Stymie continued, "and he jumped the connection. He sold a lot of their pot, too. When Ben and I started looking for a place to grow, Ben was worried that it might take too much capital, and that we should get someone in who had a lot of dough in case the first year didn't turn out. Bernard was wanting in so we took him as a partner, and now we're paying the price."

"Hmmmm, that blows."

"Yes, and since neither of us wants to sell out, we're sort of stuck like this. Partners are the most dangerous things in the world."

"Yeah, I kinda figured that out with Craig."

Bernard may have been the most fucked up person on the Buttes, but the county had all kinds. One of the extremely entertaining characters that appeared at the ranch occasionally was Grease. He was some kind of speed merchant, who looked like the typical bad guy from behind the pool hall. He'd show up, usually fairly grizzled looking, in his leather jacket, smoking a Camel non-filter, more often than not toting his two dirty-faced kids with him. He always had some shitty pounds that he wanted to off at below market rate, not that there was an established market rate for immature, poorly dried weed, but if there was, he set it. He probably only sold weed that other people had ripped off, but since he knew where you lived it was a good faith gesture to buy an occasional pound in hopes that he wouldn't rip you off too. It was interesting to see the effect he had on his kids. He came up once with some pounds of bunk and told his kids to play outside. There were various remnants of kitchen stuff laying around out there, and when we got done looking at the weed we came out to find his five year old son, Little Grease, ready for business. He had found an old gallon ziploc and filled it with dirt. Thrusting it toward us as we walked out he exclaimed "How much will you give me for this?" Like father like son.

The most amazing interlude I had with Grease, one that earned him a new name, was a year later. I can't remember where I ran into him, but I noticed that the forefinger of his right hand was missing.

"Dude, what happened to your hand?" I asked.

"Well, I was gonna go do this deal with these guys I didn't really trust," (This alone was enough to make me snicker, the idea that it was possible to do a deal with anyone less trustworthy than he was.) "so I was cleaning my Derringer to take with me, just in case. I guess I didn't realize it was loaded, and it blew my fuckin finger off! Blood all over the fuckin place! I was right, though, my buddy went to do the deal and got ripped off!" The guy must have had an angel looking after him for such an appropriate diversion to keep out of harm's way. After that I started calling him Tri-finger, or Triffinger, as if that was his last name, although admittedly not to his face.

I was down in Garberville for a game one Saturday and TS told me I should hang out for the Women's Music Festival that night. It was an annual event, alternately known as the Dyke Fest, but it was a big party with bands and shit. They had events like that down that way, because they had built a community over the years, and it wasn't nearly as remote as the Buttes. I went over to Beetle's house before the show, and he offered me a bunch of shrooms, which I ate, owing to the countrified setting. The show was at the community center, and it was pretty fun. They had a bunch of booths, like a little carnival, with food and folk music. I was getting pretty high, but it was woodsy, and everyone was smoking pot, so it seemed cool. Beetle went back and forth to the beer booth for us, and while I was lying there alone, I noticed a big commotion in that direction. I couldn't tell what was going on, so I didn't bother paying attention, but I figured it out soon after Grunt came and sat by me.

"Fuckin Dykes," he grumbled, swiggin on his beer.

"What's up Grunty?"

"Ahhh those dykes wouldn't put out in their kissing booth, so I kissed one and she got all upset." Looking at Grunt's hairy derelict face, I could understand this. "Hell, they fuckin charged 2 bucks!" Apparently the dyke manning the booth had only given Grunt a peck on the cheek for his hard-earned shekels, so he grabbed her and crammed his tongue in her mouth. It wasn't long before we were surrounded by a contingent of dykes, led by the 300 pound bearded woman known as "Burl Ives." They were looking to exact some sort of revenge, and it had the potential for all out fist fighting as they started screaming back and forth. Since Grunt had chosen to sit next to me, it was assumed that I was an evil perp myself, and I was getting the wicked vibe from the dozen or so angry women assembled. This was not doing much for my mushroom buzz. I didn't really have any option to leave, since we were surrounded, and Grunt was starting to use that inclusive behavior that people do when they are about to get in a fight and want you to back them up. I was way too high and not really in the mood to go ballistic on bunch of lesbians who probably had some justification in being pissed off at Grunt. I personally enjoyed Grunt because I'm pretty hard to offend, and he'd been relatively harmless to me, but I'm sure he had pissed off innumerable people over the years. Finally Beetle came back with our beers, and starting cracking on the dykes, in a good-natured way, and they dispersed. "Boy Grunt," he said, "you sure do know how to get a woman all hot and bothered."

We came back down from the ranch early for the Greeks, so we'd have time to take care of things in town. We needed to unload some pounds, so everyone could have their supply. I needed to score some acid and get a tank of nitrous. By this point I had acquired a 60-pound medical tank, trading for weed with someone who had ripped it off from a hospital. There was a gas shop down in San Jose that was cool about the paperwork, you just told them you worked for a dentist and they rolled you out another big blue cylinder of compressed alternate universe. Hogarth was an astro head, and worked in the planetarium on campus, to which he had the keys. We decided it would be the optimal place for a post show nitrous party. We invited a discrete slew of people, including our mutual friend, who was the first Deadhead with digital taping equipment. He had been getting some extremely good results, which I would spin copies of when I went to visit him. The shows were pretty top notch, and the boys played into our plan brilliantly with an encore of Dark Star on Saturday night. It was the second time in six or eight years and it was quite good. We all rendezvoused at the planetarium at eleven, and somehow hoisted the tank up all those stairs.

When everybody had arrived and taken a seat we began passing joints and bags around, while the lights dimmed and the galactic simulacrum came to life. We plugged straight into the sound system, so the whole room got the replay in digital surround sound. I had given up being ultra responsible for the tank by now. I liked to keep things moving, but I allowed competent individuals to fill their own bags. Manny and Willy, however, got to wrestling over the tank, which we had stationed where the stairs came up into the center of the planetarium. Someone must have been getting some nitrous, because they both fell over and you could hear the tank bouncing down the stairs. It was a peculiarly sensitizing moment for me, with my history of nitric responsibility, because I knew that if it landed on the nozzle the tank could come shooting back through the room and out the ceiling. Instead it just hit the floor below with a pang, like a church bell ringing, which was befitting of our activity. Listening to Dark Star and whipping through my dose while watching the universe come to life was unforgettable though, except that I've forgotten it.

One thing I'll never forget was that Bob Bitchin didn't show up. I ran into him at the show, and told him to come, laughing as he smiled his twinkling mushroom smile at me. I didn't see him too often, so it was great to meet there and be high together again for a moment, since he wasn't doing drugs much anymore. He was pretty much committed to his studies, racking up the grades. He had always been pretty intent on that, since his father was a UC professor and wouldn't tolerate anything less than summa. Bob still had a soft spot for Jerry though, which, living in Berkeley, had to be indulged. He ate some shrooms that night, but that had never been a problem for him. He ended up losing his pack though, or just leaving it there, which wasn't like him. I suppose it was an article analogous to Ken's ring. He went off on some Jesus trip, following Mina back to Barrington, where he told her that she was Mary Magdalene and that they needed to get it together. I suppose he was crushed by her negative rejoinder to this issue, since it takes a lot of belief in your delusion to put yourself on the line like that. Perhaps, though, he was not entirely "disillusioned."

Instead of popping back to reality, as people usually do after such excursions, Bob descended further into himself. He started getting real distant, sleeping on the roof of Barrington, neglecting school, not eating, as if an entirely different person had overtaken him. He couldn't communicate what was going on for him, not to me anyway, although everyone tried, since we all loved him. Eventually Chuck had to call his parents, who came and took him home. Perhaps the shrooms had catalyzed some internal process we couldn't foresee. School? Parents? Catholicism? I find it hard to believe that shrooms could just throw him over the edge like that. Knowing him as well as I had, it seemed more like Stymie was right. Some of us, no matter how bright, are just time bombs. The painful thing about it was too look in Bob's eyes and see that the sparkle which once animated them so, had been replaced with a dull sheen. I was worried that someday something like that might happen to me, but I had already bent my brain around like a pretzel, so I wasn't so worried that I wouldn't risk further insanity to overcome that which was already buggin me.

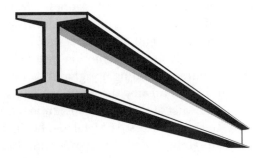

METAL

"Tell me now physician, is water the element that comes from Earth?"

"No my liege, although water does make its way through the earth, it is not the element that Earth gives birth to. When one looks deep within the earth one finds metal, and Metal is the son of Earth."

"Ore?" puzzled Huang Ti. How is this different from Earth?"

"Ore, salt, crystal, all have undergone some process of refinement within the earth, and this is the suggestion of Metal, refinement. When ore is purified, processed, shaped, it results in the tools with which you have built your empire. The axe fells the forest, the hoe tills the land, and the sword protects the boundaries."

"Indeed. And how is Metal displayed in the ways of nature?"

"Metal reflects the season of autumn, the time when harvest is made and grains are threshed, winnowing the kernel from the chaff. That of value is separated, and that without is left behind. The time of Metal is the time of the elder. When one has seen enough of the world to draw conclusions, and harvests the fruits of one's labors.

"And how does Metal manifest in the body, physician?"

"Metal is the element of the lung. The lung shows itself in the skin, the other organ of body purification, and since the nose is the portal of the lung, ailments of the sinus or breath are Metal related. When we breathe, we expel toxins and draw in fresh chi. Breath is the root of life, and it is a process of refinement. Have you experienced days, my liege, when breathing was difficult for you?"

"Ahh yes, physician, at times when I pined for things which I had lost, or that which I could not have."

"Yes, emperor. Grief and sadness affect the lung, weakening its ability to purify and replenish the body, drawing one into a withered state."

"And how might one correct this?"

"Courage, sir, is the emotion that defines healthy Metal. We see people of courage standing upright, in battle against all odds, facing losses valiantly, and turning them into triumphs."

"And what of the Metal constitution, how does one display it?"

"Those with excessive Metal may be rigid, brittle, consumed with rules or maintaining order. This may become difficult for them when the world proves itself greater than the scope of their definitions."

1

There was always a scene in the downstairs of Barrington. The politically inclined argued Marxist theory and played Diplomacy, English majors dissected books, everyone got high and engaged with or despised the various types who floated through. A variety of street people hung out there too. They had a history of hanging out there, doing drugs, and moving drugs for those who dealt with them. I didn't deal with any street dealers, so it wasn't my province to hang out with them in search of entertainment. But in an atmosphere that thrived on eclectic radicalism, I suppose that was one way to expand one's cultural consciousness. Berkeley Bob, who lived in the alley outside the kitchen, had to be ejected a few times though, since he appeared to border on becoming violent to others. He had been shooting speed for years, so it came as no surprise, particularly when you heard him ranting. He would go on unbelievable tirades, screaming at his various personalities, who would scream right back. It was his ranting that birthed the phrase, "Nazi Spies crawled on my flesh." It was written on the ceiling, and immortalized in a tape recording someone made of his late-night self-interrogation. Listening to that was always good for a laugh, but as cocaine gave way to freebase, things began to get a little more rugged for everyone.

Droz had gotten kinda tweaky on base at the Zete house, but he had moved out before the fire so I didn't see his total demise. Reiner was pretty much the first person I saw go. He must have had some kind of trust fund to do as much coke as he did, although he dealt so much that he thought he needed to keep a bodyguard. That was a clear sign of his mounting paranoia, since it's no way to be discrete, and no one would have been any less likely to rip him off or do him violence in the presence of Darren, who was actually just a rather large street person. They were something of a comedic sight, and I was told that Darren was a pretty nice guy, despite his cultivated "crazy street-person" look. The one person who found no humor in it, while adding to it immensely, was Margo, Darren's street-person wife. She would tow her children around Barrington while screaming "Darren and Pete are Fags! Darren and Pete are Fags!" Reiner, however, was the first person I saw actually searching the entire downstairs for nazi spies. Apparently they were multidimensional, because he not only looked under the tables, but on the undersides of the tables, before he opened his jacket and began searching his person for them. I was sitting in the hallway with Luigi one day after that, repeating to him the sage advice Art had given me. "You can do anything you want, but you can't Reiner out." Just then Reiner's door opened and Stymie came out, with Reiner thanking him. He had obviously dropped in to sell his old buddy some weed, since Reiner, being on the eight or ten year plan, had been in Barrington almost as long as I. I had to reassess, in that moment, and as much as it scared me, I told Luigi, "Maybe you can even Reiner out."

Oblio had managed to develop a pretty good business, and under Stripe's guidance he attempted to reinvoke Bernard's "store," concept. He had every kind of weed available, coke, some sort of opium (which I doubted the reality of) as well as a slew of new designer drugs. He bought pounds of San Pedro cactus, which was weak, sold Bromo, "gives you visuals without making you trip," X, shrooms, acid, DMT, whatever. I'm not sure how he got connected for all those chemicals, perhaps the Doc, but more excited young chemists were coming out of the woodwork all the time. DMT had a spate of popularity, since it was generally catalogued as the most powerfully psychedelic two minutes known. Everyone was telling me I should try it, the only drawback being that it was exactly like smoking a big hit of burning plastic. I found it very similar to doing nitrous and acid, but faster, and with a nasty aftertaste. It did take people on their own visionary journeys, however. Clark met with aliens who massaged him. Reiner ran down the hall screaming, "I'm on fire." The most powerful experience I had was simply watching Jake the K do a hit. It's helpful to have someone there to take the pipe away from you, since you're gone before you can set it down. I was completely straight at the time, and we were in a dark room. After Jake took his hit I set his pipe down, then watched while he turned into a luminous ball of concentric colored spheres. I decided I should leave him alone at that point.

Not wanting a hit myself, there wasn't much to do but go back downstairs and fuck Eileen. Fucking, fighting, eating, exploring our sensory capacities without consciously examining our motivations, this we did well together. Sheer physicality seemed like the best way to express our concern for and frustration with each other, and ourselves. Admittedly, she did take care of me when I needed it. I had gone wild on my discovery of mangoes the year before, and they were coming into season again so I bought a few. They are the most sensual fruit on the planet, a drug; a sweet, juicy, fruit pussy that you have to cram your whole face into. Eating mango is a sex act, and we smeared them all over ourselves. The odd thing about mangoes, which I was about to discover, is that they are related to Poison Oak. Like PO, it takes a year for you to develop the antibody, but once you do, their skin is deadly! Having smeared them up and down my face, in my pursuit of orgiastic fruit pleasure, the next day found my countenance swollen to bursting. My skin was a half inch thick and hard as leather. I went to the doctor but there was nothing to do. My ears swelled up and stood off my head at 90 degree angles, and then the pus started. My face was weeping yellow pus, constantly, for days. There was nothing I could do but lay in bed and suffer, but Eileen did her best to humor me, wiping my face down with moist rags, and not complaining too much about the fact that my pus was oozing all over her pillowcases. At least she could launder them at home.

Back at the ranch, about every three weeks, one of us would have to load up all the garbage cans and drive to Eureka to the dump. It could mean a trip to the hip city of Arcata to go to the bookstore, a movie, a sauna, whatever pleasures of town you could cram into the necessity of stocking the ranch. Of course, one occasional necessity is laundry. I was getting pretty filthy by the time Mulehorn headed into town, so I made the mistake of asking him to do my laundry. It's the kind of burden a man doesn't lay on another man, "Could you do my laundry, buddy?" But when your clothes stand by themselves, and even *you* notice that you smell like shit, it's laundry time. I had too much work to do to go to town, so I packed every thread I owned, except the shorts and socks I had on, into a garbage bag, and helped Horn load up the truck. I went about my day of weed work, had dinner, and lied around the shack with Stymie. Horn got back pretty late, so we helped unload the truck and came back inside.

"Gee Dun, I've got some bad news for you."

"What's that, you forget Mr. Brew?"

"Well the first thing I did was go to the transfer station, to get all that garbage out of my truck, so I just unloaded everything and drove away. It wasn't until I got to the laundromat that I realized one of those bags was yours."

"Oh fuck"

"I drove back to the transfer station, and looked in the piles, but they had already tractored it off somewhere. Sorry. I would have bought you some clothes, but I wasn't sure about your size."

"Guess you're gonna be lookin like your brother did at the Greek," Stymie chuckled.

"You're Fuckin A right!" I exclaimed, having no other choice.

I had heard from Dan about a guy in Miranda who had lived naked for years, so I decided right then to become Bigfoot of the mountain. It was pretty hard core to go barefoot out there, because the terrain went from rock to brush to thorn to construction scrap nails, but fortunately Horn did buy me some socks. For the next couple months I wore nothing but my boots, and my motorcycle mask if I was riding. "It's the naked man!" the neighbors would scream, but they loved it as much as I did. It felt incredibly healthy, and in the summer heat it was pretty comfortable. It was good that all the really filthy work was over with, though, or I'd have had sweaty tracks of soil amendments all over my crotch. I had always been into hanging out naked, which made it even weirder that I was still hung up about peeing. I just figured that exposing myself to whatever degree could only be beneficial.

Mulehorn's attraction to culture did make for an interesting item that year, which, in hindsight, was incredibly prescient. Michael Jackson was incredibly popular, I think BAD was out, so they had bubble gum stickers and shit all over the place, which Horn collected. Being men of the woods, we had the Stihl power tool calendar hanging by the door, sporting topless Bavarian babes in various rustic settings operating the whole line of chainsaws and such. It was a pretty entertaining calendar in its own right, but we noticed that one of the stickers had Michael's face in the exact proportion of one of the chest hefting maids. So was born our art project for the year, The Michael Jackson Transsexual Power Tool Calendar. Every month had Michael sporting huge knockers and motorized appliances. Eventually we got a picture of Jerry from the Greek up there, to make sure no taboos were upheld. It got a laugh every day, old Jerry with big hooters in a peasant skirt, making coffee in a cast iron pot over an open fire, with motorized pole saw in the background. Horn's occasional forays back to the city brought us more filmed rewards, but there was an occasional loser. To avoid the bummer films we instituted the "ten minute rule." If no one was murdered within the first ten minutes, we turned it off. There were allowances for great actors, intriguing plot exposition or dialogue, but we weren't out there watching love stories.

Dan thought we were insane for having our pack of dogs, and he was probably right, but they were pretty good. Besides Shasta, who was a small Australian Shepherd that Natalie had chosen from the pound when they stopped on the way back from Red Rocks, there was Fang, Max, Bud, Bear and Grunt, the runt of the litter. Fang was incredibly equine, so much so that we thought she believed herself to be a horse. She was the biggest, a graceful white lab that always moved in a canter. She looked more like she was galloping that running. Bud was the smartest, always looking at you with one ear cocked, as if to say, "What's up?" Max was raccoon faced and German Shepherd-ish. Bear, whom I took as mine, was a hairy mongrel, but good. Grunt was always whimpering about something, so we eventually gave her to the Face. White Dog had just appeared out of the woods that year, so after adopting him there were seven of them, which probably detracted from the wildlife on our property, but we never saw a bear, or had deer eat our weed.

The real problem was that they would go out on runs at night. It was their natural behavior, and chaining them up would have been against our ethic, as well as too much effort, which was also against our ethic. When they first went after a porcupine it was something of a problem. We did our best to cut the ends off the quills and pull them out, but Fang got it pretty bad, we had to take her to the vet to get them all removed. They calmed down after that, but eventually Shasta failed to return with the rest of them. We assumed that the rancher had shot her, since she wasn't dumb enough to get quilled that bad. Dan lived next to the rancher, and was the general liaison between the weed growers and the other locals. The rancher told him he'd seen dogs on his property and he made no bones about protecting his cattle.

Stymie was gone down to town when the pack went on its next porc attack. I think they might have killed this one, because they were **Fucked up!** Like Bud, Bear only had a few quills and we pulled them all right there, but Fang and Max were beyond belief. Fang had this trip with trying to use her arms, she'd catch Frisbees or balls with her front arms, so she not only had quills all through her mouth, but in her arms and chest. It was hard to comprehend the walrus beard that Max was wearing, I estimated more than 150 quills in his mouth. They were all down in his throat, gagging him as he frothed, but the amazing ones were those that he had driven through the roof of his mouth. They poked out through the top of his snout. Mulehorn and I were thoroughly nonplussed by the sight, which, after cursing Stymie's absence, we had to deal with. Always right on time, D&L arrived from nowhere to rescue us. Dan immediately suggested I give them all the 35-cent vet treatment, that being the cost of a 30/30 shell. Lidya immediately volunteered in her beacon of good cheer voice,

"I'll kill your dogs Sheldon!" It was a known fact that she had killed dogs and skinned them out for throw rugs.

"I don't think Stymie would appreciate that, but thanks anyway." I had to figure out a way to transport them to town, and it was puzzling me. I eventually came upon the idea of hog tying them with duct tape, which was difficult to do, since hair doesn't tape well. They were still wriggling around quite a bit, so I put burlap sacks over their heads.

Lidya wanted to go to town with me, so we loaded the dogs into the back seat of the Datsun. They still had me worried with their wriggling, so I went back to the house, loaded the shotgun, and put it in the trunk. The car was stinking with that dog fear smell, a sweaty bile stench that was practically gagging us. I rolled down all the windows so we could survive the drive, and headed down to the gate. As soon as I stopped and set the brake, Max, in a stunning act of duct tape and burlap sack defying will, hurled himself out the back window. It was clear to me that he had made a decision to stay on the property. There was no way I could risk having him bail out on the highway, and I had to respect his sense of awareness, so I got the shotgun out of the trunk.

"Want me to kill him?" Lidya asked excitedly.

"I'll kill my own fucking dog, thank you." I took Max's sack off and led him to a clear spot at the edge of the road. I stroked his neck, telling him what a good dog he was, until he was quiet. I laid the shotgun against the back of his skull and said good-bye. The blast carried his whole body off the road and ten feet down the hill into the trees. Everything was quiet after that, the other dogs didn't make a sound. We took them to the vet, who was appalled, and then we got drunk. I was having the distinct impression that Lidya was flirting with me, but I was good at denying such impressions. I don't know whether dog killing made her horny or she simply respected me for doing it. I had out-wrestled her a couple times too, so maybe she thought I was man enough. As much as she thrilled me I couldn't get past the whole Natalie deal anyway. I wasn't about to go fucking around in my newest friend's marriage. We went to the Safeway that night to load up, and were staggering around the aisles when Stymie walked in. He had just driven back from town and figured he needed to stock up the ranch. I saw him at the end of the aisle and was trying to figure out what to say to him when Lidya blurted out,

"Guess what Stymie, we killed your dog!" Oh great, I was thinking as Stymie looked at us sort of stunned. "Sheldon blasted him with the shotgun."

"Sorry man, they all got quilled again last night and Max was just too fucked up." I explained what had happened, and he understood, but it wasn't the way I wanted to tell him. After he got an earful from Mulehorn and the vet, who told him never to bring his dogs there again, I was pretty much forgiven.

The funny thing was that I thought nothing about Max's remains. The blast had yanked him cleanly from my consciousness, but after a week went by, his corpse, which was unavoidably close to the gate, was stinking like a truckload of skunks. Everyone on the hill came by to complain, so Stymie and I headed down there with a bag of lime. Since we had gotten all our groceries that same day we hadn't been out to the gate, but the neighbors were right, it stank! I had hoped we could just dump a bag of lime on him and be done with it, but we decided that burying him would be best. You could see the maggots crawling under his skin, as if it had a life of its own. It was the toughest hole I ever dug, worse than Rho Phi's, since my drunkenness had prevented any digging there, and just breathing by Max's corpse almost forced me to puke. If I had eaten anything that morning I surely would have. After that I'd always make my little salute to his grave when I came in or out.

That incident made me glad to have a pair of shorts left, so I finally broke down and bought some clothes. I went to Arcata, where they had a custom airbrush t-shirt shop. I had them create the Roachbusters t-shirt for me. It depicted a fat, smoking roach, with tar dripping off of it, and the international "no" symbol over it. It read "Roachbusters" at the top, and "I ain't smokin no roach, at the bottom," as I had come to eschew roaches as an undercaste item. In the past we had burned our faces off trying to light up roaches, rolled roaches into roach doobies, and rooted for the Houston Oilers because they had a kick return guy named Carl Roches. But even at Zete I had realized that roaches sort of knocked you out. The weed was all brown tasting to boot. If you had a moustache you were in real trouble. Stymie said it best, "If you're trying to light that you must be high already." Now that I had an unending stash of the fresh, I had to toss all my roaches. That drove people insane. We'd be driving along, smoking a joint, and I'd toss the roach out the window. "Maaan!" they'd scream, "What are you doing? I'd smoke that roach!" I'd gladly give them my roaches, but I refused to risk having one stinking up my car or my person. Fuck getting busted for a roach. I'm driving pounds all over town, who needs that? I went into a western shop for some jeans and ended up buying a black ten-gallon hat. It made me look like a Hassidic highbrain, but I could tuck all dreads up into it and pretend to be straight too, which was fun. I still liked to cruise around naked, but now I had options.

We built on a kitchen that summer, which allowed us to move the fridge and stove out of our living area, which was nice. We hadn't roofed it yet, but had the rafters up when our friend Crawdad was visiting. It was a Friday, so we were going to head over to the lake and play horseshoes, but he suggested we smoke a joint first. "Right on, but check this out," I said, in my excited "watch me" mode. I was still up in the rafters, and since I fit between the crossbeams I decided to do a genie. I pressed up into an armstand as if the rafters were parallel bars, swung back and forth a couple times and dismounted in a flip. I hadn't been doing any gymnastics for awhile, so I misjudged it, took and extra quarter rev, and landed right on my tailbone. I bounced a couple feet back into the air before I came down on it again. Like my rib, I refused to acknowledge that it was broken until got rolfed a few years back, but boy did that hurt! I couldn't even cry, I couldn't even sit in the big black chair, I just had Crawdad roll a joint and I started pounding Mr. Brew. I decided serious drugs were in order, so I rode the 3-wheeler, standing up on the foot pegs, over to the lake, and began consuming mass quantities. After a couple hours and a few games of shoes I was fucked up enough to sit down. I was also drunk enough to offer to race Grunt back down the road. Unfortunately, he had his son, Bone Boy, on the front of the bike, so when I lost it and slid into him on the same curved that cost me my rib, Bone flew off the top and broke his leg. Fortunately, he came out of it fully recovered, and still tough as nails.

I was pretty remorseful, and felt like I really owed one to Grunt, so when Stymie went down to town to finish his house purchase, (after making me swear to tape up all the plants on Garson that day) I went down the hill and got completely fucked up with old Grunty instead. I guess Stymie was watching the weather report cuz we had a wild storm that night. The wind was reported at over sixty mph in town, which meant 80 easy up on the mountain, where all our weed plants were totally exposed. Grunt came to check up on me the next morning, knowing that I was supposed to be tying everything up the day before. We hiked up the face of Garson and surveyed the damage. The Heinzers, which were bred for Hindustan and Afghanistan mountain ranges were completely fine, not a branch out of place. We were pretty heavily into those indica strains, they were more rugged and the weed was way stronger. The clones on top had been taped up already, and looked beaten but okay. There was one plant on the face though, we got the seed from the Tree People and it was the only sativa plant we had. It was completely torn to shreds. It had been a spindly thing to begin with, thin branches all arching like an upside down umbrella. The main stem of a weed grows in striations, segmented radially. The wind had torn this plant into eight different sections, all of which were laying in the mud.

Weed being weed, hemp fiber and all, the storm didn't rip anything off, it just quartered it the long way. I was bummed, a pound out the window would not make Stymie happy, but it looked as if I should just tear it out. "No fucking way," Grunt yelled when I made my intention known. "That's a weed, fix it up. You got any tree seal?" I did, and went back down to fetch it. We tree sealed every section, so that the stem couldn't mold and wouldn't get rat eaten, then nailed a dozen little rebar stakes into the ground around it. We looped green tape all around and under and across the plant until it looked like it was in traction in a horticultural hospital bed. When Stymie returned I had to admit the cost of my negligence, but the weed had already started recovering. When it started to bud every little branch turned sunward from that frame, which covered about 24 square feet. We started calling it the "Octopus," due to its tentacled appearance.

We headed out to Sacramento for some shows after that, which were fun, since I had gotten a bunch of my buddies from high school into seeing the Dead. The shows were where things revolved. Old connections were renewed and new ones were made. It was incredibly hot there, but they had set up a big shower in the back of the show that fit about 25 people at a time, soaking together under cold shower heads. You dried off pretty damn quick though, in the 110-degree heat. The even better feature of those shows was the water slide. It was next door to the show, so I didn't go until the second day, — "No ins and outs" — but I was really glad I did. Beetle was at that show and he went over with me. It was strange to be within the atmosphere of the show, able to hear it, but not within the scene. It was very relaxing, not having to deal with the mental upkeep of being in character. I went to the top of the big slide, and just as I took off Jerry started his solo in Bird Song, which I could hear perfectly. It was fantastic, sliding around through the cool wet curves with Jerry guiding the way until I splashed down into the pool. I really wanted to spend the whole show there, but I thought that I'd be ignoring my responsibility. It was good that I went back, because I ran into Jan, who had moved, and I needed to get his number. Neither of us had anything to write with, but we walked right by a cop, so Jan asked him for a pen, which he loaned us. I thought it was pretty amusing, borrowing a cop's pen to exchange information for future acid deals.

Dead tour was undoubtedly the major pipeline for acid distribution in America. The feds sure knew it. Anybody anywhere that sold LSD got it through someone that had made connections on tour. It was the travelling carnival party, the place to promote commerce. Hell, lots of shows were at convention centers, they were dope dealing conventions. I don't think the band got a direct kickback, but they had their fun, and in a way, they did. The big dealers, like everyone else, liked to be able to party with the band, which as far as I know, required that you had plenty of drugs. Like any rock stars they took an interest in drugs, and who wants to pay for all those drugs? This is what I believe caused the demise of the acid industry. The major trend toward coke had eventually been accompanied by an equal need for heroin. (When you've been up all night tweaking on blow, it's nice to have a way to mellow out.) The acid guys partied as much as anyone, and started watering down their hits to 60 mics so they could stretch their profit on a gram of crystal. These guys were selling shitty product, the original aim of which was to enlighten the world, in order to buy schmeeze and party with Jerry. Meanwhile their fourteen-year-old runners are getting all strung out. I began to see that Dead tour was not all the love groovy thing that the dreamy-eyed folks in the front row believed it was. At least Jan believed in LSD, dealt with adults, or non-minors anyway, and didn't do powders. I respected that, and I respected his opinion that shit was gonna come down.

2

It was early in the morning when the choppers broke the morning silence. We were still in bed, but that didn't last long. Dan came up on horseback to tell us that they were on the scanner, busting Ted, Rocky's partner outside the gate. They had driven in and arrested him, now they were flying in for the weed. We stashed everything we had laying around the house, and had a little powwow. We knew Grunt and Hoss would be flying through the woods hacking their stuff with machetes, because they always said they would. Our weed was pretty close to being ready, but the odds of getting busted weren't any less if you were hauling some plant into the woods than if you left it intact. They seemed to be busy with Ted anyway, and they were going into Rocky's brother's place through the BLM. After an hour or so we began to see the choppers coming off the mountain, with their nets full of weed. They had to direct the ground crews to the plants, which they'd tear out, then net it up and fly it off to the staging area. Those guys had 500 acres between them, and just as many BLM acres separating their properties, so it was gonna take some time.

The key to not getting busted, if CAMP is at your door, is running away! They may spread out over a mountain, but they only have warrants for one place. That's what the legal battles were getting to be about. They would trespass onto your property and take your weed, even though their warrant was for your neighbor. Pretty hard to stop a crew of pigs with M-16s from trashing your place, but people were trying to fight them in court.

No doubt about it though, Rocky had some weed. His operations were identical enough that they were all warranted, so the cops cut the lock and came back our way. We bailed down the hill to the pond, which seemed to be where everyone was. Hoss and Grunt had already finished a bunch of their early harvest anyway, and pulled everything that was left, so it seemed a safe place to be. Everyone brought down food and beers and we had a big party. An unintentional harvest party. Lidya and Hoss were playing guitars and singing, we were Qin up burgers and drinkin. Rocky had sent his crew over so they'd be safe while CAMP combed his place. We were watching the choppers haul it off, but relaxing and starting to have some fun when Dan pointed up and said,

"Hey isn't that old Rockyfeller hanging from that weed net?"

"Yeah, he's trying to climb back in the chopper like 007 so he can go stash his bud," Grunt chimed in. One of Rocky's crew guys got all haired out,

"Hey man, that's not funny! Those guys are going to jail!"

"Well if you're so worried about 'em why the fuck are you on my property where it's safe?" Dan shot back.

"Yeah," added Grunt, "Nobody asked you to come up here with a fuckin army of guys trying to grow a million plants. You're the ones that blew it for all of us!" That put a damper on things, so people went back to being nervous. Grunt broke the silence though, with his shouts of "Hey! Bum Out! Bum Out, Man!" That was actually rather funny. I mean, how many times has some old hippie freak yelled at you to have a bummer? Only Grunt.

Stymie had wanted to cop Grunt and Hoss's early bud, since they were known for their killer contribution to the cause of weed growing. They said they had a few pounds done, so we followed Grunt to Dan and Lidya's old cabin while Hoss went rummaging in the woods. The house sat right on the edge of the ridge, with pretty heavy forest to the East side and a clear view to the South and West. We sat there admiring the view of the valley from the picture window and drinking beers until Hoss came back with a bucket. The bud was stocious, all the more for being early, but Grunt just had a way with weed. Maybe he was so vile that his mere presence was a fertilizer, I don't know. The shit was well crystalled for early, with a heavy perfume only half masked by its newness.

"We'll have to test this, said Stymie, pulling out an appropriate nodule and whipping out some papers.

"Hell, the shit's good. We grew it!" drawled Hoss, urging to get the deal done. We passed it around and were instantly ripped, giving credence to Hoss's testimony. Stymie broke out the five grand he was carrying,

"This shit's pretty decent, I'll give you 1800 for it."

"Naah," Hoss replied, "We want 19."

"Nineteen? You sold me your weed for seventeen last year."

"Yeah, well people are selling weed in Garberville for 2000 a pound. What do you think Grunt?"

"Well I don't really care, I like more money, but I'm fucking glad I don't live in Garberville."

"How much is there?" Stymie asked.

"Two and a half."

"18."

"19!"

"18."

"19!" I was holding a bag up to the window, examining it in the light while Stymie haggled, when out of nowhere a chopper flew up and hovered a hundred feet outside.

"Fuck!" I yelled, looking at the bag and the chopper in one eyeful.

"OK, we'll take 18!" exclaimed Hoss, grabbing the cash, "You're gonna get busted!" Stymie turned to see the chopper and exclaimed in his half-deadpan cartoon way,

"I'm shitting red cubes." With that Hoss flew out the door and into the woods. We crammed the bags back into the bucket and ran off after him, splitting in another direction as soon as the woods got deep. Problem was, these weren't our woods. We stuck the bucket in an old stump and hoped we'd remember where it was when we came back. The chopper never touched down, so the party went on, which gave us the opportunity to recover the bucket at sunset, when CAMP had packed it in. When we got back up to Lizard, all of our weed was still there, untouched, which gave us reason to fire down another big bomber out of the bucket.

There was still plenty of time for our weed to finish budding, and it didn't seem like they'd come back for us, which gave credence to our general philosophy of grow good, not big. We had bought Rocky's weed during the summer, since he had unending loads from the prior year, but they were all completely uniform, and not too thrilling. It was good solid red haired bud, but it was just kind of…straight. He had his trimmers separate it into different sizes, and sold it as big, medium and small bud. Since every plant was the same as every other plant he could do that, but it seemed a little weird. We had a good range of plants, and enough proven winners to be in good stead. The Gumby weeds were just insane, baseball bats of bud with thick white hairs that had iridescent purple coloring in their centers, regular schmint factories. To go stand within them, which was easy with their girth, and squeeze an arm until it reeked, was just heavenly. You could have hidden inside them when CAMP came, if they wouldn't have busted you there. The Heinz were their perfectly solid structured selves, everywhere they grew, the purple stems giving rise to deep purple buds that reeked of grape, while the clones, in their leafy tangle on branch turned plant, had packed on incredible golden bud. They weren't quite as schminty as their indoor sisters, but the schmint was golden, not white, and as we would eventually find, the taste was incomparable.

We tried a different approach to harvesting that year, since we were living in the shed and needed to maximize the space. We pounded nails up and down the walls and strung twine like clothesline throughout the drying room. We realized that hanging individual branches would be more uniform and less crowded, allow things to dry more evenly and give us access to all the weed. It also meant you could cut the tops off plants that were done already, and leave the less developed lower branches to get another week of sun. We waited for the full moon in October, drove up on Horn's three-wheeler with some yam boxes we had salvaged from behind Safeway, and clipped our reeking treasures in the silver light. We spent all night under that moon, and the next too. We had a lot of weed to cut so judiciously, and we had to take it back to the shed and hang it all. The drying room was still my bedroom, and I loved it, sleeping smothered in skunk perfume.

(I find it very irritating when I walk down Haight Street or Telegraph Avenue and dirty little punks who've never even known bud try to sell me "skunk." There has not been skunk weed since 1984! Once CAMP made everyone switch their growing tactics it was almost impossible to get the ridiculous reeking weed. Perhaps the strains were lost too, because skunk weed was scary shit. You opened the bag, and people didn't say, "Oooh, somebody's got weed." They said **"FUCKIN A! That shit reeks!"** You ran with it from your trunk to get it inside. Your whole house stunk the minute you opened the bag. It wasn't a marketing buzzword, it was an apt metaphor, because it smelled like a fucking skunk. Most of our weed was of the heavy perfume, fruity variety, but I have encountered some weeds that you'd be scared to buy because a cop dog could smell 'em with the windows rolled up going in the opposite direction on the freeway.)

After driving my Datsun to death, (those dirt roads and all) I bought Ben's old Galaxy 500. It was a '68, with some huge V8 in it. They say the best way to lose a friend is to buy his car, perhaps sell him your car is more appropriate. In it's inaugural ride I drove Jake the K and Art up to trim for us. It was a little sketchy getting up the private road, but I made it past the gate. It had been raining a bit though, and I slipped off the road in a narrow stretch and bottomed out. Jake, who was a pretty big guy, had to either slide out my door or step off a cliff. I could have tried powering around in the mud, but it looked like I'd end up wracked against some trees fifty feet down, probably irrecoverably. It took a few days for the neighbors to winch me out, since the guys with four wheel drives were worried I might slide and take them with me. The Cowboy, as usual, was able to get the job done, it just seemed like his calling. "Tin-horn deadhead, driving that fucking boat up here into Chato's land!" He was right of course, it wasn't the kind of car that made sense up there, but it was a cruiser.

That was the season of hash. We had heard that people were making hash the year before by trimming on screens. Mulehorn, dope scientist that he was, designed frames that had silkscreen stretched over the top, into which you slid a sheet of glass. Working your weed on the screen allowed the fine crystals that fell off to collect on the glass, where you could scrape them up with a razor. I had a book on hash production techniques of the world, The Great Book of Hashish, (which I highly recommend) and I had learned all the processes. The stuff that rubbed off on your hands would obviously be the top of the line, with the golden crystal that falls off the bud next, and the green powder, or kif, that comes from smacking it around over the screen is last. They were all more potent than anything you could buy, because they were so much fresher, and the source was "the kind." We would compare our hash balls at the end of the day, trying to save them until we broke down and got completely blasted on a hit. The gold dust we'd roll into joints or pipe, and the green we saved.

Jake the K didn't smoke pot, so he was collecting an amazing hashball after a couple weeks. We all looked at it jealously and discussed it every night, until Art accused him of being greedy for not letting us enjoy it, whereupon Jake tweaked and threw it across the room. We were all in a mad scramble for the hashball but just then Bernard walked in and started complaining about something. We weren't paying much attention to him. Bernard had hired the scummiest of dirtball, hang around Barrington street weasels to trim for him. I didn't even want these guys to know I was a dealer, and here they were in our growing scene! He told them to forage at our place, since he wasn't providing food either. So much for the trimmers' dream of free cocaine and champagne. Bernard finished his bullshit and left, but we never found that hashball. Art always suspected that he had pocketed it in the confusion, because it did seem to bounce toward the door, and he always had that sort of timing.

Jake did redeem himself before he left though. On the eve of his departure he baked a pan of brownies. The recipe makes allowance for baking at altitude by adding three tablespoons of flour. We had such a huge stash of kif by then that Jake packed three tablespoons full, about 18 grams, and added them to the mix. I had agreed to take him down to the Greyhound station, so the next morning we got up and got ready to go. Bernard needed something so I begrudgingly agreed to take him too. It was pretty early and I was hungry. Dave was cutting out a quarter of the pan to take back to town with him, so I ate a couple squares, not thinking about the fact that they were gram each brownies. I took him to the bus depot without a hitch, then headed up to Eureka to get some supplies.

Eureka is sort of strange town, a redneck remnant of the logging and fishing industries' once great commerce. The highway splits into two main roads, which zip through town in opposite directions. There's another road that runs between them, and for some reason I had turned on to that one when my car died. I tried starting it again and again, but I was just burning the battery. I looked at Bernard, who hadn't said a word all morning. "Maybe... it's... the... alternator." I was starting to feel a little desperate, like I didn't want to be stuck anywhere with Bernard, so I popped the hood and dug around. Not that I would have known, but I couldn't find anything wrong. While I was standing there I began to notice an inordinate number of cops cruising by. I realized that the middle road housed both the Sheriff's and the CHP offices, and that they were rolling by every five minutes. Not only was I a freaky white rasta, I suddenly remembered that the Galaxy was something of a safe, too. I had bought three pounds of Grunt's old lady's weed and stashed it in the trunk. Now I had something to be paranoid about.

Bernard went on being his weasely self and my car continued not to start. I walked over to a little auto shop and they said they'd send a dude to look at it in awhile. After an hour and a half of watching cops go by, sitting in silence with Bernard, a mechanic pulled up, popped the hood, did what I had done, nothing, and told me I'd have to bring it in. I didn't want to have it towed a half block, so I tried to push it, but it was a beast, and the power steering wouldn't work. So we sat. I didn't know why I was tweaking so hard, but it became apparent that Bernard was an agent of Satan, and that I may need to kill him and be done with it. If I sat there getting eyeballed by pigs much longer they were gonna bust me for something, so it might as well be something worthwhile. My mind was on fire when I cranked that thing so long and hard I thought I'd break the key. I stomped on the gas again and again and a VroooooOOM! Out of nowhere, it fired up.

We had several errands planned that were now moot as far as I was concerned. I turned that thing around and beat it down to the Barneveld Safeway. My heart was pounding the whole way, but I managed to round up a food stash. I still knew what was important. We left the Safeway and I drove up to Lawson, which was only about five miles, but the curves were getting to be too much for me. I was out of control and had no idea why. Against all my judgement, but with little other choice, I asked Bernard to drive. We switched places and began to float down the road. The fog was already in the valley, so we were taking the curves hard as they appeared out of nowhere. It seemed as if he wasn't in control, but simply drifting along. I was seeing colored visuals against the white base of the fog, but still hadn't figured out why I was so high, or even that I was high, it was just how it was.

Bernard, the agent of Satan, who hadn't spoken three sentences all day, was driving us to our death, and since I was incapacitated there was nothing I could do about it. He headed up the hill below Lick Ranch, and into the straightaway beside it. He was picking up some speed, but the fog was too thick to see through. We broke through a patch and were right inside a group of horses that had gotten through the fence and onto the highway. Bernard stomped on the brakes, while this one horse stood dead ahead and stared down at us. I could see it coming in the windshield and crushing us, but we skidded to a stop about three inches short of breaking its legs. It snorted at us before galloping off across the road. Now I was fucked. I knew I was in no shape to drive, but apparently neither was my pilot, who was straight! I just had to hope Onnggh Yaangh was with me. I guess it was, because the road only held more hairy curves and we managed to get back to the ranch alive.

I was tweakin, and it was getting late. I hadn't eaten since the brownies I had for breakfast, but as is the case when you eat weed, I was entirely oblivious to the relationship between the brownies and my tweaking. All I knew was that I was starving. It was late enough that those guys had already eaten and nothing was left. I had brought home a load of groceries, but I needed food now! I looked down on the counter and there was still a half pan of brownies, so I ate half that! I wasn't hungry anymore. I had a Mr. Brew and explained the traumatic events of the day, which seemed far behind me, but things were still a little strange. I began to feel as if I were at sea, rocking back and forth. Stymie and Horn went to bed, but I was glued to the black chair, as it pitched and yawed on an invisible sea. I was gripping the armrests so hard I left indentations in the cushions, but I had to hold on!

I went on like this for hours, lashed by storms, swells crashing over the foredeck, "around the horn and around perdition's flame." Finally at about four o'clock, I was able to crawl upstairs to my bed and crash. I got up the next morning kind of latish, about ten or ten thirty. I went downstairs and told Stymie I'd get right to splitting this cord of firewood I promised to do the night before.

"Ahh don't worry about it."

"What do you mean, it's October, we gotta get that shit done. Besides, I love splitting wood."

"That's alright, we did it already."

"No way, it's 10:30, there's no fucking way you chopped all that wood already."

"We did it yesterday."

"You said last night it was still there."

"No, that was the night before."

"What do you mean, the night before, I just got up."

"You never got up yesterday."

"OH SHIT! You mean it's Thursday?"

"Yep. Pretty strong brownies, huh?" We baked up another batch before heading down for winter, but Stymie bagged them up before I could eat any more.

Our weed was killer that year though. Everyone likes to say that their weed is the best, and each person does affect their weed with their personal vibe, so it gets them the highest. But there weren't many people higher than Stymie and me, and we had the jones of our whole community assisting in the vibe. I never met anyone who didn't think that our weed that year was some of the best they'd ever had. But one of the things about being a serious doper is appreciating the varieties, and their different effects. The Heinz plants turned out what was generally known as "the grape," for it's Welch's concentrate flavor and possibly the very satisfying way it made you feel, like a ripe grape hanging on the vine on a warm Napa evening. The clones were an entirely different story. What yielded a chemically taste with a soporific buzz indoors, became known as the Juicy Fruit. It tasted as sweet as the gum, with a delectable electric buzz when grown outdoors. The plants were all a pound each, which is what you want in the industry. I've heard of plants of up to four pounds, but they were probably using Rapid-gro and Bloom. The biggest organic plant I've seen was three pounds, but it was grown in a gardening junkie's compost pile in the full sun on a south facing hilltop. The giants of Gumby had a different but similar taste and effect to their ancestral Heinz, and they cranked out about a pound and a half each. The Octopus' bud was all skinny little pencils of sativa, but it defiantly produced two pounds, the biggest yield we ever had.

3

I had never been very lucky with my mail orders for reserve seat Dead shows, (maybe they knew I was a bummer) so I had left money with Luigi when they announced Halloween. It was at the Berkeley Community Center, where we had seen Ravi, and they were playing six nights, which is a pretty long stint. It was right around Luigi's birthday, and he told them so in his order letter. They came through with pairs of 2nd, 3rd, 4th, 5th row tickets, except Halloween, for which we got six in the 12th row. Not bad. Those shows were great, very Berkeley. They had a Vivoli's booth in the hallway, where you could get the original and ultimate handmade gelato. There was an espresso stand too, so you could get jacked up for a tenth of the price of coke. I was laden with awesome bud, freshly trimmed Grape and Juicy Fruit, and when they played the most thumping "Let it Grow" on the second night, I threw a big golden bud at Phil. I should have tried to hit his hand, since he was preoccupied with playing, but I was worried that would upset him, so I sailed the bud right by his face. It slid behind his stacks and some roadie snagged it, so I doubt Phil ever got any, but maybe he did. There was certainly enough for a few spliffs.

I saw Jan and got a fresh load of bottles. He also gave me a present, string. The string had been removed from a drying box, where sheets of blotter are laid out to evaporate after they've been dipped in acid. After so many thousand hits are dried, the string gets crusty from absorbing acid, so it's removed. Jan would cut it into pieces and give it away, a mystery dose. You could never tell how much was on it. I had given Willy a piece of string on New Years Eve, which he said began to burn his tongue so fast he had to spit it out. He still came on almost instantly. Stymie flossed with his and got high. I decided to eat a piece for Halloween, having wrapped my dreads into a point to fashion myself after Zippy the Pinhead. The piece I ate was so crusty that I couldn't coordinate my tongue to spit it out after it started burning. I reached into my mouth to pull it out, but couldn't tell my finger from my tongue, so I ended up swallowing it. I was coming on like a cyclotron. Horn's girlfriend was dressed as Indira Ghandi, who had died that week, and I couldn't tell if she was alive or dead herself. As I started mingling around the lobby, I realized that perhaps I was Zippy, since my brain seemed totally useless, and I began to worry that I had gone from potential scion of the Dead scene to burnt out casualty and laughingstock. It was good to be able to find my seat, because I was riveted to it for the first set.

I was having that feeling, like my body was a big grinding electromagnetic device, just buzzing along, almost high enough to forget my ridiculous paranoid ego bullshit, but not quite. The BCT was another one of those theaters that seems to turn into a space ship when the lights go down, and we were heading into another universe, for sure. I survived the first set, white knuckled, and tweaked as I was, managed walking around during the break. Everything was flowing by like a river, moving at different speeds, with eddies and rapids varying the flow. People were either in costume or tie-dye, so it was a totally bleeding visual experience, with snatches of conversation and music bouncing off the walls in a jumble. Fortunately for my friends, I had rolled a bunch of doobies before the show, so all I had to manage was getting my case out and lighting one before we were graced with the stunning puffage. There was something momentarily calming about a lungful of the grape, before it added to the already disorienting effect of the LSD, but my autonomic nervous system knew that smoking everyone out was both a necessity and the only possibility of not appearing so completely blown away. I don't know why I should have been embarrassed to be blown away after eating crystal LSD, but I was so invested in handling it, whatever that meant, that I didn't have permission. The tapers motto: "Peak don't tweak," was hard to live up to.

The second set started off with Touch of Gray, which freaked me out, since I had used that as an alias to get my phone number at the new house with Stymie. It was a song about being jaded, which I certainly was, and a heroin addict, which I certainly wasn't, but I still took it personally. They rolled around to playing Ship of Fools, which my distorted auditory sense turned into a real piece of torture, with an accusatory sound to the tag line. Yes, we were sailing on a Ship of Fools, and it was time to sail away. I couldn't hack it anymore, but by my own rules I couldn't leave the show, which would somehow break the bubble. I don't know how I formulated my personal rules of acidified conduct, but once I did, they were law! I went upstairs to the outside balcony, where I could hang out alone at that point. Eileen followed me up to see if I was alright, but I wasn't and there wasn't anything anyone could do about it. Of course, as soon as I split, they ripped into one of my favorite Bob songs, I Need A Miracle, so I went over and leaned on the ventilator grate. It was a duct about two by three feet, which went straight down into the theater. It actually sounded pretty good, so I lied down on top of it. That's when I left my body in the October chill, floated down through the airshaft, and hung out on the ceiling of the show.

I was enjoying the show from my new vantage point when my other dreadlocked friend, Smurf, happened upon my vacant seat and climbed in. I don't know what he dosed on that night, but I felt like I had left an acid burn there, since I didn't know him to have this sort of problem before. Of course, everybody has their own trips, that's what makes the show so "fun." Luigi later told me that about halfway through "He's Gone," which I felt was a clear indication of my having left the fold, or died myself, Smurf saw Jerry, in the golden stagelights, appear to be dying. Once the drum solo started Jerry left the stage, which was enough to cook Smurf's gourd. Luigi told me his arm went numb from being squeezed so hard by our terrified friend, who kept whispering "Jerry's Dead!!!" Poor Luigi, in the cute Dancing Bear ears that his girlfriend had made him, trying to have a good time while all his friends were losing it.

After the drums got underway, Kip, who was up from LA and had eaten some string also, wandered out the front door and right up to some cops, whose blue uniforms didn't mean anything to him. He told me later that they seemed like friendly guys, who offered him a ride. They took him to the hospital, where they went through his wallet, got his info, called his aged parents in San Diego, and told them he had been taken to the hospital under the influence of LSD. Then they made him drink a gritty black liquid, which he said was like DMT in reverse. I believe it was some Thiamine concentrate, but he said he felt like he was ripped off the dark side of the moon and stuffed back into his body. He took about five minutes to figure out what happened before calling his parents and telling them that he was in LA and it was just a Zete fraternity prank.

I sat out the rest of the show, "Morning Dew," "Saturday Night," "Satisfaction," everything I could possibly want to hear, with my body on the duct and mind on the ceiling. I think Eileen spent a good deal of time there with me, at least she was there after the show. Unfortunately, I couldn't figure out how to bring myself back into my body. The security guys were coming around trying to get us to leave, but I refused to move my body while my consciousness was stuck at the other end of the duct. Eileen found Terry and together they pulled me away, protesting with every stumbling, robotic step my now completely brainless body was making. I was petrified by the fact that I was leaving my mind at the show, and tried to convince them to let me stay until I recovered it. My Paleolithic language skills were far from sufficient to describe my disembodied situation, however, and it probably would have been taken as simply another hallucination anyway. They dragged me the half dozen blocks back to my new house, Stymie and Ben's place, where the party was already beginning to rage. With every bag of nitrous I tried to project myself back up the street to reunite with myself, but no such luck, I could only get farther out. Now I understood, I want my brain back!

I finished off the tank the next morning, after the sun had come and everyone had gone. There were a few bags left, so it was sort of a cumulative excursion. It gave me a interesting slant on the nature of existence, which is usually forgotten upon return to waking consciousness. For some reason, I went into the small closet in Stymie's room, instead of dragging the tank out. As I was whipping out I realized that to be an individual was a process of deviation. So many things are done in common with others, but a turn here or there makes for a slightly different outcome. I decided, in my nitrouspheric state, that I should deviate so many extra turns that my individuality would be completely assured and unrepeatable. While draining every cc of gas from the bag, I did a headstand in the closet and walked my feet up the walls, then worked them around to screw myself like an auger into the floor. In my mind I was sort of wormholing through these levels of consciousness in an amazing pattern, but in physical reality, I almost broke my neck. I really did feel I had achieved something, some otherwise unattainable level of mind exploration, but my neck was fucked up for weeks, and I was no closer being whole.

4

With trimming over and T-day approaching, I made a plan. Stymie was headed home, and Ben was going to his sister's, leaving me with the run of the pad. It had been one of the best years I'd seen, so I felt pretty thankful, which spurred my decision to have T-day there. It looked good for a family gathering, since Ivan was now living on my couch. He had finally got fired for being tooo wasted, and ignoring my advice, moved in with my parents. That only lasted until he got fired from his next job, for being drunk, on the first day. I figured he was safer with me, where I could feed him a 12-pack every day until he got himself together. I told my mom that I would cook, went to Berkeley's produce heaven, the Bowl, and bought everything I could imagine cooking. I stuffed the turkey with a fennel dressing I dreamed up, then barbecued it on the Weber. I cooked up veggies and mashed potatoes, made gravy and cranberry sauce, all that stuff. I laid out a bunch of snooty cheese and appetizery things to go with the champagne I bought, and opened a few bottles of Ben's cousin's wine, which was excellent, so they could breathe.

I hadn't spoken two words to my parents in the last year and a half, owing to their unhappiness with my career path, and I was determined to show them up. All the things they expected of me, at least in terms of being cultured, I was going to display. Of course, I was also able to do it with an opulence that my career choice allowed for. When they arrived and found that I had all the cooking under control they were slightly taken aback. My father was appreciative of my hors d'oeuvre layout, and the champagne. He and Ivan watched some of the remaining football while I finished things.

I was getting pretty close to being ready when the doorbell rang. "There they are! My special guests." I ushered in Dan and Lidya, who I had expected a little earlier. They were on their way to Lidya's parent's house, looking all fresh and holidayish, but they had something for me. I introduced them to my folks, "These are my friends, Dan and Lidya." They all shook hands, and made small talk while I got them some champagne. They were a little late and needed to get on to Lidya's, so we decided to commence with things.

"Hey mom," I said, "I've got to buy some pounds from these guys, wanna come in here and check this weed out?"

"Uhh, I don't think so, son."

"C'mon mom, you like flowers don't you? These are nothing but the flowers of weed plants. Very nice weed plants." I couldn't get her to attend, so we went into the closet and broke open their bucket. It was full of the Grape, from Sherwood. I handed them a load of cash to count, took a bud, and went into the kitchen. Squeezing it in my hand I held it up to my mom's nose, "Smell this ma." I watched her squint as she pondered the mysteriously sweet smell to which she was a foreigner. I opened my hand to show her, but she couldn't take a wholehearted interest, so I went back to my room and finished things with D&L, wished them a Happy Thanksgiving, and sent them on their way. We moved on with dinner soon after they left, and my attempt to display the honor of my profession did not impinge on our enjoyment of our meal or each other.

When we had made it through dinner, my mom's pies, and coffee, I dug in.

"You know folks, whenever we have Thanksgiving at your house, we all go for a walk after dinner and smoke some pot. But here at my house, we don't need to go anywhere." I broke out a bud of the weed I had just purchased and meticulously cut it apart before rolling a perfect bomber. I was thoroughly compelled to display the elegance of my work, and invited the folks to join us. "You've both smoked tobacco, just taste this," I pled, as I fired it up with a French inhale and a smoke ring. I passed it to Dave as our folks eyed us. My dad sat there silently, and deferred as Dave offered him the doobie. I think we were more intent on our mom because there seemed to be some possibility there. She was always the more open and good-humored of the two.

"C'mon mom," Ivan said, "Enjoy yourself." He slung back in his chair and toked so hard that it ruptured his lungs. He started coughing his guts out, turning red, and drooling, as his eyes watered.

"You don't seem to be enjoying it very much," was my mom's curt response. We sent it around again but the folks got too uptight and decided to depart.

"You know, it's not like we're different people than we ever were. The weirdest thing is how differently you act now that you know we get stoned. I was high every day in high school and we had great talks and laughs, but after you busted me you started acting all weird to me, as if I was somehow different."

"Maybe I just realized how different you were." They got their coats and thanked me for the meal.

"You don't have to go, we can play Scrabble," I coaxed. It was too late though, the bridge had been broken again.

5

I'm not sure how it came about, I was probably up on the ranch when it started, but Oblio had begun dealing heroin. I certainly knew enough folks from tour who were using, but no one in Barrington had ever dealt it. It wasn't in the program of mental experimentation. As much government drug propaganda as I had refuted by this point, my understanding of heroin was still thoroughly negative. It certainly had no place in my Barrington. I tried not to be too freaked out about it though. After all, I had other friends who used it, and it wasn't like they were shooting up. It was the shitty Mexican heroin, tar, schmeeze. You smoked it on a piece of foil, which probably had you more at risk for Alzheimer's than the streets-crime-prison associations generally linked to it. Still, it unnerved me to see my young friends doing it; or talking about it, since everyone hides when they do it. At least in the woods we smoked our opium out in the open. We grew it, knew it, and when we ran out, that was it. There was no heading down to Oakland in the middle of the night, or even easier, to Oblio.

On the other side of the drug spectrum, that was the first winter I went to Pinnacles, with Art and Clark. Clark was in his second year at The B, a little shy, but smart, and a total stoner in high school. He had done a bunch of outdoor adventuring, and was always looking for partners for wilderness exploration, which totally fit my model of glorious living and dying. Art had wanted to go somewhere to dose where we could watch the full moon set and the sun rise on the winter solstice. We were looking for a place that would have a good view, without any clouds or fog. Clark suggested the Pinnacles, which is a volcanic park that's famous for its rock climbing. It got cold enough there at night that it was totally clear, and from the tops of the rocks we would have a 360-degree view. We loaded into the Galaxy and took off at about seven o'clock, which, after doing some food shopping in Salinas, put us there around 11. The drive in was on an insanely curving one-lane cliff side road, coming out of ranchlands east of Soledad. There was no one there but us, so we set up camp, squirted down some doses, and began hiking.

The moon lent an iridescent glow to our surroundings as we ambled over the bridge that takes you away from the campground and into the park. Crunching down the gravel path we entered the chasm between two huge walls of rock, winding our way between boulders of various sizes as we headed in. We came to a widening of the path that displayed the extreme climbing. Huge vertical walls of granite loomed over us, covered, as everything there was, with lichen. The lichen gave color to an otherwise gray environment. At first it appeared merely as gray green, but the more we looked, the more we noticed the yellow variety, and the rust color on the granite faces was lichen as well. There was white, and black, and blue, and all of it growing on everything, its hexagonal overlay pattern expanding infinitely under our scrutiny. We descended into the caves, tripping in the darkness, then hiked up to the Balconies, meandering up the trail for hours in the silvery glow.

We wandered around on top, from boulder to boulder, until we found one that made a nice resting place. We were exploring its contours when we found an unexpected omen. There, on a small spur coming off of it, was what appeared to be a large frog, burned to death. We couldn't see it very well in the dark, being on the far side from the now setting moon, but it definitely had four legs, a head, and an amorphous burnt shape. Clark and I immediately began spinning off into the What bizarre Satanic freaks were here before us, and are they still here? mode, while Art, ever pragmatic, started kicking the poor dead thing. He put a few boots to it and its now solidified seared flesh popped off the rock. He picked it up, held it up in the moonlight, and displayed to our slightly improved cognition that it was actually a GI Joe or Big Jim action figure. Now we knew that whatever other freaks came up here were just like us! Death to GI Joe!

We were right on time to see the moonset. While I came to later describe the lichen as being everycolor, the spectral panoply of the solunar event was like nothing I've ever seen. As the moon dipped it turned the sky every possible shade of indigo, violet, blue and green, while the sun lit the East with yellow, orange and red. We rotated again and again, the three of us, leaning back to back with our arms linked, infused as a trine of consciousness, observing how each degree of the horizon held a slightly different charge. Maybe we were looking out on heaven. Clark and I broke off and began to do an interpretive dance to greet the dawn. In the usual mirror dance, you try to reflect the actions of your partner, but Clark and I were able to merge so completely with each other that we could actually feel each others' nerve impulses, tap into each other's system and direct each other's bodies to follow our thought. It was electrifying, dancing in that energy flow against the backdrop of pure color.

When the moon had given up precedence we broke out the bag of granola that we bought in the Safeway in Salinas. It was the old Vita-Crunch, the original granola, which gave our jaws some exercise in the dawn's chill air. I don't think the citizens of Salinas were too big on granola, cuz the shit was rock hard. It was probably on the shelf for years. It was a welcome crunching though, until we all heard a **Crack!** to which Art responded, "Uhhn. I think I just broke my tooth!" He spit the handful of half chewed granola into his palm, a steaming chunky load that quivered like a slug, and began to inspect it, which was unbearably funny. Clark and I were howling as he fingered through it, held a nut up to the light, and voiced his disappointment, "That's not my tooth." He kept sorting through the goo until he came up with another piece, "Now that's my tooth!" Knowing Art, I knew I'd be in for a morning of acid drenched empathic dental pain, but I was laughing so hard I was crying already.

That trip was a positive change, for me. Except for some worry about the toasted frog, I wasn't tweaking too hard. Things can be sort of naturally frightening on acid, just because they seem so unknown from moment to moment, but it was clear that the psychedelic landscape had been spewed forth by the planet, and that we were within its energy field. I still had my own personal issue of being unable to pee, but I'd just disappear off the trail for as long as it took me to get away from myself. Even though I was intensely connected to Art and Clark on a consciousness level, I couldn't really tell them about that. It was just too devastating. What, after all, is the point of being a man if you can't just whip it out and pee? Women have us all beat down in the orgasm thing, and as much as I've loved my life of action and adventure, I have all the injuries I need to show for it. No, this was just going to be my monkey, my private hell, to suffer through, to test my endurance, to give me a new game, but never to acknowledge. It was just too big a rent in my façade. I desperately wanted to be healed, but the only possible answer was to take the same train that had derailed me. Through my own hypothetical construct of consciousness, I hoped that I might possibly be able to dose hard enough to regress myself to before the point of getting all weird. Although eating crystal at Halloween hadn't helped, it had in fact made me more clear about the damage being due to separation from my body, and my need to get back into the proverbial airshaft to reconnect.

I considered writing something on my hand when I dosed, to the effect of "You're just tripping," to remind me when I started to geek out, but that would be an obvious admission of not being together. I went through the next bunch of shows hoping to correct my state, but I only seemed to get on to a new deluxe paranoid trip. It wasn't just that I was the unknowing or unwilling child of Satan anymore, things had moved beyond the point where I could claim my title and do anything with it.

My years of vegging had brought things to a dull lethargy, and it was time to end that. Since Raygun hadn't dropped the bomb, I realized that I must be the bomb myself. I became certain that the incorrect sequence of thoughts on my part would turn my brain into a thermonuclear chain reaction. There was certainly enough atomic matter in my brain to melt down the world as we know it, and it worried me! Must—not—think—bad—thoughts!

The wrong interaction with some other tripping deviant in the hall would send me spinning. Anyone could be an agent of the forces of destruction, trying to trick me into wiping out the planet!!! Who knew who I might be up against? Art and I had once run into these guys in the ramps of the Oakland Aud, which had winding ramps rather than stairs. It was New Year's, and they seemed to be focusing on making whoever walked by forget where they were going. They were doing a pretty good job too, because everybody winding up or down would slow down or stop, and look around confusedly for a second, while these guys laughed. There were some dangerously powerful high-brains out there. If only I knew the sequence, I could know that I wouldn't stumble over it. But to know it would be to set it in action, like opening the red envelope in Fail Safe. The only safe and practical answer to this dilemma was that I should die.

It wasn't at all that I wanted to die, it just seemed the only way to protect my friends from such potentially hazardous material as myself. I suppose I had come to this conclusion in the past, but never with such conviction. The Dead play plenty of songs that you could mistake for the announcement that your time was up, and I certainly had considered at various times that I might be dying, but it was becoming a need. "You know he had to die." A large part of the LSD experience deals with negotiating your death, in some form or other, so it's not uncommon to have the feeling that you are dying or have died. This is quite unlike the panic driven feeling of needing to die in order to keep from destroying the world. Indoor shows really seemed to bring this out in me. There was just no knowing that the outside world existed. At least at the Greek you could see the stars, the trees, the bay, but indoors it's just you, the band, the freaks, security, the bar and the bathrooms. None of these were particularly prone to avoiding my sense of doom. At the core of my being I knew that most of all I loved all these people, my friends, the band, everyone there, it wasn't just about being a good hippie. Hell, I was a bad hippie, hypercritical, jaded, derisive, elitist, egotistical, but I really loved these people, agents of Satan, dupes, or whatever they might be. I just couldn't allow myself to feel it. Maybe I was the reason for the general slide into heroin use, I couldn't imagine that everyone else was so tweaked that they needed to do heroin to stay detached. No one else could possibly imagine himself to be in the position of power my delusions had me occupying. (I Hope!) They could all be getting bored, however, with waiting to see if I'd ever fulfill my destiny.

6

Dan had asked Stymie to kick in to buy a tractor, since he was serious about doing all the roadwork, and had heavy equipment experience from his early days as a runaway in LA. That and the balloon payment on seven were due for the winter, so I was volunteered to make delivery. I had to take the truck, there was no way in hell the Galaxy would make it beyond Dead-Head hill and back. It was the usual winter radical mud drive down, so I left the truck parked by the creek, both to sneak up on them and to make sure I could get out. I stashed a few things they wouldn't see too often back there in my pack, like a fifth of Stoli 100 proof, and started walking. It was a crisp black night, but I had been there enough to make my way down the footpath through the creek without biting it, losing my way in the brush under the oaks, or stepping of the trail and falling down the hill. There was just a light from a DC bulb over the sink illuminating the cabin, but I could see them doing dinner so I kicked in the door, "Surprise!" It was always good to see those two, they just made you feel like you were home in a real sense. They were so far removed from the world that you had no choice but to just be yourself. On the earth with the salt of it.

They knew one of us would be coming sometime, but without a phone time just passes in its natural flow. We cracked the Stoli and made some drinky-winkeys. Civilization hath its charms. I handed them the bag of cash,

"Happy New Year! Ho, Ho, Ho."

"Can we hang stale gingerbread men from your dreads?" Lidya chided.

"Yeah, give those bugs in there something to eat you old rope head."

"Hey man, I wash these things every year! The only bugs I get will be from sleepin on your couch."

"That's right, you better have your own fart sack."

"Yeah I know, it's like a body condom to protect me from where you've had sex."

"Or where Grunt sat, take your pick." Dan had a nice bed of coals going, and whipped out some steaks cut from the cow he had raised that year, Mooey. He grilled them over the open flame with a little cage on a stick thing, making the best steak I've ever had. It was nice and wintry, so we stoked up the fireplace for our after dinner entertainment of drinking Stoli and smoking the fruits of our labor. They told me they were going to head down to Baja when it got really shitty up there, since there's not much to do in the snow, and they had earned their vacation. They thought I should come down, but I was never big on the idea of going to Mexico.

Mulehorn and I got to discussing the idea of a vacation though, as we wintered in town. There were always plenty of cultural activities there, movies at the UC, the PFA, wherever, concerts, clubs, etc., but it wasn't quite as adventurous as going somewhere. I hadn't really been anywhere in a non-Dead related context for some time. The Dead do encourage you to travel, but you're always heading to the next show, until you're drifting back home. We decided Baja would be cool, since it was a popular vacationing weedgrower spot and we could meet our buddies. We drove the galaxy to Kip and Carl and Bam-Bam's place in LA, The Stoner Pad, thrilling them with the stunning grape weed, offed a couple of pounds, mailed my cash back and caught a flight to Cabo. We took a cab from the airport to San Jose, which is the little town by the airport. The cabby was a riot. When he flipped down his visor it exposed several stickers of pigs fucking with captions like "Sexo!" and "Puerco!" We were expecting him to take us right to a whorehouse, but such decorations were considered thoroughly respectable. We hung around town for a couple of days, getting used to the siesta pace, checking out some bars and restaurants, wandering through town, swimming in the ocean, scoping out the sick disco at the big hotel, but there was no sign of our friends. It wasn't as if there had been any way to contact them and make a plan, either before we left or after they arrived.

We were walking along this frontage road in the blazing sun, getting a little bored, when their truck drove by. Fortunately, Horn recognized it. We started running down the road after them screaming until they saw us and jumped out. "It's a freaky carpet headed dude!" We hopped in the back and began our chauffeured luxury tour of Cabo. Riding in the back of a sweltering Toyota pickup down brutal donkey trails and pocked up freeways, ai yi yi. The first thing Dan asked was if I had brought any weed, since he had smoked his already. I figured it was a bust, particularly with my hair, so I didn't.

"What the hell fuckin kind of rastaman are you boy!" he yelled at me.

"Boy hell, ten foot dick, bucket 'o balls, wipe my ass with a cactus," I replied, taking a page from his own book.

"Sheeit, they don't care about dope down here."

"Bummer, man, I could fly back to LA and get what I left in my trunk."

"Ahh, let's just get some tequila." So we did. We got sufficiently fucked up and crashed back at our hotel. The next day we headed out to the West side to find some out of the way beach and camp. We bought a bunch of grub, a case of Ballenas, and got outta town.

Dan knew this great beach, completely deserted, spotless, with one little tree to park under. We snorkeled all day, with occasional breaks for beers and food, but after a day my skin started to freak out. By the next morning I had developed a case of prickly heat. I had never been out in sun like that, and I had these little red bumps all over me. I tried to stay in the shade of the rocks as long as I could, but that wasn't very long. I would combat it by staying clothed in the water and drinking beers. We were sitting there in the afternoon when a VW 411 station wagon pulled off the highway, sat for a moment, and then bombed down the hill and all the way up the beach, burying itself in the sand. Three teenage surfer guys get out screaming, and the driver, who had seen Dan's 4x4 before heading down to the beach, jogs over to us.

"Hey I got stuck, do you think you could pull me out?"

"Hell fuckin no, I spend all year pulling assholes out of the mud. I'm on vacation." The kid's jaw dropped so far it could have dragged up a load of sand,

"But it's my mom's car!" he cried, as if that made us responsible.

"Yeah, well there's a phone about forty miles down the road, maybe you should walk down there and call her.

"But she'll kill me," he pleaded, unable to detect sarcasm.

"Maybe you should have thought about that before driving her car down on the beach like a fuckin idiot. Your not allowed here anyway, the federales will impound your car if they see it. That's why I hid my rig under this tree. I'm sure as hell not gonna get it stuck out there!"

The kid was just about to start crying when Lidya jumped up. "I'll help you push it out!" With that she ran over there, with the kid tagging along, and Dan just relaxing in what little shade there was, mumbling about tinhorn no nothing punks from San Diego. They had buried it pretty good, and Mulehorn and I had to be a little more liberal about helping, since we relied on Dan to pull us out during the year. It was funny though, because Lidya was so much tougher than these surfer boys, she pushed one side out almost by herself. We decided to pack up and split after that, our privacy having been invaded. We headed back to some bar, where I discovered the banana daiquiri, which became my stock drink for the rest of the trip. So satisfying, food and drink combined in a thick frozen concoction that feeds the brain while slapping it around. Mmm-mmm. They had very aesthetic glasses for them too, coke-bottle thick, dirty Mexican barware glass. It was heavenly. I got fucked up enough to tear a huge leaf from the aloes growing out front and goop it onto my tortured skin, but I wasn't nearly as fucked up as I would get.

We were walking around on the beach the next day, when an old Mexican man approached me. He was all dressed in white, as was everyone there other than I. With no white clothes at the time, I was totally unprepared for the furnace like conditions or my prickly heat, which made wearing shorts uncomfortable. In the 110 degree sun I had on my work boots, black jeans, my red Badger T-shirt (the one from Badger comics with a paw mark ripped across the front) and my black ten-gallon hat. This old man eyes me in amazement and asks,

"Tu eres indigeno, de Norte America?" I looked right through him, dead serious, and dropped my voice an octave.

"Sí. Yo soy un Apache." The guy was so embarrassed he almost had a heart attack. It's bad form to ask a silly question like that in a culture where people have some modicum of respect for each other. He was rattling off his Spanish apologies when I started laughing. "Yo no soy un Apache, yo soy un loco gringo!" He had one of those shocks of recognition, where the grin slowly crept up over his face until he broke out laughing, then became my instant buddy, demanding that I come to his restaurant that night,

"Con todos sus amigos," where he would make a fabulous traditional meal and serve us free margaritas. We went over to Hector's house, since he had bought into the little community above the surf break there. It was a beautiful little villa, with a palapa to keep cool under, and a serving window from the kitchen so you could just hand drinks out to the patio. Hector wasn't there, but his partner Grits was. In the evening we piled into his old Ford station wagon, El Rojo y Azul, a two colored junker perfect for Mexico. We stopped by the beer store for a case of Ballenas, where I inquired of the proprietor as to the existence of drunk driving laws. Everyone seemed to be driving with a beer in hand, so I wondered.

"Oh no, senor, is illegal to drive drunk."

"Well, when are you legally drunk?"

"When you can no longer drive. Ha ha ha." There was a law we could respect.

We showed up at the restaurant, the four of us, Grits, and some girl we met at the beach. The owner was in the back, but there was a waiter to welcome us into an otherwise vacant dining room. "Good evening, I am Proto. I am a famous singer on the mainland, but since my old friend has opened his restaurant here, I came back to help him until business gets big." He started eyeballing Lidya like he was Don Juan, which was really a crack up, since she could have easily kicked his ass. We told him we wanted our free margaritas. "Yes, but first let me play for you." He whipped out his guitar and began belting out some love song while hovering around Lidya, who was cracking up. This guy's idea of being a famous entertainer was getting the gong on *Sabado Gigante*. We finally got him to make us a round of margaritas, but free was not cheap enough.

They were nasty. He must have dipped the whole glass in salt. Proto took our orders while the owner came out of the kitchen and greeted us. He looked kind of fucked up, but I wasn't in much shape to be making that judgement call. Proto started playing some more songs, in the direction of Lidya and our female guest, and started to become pretty entertaining in a ridiculous way.

We ordered more smegaritas, which were bad enough to get us to demand the bottle of tequila and pull beers out of the car. I don't even think they had chips and salsa to keep us alive, so we were starving and drinking. I went to take a piss, wandering down the hall by the kitchen to where the sign pointed out to the back. I think I may have missed the door, but it seemed like the right place to take a leak, against the back wall in a junk strewn lot. As I walked back in I noticed that "el chef" had a bottle of tequila himself, and was in no hurry to keep it full. He hadn't even started on our dinner, which Proto was lobbying for on our behalf. I stumbled back to the table, "You've got to check this out." We took turns wandering back to watch them argue as the chef got more fucked up. They were practically brawling back there. By the time our food came we were in hysterics. It seemed that the "specialidad de casa" shrimp had been around past the "sell-by date," since they were more completely dredged in salt than the smegaritas. Completely borracho on Tequila and beers, ears suffering the assaults of Proto's lacerating vocal accompaniment, our mouths were now being poisoned by long dead sea creatures that had been posthumously tortured in a frying pan. We took turns tasting each other's food to see who had the worst. We looked back in the kitchen and the old man was curled up on the floor with his bottle, but Proto was just as proud as ever, asking if everything was okay with our meal as we staggered out the door.

We had a great time, snorkeling, drinking, going to the little carnival where we won everything, Dan gambling on the tarot wheel and I at the pitching booth, hitting some poor Mexican in the face with a beanbag until he had a bloody nose. I'm not sure if it was "the best worst meal I ever had in my life," which is how I described our encounter with Proto, or the pescado pizza the next day, but Mexico finally caught up with me. I spent my last day there erupting from both ends and polluting my hotel bathroom, since the toilet, of course, refused to flush. Completely gutted out, just looking at the airport bar made me hurlish. I could only sit there, sweating, with the iguana I had won at the carnival, painfully awaiting the return to my nice clean country.

7

Stymie drove up to the ranch around March to get the rest of the weed he had buried. There were six pounds of Juicy Fruit left from Garson, which were all ours. We hadn't brought down much of that weed yet, we wanted it to cure enough to be as amazing as it could be. It's interesting to note how you can be so professional at one end of your business and so slack ass at the other. Somewhere down by Santa Rosa Stymie looked back in the bed of his truck to find that the duffel bag with all the weed, which hadn't been weighted or tied down, was gone. He turned around, bombing back Northward to Healdsburg, where he found the kitchen garbage bags in which the gallon ziplocked qps had been stowed, blowing around in the bushes on the median. Apparently the pillowcase which contained them all had been blown out of the truck, and someone had discovered it before Stymie noticed. It was devastating, four or five grand down the drain for me, and twice that for Stymie, but the money was secondary. There was just no replacing that golden clone bud!

The dough, however, was recoverable. It would take a few months, but we got right to it. I was running up to the Freaks' every week for ten pounds, flailing them out at the B, packing the cash in a Pepperidge Farms cookie bag, Milanos, and driving. Driving, driving, driving. I was in Stymie's truck, heading North past Willits one night, it was after midnight already, and the pigs pulled me over. I wasn't doing anything except perhaps fitting the profile. What profile I'm not sure, since Stymie's truck been falling apart over the years. Have you ever seen a Toyota SR5 without a piece missing or dented in? Stymie's had every mark I'd seen on any of those trucks, missing both rear bumpers so the frame pieces jutted out, tailgate bailing wired on, smashed mirror, caved in front quarter panel, missing front grill, missing headlight assemblage, it could have made a great ad for Toyota. It certainly didn't make me look affluent. I asked the cop why he pulled me over and he told me I was driving in the passing lane. I was in the left lane of two lanes on an empty highway, BFD! He asks me for the registration and I open up the glove, which they flash their mag lights into. It's loaded with crumpled ziplocs full of white. The fuckin pigs jacked up like they all did espresso enemas.

"May we look in your glove compartment?"

"Sure," I replied. They go charging in there and pull out these bags, which were all full of used Kleenex. That really took the starch out of their collars. They could have drug tested the snot and come up with something, but they let me go. I had thirty-five grand under the seat, but they never thought of that. Cops just don't think the way other people do. I began to realize that as I drove more, and I felt a little safer.

I set some record times for the drive to the Freaks' and back with ten pounds, but sometimes you'd have to wait out the rain, or wait for some more pounds to arrive. I've had nights were I didn't leave there until 11, drinking Pepsis and winding through the redwoods in the rain. Heading down those long boring stretches with only the whine of the engine to keep me company, saying to myself don't fall asleep, don't fall asleep. I got home on one of those nights and fell in to bed. As soon as my head hit the pillow I was driving again. It was dark, and I was tired. I started to fall asleep. No! I jerked up, sloshing awake in my waterbed. Whoa. I went right back into it, falling asleep behind the wheel, No! waking up again. This repeated until finally I was asleep, driving, falling asleep, and I told myself, Just crash it into this building. I turned right up off the highway and into a big brick wall, and drifted off.

On one of those runs I scored some weed that came in a white bag. Stymie was kind of upset, but we poured it all out and it wasn't shaky, which I knew before I bought it. We smoked some though, and ended up stashing a quarter pound, it was such fantastic weed. We never saw any more, the next week or after that. We just had our one stash of White Bag to sustain us through the loss of the Juicy Fruit. We got very into stashing that year, which we always had, but it was a bumper year. We had mason jars full of bud for our personal collections. As Stymie used to say, "Beats the hell out of collecting stamps!" Masters of weed science that we were, we investigated every kind of combination. A third of this, that, and the other weed, a dusting of hash powder. Stymie scored this amazing Pakistani hash from one if his friends. It was unlike any imported product I've ever had, obviously smuggled direct, not commercially. It was soft and gooey, with a mocha flavor. We'd roll that in combination with the White Bag and almost be knocked out. It was luxury living at its finest. We were undisputedly the weed kings of Berkeley. Art even started calling Stymie "Weedneesh," since the Rajneesh freaks were making such scene, and he always had a bud that would reveal cosmic truths. (If only we could have gotten all the rich women in town to give us their money and have sex with us.)

I was sitting around at the Freak's one day, waiting for Beetle to track down some pounds. TS and I were talking about something he had been doing in Garberville when it dawned on me, Garberville was where Mr.

Ching had moved all those years ago. Gville is really the center of Southern Humboldt, and is the generic title given to describe any of a dozen different one horse towns and their environs. It was the equivalent of asking someone if they knew Joe Blow because they were both from LA, but I had to ask,

"Hey T, do you know a guy named Ching?"

"Ching? Of course I do. He's the only Chinese guy in Humboldt county."

"Do you know where he lives?"

"Two miles up the mountain."

"NO Fucking way!"

"Go check it out." I hauled out of there and up the mountain, turned in at the old cattle guard, rolling slowly up to an old one room cabin.

"Hey Ching?" I called out. The door swung open, revealing a kitchen with a table inside. Mr. Ching stepped out and looked at me querulously.

"Can I help you?"

"It's me, Sheldon." His eyes widened as he saw through the dreads and the beard and the ten inches I had grown. As usual, he burst out laughing.

"Ho dude, what happened to you?"

"I gotta Jamaican make over, baby!"

He popped out a couple of beers, introduced me to his kids, who I hadn't seen since they were infants, and took me for a stroll. He had done really great work homesteading his place, built a great garden, planted fruit trees; his few killer plants were hidden so well I walked by them without even noticing. He had made a pretty good life for himself away from the city. He still taught, did volunteer work, all the things he was cut out for. But he was doing it here in this beautiful country, where there seemed to be fewer repressed people to argue with him about actually teaching. It was a joy to see him again, and to know that he was doing just what he wanted. I told him I was running loads with the Freak Brothers, which cracked him up. "You fuckin crazy white boys," he laughed at me, but it was good in that it made occasional visits a breeze. It was also exciting to see life cycle around in such a way as to return my mentor to me.

Maybe just talking to him made me realize what might be possible in life, in terms of a socially responsible counter-culture existence, and just how far from that ideal my world was becoming. Paranoia and traumatization were one thing, but those were personal problems. When I wasn't in my delirium, I liked to think (except for the fact that Reagan, republicans, and religious retards were running things) that the rest of the world was okay. The more I dealt with my taper friends, though, who were always grinding up bindles of coke, and doing shmeeze with the fat man himself, the more I noticed how the scene really was. There were thousands of star-eyed, love struck kids and adults out in the crowd every night, thinking that the Dead was such a groovy evolutionary peace and love thing, while the band was actually about as sick as the Stones. The acid taking, consciousness-promoting bandwagon had become a front for massive coke and heroin abuse, and I wasn't exactly standing on the sidelines. When they played the BCT again that spring I got an idea of how far things had gone.

They had opened that show with "Terrapin Station," a slowly rolling anthem of lyrical ambiguity. It churns its way through its story, building up to the room-rumbling refrains of "TERRAPIN!" the mysterious destination of Deadheads. It had been awhile that Stymie had been singing it as "HEROIN!" and I found it a substitution not devoid of humor. At some point I grabbed Luigi to go smoke a joint and talk. We walked upstairs to the very last row of the balcony and sat down.

"Is it just me, or are they sucking?" I asked him.

"I think someone cut Jerry's schmeeze with methadone, he's been stuck on the 'ta-diddle' lick for the last three songs," he agreed.

"Do you think some crank would help?"

"I can't imagine that more drugs will make a difference. No."

I rolled up a bud as we exchanged observations about the band's weak performance, then fired it up. It was nice to be alone, with a pal, talking shit in the undisturbed remoteness of the back row. There seems to be a curve, around which your star-eyed love for the Dead gets lost behind a few "cosmic revelations," shall we say, and you wind up becoming jaded. It's not such a bad thing, it gives new meaning to the shows. You can insult Jerry, like Bagel would, or think of funny lyric substitutions, or just rag. Still, the glory of that one show, where you were too high to realize it would never be that groovy again, was forever etched on your mind, hoping for a repeat. A return to innocence. If it weren't, we'd all have to wake up to the fact that our jaded commentary was true, and to still be going would mean you were an idiot. Of course, one had one's social rounds to make as a dealer. If you paid taxes you could write it off as a business expense.

Luigi and I were still puffing along when out of nowhere a foot appeared between our seats. It had a shoe on it, it was attached to a leg, but its presence defied logic. We turned around to discover that a black scrim had been hung between the row we were in and the actual last row. In the darkness it simply looked like the wall was draped, but when we looked right up against it we saw people smoking heroin in the back row. The band had arranged for a secret section where people could do heroin! This was too much! The most glaring thing for me, was that Eileen and Mina and Terry had started using it, along with their other trust funded girlfriends, all of whom seemed to have less than positive emotional associations with their fathers. Not that mine were that great, but I had always leaned more toward blowing my head open than locking myself in the closet. Perhaps, with my head as blown open as it was, I didn't make too good of an example. Mina accused me of being painfully square one day, when I was carping on her for doing heroin. "Why don't you just get off your uptight boojwah middle class trip?" How could she say that to me? I, who had given her LSD when she was still a shy 16 year old private school girl.

I was ruminating on this question, that perhaps my ideas about drugs had become superfluous, that I was old and boring now, and afraid to get with it, when Jerry played in town. The Keystone Berkeley was a shrine of sorts, a big enough club that serious bands had played there for decades. It had maintained its old Berkeley funky feel, an open room with a bar, devoid of any trendy attempts at club style. It had an upstairs balcony, which was divided into a section of tables, where you could watch the show in the darkness, and the back area by the stairs, which was a mingling spot. In the darkened tables of the balcony was where people liked to do heroin. The Menace had been after me for awhile to try it, he had been balancing his cocaine use with it for some time, as were most of its new devotees. A thorough search of The Menace's belongings would generally find an eighth of blow, a quarter tenth of heroin, a quarter ounce of weed, a thousand hits of acid and a pound of mushrooms, owing to his personal habituation and large East Coast mail order biz. I enjoyed Dennis, he was a rager with a great sense of humor, and I figured that if I were to try heroin with anyone, he would be the best.

"Welding!" (he liked to call me that) he shouted, when I found him at the bar. "Beer?"

"Sure Denny, but I've got a proposition for you."

"What's that?"

"Let's smoke some heroin."

"Whoahoho, buddy boy," he said, his eyes opening behind his rose colored glassed, "what's got into you?"

"Nothing, just figured this would be the place to do it, and you'd be the man to do it with." There is something primal about turning other people on to drugs, sort of a deflowering process, and I could see his wheels turning with the idea of getting me high, since I was such an anti-powder campaigner. "You got?" I inquired. He looked around to make sure no one was listening, then leaned over,

"Yeah, yeah, let's go upstairs."

"Okay," I said, following him to the back, "but one thing, we have to do it in the open." That stopped him. He turned around and looked at me,

"What do you mean, Shel?"

"I don't want to go hide in the dark and shit. If I'm gonna do heroin, I'm gonna do it like a man. Right here in public, where everyone can see me, okay?"

"I dunno, man" he replied, with that vaguely laughing—you're not serious—look on his face. We sat down on the bench at the top of the stairs. It was right in the middle of everything, people heading up and down, dancing, sitting at tables.

"If I'm gonna do heroin, I wanna sit right here and do it."

"Shit man, that's crazy."

"What do you mean, Menace? Who in here is gonna give a fuck?" We got up and sauntered into the darkened front half of the balcony, where he felt more at ease.

"Let's just move over to the corner, where it's cool."

"Naaah. I told you man. I'll smoke a bunch of heroin with you, here tonight, but it's gotta be right there on the bench. You think it over." I went back downstairs with my beer, alone, although I bumped into him a couple more times during the show. He eyed me nervously, pondering his own paranoia no doubt, but I couldn't get him to do it. That's when I knew I was right.

Still, being right about heroin didn't help matters much, since Eileen was doing it. Despite my overall lack of sensitivity, I couldn't help but be stung by the fact that my girlfriend wanted to do heroin. Heroin is about ignoring everything, being unaffected, not allowing any feelings to get in the way. It was not only against my belief system, it was against me. Yeah I was high all the time, but I had locked myself out of my emotions, as a conscious decision, drugs or no drugs. I didn't think that weed locked me out. Perhaps I was mistaken. Maybe smoking weed all the time made me unavailable. I certainly hated it when I'd smoke a barrel of some incredible shit and Eileen would call to discuss some emotional crap. It would totally ruin my high — to get dragged down into my body like that, and it seemed like she had radar, she'd call right after I toked one. I suppose that's the good thing about heroin, you get so out of it that your travels are uninterruptable.

At least in my misunderstanding I believed that my drug use was directed toward some kind of heightened sense of awareness, which is not an error you can make about heroin. This argument, however, only expanded the rift between Eileen and me, making it easier for us to stay high in our own ways, coming together only for the sensation of fucking, feeding and fighting. A girl can really take a pounding when she's all doped up, and it's the kind of drug that's easily hidden. If you haven't done enough to be nodding out, you're still fairly under control. No one's checking your pupils in the dark, and I was stoned enough not to notice Eileen's use until it became obvious. Still, we were connected somehow. As much as this, or any other of her negatively perceived qualities tormented me, (in my egotistic view of her as a reflection on me) I couldn't leave her, and she didn't want me to, so as much as we duked it out, we stayed together.

§

When it was time to head back up to the ranch for another year, I was pretty invested in being up there. I took a bunch of my stuff with me, including my nun-chucks, which had somehow survived the fire and my ensuing itinerant period. They had been made a federal offense, so I thought it wise to get them out of the house. I wrapped them up in a shirt and stuffed them in one of my rubber rain boots, which are mandatory attire in Humboldt. I put all my shit in the trunk of the Galaxy and hit the road. I was going to go in the back way, having arranged to meet Jackson back in Roseville to party for a night before going to Chico where Ed was drinking his way through college. I had imagined that I would go to the DMV there to register my car, since it was such a pain in the ass in Oakland, and it needed doing. I was tooling down Interstate 80, cranking my stereo, when I saw the red lights flashing in my rearview. Fuckin cops. This CHP pulls me over, although I was hardly speeding, and tells me my tags are out of date. I explained to him that I was on my way to get them, but who hasn't heard that. He looks at me, and decides I'm extra freaky, like, maybe he has a bust.

"Are you carrying any contraband or illegal weapons?" he asks me. No one in my entire life has ever imagined me carrying a weapon, yet there I was, with my chucks in the trunk.

"No," I replied, disgust beneath my disdain.

"I'd like to search your car, sir." It's a tough decision, whether or not to argue with them when they pull the police state crap on you, but there was nothing in my car, so I agreed. He made me get out of the car, go back to his, put my hands on the hood, and let him frisk me. This is all for having dreadlocks, no roaches in the ashtray, no nothing. Okay, I had one week expired tags, but hey, get real. I was standing there, hands on his car, thinking, fuckin pig, when he started going through my back seat, and I had to laugh. My back seat, or the footwell back there, was completely full of trash. It was one of my efficiency theories that one should use the entire rear area as a trash bag, cleaning it out only when necessary. This pig was going through all my old sandwich wrappers and chip bags and Pepsi cans and shit, just diggin through there like a raccoon or something.

He finally gives up on the trash and I see him open my backpack. Oh fuck, I did not give him permission to search my pack, but it's a little late to argue that point. He fiddles about in there for a while, and I can't see because he's behind the front seat. After an exceedingly long search he walks over to me with a bag of weed.

"I thought you didn't have any contraband," he says, which was obviously a lie, cuz if he thought I didn't have any contraband, he wouldn't be diggin through my trash like a fuckin maggot.

"Officer," I groaned, "that's just my stash." Since having less than an ounce was practically legal I didn't think much of it as a crime, but I was attached to the weed, which was Mulehorn's pepper weed. It was a super airy bud, which tasted just like pepper, and there wasn't very much of it. He gives me his cop glare, walks over to the side of the freeway, dumps out my baggie, and crushes the buds under his cop shoe. He lifted his foot, and the weed, which was extremely dry also, had been ground into a powder. Just at that moment a breeze came up and blew the whole quarter ounce pile away. My jaw dropped with the instant bummer of it, and he got his pig satisfaction. He let me off with a fix-it ticket for the registration, and I drove away. I kept my eye in the rearview though, cuz I was still sweatin. He had taken a mighty long time in my backpack, so I crammed my arm down in it to grab a little pouch that was sitting just below the weed. Keeping it low, and watching in the rearview for the cop, I unzipped it and fingered through the stacks. I thought he might have pilfered, as cops are wont, but my 15 grand was still intact. The cop was so stoked on his little weed bust that he missed all my cash. Of course, my weed was gone, which was a bummer, but Jackson understood. I was upset though, to have driven a hundred miles to smoke out my buddy and have no stash. I pulled my pack apart, fishing into the cool side pockets that it had, and then remembered the secret pouch. I reached in there and pulled out a quarter ounce chunk of black hash, which had to be at least eight months old. We were blown away, both by the discovery and a fat pipe load, but I was doubly so, since the feds had bumped hash up to Schedule 1 that year and that pig could have really fucked me. Once again they were on another wavelength.

I left the next morning, swung up to Chico and spent another day getting wrecked with Ed. It only took me five minute to register my car there before heading west to the ranch. That was the kick-off to another year of weed growing, almost as if there were a old world festival to bring honor and glory to the years efforts, something like "The Day of Narrow Escape From the Pigs." It was back to work again, time to bust a gut, shed the winter coat, wallow in shit. Speaking of shit, Bernard came over to complain early on. He was particularly upset because during the winter someone had come up, "Supposedly to visit Ben," as he suspiciously put it. He had met him in the meadow, told him to leave, and when the guy told him he was there to see Ben and to stop bugging him, Bernard punched him in the mouth. Whoever he was, he was rather distressed after that, and left.

"Oh great, so you're just punching anyone who comes up to visit?" Stymie asked facetiously.

"He. shouldn't. have. been. here." Bernard said, stridently. "Ben. doesn't. live. here. I. want. to. know. who. he. was."

"Maybe you should have asked him." The pigs may have been escapable, but the asshole land partner was still right there.

We had a plan to expand that year, cutting back on Garson a little so we could go down to Sherwood and grow. Dan's original agreement to give a share of the Sherwood crop to Stymie and Bernard was over, so we had to do it ourselves. We went down there to select a place, surveying what areas were discrete yet accessible enough that we could get water to them. We discovered a reasonable east-west slice between some firs, where we put in about 10 holes in three patches. We redid the holes up on Garson, as well as all the patches on Lizard, topping off the old dirt with a load of fresh turkey shit, blood, bone and lime. We had gotten a jump on things by starting our plants at home in the garage and leaving them under Ben's care while we put the mountain together. Of course, we made time to thrash with the neighbors, inviting them up to kick off our new season of film.

We had been there working for a few weeks when Bernard came over to the shed, completely flipped out. He accused us of hiring hitmen to take him out in what was, unfortunately, a failed attempt. He had burned Katrina the year before, deciding not to pay her for growing all his weed while he was down in town fucking some bimbo, so she had split. He drafted his sister and her boyfriend to be his new weed slaves, and they were living down at the Dollhouse, the little cabin he had built for Katrina on the property below the Dead Shed, which is what the neighbors called our place. Bernard had been gone for the weekend, as he always was when the roulette ball was about to land in his slot, leaving his sister and her boyfriend there alone. A couple of rugged dudes had driven up in a Lincoln or something, entered brandishing pistols, and tied them up with duct tape. They questioned Bernard's sister about his whereabouts, which she unfortunately didn't know. They had a variety of torture devices, which they didn't use on their hostages, but were apparently prepared to use on Bernard. After a day and a half of this, peering out the window whenever someone drove down the road, they decided to split. Bernard came back to find his very distressed sister, who was now unwilling to do his work for him. He was totally freaked out by it (probably because he couldn't scam anyone into doing all his work for the year) so he borrowed a gun from Dan to "protect himself." A year later we found out that the clone guy had come to visit Ben in early spring to see how outdoor growing worked. I suppose he was the first of the industrial weedgrower trend, and similar to Bernard, in that he was more attached to the financial enterprise than the product. He seemed perfectly okay when I met him, but he had some hardcore associates from his youth in Reno. They had been asked to repay Bernard's impoliteness, and chose the wrong day. After that Bernard was even weirder than he had been before.

It was hard to be sure what really happened. We never saw Bernard's sister, and with his pathology it was hard to believe him alone. We imagined that if it had actually happened it was Bernard's own behavior being visited upon him. No big, we just went back to work. As things progressed down at Sherwood, we were warned by Dan that the deer were heavy down there, since it was further from the population base of the road, and bordered more uninhabited property. Deer will fuck up your weed, which can be crushing after you've spent months working and expecting a payoff. The pigs are bad enough, but if some animal that you could have shot eats your weed, that's a bummer. Not that we wouldn't like to kill the pigs, but you have to be reasonable about some things.

We didn't usually plant until about July, when the plants were starting to outgrow their containers, and we didn't start working on the fences until after we planted. The thing about July was that it was about the time opium poppies are ready. Lidya had filled in a section of her compost area with poppies that year, and they were booming. Huge flowers of red and purple, with their various gradations, waved at the end of six-foot tall stalks. The poppy is an interesting plant, yielding a seedpod that hides within a cup of huge, beautiful petals. If you showed one to your mom she'd have them in her garden the next year. Lidya's green thumb had worked it's usual magic, you'd walk out there in the late morning, eye level with a giant poppy, lean it back to see past the flower petals to the pod, and a huge bumblebee would fall out, completely wasted from the pollen alone.

Dan was a serious master of O-cropping. He took to the plant science the way he did everything, raw and professional. He'd wait until the sun was up enough to dry the dew off the pods, to get them warmed up and swelling, before dragging his razor across their surface ever so lightly, perforating the outermost layer without breaking the skin, which kills the plant. The white milk would bead up instantly, oozing into a line that sat on the pod to bake in the sun. At the end of the day, or even days later, he'd scrape the dried brown resin off the surface of the pods, like dope plant caramel for candy craving kids. The longer you left the resin on, the more the sun's baking would purify it, but Dan had a direct method too. He'd get a spoonful of the goo, add water, and boil it into a dark crystalline form. He'd chop that up with a razor and put it in the glass pipe, or roll it in a doobie, the paper of which he'd wipe with the goo.

We'd take the truck down there every day to do our fence work, but it wouldn't start until we'd had a session. It was hard to imagine working after getting so thoroughly whacked, but that's probably one of the reasons opium became so popular. We'd crank out hardcore days of posthole digging, ramming fence posts, and stretching wire in the blazing sun without a second thought. After that job was done we simply made excuses for having to go down there, until the crop ran out, at which point we had to kick the habit and go back to smoking plain old maryjane. We loved hanging out down there though, just to be around the cowboy. It was always entertaining to see the human contradiction of runaway-hippie-dope-dealer turned redneck.

"Hey you freaks," he'd start in, "I found a bag all full of moldy weed. I hear them Deadheads'll pay extra for it."

"Yeah, that's why we're down here every day, smokin your shitty goo, cuz it tastes like toejam!" I'd reflexively insult.

"Goddamn right, I bought it off a nigger at the bus station," he'd say, topping me in mock self-deprecation.

I started to make daily rounds to Sherwood on the bike, both to check the plants and hang out. I'd bring a couple Mr. Brews, smoke a fat one and watch the sun set over the ridge with D&L. As soon as it fell out of sight I'd get on my bike and roar up the road to the pond, where I could watch it set again, but with a commanding view of the shadows creeping over the valley. After it had peaked I'd fly on up to the Dead Shed, where it would be gin and tonic time with a doobie on the back balcony. From there you could watch the sunset through the trees, which filtered the light in a kaleidoscopic display. When it got dark at the shed, if it wasn't my day to cook dinner, I'd hop back on and roar up to the top of Garson, where I could watch the sun set on the ocean, 40 miles away. You could see all the cloud patterns, tingeing red and pink and purple, while the sky went through its prismatic display of hues. On clear days there'd be a layer of sea green that I'd never known before. It was certainly not an aspect of the city sky, and it was beautiful. It was a perfect meeting of the modern conventions of bud, booze, and motorized transportation, with the stunning splendor of the wilderness.

I was over by the Gumby one day when I ran into Bernard. He had calmed down some since the hitmen came, and I actually had a conversation with him. I asked him about dealing in Barrington and how much acid he had taken. He told me that he had never dosed.

"What?! You've never taken acid? Did you sell it?"

"Yeah."

"How could you sell acid and not do it?"

"It… didn't… appeal… to… me." It made sense, in the fact that no matter what trip you go off on from taking acid, you always have a greater sense of your impact on people. I think it makes you more careful about your potential karma, because you can see it come back pretty quickly. Even that, however, can be ignored through massive heroin consumption. Perhaps that's what spurred the massive heroin consumption on tour, imagined karmic avoidance. We got to talking about Oblio and his scene in Barrington, and Bernard asked me if I ever did heroin.

"No way, that shit's for losers. You get more fucked up on O anyway, and you don't have to deal with any scumbags."

"Yeah, but you could buy a bunch pretty cheap…" he said, his speech pattern evening out as he leaned toward reverie, "and have enough to just do the same amount every day, to maintain the same high. I think about doing that… just scoring a big load of heroin… and doing a little bit every day." It was apparent to me that he had thought about it.

"Yeah," I said, looking at him in this new light, "I think a lot of people say that." I was impressed at how imbedded in the weed trip Bernard was, while being diametrically opposed to, or ignorant of, the general thinking and understanding of the dope culture. I guess that "totally out of it" would be a good description. I think a lot of the problems we had with him could have been corrected by slipping him a 250 mic dose. Unfortunately I was also a raised-in-Barrington professional LSDealer, so that kind of shit was beyond the outskirts of my moral code.

9

Ballbusting, however, was respectable. Exploiting every weaknesses in everyone's façade, it was a revered tradition in the woods, one you either excelled at, by developing a thick skin and a sense of humor, or cracked. Bernard was more of a cracker. He did shit to try to break balls, but mostly he whined. He seemed to be more intent on driving us off the property though, as the year went on, which led to confrontations that weren't within the code. I was bombing down the driveway on Ben's little BMX bike one day after lunch. I was a little gutted out from peanut butter overkill, but not so much that I couldn't take my flying leap off the berm. I landed clean and was headed down between the trees when Bernard jumped out from behind one and shouldered me off the bike. It completely knocked the wind out of me, so all I could do was lay there.

"I. want. you. to. leave!" He shouted.

"Fuck You," I groaned. He kicked me in the ribs,

"Pack. up. your. shit, and. go. home."

"This is my home."

"No. This. is. my. home, and. I. don't. want. you. living. here. anymore!"

"You'll have to take that up with Stymie, I work for him."

"No. This. is. between. you. and. me."

"Well then, I ain't leavin. You can fight me every day, maybe beat me, but you can't make me leave."

"You'd. better. watch. yourself."

"Yeah, I guess." He strode off into the forest, leaving me to pick myself back up out of the dirt.

It was obvious that he could get to Stymie and Mulehorn if I weren't there. He was kind of gnarly, working in the woods and living on his miserly diet of canned Jack Mackerel and sauerkraut, but I figured that if I couldn't kick his ass outright I'd take a beating every day rather than back down. He was doing a better job of cracking Mulehorn, but never got violent with him or Stymie, which might have been more effective, since they hadn't had the training my brothers gave me. I asked them if they wanted me to fight him, since he was definitely going for them by trying to drive me off, and I owed him one now, but they wanted to keep it as mellow as possible, so I just kept an eye out for him. He definitely went for that hiding in the woods shit. I probably should have pounded him of my own volition, but I didn't want to escalate things for those guys. I figured I'd get my chance sooner or later, on my own terms, and it was good enough to know I was breaking his balls.

When Bernard wasn't around, and he stayed fairly well hidden, it felt like it was all our place, and beautiful. I invited my friends to visit, and had great times when Clay, Luigi, or even Eileen visited. Nothing like sex in the sunshine next to a giant weed to improve your relationship. I felt secure there, in who I was and what I was doing. It was "Sugar Mountain" made of weed. We started having barbecues and horseshoes every Friday. D&L and Grunt would come up, sometimes the Tree People or a Rockyfeller. Hoss and Hector had moved off the mountain that year, as well as Rocky's partner that got busted, so it was good to have regular social activities to keep the community together. Whether he was around or not, Bernard never came.

We kept dealing through the summer, making our runs down to town every ten days or so. When the Freak Brothers started running out, or it would take too much time to visit them, we'd have Rocky and his brother bring up a load. Despite CAMP's pillage, Rocky had still gotten a couple hundred pounds out of his places, which he had graded by bud size and sealed in seal-a-meal bags. It was kind of weird, dealing with his generic pot, of which every bud was the same, but were sold in pounds that went up a hundred dollars for the size differences. We bought our usual ten pounds one day, breaking a bag open and smoking a bud out of it.

"Pretty good, huh?" Rocky tentatively inquired to assure himself of his dope growing mastery.

"It's okay, Stymie replied, breaking out an extant bud of our golden clone weed, "Try some of ours." I had never smoked any pot with those guys before. Rocky was usually going about his business and didn't seem like a serious dope smoker, although his brother was. We handed them the twenty something grand to count and rolled one up. Lighting it up infused the room with the heavy sweetness that we used to sugar coat our lungs before passing it to those guys. By the time it had gone around twice they were completely red-eyed, and then the fun began. Rocky's brother was so Chinese he could hardly see. They were each trying to count a bundle of ten grand but couldn't get more than three stacks done before they'd fuck up and start again. It went on for awhile, miscount after miscount, while they looked more and more glazed. I'd take a stack from them and whip through it to make sure it was right, before handing it back for them to recount, but eventually they just gave up. "We trust you guys," they told us, but they just never had to deal with getting that high.

Jan's prediction about the downfall of the acid network seemed to come true that summer, and I can't say it was a great loss. Maybe if we lived in a society where freedom of thought and spiritual health weren't already suppressed, the original ideals of the acid generation, to expand our consciousness and create a free society, could have flourished. The state of decay we were reaching in the repressive Reagan era had brought the once hoped for salvation of the west, LSD, under the control of a bunch of junkies. I heard that the feds blasted Mex in the parking lot of Spenger's, Berkeley's once famous fish house. BT on the other hand, apparently unable to afford his powder abuses through product sales alone, had taken his dosing to the logically criminal extreme. Believing himself invisible, he began to rob banks around Los Angeles. I'm not sure if he dosed for his robberies or was under the veil of invisibility all the time. I hadn't seen him for a while. Robbing banks in broad daylight is no way to avoid detection by the police, however, so he went down too. The gel factory was still working, but my childhood connection had moved on to coke too, and I didn't like their product much, especially after a thousand hits I Fed Exed got ripped off. I guess FedEx was a more acceptable loss than the feds, but it was a bad sign. When their man in New York stepped out the window of his 18th story apartment with a flight bag containing a hundred hits, a walkman, and some Dead tapes, I think that even they might have had an inkling that the end was coming. But not the end I had anticipated for so long. No, despite his abuses, Raygun wasn't destroying the world in any atomic flurry.

Oblio too, had gotten to be a thorny issue for me. I'd be delivering pounds to him while he was having congress with all sorts of folks in his room. Yeah, I was uptight, but I really didn't want a bunch of street dealers to know my biz, and he wanted to do his deals in front of everyone to show how politically correct he was. He was taking Bernard's concept to the next level. As more people got deeper into heroin though, the vitality of Barrington began to wither. Of course everything changes, but it was no longer the playground of my youth, nor the hub of counterculture progressive thinking that it once seemed to be. It was rapidly becoming a hangout for street dealers and junkies, one that invited young people not to throw away their propaganda-fed social constructs and redefine society, as it had in the past, but to descend directly into nihilism. I had taken a longer road to nihilism, and I could see how the shortcut worked. Once you learned to avoid your feeling of regret about becoming a junkie, (and by then you've become accustomed to avoiding all sorts of feeling about your life) you become dependent on avoiding it. There's only more regret, sadness, despair, disconnection, whatever negative emotions you have, piling up outside the closet door. So you stay in the closet.

My friends hadn't started banging yet, but I knew it couldn't be too far away. I had watched Art and Bill Crooks shoot up once in Eileen's bathroom in 207. Art had been crashing on our floor, and had procured a load of MDA. He had been in the army in Germany in his youth, where he sold heroin, and shot cocaine for awhile too. He was someone I utterly trusted though, because he understood the drug, and made no pretense about the downside. He liked to get high, and get off, and knew there'd be costs. It was pretty gnarly to watch those guys jack it in, particularly with a drug I had never associated with that kind of use, but they got off in a hurry, way off! Once you start stickin I suppose you realize that all your smokin and snortin ain't shit.

16

That summer came to a glorious ending though, starting with my 23rd birthday party. Eileen and I had been frequenting this sushi bar up the street from Barrington, to the point that the chefs and I partied all the time. I was so impressed by their creativity one night that I took one of their porcelain bowls and put a bud in it for them. They amazed me by responding in a totally Berkeleyan fashion, creating a foil pipe in about eight seconds and toking it up right behind the bar. I dropped a lot of cash there that year, and the owner closed the restaurant so all of my friends could party with me. They made me a whole fish, over two feet long, by covering a cleaned skeleton with pieces of sushi. We went wild, swimming in sake, ordering whole platters of unagi, hamachi, tobiko with quail egg, smoking bombers between onslaughts of fish. Ivan got so fucked up that he passed out in his plate, allowing The Menace to create a brilliant comedy routine.

"Yo, Ivan, can you give me a ride home? Whaddya think man? It's gettin late, the bus quit runnin. Hey, Hey IVAN! Can you give me a ride HOME?" He went on like this, elbowing Ivan for effect. "Yo Ivan, can I buy you a drink? Jest one more for the road, eh buddy?"

The following weekend was Labor Day, and the five-year reunion for Roseville High. I had never heard of anyone having a five year reunion, and as much as I would normally eschew such a thing, I knew I had to go back and paaaaarty! I dressed in my most psychedelic rags, packed an oz of the finest Grape, Juicy Fruit, White Bag and T-Rex buds, (five or six was all it took) and headed home, if I could still call my folks' place home. I hooked up with Don and drove over to the Carpenter's Hall, which was done up festively, greeted the girls I hadn't gotten along with but were now married to my friends, and went about shocking everyone with my dreads. I hit the bar and got rolling, dusting out the cobwebs and getting reacquainted with old friends, playing my freaky dope dealer image to the hilt. There was a buffet, and I lost my seat while I was up getting my plate. No big, I ended up next to the girl who wore the tightest jeans in school, Betty Kepler, and her husband. She was always fun, and there were a bunch of friends around, so we had a pretty good time. When dessert was over and the tables were cleared, it was time.

"Who want's to paaaarty?" I yelled, whipping this gallon ziploc of bud out of my pack and waving it like my freak flag, high. I reached in and pulled one out, squeezed it and inhaled the perfume of grape, looked down, and saw a cop badge in my face. It was Betty's husband's.

"Look man, whoever you are, I'm a policeman in the Bay Area, and I'm here on vacation, so I don't want to have to deal with this shit! So why don't you take your dope and get the hell out of here!"

"Hey, no problem, man, just tryin to have some fun at my reunion. I'll just leave right now." I stood up and walked out to the back parking lot, where Don and I parked, and went over to his car. "Just let me into the car Don," I told him, "I'll roll a few bombers and stash my weed. He can't bust me for smoking a joint." Almost immediately I was surrounded by half the football team.

"Hey man, you want us to go in there and kick that guy's ass? He can't talk to you like that!"

"Naaah, it's cool, I'll just twist these up and go blow it in his face." I rolled up some spliffs and went back inside, but it looked like there had been a riot; or fear of a riot. Apparently, Betty had dragged her husband out, screaming "You can't talk to Sheldon like that!" Seeing this, all the straight people hurriedly followed suit. I hadn't noticed, since we parked in back, but the place had cleared out except for the OH club and our friends. We smoked bomber after bomber and drank until the bar went dry, after which we restocked at the liquor store and went to someone's house. When we completely torched, about two in the morning, Jackson screamed, "Who wants to go to Reno?" To which Ed, Clay and I yelled "I do!" So we piled in Ed's Impala on hit the road.

I wish I could say I went to the Mustang ranch and had my money sucked out of me, but I just threw it away. I was doing better than Ed though, whose gambling compulsion was taking hold at this point in life. When we had all gotten down to brokeness, I still had 100 bucks left, which I intended to spend on breakfast for all of us, but Ed demanded that we go to Circus Circus. The sun was up and none of us wanted to gamble any more, but Ed was insisting that I loan him more money so he could win it all back.

"C'mon Sheldon," he pleaded drunkenly, "jess loan me fifty and I can make it back."

"Man, you lost the fifty I loaned you already, let's go to Rosie's and get some breakfast!"

"No man, I'm tellin you, we'll go to Circus Circus and I'll win it back, you'll see."

"I'm so wasted I can't see anything as it is, and I don't think you can see too well either, let's go eat!" Jackson was passed out and Clay was just laughing at us when we pulled into the parking lot.

"It's one dollar," the attendant told Ed, who was at the wheel. He got out his wallet but it was completely empty,

"Man, loan me a dollar so we can park."

"Dude! You don't even have a dollar to park and you want me to loan you fifty bucks to blow on blackjack?"

"Look man, we're not getting out of here until you pay the lady and loan me fifty bucks," Ed fumed in that restrained yet vaguely psychopathic manner of alcoholics. It was too funny to take seriously, so I gave him a buck, we parked, and he burned the rest of my cash. I had enough left for a tank of gas and a couple shitty burgers on the way out of town, but I got years of mileage out of hassling him for that.

WATER

Water, as you had assumed, is the last of the elements, my liege. That which moves constantly, seeking the deepest point."

"Yes, I had imagined that the cycle of life would be impossible without it, but how does Metal yield Water."

"Temperature. In the cold of night, condensation forms standing drops of water on metal, and heating metals to extremes liquefies them, so Water is the child of Metal."

"I see, and what does Water represent?"

"In the cycle of nature, Water is the time of storage, of winter. It is indicative of cold, and the North. Water is death, when all forms retract into the earth, storing what they can for a new beginning."

"Is death not permanent?" asked Huang Ti.

"Only in the physical realm of appearances, my liege. The tree loses its leaves, but the sap stays at the core to feed it in spring. Water finds the deep point, but is transformed by the earth to nourish Wood. The spirit of man rejuvenates as well, but after so many cycles of change it moves on to another form. Many see Water expressed as money, but even more valuable, it is wisdom. As such, its value only increases, particularly through the act of sharing it with others."

"Where does one find Water in the body, physician?"

"In the bladder!" laughed Chi Po. "The bladder is attached to the kidneys, the organ of Water. Water creates the bones and teeth, the reproductive organs, the deepest structures of the body. It controls hearing, the deepest sense, which is ours in the womb, and opens into the ear, which is shaped like a kidney. The kidney is very important, as the home of Water it regulates the life energy gathered from lifetimes before this. The strength of the Water is what determines our own strength, health, and longevity. It controls the development of the body, and reproduction. This is why I advise you to sleep with no more than four of your concubines in a week, to maintain the vitality of the kidney."

"HA! If that is how I should die, then I will die!" erupted Huang Ti.

"No," corrected Chi Po, only age yourself before your time, and rule from infirmity."

"A doddering old king is quickly overthrown," said the now reflective ruler.

"As is the integrity of the body, when water has been weakened," interjected Chi Po. "When Water is diminished, one has no sex drive, or will power, and one is beset with injuries.

"Tell me then, physician, how does one tonify the Water element."

"Many men seek Water through herbs, and some through horns and organs of powerful animals, but the key to Water is never to deplete it. Like a well that is overused, the quality of the Water will be impure. One must save Water always, and never squander it."

"What depletes Water, physician, other than excessive sex?"

"Fear. Fear goes to the core of the body, draining chi. When we are very afraid, sounds enter the ear and terrify us, we feel cold, and our teeth chatter. We must train ourselves to maintain calmness, avoiding unnecessary excitement. Excessive behaviors, accidents and injuries all affect the kidney's ability to store chi and rejuvenate the body. Strong drink and intoxicants also deplete the kidney chi, making it difficult to be resolute. To lead a full life, one must protect one's reserves and strengthen them through internal practices. In harmony, Water plumbs the nature of death, with the strength to bring that knowledge back to life, and start the cycle over again."

1

As September came to a close, harvest loomed ahead. We were hanging around the shed after dinner one night, toasting a rube and drinking a beer, settling into the evenings feature presentation; "The Treasure of the Sierra Madre." We had watched it before, but it rode the top of the rerun list, being the epic saga of partnership. Dobbs and Curtin had just finished beating the crap out of the swindling construction boss to get their dough when Dan drove up.

"Hey you guys, there's something weird going on. I drove up to the gate and found this flashlight there, it was still on."

"So," ventured Stymie, "maybe somebody dropped it."

"Of course somebody dropped it, but who the hell would use a flashlight? When you drive in your lights are all you need, and if you were on foot you wouldn't just leave it lying there. I think someone was sneaking in to rip off, and I scared them when I drove up. They might have cut back over the hill toward the rancher's." Stymie refused to be talked into paranoia.

"Who'd come up here to rip off?"

"Who the hell knows? Fuckin Grease! Maybe those guys who came up for Bernard."

"If it's those guys I'll make 'em some drinks," Horn joked.

"Yeah, well it felt weird to me, and you guys are the closest to the gate, so if they did come to rip off you'll be the easiest." We brooded over this fact for a moment before Stymie replied,

"They'd have a hard time heading cross country over Garson, if they ran off that way from the gate. I doubt they'd find any patches in the dark, anyway. More than likely fall off a cliff."

"Hang out and watch this movie man," I interjected, "it's the shit!"

"Naaah! I'm gonna go tell Bernard and Grunt."

"Worry, is the furthest thing from my mind," Stymie refrained, taking a toke and hitting the play button to see Dobbs & Curtin shake hands over their newly formed partnership. (ba ba baa, ba ba Baa, ba ba BAA) (For those of you who've never seen the Treasure, I can only recommend it as the most important film ever made for people who plan on living life. Dullards and toadies can ignore it if they choose, but for anyone that ventures into any sort of business or partnership, its sublime outline of the parameters of human behavior makes viewing mandatory.)

No one kicked in our door to rip us off that night, nor did the remaining dogs make any more noise than was ordinary. I got up the next morning, late as usual, but early enough to start my watering chores before the sun broke the tree line. I walked down to the upper patch, where I was met by the unlikely sight of the sheared off stems of all our weed plants. I ran back up the hill to the shed, to roust Stymie & Mulehorn, noticing as I went that a trail of leaf led away down the hill toward the Dollhouse. We frantically headed down to the Upper and Lower patches, then followed the leaf trails, not toward the road, where a rip off would probably return, but toward Bernard's. We were halfway down the hill toward his place when he came out of the woods, brandishing a pistol.

"Hey," Horn started in, "our weeds been ripped off and there's a trail going down to your cabin."

"Well my weeds been ripped off too and I think you guys did it."

"Well we want to look at your cabin."

"Get away!" He fired a shot into a tree by Mulehorn, which was definitely enough to change our plan. Horn rode down to Dan's while Stymie and I checked the other patches, which had been picked clean, except for Armageddon, which was too much effort. Still, the odds were astronomical that anyone would find all of our patches, and Bernard's, and haul all our dope out on foot. Dan and Lidya came up, but Bernard wouldn't let them come into his house either, which was definitely weird, since they had always attempted to maintain neutrality regarding our affairs. We went over our options, but short of blasting Bernard with the shotgun there didn't seem to be any way to find out if he had our weed. It seemed pretty obvious that he had done it, but after watching the Treasure, "You'd all have to take out your cannons and blast away, so that no one would have anything over the other two," it was apparent that we weren't gonna kill him. We weren't criminals, we were hardworking hippies who happened to disagree with a dumb drug law. If it took killing an asshole to secure our fortunes, well, we'd be a little less fortunate. It was a bitter pill, but we dug up what stash we had buried in the woods, packed up our shit, and split.

We came back a week later, since we still had some plants left down at Sherwood, and got the full lowdown from Dan. The day after we left, the cops, Sheriffs and CAMP all showed up with warrants. They said that some guy had wandered into the Eureka Sheriff's claiming that he had come up to Caldwell with his partner to rip off some weed. He said that they were chased off the mountain, got split up, and that his friend, who had taken him up there in the first place, never made it back to their car, which they parked on the BLM. He never returned to his home either. It turned out that the guy who disappeared had worked for Hector several years before, so he thought he could find the way in. The cops walked the property, looking for a murder scene, but never found anything. CAMP took what little remained of our weed, so we pretty much ate shit. The cops never found the guy, or his body, he simply disappeared.

Dan had tried to remain neutral in our arguments with Bernard, but he was more than a little concerned a few days later, when he asked for his gun back. "I lost it," Bernard told him. It wasn't the kind of thing you lose, unless you needed to, and he certainly had it when he was shooting at us. When I heard all this I began to think seriously about killing Bernard myself. Art, who had been trained to kill people by the government, offered to dispatch him as a gift to Stymie, but I had a more personal motive. It takes a lot of resolve to actually kill someone though, and we were really just peaceful hippie dope fiends, so we harvested our remaining crop from Sherwood and finished out the year taking care of that. At least we came away with something, something I'll never forget, like old Howard laughing his head off at the end of the Treasure; "Call it God or fate or nature or whatever you will, but it's sure got a sense of humor. The gold's all blown back up to the mountain. Ten months of sweat and hard labor's the cost of that joke, Aaa ha ha ha ha ha!"

Our crop loss certainly knocked me down a peg. With my capital thusly depleted, my plan to buy a neighboring parcel with Stymie was moot, and growing on Lizard again looked unlikely. Furthermore, the biggest customer in town was Oblio. It was hard to sell pounds to him, knowing that he had twenty-five grand in the pressure cooker he kept chained to the radiator. I was so pissed off by the state of affairs, that the fuckin scumbag Bernard had ripped us off and driven us out, that Oblio had single-handedly turned Barrington into a junkie shithole, and that the respect, honor and ideals of the trade I had been born into seemed to have fallen by the wayside, that I felt I had to do something. I formulated a plan, one to correct the injustices of the past year. It wasn't a simple revenge plot, as with Bernard, it was necessary to protect future Barringtonians from what should have been forbidden knowledge.

I would go to Oblio's room, lock the door, and physically pound him into remission. It wouldn't take much, as he was a skinny junkie and I was pretty buff from weed work, but I was furious enough to thrash anyone that got in my way. I'd take his keys, steal all his cash from the pressure cooker, go through the closet and take all of his weed, dump out whatever powder I came across, and then cram his ass out his third story window. Who would fuck with me? Who'd call the cops? Nobody. Even if they did, the cops would probably give me an award. Sure everyone would be upset, since their schmeeze connection would be out of business, but that was an acceptable loss in my book. Every day I spent around Barrington was one I wrestled with enacting my plan, but as with Bernard, it would be giving in to being something I could never be. Even in justice it was beyond my hippie ethic, so it remained a fantasy, a fantasy of a just world.

2

New Year's that year went beyond the others in every way. First of all, they moved the shows to the Oakland Coliseum, which was huge, and they still oversold it. It was packed, and security was none too friendly. It was a big hassle to travel around from section to section, which is the essence of the Dead show. I never stayed in one place unless I was right up front. Eileen and I both dosed for that show, and she started freaking out before I did. I had been in a hurry to go and dropped some liquid on a piece of bread. When I got it out of the ziploc at the show, I couldn't tell which part had more hits. Eileen took one corner, chewed on it, and spit it out, saying it tasted too strong. I called her a wimp, so she scarfed it down, whoops. After awhile she told me that she thought she was higher than I was, and for once I had to concede. Perhaps just being inside was spooking her, but we both went through periods of starting to tweak and talking each other down. I told her that I'd take her home if it was getting too weird, and after a few bouts back and forth, I was certain we should leave.

We made it as far as the hallway, where she ran into her friends, which normalized things for her. I was certain of the imminent nuclear meltdown of my brain, so I demanded that we leave before she started freaking out again too. It was terrifying to think that I would leave the show before it was over, it simply wasn't allowed. I really had to gear up because I knew that all the agents of Control and Chaos would be trying to convince me to stay and have fun or detonate myself, and I wouldn't know who was who or which option was which. Eileen was back to enjoying herself by the time I insisted that we make our move, but she agreed it would be better for us to escape. Better in what way was the question. I felt very strange leaving the show, like I had walked out of something that I could never return to. On a physical level it felt like I had broken through a membrane, and was now standing on the outside. Mentally, I was very uneasy about what lay ahead, beyond its ruptured hull.

My first objective was to get back home, to where it was relatively safe and under control. I could deal with suffering through my own torment at the show, but I had some level of commitment to Eileen, and I would do whatever I needed to do to protect her. We had taken BART, which was already closed, having decided that year that it was no longer economically feasible to stay open all night on New Year's Eve. I was stunned to see a cab parked right out front, and wasted no time hopping in it. The cabby, who was of some Arabic denomination, smiled as we got in.

"Where to my friend?"

"Berkeley, and step on it." He pulled away from the curb, accelerated through a section of parked cars and locked it up. We skidded to a halt about eight inches from hitting the cop car that was headed perpendicular to us at the next corridor. They drove by with a stare, but didn't stop. The cabby turned around, eyes wide from panic, and screamed at us,

"Are You High? I cannot drive if you are high!" I had never heard of anyone so clear about the fact that their own mental state could be waved out by another's aberrant brain pattern, a contact high.

"No man, I'm fine," I practically shouted, my need to escape forcing me immediately into straight mode.

"Okay then, I can drive." We pulled out and on to the freeway with no problem, and then we were rolling. He had a nice cab, all red velour interior, tuck and roll, it felt strangely sumptuous, like a bordello. It started to get warm inside, hot, sweltering, Eileen and I tried rolling the windows down, but the power was off. It was like a furnace, of red velvet, with a bizarre Bedouin at the wheel. As I lapsed back into being high I could no longer tell whether we were within the lanes. He seemed to be weaving as we floated down the freeway, but I didn't want to disturb him. I had to try to maintain straightness if we were going to survive, but it was obvious now, we were on Saudi Satan's flying carpet.

As we approached the Oakland cop shop I started to panic.

"You're not taking us to the police station are you?" Saudi Satan turned around with an evil leer, glaring right through me, and replied with a ferocious facetiousness that implied he knew exactly who I was and what was going on,

"No, why should I take you to the poleese station?"

"Oh, no reason, just go ahead to Berkeley," I stammered.

"Where in Berkeley?" he snapped. I was too freaked to have him take me home, so I told him,

"Ashby BART."

"BART stopped running," he replied suspiciously.

"Oh that's okay, I left my car there." We made it the rest of the way without any lapses, but when he pulled up there was a pimp waiting there. It was already close to one-thirty, no one else was around, and it seemed a strange place to be. The cabbie pulled right up to him and said, "Hey boss!" I just handed over the cash and started walking, while they began a conversation. I had escaped the Satan ride, but I knew that leaving the show had caused some impact. It was wet around all the trees in the BART parking lot, which I took for a sign that my breaking out of the show had ruptured the cellular fabric of the planet. It was obvious that they were all bleeding from internal injuries, and this really panicked me. Oh no! All the trees are dying. I've killed the planet! We snuck back in fear along darkened streets to my house, and straight to my waterbed, crawling into its womblike safety in the darkness.

I maintained my pretense at non-existence when Stymie came home, but eventually the phone rang, and answering the phone was a Pavlovian dope dealer response. It was Dave, calling to see how I was and if I wanted to head over to the ocean for a polar bear New Year's Eve dip. It seemed like a good idea, and he was safe company, so I had him come over and we drove out there. Eileen thought we were insane, but I was happy to be at the beach, where she sat with our clothes while we entered the freezing water, naked. With each step I felt that I would be swept away and drowned, but after what I had done that night, I felt I deserved it. It would be okay to die with Dave and Eileen watching, I figured. Dave just kept singing his pagan song, "Mother of the waters of the world, return return return," as we got up to chest depth. At that point I could no longer breathe, but there was no more keeping my head above water, so I finally gave in to my frigid death. As soon as I went under my fear was swept away from me, my body temperature evened out, and I found myself swimming further out into the waves. It felt fantastic, like the earth had accepted me. It was an unexpected turnaround, but one that allowed me to return to normalcy and meet the New Year's dawn with a sense of peace.

3

My relationship with Eileen still worried me though. For a long time I had believed she used me as a method for achieving a social station, which is something I feared about any possible relationship. (cuz I was soooo cool) She didn't want to smoke all my dope, (my primary relationship fear, being used for my dope, was based on my only certain point of self esteem) but I wondered on occasion what she was getting out of being with me. (Probably not as often as I wondered what I was getting out of her, but a fair amount nonetheless) Despite her slide into heroin use, or perhaps because of it, she was really looking for a sense of emotional intensity, which she later told me I provided like no one else. "You could never tell what was going to happen. You could be really mean to me, or really nice, or take me places, or be freaking out, like the world was ending. It was a big adventure, and it could always be the last time. That made it exciting." I still felt chained to her in some inescapable way though, not like I was in love, but in some intangible energetic sense, and through my fear that she might expose me for being as tweaked as I was. This took up more of my energy than anything, fearing that my friends, or anyone, would find out how completely tweaked I was. Eileen, who had seen my grandiosity at its height, and kept my pee thing secret for all that time, was enough in contact with everyone that she realized my tweaks were not that much greater than anyone else's, only enlarged by my sense of immensity, and my overkill on LSD. But I was always so concerned about maintaining my imagined social station, whatever that was, and how her behavior reflected on me, that I was an incredibly nazi to her. She was rather boisterous, and I was always thinking that her speech or actions would be considered unbecoming by someone. God knows who, because in the final tally no one really gives a fuck what people do, and people who do are pretty much assholes. I guess that made me an asshole. Shit.

As it is wont to happen, whenever two people spend as much time fucking as we did, we got pregnant. It doesn't matter what barriers are placed between the hot jiz rivets and their intended target, eventually one of the trillions blown will find its mark. We used everything too; pills—which lead to even more hormonally oriented emotional lability than usual; diaphragms—which get knocked off; condoms—who the fuck wants to use a condom? the cervical cap—which occasionally grabs your dick head like a rubber vise, producing an orgasmically stunning sensation I find hard to recommend; but eventually all forms of contraception give way to either their own percentage failure rate or your failure to use rate. Pregnant, and I had still had sex with less than ten girls in my life! That may be why guys are so reluctant to believe in love. To really fall in love, as it is written, would mean the end of all your fantasies of having sex with every girl on the planet. It's almost as if you'd have to give up on life itself to fall in love, or even worse, to get married. With all the time I had already spent trying to escape Eileen's hold, I was not going to end up married with a kid, or having a kid floating around out there without me.

With all the personal torment that I was subjecting myself to, I couldn't with any reasonable conscience bring someone into this world for whom I would need to be responsible. How could I raise a child with my paranoid tweaking? A son I couldn't pee in front of? I'd rather die. But despite being a Women's Studies major, whose shelves were lined with books detailing the accounts of how women were oppressed in every way, but primarily by their lack of reproductive choice, which accounted for their inability to complete their educational or professional goals, despite all that, Eileen wanted to have my baby. The arguments I had with her to convert her academic knowledge into the present reality were brutal. "I could raise a baby on my own and finish school," she protested, but I was adamant.

I felt that part of her desire was a heroin induced quality, although it could simply be a human quality, to desire something to hold on to and to have a fantasized, self-defined relationship with, which any parent knows only lasts until the child decides to determine the relationship through his or her own perspective. Heroin was the trump card, finally, "You're on fuckin heroin and you want to have a baby! Wake the fuck up!" Perhaps having a baby would have given her incentive to clean up. She wasn't particularly strung out, just smoking it every day. At least she wasn't shooting, as her friends had started doing. I like to think that it's helpful to make a conscious choice about having kids from the outset though, so we finally got an abortion. I was as good about it as I could be, bought her a ton of chocolates, brought her food and magazines and whatever she wanted while she recovered. I even let her do schmeeze. I did really care about the girl. I wanted her to at least be able to finish college, which I hadn't been able to do. I could tell that the abortion had done something to us though, elicited some communal pain which made us closer in an odd way, like we were attached to something besides each other.

4

'85 had definitely been a bad weed year. Not only did we have a diminished supply from being ripped off, but CAMP had been very active, leaving us with little to choose from in the following spring. Stymie had made the terrible mistake of buying some bunk off of Grease. I begged him not too, "Dude, it's Trifinger weed!" Usually he had more sense, but after the rip-off a load of cheap weed seemed like a good thing. Even with weed as shitty or non-existent as it was the next year, nobody but nobody wanted that bunk. He sat on it all year, which was a terrible loss in operating capital, although we survived. It began to bug me though, my pitiful stash, since few of the hundreds of pounds I copped had anything worth saving. I was also up against the bummer of watching my friends, who were graduating and getting jobs and such, spend the money they actually worked for on bunk dope. I began telling my customers, "If you paid this much for it, it better be bunk," since quality and price had become inversely proportional.

I felt embarrassed to have such lame weed, but people demanded it anyway. This worried me. I had tried to elevate everyone to my level of weed snobbery, but people would smoke whatever came through, and even get excited about the indoor, which I found patently boring, because it got them so obliterated. It finally dawned on me that I was making quite a comfortable living from my friends' refusal to attain my level of disdain. In college it wasn't such a big deal, of course you used your loan or grant money, or your trust fund or whatever you had to buy dope with because you had to party. But to actually work a job that bored you so much that you had to smoke negligible weed all the time was a horrifying concept. I certainly tried to uphold my level of quality, offering the best of the not so great weed that was available, but the fact that it was sucked up without much complaint worried me.

The Dead did a big show that summer with Bob Dylan at the Oakland Coliseum. It was outdoors, like a Day on the Green, so they could cram some hundred thousand people in. I took my buddy Jael, since he was a big Dylan fan. We arrived fashionably late, as was my custom, but also due to getting a flat, on which I drove the last miles to the Coliseum anyway. "Neither rain, nor sleet, nor hail, nor snow, will keep a Deadhead from the show." The lawn was packed with heads, awash in tie-dye, resembling in their proximity to each other a multi-colored pile of maggots wringing a piece of green meat. Knowing I had friends in front, and never one to be disturbed by frottage, I surged into the crowd, trying to leave an invagination trail for Jael to follow. I had always eschewed being followed at a show. If you couldn't slide past the sweaty bodies as they writhed, or hit the gap as they opened and closed, you would be left out. But Jael wasn't a Deadhead, so I tried to keep an eye on him.

The first set was already rolling along, so people were moving, but no one was very happy about my taking up space that they had stood around so long to claim. We stopped about halfway to the front, standing on the edge of a blanket that someone had laid down to mark "their" territory. He was a really pushy guy from New York, who started going off on me about how I had to move because he had waited all day to get this space and laid down his blanket yadda yadda yadda. I was like, "Dude, you're in my backyard, no one owns any of this space, and I'm just here dancing. If you want to be uptight at the show go see them in New York." This really pissed him off and he began telling me that he was ready to fight for his space, which is totally antithetical to Deadhead consciousness, so I laughed at him and moved forward enough that I could share a joint with some other people and just blow smoke at him. Folks usually didn't complain too much if you got them high while you stood around, but I kept moving anyway.

I eventually got about thirty or forty feet from the stage, and I could see Hogarth, but I couldn't move an inch. I couldn't even raise my arm to smoke a joint. I ended up crowding against a couple of guys who were trying to tape the show. I had met one of them before, as he passed back and forth between the coke filled rooms at my taper friend's, but he didn't recognize me. He started getting hairy right away, exclaiming that he was taping and I couldn't go past him. I told him I needed to get up to my friends, and that I wouldn't touch his equipment, but he refused. This really pissed me off. The Dead allowed taping at the shows by this time, but only in the designated taper section, which he was a long way from. Knowing the guy was a coke weasel, I just told him to fuck off. He actually told me "Look dude, I'll kick your ass," which I found immensely entertaining, not for the simple fact that I would have killed him, but because you couldn't even lift your arm to throw on anyone. This gave me the distinct advantage in that my height would allow me to shatter his nose with a head butt. Before we could resolve it with violence however, Dylan came out and began to play.

Hogarth had seen me and was trying to get me up to come up to where he was. Since he vaguely knew this dickhead too, he tried to infer by hand signals that they should let me pass, but they weren't moving.

It was apparent pretty quickly that Dylan had been herowhining with Jerry during the break, because he was playing like shit. Not that his guitar playing was ever much to speak of, but he was so out of it that they turned his guitar off in the PA mix. He was forgetting lyrics right and left, so Jael, with his encyclopedic knowledge of Dylan songs, started singing everything loud and clear. This is when the taper dude freaked.

"Hey man, I'm taping here, you've gotta tell your friend to quit singing!"

"Sorry man, he's real into Dylan, and I think he's high on something, I wouldn't want to bum his trip."

"Please, please, I'll give you tapes!"

"I've got friends taping digital off the board, so fuck your tape." They played another couple songs, with Jael holding down the vocals, before the taper dick realized he could simply let us move ahead of him and cleared a path for us.

"Thanks," I spit, as I squirmed my way up to Hogarth and lit a fatty.

That show was pretty much it for me. If I had seen the set list without hearing their entirely lackluster performance I'd have thought it was the greatest show imaginable, but it truly sucked. For all my paranoid tweaking at shows, I had never been physically threatened by anyone, except for that biker in Reno, but you expect that from bikers. The idea that NY dorks were coming in droves to take up air at my shows while the band continued their downhill spiral finally connected with the fact that they hadn't written a song in three years and kept whipping out covers written by an obviously useless junkie. Completely freaking out every night behind LSD fantasy and megalomaniac paranoia I could handle, being straight enough to see what was really going on was too totally lame, so I retired from the scene.

5

There was only one thing left on my list of "must dose here" activities, Pinnacles. We did our usual drive in, dose at 11 thing, but this year we went up the High Peaks trail, rather than the Balconies. It seemed like a mandatory route for tripping, the words indelibly carved into the wooden sign at the trailhead, and thence on to your nervous system. There's a bench at a fork in the trail, where you can follow the High Peaks or go back down some other ridgeline. We were coming on pretty hard by the time we got there so we sat on the bench to watch the stars. It was the night before Thanksgiving, and shooting stars were falling into the atmosphere with astounding regularity. They were burning their way across our visual fields when I came to the conclusion, a rather rare one for me, that these must be spirits, being born into our world. This gave me some measure of confidence in the idea that we should walk the entire High Peaks trail, which was supposed to be carved through tunnels at the top, before descending the miles back to the underground caves.

Art had his dog with him, and didn't want to go over the top, so Clark and I went alone. It wasn't long before we took the turnoff to hell, at which point I realized that Clark, my pleasant young companion, had become an agent of Satan. His skin had taken on an orange striped quality, and he was wearing his shades in the moonlight. When he took them off his eyes had become glowing yellow, and I knew that he had travelled back in time from the land beyond the atomic destruction of the planet, where only ghouls survived. Art was gone, dead to my reasoning, and the idea that my remaining friend was a post-atomic ghoul left me with no alternative but to destroy the world or die myself. In his jolly way, and through my unreality filter, Clark implied that the world would be a fine place after we returned. All I could imagine was a nuclear wasteland, which we were preparing to exist in. I desperately wanted to run away, to go back to the car and drive back home, but I knew that such a move would be the trigger. As usual, I had to wait it out and figure out an escape.

It seemed that the only possibility for survival was to go forward, through whatever lay ahead. In my mind the world that I left behind could only exist by my finishing the path I had started. My dialogue with Clark went through its suspicious turns, whereby he invited me to return to camp with him, but I knew that meant certain destruction, so despite the freezing cold at the top, the clouds, and the uncertainty of existence beyond, I followed the High Peaks. I must have sown the seeds of paranoia in Clark's mind as well, because he eventually turned back and left me there to die alone. After cresting the trail I came to a footbridge. It had railings made of three inch steel pipe, which, like the planks, were covered with dew. It was almost freezing to the touch, and its resemblance to the condensation that forms on a nitrous tank assured me that I was entering my own personal purgatory, condemned to wander mindlessly for all eternity, The land beyond, where nitrous is air; Xanadu!

I hiked onward through the fog, as the clouds settled on top of me. The trail continued up sets of steps cut out of the rock by the intrepid park laborers, but obviously meant only for me. Along the edges of cliffs I wandered, gripping the freezing railings that had been pounded into the rock, designed to prevent accidentally slipping to the certain death that I considered purposely hurling myself to. But I was already beyond death. Helplessly lost in a land beyond time, I sat down in the dirt, which was strewn with lichen covered rocks. Staring at this micro-landscape I realized that the contours of the rocks were a map of the park. If I could follow the trail laid out in this rock pattern, I could find my way back, or forward, to save the planet from destruction. I crawled around the spot on my hands and knees to get an understanding of its scale, but realized that I was wiping it out as I went. I was fractured with despair as I saw that my entire past had just been wiped clean off the map. I lay down in the dirt, hoping that the cold would carry me to death, although I knew I was condemned to the fog shrouded dimness forever.

Looking at the little rocks strewn in front of my face, I realized that they were alive, like barnacles, slowly opening and closing. I had other experiences which taught me that rocks were alive, forms of planet consciousness moving in an entirely different dimensional speed than our own. I took hold of one of my dreads and plugged it into the mouth of a rock, which clamped down on it, before opening the valve that sent warm gas flowing into my brain. It was the breath of God, of consciousness, speaking directly into me, revealing all. As I lay amongst rocks I felt the universe open up before me. It seemed that I was attached to a spirit, the spirit of Eileen's & my aborted child, which had followed me the rest of the year looking for release. I could feel it, on some deep level, and was able to witness its birthing. It separated from me, through the womblike nature of the planet, the cracks in the rocks of Pinnacles, to float out into space and on to another life.

I had lost self definition enough that I was the planet, birthing this spirit into the universe, which was an unbelievable cosmic energy transference. I felt like I knew what it was to give birth, and to have had an abortion. I also felt the sense of forgiveness that the spirit had for releasing it. In some pure wave of bliss, perhaps it was communicated that I was loved. This was difficult for me though, since I felt like my heart had long been frozen. As I lay floating in the blackness though, I became aware that I was in an operating theater. I could feel the surgeons of another dimension opening my chest and replacing my old frozen heart, like a burnt out atomic battery, with a new one, a sun plucked from another galaxy. It seemed like a ridiculously expensive procedure, wiping out a whole galaxy to keep me alive, but perhaps my purpose on earth was still worth the expense of Atomic Open Heart Surgery. When I found my body again, I rolled over to get up and found a horse chestnut on the ground. It was about palm sized, a smooth golden skinned translucent nut, through which I could see the developing form of its potential plant. I took it as a sign, that the spirit had left a symbol of rebirth here on the planet.

I awoke from this state with a clear directive to go forward. I recovered my dread from the God portal, dusted myself off and headed toward the tunnels. I was still nervous about entering them, but step by step I made my way through the pitch-blackness, feeling the walls with my hands. Emerging from them was like being born into the world again. I knew that I had passed the point of destruction, and in the faint rays of dawn I could see that the planet was safe. I hiked the miles back down to the caves, and found Clark and Art there as the sun was coming up. We explored the caves until we found a wall that acted as a seepage. Water rolled down its face from a spring behind it. It was an unmistakable sign that the planet was a living being, and I licked the water straight from the rock, as if I were eating planet pussy, and I never felt more alive.

We went back to camp in the dawn light and made some tea. I whipped out a bag of Vita-Crunch and began to chow down. **Cruuunchh!** "Oh my God, Art, I broke my tooth!" As it was on the bus, the karmic cycle had come around with predictably funny results. It was Thanksgiving day, so before we left I called my mom from the payphone to tell her I loved her. I told her I was at Pinnacles, and she replied that she had been there as a girl. My family! I thought, feeling oddly connected. I asked if there was an incredibly winding road and she remembered, "Yes, it was so bad that I threw up and had a terrible time there." Oh yeah, reality. I guess there are just some things I'll never be able to share with my parents, but Pinnacles was not a place for the uninitiated.

Back in town I had arranged a big T-day party at Eileen's house. She made an incredible meal and we had everyone over, Stymie and Horn and Manny and Willie and Dave and Luigi and Art and Clark, all of my dope friends. I was so charged from the Pinnacles that I knew I just loved them all, and Eileen too. I gave her the Horse Chestnut, as a symbol of our year's trauma, but without having been there, I don't think she could quite grasp its cosmic significance. Perhaps she was too used to my assigning cosmic significance to things that seemed mundane, perhaps there is no knowing the depths of another's experience. She kept it, nonetheless. As for me, it didn't matter that I was a freak, or couldn't pee, or anything. I felt so alive I was electrified, and although I didn't want to anymore, I could have died happy. I did feel sort of bad about wasting a galaxy though, so I decided I should put more effort into achieving something.

I wish I could say that I ended my career of tripping on that high note. It was what I was looking for, in the Grof paradigm I had completed the four stages and had a brilliant rebirth. The ecstasy from this resolution was intense and long lasting, but I wasn't miraculously healed. My self-consciousness was still there, affecting my freedom to exist comfortably in my body. Though there was some overwhelming sense of universal love, I was still somewhat at odds with Eileen about my whole perception of the world. One amazing thing about that trip was that having worn my polypropylene underwear for a day, it became like a second skin. It numbed my body in a way that precluded sensation of touch, except in my hands. My hands became so sensitive that I wanted to have sex with this new skin on, focusing all my sensation away from the generality of my body. Eileen thought this was too weird, demanding that I take off my clothes before getting into bed. It was discouraging, but it brought me some resolve, and remembrance.

Although Eileen tripped, she wasn't into exploring things the way I was. I had felt this early on, in the Zete days, but when I collapsed in need of someone to trust, I had to overlook it. I eventually hoped that I would be able to reverse the effects of time, moving my psyche back into a place of completeness, to my pre-Zete clarity, where I would no longer need her. You have to take a lot of drugs to imagine you can reverse time, but I kept trying. It was clear that I couldn't go on with her, but even after my cosmic abortion, I still felt as if some unseen force connected me to her. After talking to the crystal lady on Telegraph Avenue one afternoon though, I realized that I was carrying the connection all the time! I walked down Haste Street and ripped off my crystal necklace, spilling the purple beads along the sidewalk before I threw the stone into the sewer. The yoke was broken, as if all of Mr. T's gold chains were lifted off of me. I finished what I needed to, helping her move on to a career that I hoped would overcome her interest in heroin, which it did. Once ensconced, she didn't have the energy to argue with me about my moving on myself.

Things kept changing, as they do, but weed remained my faithful ally. Maybe it helped me ignore things, or helped me make sure nobody else could tell if I was tweaking, but it certainly upheld my lifestyle. Stymie, in a totally uncharacteristic move, met a girl, got married, and retired. I took over his ends and ran the faucet. I was getting pretty bored with dealing, since the days of exciting bud had all but ended, but there were still a couple of professionals left up north, and for awhile we were the American Weed Company. I was making enough dough to think about doing something with myself, until Bernard narced out the Cowboy with an anonymous tip letter to the sheriff, which totally fucked up our trip. I was pretty worried that the pigs would follow the lead down to me, but Bernard had done such a good job of painting Dan out to be the evil "Mr. Big," that they didn't investigate any further. The pigs really wanted to ream him, and it made me wonder what could happen to me in that situation. It's pretty hard to bounce back when all your money gets swiped, your property gets seized, and you wind up in hella debt to your lawyer. With my professionalism and lack of criminal history, I might still have been safe, but I started to explore legit business opportunities anyway, having had about all the paranoia I could handle for one lifetime.

The dosing had definitely left its mark, and no matter what I did, I still had the burden of the psycho-physiological affects of my wild years to deal with. Perhaps it would have been easier to have a good trip if I only ate one hit, but that was far too wimpy. If I couldn't overdose, I couldn't dose. But Jan got set up in an FBI mail bust, which put an end to my trusted acid supply anyway. Without him, or going to see the Dead, my trips became far more sporadic. As much as I was committed to the idea of reorganizing my mind by dosing hard, it wasn't really achieving the desired effects. I began looking into other methods of retuning my mind, particularly meditation training. Grof's development of Holotropic Breathwork was valuable too, and my sessions had serious near-death nitrous parallels. Without acid to blame it on though, I couldn't pretend that it was just the drugs, and had to reframe my thinking about the whole question of consciousness and drugs.

Yin & Yang

"Refresh my memory, Chi Po, on the subject of yin and yang, in light of what we have discussed," Huang Ti requested.

"Yin and yang, my liege, are the two poles into which the cosmic unity divided itself, while remaining essentially indivisible," Chi Po began. "Yin and yang transform each other, as day turns into night and summer into winter, always inseparably linked. When the transformation cannot be made smoothly, one collapses into the other, as the boisterous drunkard collapses into slumber. It is from the interaction of yin and yang that all things are formed, including the five elements."

"Do you mean then, that there is a yin and a yang Wood, for instance?"

"There is a yin and yang to all things. The leaf and trunk of the mighty oak, which is which?"

"The trunk is yang, obviously."

"How so?"

"It is more masculine."

"Perhaps, but the function of the leaf, to draw energy from sunlight, is more yang than the storage function of the trunk. Both are yin, both are yang, neither could exist without the other. As yin and yang flux into one another they go through stages, the stages that describe the five elements."

"How divinely complex."

"Complex, yes, yet deceptively simple. These inseparable divisions can be seen in all things, and occur on levels beyond those we can see."

"And in people?"

"Those of yang constitution tend toward excess, those of yin constitution toward stillness. The five elements all act to control and balance each other, but no one is born with an even distribution, so the tendency toward yin or yang, or an elemental imbalance, should be noted before it can lead one to detrimental behavior. In all things, returning to balance, even when the natural character of one's birth chart is imbalanced, can only be for the good. Man's spirit is a reflection of the heavenly force, yang, while his body is borne of the earth, yin. Man is the fulcrum between these two energies, heaven and earth, yin and yang. By understanding this, and the pattern of the five elements in one's life, one can know the time for each activity, for excess and stillness. Most importantly, he will know how to return to center."

1

It makes me sad to think that I took something that was such a blessing to me, a spectacular kaleidoscopic eye-opening wonder, and turned it into an inescapable nightmare. In discussing LSD use and abuse with my friends I'm glad to report that none of them had quite such insanely paranoid experiences, so I expect that mine only came from doing too much and in the wrong state of mind. For some there is a natural progression, however, in the search for elevated states, which leads to trying different things, or in the case of acid, increasing the dose. As is the way with our macho western ethic, the dose becomes more important than the experience. The idea of seeing how much you can handle, however, is ultimately ridiculous, since the purpose of LSD is to help you let go. Being in control is impossible, and that's one of the things that LSD is here to show us. You can be in the flow, but no one is in control. Those who pretend to be are laughable, and like I did, probably have to lock themselves in their rooms when they get home and take off their masks. The more I tried to dose and be in control, the more out of control everything became, and the more I tweaked trying to deny it.

Why would anyone subject himself to all that punishment? It's a question I ask myself on occasion, but I was desperate as I was to be healed, and return to the glory of being transcendentally high, I was afraid to admit to anyone that I was "mentally disturbed," and felt that there was nowhere to get help anyway. Perhaps if I lived in a culture that respected and honored drugs I could have learned what I needed to and left the rest. I'll never know for sure, but I do know that there are much more intelligent and responsible ways to use psychedelics.

We're all searching for some meaning in our lives, something the usual channels don't offer. Psychedelic experiences provide a distinctively different and deep view of what life is, and how we might go about living it richly and responsibly. **There are dangers, however.** Art Kleps, Timothy Leary's neighbor at Millbrook, and founder of the acid-sacrament eating Neo-American church, said something I always liked: "Acid is no better than the traditional methods, (meaning meditation) it's just faster and sneakier." I'm not here to tell you to go out and trip, but if you're reading this, you've probably thought about it. I don't expect anyone to do what I've done, or Dr. Space has done, or probably a lot of people that are still okay have done, but with a little clarity about the issues no one would have to.

In Wizard of the Upper Amazon, a book chronicling the shamanistic life among the Brazilian rainforest natives at the turn of the century, the legend of the first man to take ayahuasca is told. He took way too much, and got blown away, with no one to help him figure it out. He didn't have a choice. Over time, the cultures that productively use entheogens have developed distinct objectives for usage, and trained leaders with deep understanding of the symbolism evoked by the plants and the group setting. Unfortunately for us westerners, there is no source for mentors to trip with, and we mostly rely on our "more experienced" friends. When I began leading my group sessions I had no fucking idea what I was doing, other than trying to get incomprehensibly high, and I must apologize to everyone I dragged (drugged?) along with me, however willing they were. When I realized that I had given up the leadership of my personal quest to the Dead, who were on a whole other mix of drugs (and didn't want that role anyway), I really had to wonder what the hell I had done. I'm over my period of blaming them for my own stupidity, but I wonder how much less destructive I might have been if there had been a responsible avenue for my induction. I also wonder if we can create such a framework for the generations to come.

Trying to inculcate a sense of respect for drugs and their effects is our responsibility. I ridiculed the idea of having someone guide me on a trip, because I knew I could handle anything, and I thought a trip was a trip, not a gateway. Believe me, it's a gateway, one we are generally ill prepared for or have no interest in. People used the expression "See God," for a reason. Taking psychedelics opened up their perspective to the universe as a conscious entity. You don't necessarily need someone to "guide" you there, but it's very important to have someone sitting with your body while you're out, and it helps if they know the terrain. I laughed when I heard Bob Weir doing a public service announcement warning people about taking acid, thinking he was being facetious, but I realize now that he saw enough negative results to be concerned. As a born atheist, looking for purely intellectual awareness, psychedelics threw me up against some things I was not very well prepared for, like the fact that expanded consciousness demands a spiritual perspective. If you would rather not take a step in that direction, don't. If you think you do, do some reading. Research what people say about preparing for such states and do your best to recognize the potentials in them. I'm always impressed by people who tell me they dosed once, had an incredible visionary experience in the wilderness somewhere, and never did it again. How valuable to have gotten what they needed out of it, and not to have fallen into the trap of doing it for entertainment purposes alone.

It seems to me, though, that everyone wants to get high. The animal kingdom is rife with examples, not just Rho Phi, but birds that ferment berries, cats eating catnip, deer eating weed. People are no different, they only differ in what kind of intoxicant they prefer. This boils down to socialization and safety. Most cultures have a respected and locally obtained mind altering substance. Think about coffee, it's easy for people to accept this drug because they are socialized with it. They feel safe doing it. The prevalence of alcohol, despite its high potential for accident, injury, violence, and death, is due to our acceptance. The cultural message (on billboards and during ballgames) is that alcohol's a cool way to alter your consciousness. Altering consciousness isn't all about meditation, psychedelics, or scientific research, it's about taking your mind to a different place. The question is not so much why we want to change our thought process, that's a biological imperative, perhaps even an evolutionary imperative, because it's beneficial to think in different ways, no, the question is whether we do it to explore ourselves or avoid ourselves.

Obviously, the majority of mind alteration goes on in the avoid-self category. Even the drugs that have consciousness expanding potentials are treated in the consumptive manner that everything in America is. For me, LSD became a "have another beer," kind of drug. Geared as I was to extremism, and searching for uncharted realms of consciousness, it's no wonder I blew a gasket. I'm an isolated case, but without a shift in our cultural consciousness, it may be difficult to develop reasonable perspectives regarding use and abuse. We do need training in recognizing our own minds, but it is becoming more widely available, and with a little help each of us can begin working toward our own highest levels of awareness. I'm not saying that occasional use to goof off or change your perspective is a bad thing either, it's just important to know what you're trying to achieve, and pay attention.

Drugs all have their different functions. Heroin masks the despair of desperate living, and as much as I have always eschewed it, I understand why it has held sway for over a century – people are in pain! And it's the people who hurt the most, beaten down by all of our socialization games, people who need the most kindness and forgiveness and help, that become the junkies we hate and fear and despise. Cocaine adds excitement to vacuous living. Do enough coke and doing nothing seems like an accomplishment. Once the rarified choice of the elite, the crack years redefined it in terms of poverty, and the poverty of the soul that follows it. Crank, "poor man's cocaine," lets you work from dawn 'til dawn, and party all night long, and while it's now the biggest threat to Democracy, it's only a step away from the millions of medicine chests full of prescribed amphetamines, a nation full of Ritalin kids, and the armed forces' "Go Pills." Alcohol loosens you up, to the point where none of my uptight hippie bullshit (or even a modicum of tact) can survive. For many people, it's both the wall and the only way to take down the wall. It's also implicated in 85% of violent crime, 41% of traffic fatalities, and roughly 25% of our annual health related expense, but we learned the futility of making it illegal almost a century ago. Chocolate's theobromine acts both as a stimulant and delivers the recently discovered neurochemical, "anandamide," giving emotional warmth. Sugar helps generate serotonin, which controls neurochemicals that create pleasure and block pain. Coffee delivers caffeine, expanding blood vessels in the brain. Tobacco releases acetylcholine, making you feel intelligent and heroic, until you run out! It also kills more people every year than the next five causes of death combined, so I suppose there must be something appealing about it.

Psychedelics work in a variety of ways to expand sensory capacity, often take you beyond the superficial level of consensus reality to field consciousness, and a deeper awareness of your self. In its years as a therapeutic agent, LSD had tremendous successes, and proved the greatest agent in recovery from alcoholism. It was Bill W's 11th step. Ecstasy too, has fantastic therapeutic value, dissolving the imbedded fears and walls that we hide ourselves behind. (Although I probably would have abused it too, I wish I had known a therapist using it when it became available, as it might have done a lot to ease my paranoid defensiveness.) In a society so stratified with fear as ours, there's no wonder it's become so popular that people have trashed themselves on it. Mushrooms, mescaline, ibogaine, ketamine, DMT, all of these have incredible healing and spiritual potentials, and despite the DEA's insanity, these drugs are finally being studied again for therapeutic use.

Weed, my ally, is another tricky one. The much decried dangers of marijuana were never actually tested or proven, but the association to Mexican immigrants and the Negro community, with their "hedonistic criminality," was enough to promote the Reefer Madness campaign in the thirties. The evidence supporting legalization has been collecting dust since Nixon had the first study done on marijuana in '68, and is finally being acted upon by various rational countries. Pot doesn't lead to harder drugs, it just makes you realize you've been lied to, which makes you suspect that everything you've heard about drugs is a lie. It's the lying that leads to harder drugs. Making drugs illegal, as governmental policy pundits have pointed out for decades, only keeps them expensive and dangerous, but the anti-weed hysteria rages on. A drug awareness pamphlet, recently penned by a Utah senator, states that the signs of marijuana use may include "concern for the environment, or taking up political causes." How unfortunate, that to have a functional brain is to be suspect of drug use. Why would your children care if their air, water, food, and land were polluted? They must be smokin' dope! Oddly enough, in a country that once prided itself on its political astuteness, only the dopers are concerned enough to pay attention to reality anymore. If being branded a stoner is what it takes to be part of the solution, I guess I'm on the stoner team again.

But I don't feel like being on the stoner team anymore, I've become tired of its limitations. Good weed can bring you up to a psychedelic level, but it can also enable you to ignore whatever lies outside your stoner tunnel vision, much like alcohol allows those who are amped out on "corporate mind" to disengage completely at the end of the day, without ever having to consider how "corporate mind" affects them. And it's not just the people with straight jobs that fall under this spell. Dealing itself is a job, plain and simple. I used to laugh at the Navy ads, "It's not just a job, it's and adventure!" because they applied so well to dealing. But lately I've been thinking, *It's not just an adventure, it's a job!* It has its thrills, its glory, its power, and in its way it seemed to inspire creativity, but eventually it's just a job – a job that allows you to stay high. To look at it any other way is a lie. To imagine that you're fighting the system by selling dope is pretty deluded, when you look at the state of the system. For the most part you're just keeping people high enough to ignore how shitty it is. The job pressures of dope dealing get to be a hack, too. You've devoted your life to everyone having fun, but that's your job. You can't just kick back and get high when that's your job, you have to do it better than anyone else, or be paranoid about doing it, and that's a drag.

But dealing is a subculture unto itself, an unstoppable industry, a drug that creates it's own incredibly powerful addiction. People become addicted to the game. You may come in for the free drugs or the money or the prestige, but you stay for the game. There's always the element of risk, subtly altering the polypeptide activity in the brain. Dealing is a buzz! You can get ripped off, or busted, or everything can run completely smoothly. Even if everything does run with clockwork precision, as my scenes did, you always have to imagine the possibility of danger, which promotes the buzz. That's why people move up from dime bag to boatload, it's big time commerce, with an edge of - In your face, pig! Of course, the money gets to be fairly attractive too. When you call the shots, stay out all night and sleep as late as you like, or do whatever you want to do with a steady stream of tax-free cash, it's very difficult to consider other careers. So much for the Protestant work ethic, which has been promoted as intensely as the Horatio Alger myth, as a way to keep people invested in work for its own sake. Drugs, and drug dealing, make discontents, seeing through the purposelessness of the greater part of our culture, and this does not support the corporate structure. That's why they're illegal. These discontents, if self-avoidant, are satisfied with staying wasted, at whatever cost. The self explorative malcontents, however, often come away with a vision and desire to improve society. The real job is facing the obstacles, bringing the vision to fruition, and not spacing out behind the drug.

2

Apparently, there are actually people who think that weed is evil, and while I've seen users become lethargic, dull-witted, pathetic bores, and dealers become paranoid, power-mad, usurious scumbags, those are pretty extreme cases. A lot of folks are okay with it, and I'd hate to see it disappear. It grows all over the planet! And while other plant based entheogens occur within specific areas, they all seem to talk to the people of those regions in a spiritually uplifting way. No, the problem is not that the evil _____ (insert drug here) exists, it's that we as people stand so far away from knowing ourselves that we are ripe for addictive use. Speed, downs, coke, heroin, cough syrup, shoe polish, correcting fluid, paint, cold remedies, airplane glue, antihistamines, aerosols, antiperspirants, butane lighters, how many of these would you outlaw to prevent the people in every community from abusing them? Drugs are merely a symptom of our larger societal problem of alienation; spiritually, from the planet, and from our selves.

There are a lot of people out there who like to get high, one way or another. Since Reagan trashed the place there's been this big hush around that fact, and I'm tired of it. It's not that I think getting high is the most responsible thing in the world anymore, or spend much time at all doing it, I'm just tired of everyone thinking they need to lie about it. The number of parents out there lying to their kids about the fact that they have or continue to smoke pot is ridiculous. It's the same kind of behavior that implicitly promotes the idea that kids should be lying to their parents about their own dope smoking. This is not what a generation of smoking dope was supposed to promote! Are you afraid your kid's teacher will find out and report you? Take it from me, your kid's teacher has smoked pot!

I have smoked weed with or sold dope to engineers, accountants, stockbrokers, businessmen, chemists, laboratory scientists, mechanics, drivers, dispatchers, cops, yes cops, lawyers—dozens of lawyers, judges, university professors, IRS workers, musicians-—duuuh, professional athletes, actors, singers, dancers, technicians, journalists, authors, personal trainers, salesmen, office workers, computer engineers, programmers, systems analysts, driving testers, plant operators, politicians, plumbers, maintenance men, gardeners, arborists, farmers, prison guards, doctors, ad men, carpenters, construction workers, garbage men, masons, roofers, MIS specialists, entertainment industry execs, and every other kind of everyday, backbone of society American you can imagine. Oh yes, and teachers, elementary school teachers, kindergarten teachers, high school teachers, Sunday school teachers, after all, teaching is about expanding your mind. It may relieve you to know that I have never smoked weed with any airline pilots, brain surgeons, or encyclopedia salesmen. But when you consider that I sold at least a hundred times as much weed as I smoked, and that there were thousands times more pounds grown every year than I ever saw, there's no telling who's been high.

I was a weird kid, growing up, and when I looked at America, the idea of being normal was anathema to me. When I discovered drugs, I thought I had a line on full-time weirdness, and in some sense I did. But everybody's a little bit weird, and I'm realizing now that taking drugs is normal! Any time you do something all the time, it becomes normal. If you're frying all the time, that's your normal mindset, as weird as it may be. And when you need to avoid your daily state of mind by plunging onto drugs or alcohol or TV night after night, you're engaging in pretty normal behavior. Booooring! Consider the 50 million people on anti-depressants, or any of the slew of pharmaceuticals we rely upon to be "normal." I find "normalcy" highly overrated. If being "normal" means suppressing whatever is disturbing you, you've got a problem. Deal with it! Remember, everyone's a little bit weird, so let's all just be proud of it. Maybe then we can give each other (and ourselves) the acceptance we all so desire.

I'm happy to be lobbying for weirdness, as a true expression one's individuality, although it feels hypocritical telling people to rethink their drug use. Smoking pot was such a ritual that I feel remiss at not doing it, but it's hard to get stoned if you don't do it all the time. I may sound like a pussy, but I get blown away. I can get paranoid when I'm with my best friends! I can laugh at it now, since I'm not carrying a ten-year sentence in my backpack, but it bugs me. I always liked my weed strong, but after a couple of hits my once competitive verbal skills can be relegated to mush mouth. I see friends that I haven't seen in years, get too high, and have to go another couple years before we can have a conversation, and that sucks!

I also realize that I've blown off a lot of opportunities because I was too busy getting high. Things I always wanted to do, and could have done, fell behind the next doobie into a dusty corner behind the bookcase. In Chinese Medicine they call weed "The Drug that makes you Eat your Children." I had to laugh when I first heard this, but thinking about it shut me up. Children are metaphoric of projects, ideas, anything you would give birth to. I had ample opportunity to go back to college, get into television, get my professional scuba certification, whatever. Between my sociopathic paranoia and my brain-numbed fear of testing my ability to learn again, it was much easier to just get high than do anything. I think weed makes it easy to ignore your situation until it's too late to do anything about it. And dealing? It's unthinkable to take an entry-level job when you can just pick up the phone and rake in the dough.

This is all my own experience. I know I fucked up! I don't expect anyone to do what I've done and I expect plenty of people reading this to laugh at what a tweaker I've been. My bent may be different than yours, but if you're doing drugs, you'll probably push yourself up against whatever limitations you have, until you're forced to deal with them. I have spent most of the last decade meditating, observing, clearing and healing the burdensome expense of how much "fun" I had in my youth. Now I know when I'm having fun, and I'm not afraid to admit it when I'm not. Writing this has made it abundantly clear that some process was underway that prevented me from noticing the signals that were as bright and loud as meteors crashing through my living room. I see the places that I denied my own sworn reasoning, and that scares me. My promise to myself that I would stop smoking weed if it ever became a health concern was quickly mollified by the use of aloe vera juice. My decision to take LSD annually as a visionary exploration quickly went over the edge into weekly Frydays. My intention to quit dealing after high school would have been easy if I hadn't been busted, but isn't being busted a good enough reason? Isn't going insane behind nitrous and having your house burn down a good enough reason? Isn't getting ripped off by your psycho neighbors who are murdering people a good enough reason? If you're not running away from yourself I'm sure that they are.

It would have been nice to recognize this before I pounded my brain into slop, but I doubt that it was the effect of the drugs so much as it was my doing them stupidly. By slamming myself up against my psychological limitations without a guideline for change, I was wringing my brain pretty hard. Sure I'm still fairly witty, pretty quick, I wrote this book, but I know I'm not as fast as I once was, and that irks me! Having become paruretic kills me! I'm one of the most sociable people I know, but for years I had to balance that out against the impossibility of simply taking a leak! Try partying at your friend's house knowing you'll probably have to leave to go pee in the neighbor's bushes. And remember, **partying is your job!** Hundreds of concerts, clubs, trips, travels, events, where you're too high to pee! I'm much healthier now, but I wonder what I could have accomplished had I gone another route. I might have taken a different path to ignorance, and back around to self-awareness, there's no saying. I like to think that I wouldn't have had to make it so difficult to be a human. It all comes back to the work of knowing yourself. I still believe there are ways to experience altered states and lead conscious, clear, contented lives, but it doesn't happen by accident.

So what, to all this, you ask. The usual leftist strategy, I reply. Decriminalizing drugs would give everyone the opportunity to use them in an intelligent and legal capacity, within whatever guidelines may be established, hopefully under the advice of experts. Several of our European allies have legalized or decriminalized marijuana, although I've never seen that fact reported in the American news media. The allowance for use of psychedelics, for adults only, or perhaps as part of a coming of age ritual, and only after certain preparatory requirements are met, could only benefit our largely addictive society. The results of LSD experiments have been consistently positive in cases of addiction and alcoholism intervention, as well as for those with terminal conditions, (such as life itself) but its use even for research has been denied since the Reagan era began. This is what pisses me off. In a somewhat smarter society, one not so motivated by fear and greed, one that wasn't profiting from drug cartels, or feeding taxpayer dollars into useless prisons, perhaps we could have an educated, responsible, productive populace that uses drugs to promote those ideals. Perhaps young people like myself could experience the creative and spiritual potentials that lie within our grasp, without having to burrow into the underworld and turn their backs on society in order to eat of the "Tree of Knowledge." Maybe, in a free society, we could learn to use these drugs effectively, to learn our lessons, have our fun, and carry that awareness into the world. It's something to hope for.

Afterweird

One thing I have come to recognize is that there are other levels of reality, those described by seers, shamans, and psychics, as well as tripping hippies. My intention to understand the productive uses of altered states of consciousness has finally come full circle. I spent ten years meditating before I first wrote this, and since then I have experienced tremendous healing with shamanic work, while my research into the history and protocols of psychedelic psychotherapy has shown me its unassailable value as well. (I only wish it had been available to me when I first needed it, or was accepted now.)

Whether you choose to use them or not, it's imperative to recognize that **Drugs Are Tools, Not Toys,** and need to be respected as such. Using tools requires a plan, a purpose, training and safety equipment. Using shamanic tools requires Intention, Consecration, and Integration, as well as knowledgeable Helpers. We have the potential to use these tools to better ourselves, if only we're allowed. The government may not want us to learn how to use them responsibly, so that our only option is to get fucked up, but using drugs is defying the government, so if you're going to use them, learn how to use them correctly. Obviously, no one is sitting in a cave for 20 years in order to have a mystical awareness when they can score some blotter and get their mind blown tonight. But despite our cultural love for being too high, drugs are best used in a focused context, and focusing takes practice.

I have been able to translate some of my visionary experiences into meditation tools, and work with them in powerful ways for healing myself and others. I'm not done yet, nor do I believe that there is ever a point at which there will be nothing left to work on, but I'm paying attention now, respecting the work, respecting myself, and committing to my own clarity. The discipline of daily meditation is far different from the explosive nature of a fat dose. It's a very different high, focusing one's conscious, but it's quite rewarding, and no one's trying to bust you for it (yet). Anyone who has dosed can tell you that you always have to come down, and that's never really fun. While meditation is great preparation for psychedelic states, the thing that appeals to me most about it is that I never have to come down. And for someone who has invested as much as I have in being high, that's a wonderful feeling.

PS

In revising this book, I've been struck by my youthful homophobia, which glares at me now, but I feel would be dishonest to edit away. I'd hoped, in writing it originally, that the subtle threads that tied my antagonism together would be clear, but I want to take a moment to apologize to anyone who might take offense, not recognizing the psychic imprint my father's fear put upon me, the cultural promotion of this fear, and its tremendous expansion during my psychedelic states, which demanded my violent rejection.

I'd also like to apologize to anyone who has suffered as a result of knowing me before I had the awareness to write this book.

Peace.

Glossary

ASC: Altered State of Consciousness. Used to describe both meditative and drug-induced changes in perception. Also Non-Ordinary State of Consciousness.

Ayahuasca: Both the prepared beverage of, and the plant from which the word translates. "Vine of souls," banisteriopsis caapi.

Ballenas: Quart bottles of Pacifico beer (literally, Whales).

BLM: Federal Bureau of Land Management. The Government agency in charge of Federally-owned land that is not a specific property of any other Federal entity.

Bomber: A large marijuana cigarette. (Spliff)

Bong: A simple water pipe consisting of a bottle or vertical tube partially filled with a liquid (water or liqueur) and a smaller offset tube ending in a bowl used for marijuana or hashish. The water cools and filters the smoke; use of an alcoholic liqueur (instead of water) adds alcohol vapor to the smoke. (From Thai bhaung.)

BÖC: Blue Öyster Cult, a popular heavy metal band of the '70s.

CAMP: The U.S. Government's Campaign Against Marijuana Planters.

Carburetor: A hole in the stem of a bong, which allows you to control the vacuum pressure against the bowl, and the ratio of smoke to air inhaled.

D5: The standard of portable recording, before the arrival of digital tape.

DMT: Dimethyl-tryptamine: Powerful psychedelic found in ayahuasca, numerous plants, and the Pineal Gland!

Doobie: A marijuana cigarette. (Joint, Rube)

Dose: To take LSD, derived from Threshold Dose, the scientific term for the amount of a drug needed to produce the intended effect. Originally 250 micrograms in lab tests, hits available on the street were generally 100 micrograms or less.

Dune: Frank Herbert's novel of galactic politics.

Eleusis: Ancient Greek rite of Soma ingestion.

Entheogen: Term coined by R. Gordon Wasson, referring to the felt presence of indwelling divinity in psilocybin mushrooms, expanded to all such plant based substances.

Felch: The most depraved sex act known to man.

Fart Sack: Sleeping bag.

Freewheelin Franklin: One of the three Fabulous Furry Freak Brothers, whose motto is, "Dope will get you through times of no money better than money will get you through times of no dope."

Fat man: Jerry Garcia.

Front: To sell drugs on credit, usually in quantities to be broken down and sold by the frontee.

Hit: A dose of LSD, usually on blotter paper or gelatin. Also a toke of weed.

J - Joint: A marijuana cigarette. (Doobie, Rube)

Kif: Green hash powder, usually pressed into slabs for industrial sale.

LB: A pound. (The dream of Stymie, to roll the LBJ)

MDA: Methyl-deoxy-amphetamine, The Love Drug. Forerunner of MDMA, popularly known as Ecstasy.

Nadsat: Language used by Alex and his droogs in A Clockwork Orange.

Off: To get rid of, to sell.

OZ: An ounce.

Paruresis: Psychiatric term for pee-shyness as a psycho-social disorder, characterized by a marked inability to urinate in the presence or proximity of others. Studies indicate it may affect over 10% of the general public.

Power Hitter: A device to trap the smoke from a joint and blow it back through when you take a hit. "Onward through the fog."

QP: A quarter pound.

Rube: A marijuana cigarette. (Doobie, Joint)

Schmeeze: Smokable heroin, Persian.

Schmint: The crystallized resin deposits that form on bud.

Spliff: A large marijuana cigarette. (Bomber)

Staja: Nadsat for prison.

Taper: Someone who makes bootleg recordings of concerts.

Toke: to inhale marijuana smoke, from a joint, pipe, or bong.

Wheel: A dealer in the central position to the market. Everything revolves around the wheel.

White separated: LSD that has been taken through an extra purification process.

Resources

Drug Books
LSD Psychotherapy, The Holotropic Mind, or anything by Stanislav Grof
Pihkal,Tihkal, by Alexander & Ann Shulgin
Acid Dreams, by Martin Lee & Bruce Shlain
LSD, My Problem Child, by Albert Hoffman
Teonanacatl, Ayahuasca, or anything by Ralph Metzner
Food of the Gods, by Terrence McKenna
The Secret Chief, by Myron J. Stolaroff
Wizard of the Upper Amazon, by F. Bruce Lamb
Illicit Drugs, Paul Gahlinger
Pharmacopoeia, or anything by Dale Pendell
Under The Influence, edited by Preston Peet
Tripping, by Charles Hayes
Drug Crazy, by Mike Gray

On Chinese Medicine
Between Heaven and Earth, by Beinfield and Korngold

Websites: Drugs, Consciousness, Policy, Research
www.adopedealer.com
www.maps.org
www.dancesafe.org
www.drugwarfacts.org
www.drugpolicy.org
www.usdoj.gov/dea/directory.htm

www.erowid.com
www.mpp.org
www.stopthedrugwar.org
www.cognitiveliberty.org
www.holotropic.com

On Paruresis
www.paruresis.com

Ab☮ut the Auth☮r

Photo by Pops Norberg

Author, performer, producer Sheldon Norberg can be found staging his solo-show, *Confessions of a Dope Dealer,* and lecturing about drugs at colleges around the country.

Find out more at **www.adopedealer.com**

Metaphysician, hypnotherapist, bodyworker, (astrologer and shaman in training) Sheldon Norberg still resides in Northern California.

Dope Dealer Sheldon Norberg is now retired, after finding that so many hats are difficult to wear with dreads. All of him was shocked to realize what his parents never could have known, that the ebonic anagram for Sheldon is – He on LSD!

Order Blank

If you liked this book, and would like to pass one on to someone else, please check with your local bookstore, online bookseller, or copy this form:

Name_____

Address _____

City _____State____ Zip _____

Please enclose $19.95 plus $5.00 (postage and handling) and send your request to:

> North Mountain Publishing
> P.O. Box 3267
> Oakland, CA 94609-0267

California Residents, please add $1.70 sales tax to the purchase price.

For more than 5 copies, please contact the publisher for multiple copy rates.

T-shirts, sweatshirts, posters and more information available at www.adopedealer.com